OKANAGAN UNIV/COLLEGE LIBRARY

02744529

D0583933

DATE DUE

DEC 1 0 2001	
MAR 2 7 2002	
OCT 1 0 2002	
FEB 1 8 2003	
FEB 1 6 2004	

BRODART   Cat. No. 23-221

OKANAGAN UNIVERSITY COLLEGE
LIBRARY
BRITISH COLUMBIA

Shamanism

The Neural Ecology of Consciousness and Healing

Michael Winkelman

BERGIN & GARVEY
Westport, Connecticut • London

Library of Congress Cataloging-in-Publication Data

Winkelman, Michael.
    Shamanism : the neural ecology of consciousness and healing /
Michael Winkelman.
        p. cm.
    Includes bibliographical references and index.
    ISBN 0-89789-704-8 (alk. paper)
        1. Mental healing. 2. Shamanism. 3. Shamanism—Physiological aspects.
    4. Altered states of consciousness.   I. Title.
    RZ401. W56 2000
    291.1'44'019—dc21   99-040489

British Library Cataloguing in Publication Data is available.

Copyright © 2000 by Michael Winkelman

All rights reserved. No portion of this book may be
reproduced, by any process or technique, without the
express written consent of the publisher.

Library of Congress Catalog Card Number: 99-040489
ISBN: 0-89789-704-8

First published in 2000

Bergin & Garvey, 88 Post Road West, Westport, CT 06881
An imprint of Greenwood Publishing Group, Inc.
www.greenwood.com

Printed in the United States of America

∞™

The paper used in this book complies with the
Permanent Paper Standard issued by the National
Information Standards Organization (Z39.48–1984).

10 9 8 7 6 5 4 3 2 1

Material used in Table 2.1 has been reprinted from *Shamans, Priests, and
Witches* by Michael Winkelman from the Anthropological Research Series,
Arizona State University. Used with permission from Arizona State University
Anthropological Research Papers.

Contents

List of Illustrations

Preface

Shamanism, one of humanity's most ancient traditions, has recently reemerged in contemporary societies' religious, spiritual, and healing practices and consciousness traditions. Although specification of the basis and the nature of shamanism has often been vague and ambiguous, there is a broad recognition of a primordial natural form of healing and personal development with continued relevance for today's world. The importance of these universal phenomena of shamanism and the alterations of consciousness involved have traditionally been attributed to the supernatural and spiritual domains. With the rise of modern science and an atheistic materialism, shamanistic phenomena were denounced as fraud, trickery, and delusion. Psychological explanations portrayed shamanistic phenomena as forms of mental illness, dissociation, hysteria, other psychopathologies, and mistaken magical cognition. It was presumed that shamanism and its practices, like other aspects of religious thought and behavior, would disappear with the spread of modern rationality.

Just as it seemed shamanism might slip into its final demise with the expansion of modern rational bureaucratic consciousness, these practices reemerged in modern societies. The widely heralded decline in religious behavior in the twentieth century was corrected as a misperception. Although traditional religious denominations and churches continue to decline, religious participation has been growing in sects and cults. These latter range from indigenous groups such as Pentecostalist and "white shamanism," derived from the Native American spiritual traditions, to a variety of Eastern import religions—Unification Church, Transcendental Meditation, Hare Krishna, Buddhism, Hinduism, and others. Scholarly investigators have often characterized people's attraction to religion as a reflection of its role as a source of refuge and comfort to the downtrodden. But the adherents to the new religious groups, particularly the alternative religious-healing practices and foreign-origin cults, are disproportionately people from the economically well-off and educated middle class.

The attraction of alternative religions and their healing practices is supported by new perspectives on shamanism provided by the emergence of the fields of consciousness studies, transpersonal psychology, and the anthropology of consciousness. These perspectives view shamanism as involving techniques for the alteration of consciousness to support healing and personal development. Ritual activities are increasingly recognized as complex ethnomedical practices that provide important cultural healing resources. Investigations of shamanistic practices reveal their ability to manipulate physiological processes, psychophysiological reactions, personal experience, and social psychology and relations. The emerging understanding of shamanistic practices locates their foundations in human biopsychological potentials and in concerns with identity, emotion, attachment, sense of self, and personal conviction that transforms consciousness.

A NEUROPHENOMENOLOGICAL APPROACH
TO SHAMANISM

This book examines the psychobiological and psychocognitive foundations of shamanism and related universal traditions concerned with the therapeutic alteration of consciousness. The perspective articulated is a neurophenomenological approach that links neurological structures and processes with cultural practices and personal experience. Shamanistic practices induce extraordinary experiences and healing by producing integrative relationships among brain systems and psychocultural beliefs. These experiences reflect the simultaneous elicitation and integration of normal modes of information processing and consciousness that do not ordinarily occur together. These altered states of consciousness (ASC) nonetheless involve normal integrative psychobiological processes elicited by many procedures.

A primary focus of the psychophysiological effects of shamanistic ASC is in the limbic system, or the paleomammalian brain. This brain area emerged in the evolution of mammals and provided a number of distinctive developments. Shamanistic healing is based on manipulation of processes and functions of the paleomammalian brain—self-identity and social identity and their attachments, emotions, meanings, and references. Shamanistic ASC elicit processes of the paleomammalian brain and induce a systemic integration of information-processing functions across the functional layers of the brain, producing limbic-cortical integration and interhemispheric synchronization.

Shamanistic healing practices achieve this integration by physically stimulating systematic brain-wave-discharge patterns that activate affects, memories, attachments, and other psychodynamic processes of the paleomammalian brain. This activation forces normally unconscious or preconscious primary information-processing functions and outputs to be integrated into the operations of the frontal cortex. This integrates implicit understandings, socioemotional dynamics, repressed memories, unresolved conflicts, intuitions, and nonverbal—visual, mimetic, and presentational—knowledge into self-conscious awareness.

Another central aspect of shamanistic healing lies in what has been called "medicine's symbolic reality." A universal aspect of the healer-patient relationship involves the positive transformation of the patient's well-being through symbols used by the healer and the expectations for improvement that they represent. This relationship symbolically manipulates physiological levels, a fundamental mechanism of shamanistic action derived from linkages among the mental and biological systems through attachments and affects. These processes, manifested in psychosomatic and psychoneuroimmunological phenomena, are central to shamanistic healing and are increasingly being recognized in medicine as an empirically effective "religious healing" reflecting the consequences of a "biology of hope." Cognitive science and philosophy address these as "top-down causation" and "supervenience."

Understandings of shamanism and ASC are shifting from their mischaracterization as atavistic and delusional to a recognition of their central role in the evolution of human consciousness. Shamanism represents adaptive potentials, an enhanced operation of consciousness derived from integrative brain functioning. Shamanism was the first human institution that systematized this integration, and its potentials and processes still have important implications for humans. These potentials provided the basis for the evolution of synthetic symbolic awarenesses in early evolutionary periods of modern *Homo sapiens*, providing a basis for human development in the mythological systems representing self, mind, other, and consciousness. This is exemplified in the soul journey and in guardian spirits, which constitute forms of self-objectification and role taking that expand human sociocognitive and intrapsychic dynamics. Similar processes are found in the classic shamanic motif of death and rebirth, which represents the development of self through the symbolic death of the old self to permit the emergence and integration of a higher-order self.

This book presents a neurophenomenological perspective on shamanistic practices and their effects on consciousness and healing processes. This neurophenomenological approach deliberately articulates the relationships between two complementary realms of information: (1) personal phenomenal experience, and (2) knowledge of the brain structures and functions. This synthesis bridges what have been traditionally considered separate fields of endeavor: the religious, spiritual, or mystical on one hand and the material or physical on the other. The integration of the complementary perspectives provided by the conceptual worlds of the mystical and contemplative traditions on one hand and, on the other, the knowledge of the brain provided by the neurosciences is necessary for understanding the nature of shamanistic phenomena. The experiential domains reveal a natural symbolic system that represents aspects of consciousness, self, mental processes, and psychosocial emotional dynamics. Shamanism evolved as a practice for symbolically and psychophysiologically manipulating the biological substrate to enhance well-being. The meditative traditions extended these potentials in examining and controlling the attentional, perceptual, and conceptual processes underlying consciousness. These traditions are examined by integrating neurobiological and symbolic perspectives, explicitly relating neurophysiology to experiences and symbolic processes in order to provide a basis for illustrating how shamanistic healing practices achieve their therapeutic effects.

ORGANIZATION OF THE BOOK

The book is organized around three major concerns: (1) a cross-cultural perspective on the nature and the basis of shamanism and its relationship to other ASC healing practices; (2) a neurophysiological perspective on the nature of shamanistic ASC and the characteristics of the integrative mode of consciousness that they produce; and (3) the physiological and psychological mechanisms of shamanistic healing. These approaches illustrate that shamanism reflects the natural or neural ecology of human consciousness and healing.

Chapter 1 provides an overview of the anthropology of shamanism and altered states of consciousness and of their relationship to the brain organization and function. A general model of consciousness is provided to exemplify the specific aspects of consciousness addressed in shamanic practices. The model shows that shamanism is concerned with the socioemotional and self functions of the paleomammalian brain and with cognitive capacities based in presentational symbolism, metaphor, analogy, and mimesis.

Chapter 2 examines shamanism by integrating cross-cultural and neurognostic perspectives. Cross-cultural analyses indicate a form of magico-religious practice, which is largely confined to hunter-gatherer societies, that has a worldwide distribution and that shares fundamental characteristics, which justifies the conclusion that shamanism is a psychobiologically based phenomena. The universals of shamanism are examined from neurognostic perspectives, illustrating psycho- and sociobiological bases for the structures of soul journeys, spirit perceptions, guardian spirits, death and rebirth, and other forms of shamanic cognition. The contributions of these potentials and practices are examined in terms of sociocultural and cognitive evolution in modern humans.

Chapter 3 provides an overview of the psychobiology of ASC, relating their characteristics to the general functions of the brain. The biological basis of the integrative mode of consciousness produced by ASC is contrasted with other modes of consciousness (waking, dreaming, and deep sleep). The specific psychophysiological functions of ASC are addressed, and the primary variations of ASC cross-culturally are illustrated. Shamanic soul journey is analyzed in terms of the physiology of induction procedures and the phenomenology of the experiences that illustrate their role as symbolic processes. Possession is addressed in relationship to the associated psychosocial conditions and in comparison with recognized neuropsychiatric phenomena, including temporal lobe syndromes, ictal personality patterns, and multiple personality disorder. Meditative forms of consciousness are examined from neuroepistemological perspectives that illustrate them to be natural, or innate, forms of cognition. The basic aspects of meditation are shown to affect perception, attention, cognition, emotion, and epistemological processes.

Chapter 4 reviews the physiological bases for shamanistic healing, placing them in the general context of the psychobiology of ASC. The psychobiology of ASC involves physically and culturally mediated forms of adaptation to stress and psychoneuroimmunological responses that are reinforced by procedures that elicit symbolically and socially mediated opioid release. The therapeutic effects of hallucinogenic plants are examined in relation to their interaction with serotonergic mechanisms, suggesting their functions as "psychointegrators." Therapeutic effects of shamanistic practices are illustrated through an overview of assessments of the effectiveness of meditation in managing a variety of health conditions.

Chapter 5 examines the psychophysiological effects of shamanistic healing, particularly the role of rituals as procedures for altering physiological, psychological, and emotional responses. Shamanistic healing's utilization of biological processes and development of neurognostic potentials underlie its ability to produce symbolic penetration of physiological systems, altering their responses. The religious dimensions of shamanic healing are reviewed to illustrate a wide range of intrapsychic and sociopsychological mechanisms. Modern illness characterized as "spiritual emergencies" and contemporary spontaneous religious experiences are analyzed to illustrate their shamanic roots and the continued relevance of shamanic therapeutic paradigms. Similar processes found in possession and meditative traditions illustrate their continued relevance as therapeutic resources.

The perspective on shamanism offered here locates its foundations in brain systems, neurology, and the psychosociobiology of human consciousness. The practices of shamanism produced a human cultural evolution, exploiting biopsychological potentials through ritual activities that focused and utilized these potentials in adaptive ways. The ways in which shamanic practices contributed to human development are presented here within a framework that emphasizes their biological foundation, as well as their ability to manipulate that psychobiological basis for enhancing human well-being. This linkage of shamanic practices to human psychobiology and psychocognitive potentials makes shamanism part of the natural ecology of human consciousness, with continued relevance and consequences in today's world.

Acknowledgments

A number of individuals have contributed to this work, directly and indirectly. Charles Laughlin's neurophenomenological perspective is a guiding influence throughout this book. I thank him for that and for his comments on specific chapters. Harry Hunt's work, particularly his book *On the Nature of Consciousness*, provided crucial insights incorporated here. I also thank Stanley Krippner for his encouragement of my work over the years and for his insightful perspectives. Thanks are also due to Marilynn Bubb for assistance with word processing and proofreading.

1

⌇

Shamanism and Consciousness: An Introduction

CHAPTER OVERVIEW

The anthropological study of consciousness has been primarily concerned with phenomena associated with *altered states of consciousness* (ASC), particularly shamanism and possession. A neurophenomenological framework linking biology and experience is necessary for understanding these behaviors for altering consciousness. The necessity of neurophenomenological approaches for understanding consciousness is illustrated by the linkages of the experiences of organisms with the brain systems that mediate experiences and their forms of symbolic expression. Cross-disciplinary, linguistic, and etymological perspectives illustrate that consciousness is fundamentally concerned with "knowing systems." A systems model links biological and constructed aspects of experience and consciousness to illustrate the structural foundations from which a variety of forms of consciousness are produced. The fundamental properties of these knowing systems include self, other, representation, and motivation and are directly related to the practices and experiences of ASC, shamanism, and possession. Shamanic ASC focus on adaptations of the internal environment of self, other, and cultural systems of meaning to neurognostic structures of consciousness. Shamanic ASC are concerned with

imagetic representations of salient emotional memories and representations of self; motivational systems central to self, emotions, and
others; and mythological and neurognostic interpretative structures
that provide the basis for modeling self and consciousness. The
paleomammalian brain and its protomentation and emotiomentation
processes are a foundation for the emotional, personal, social, and
cognitive mechanisms of shamanistic practices. Shamanic practices
are primarily focused on affecting functions of the paleomammalian
brain and the integration of those functions with other brain systems.
These integrative processes are manifested in analogical thought and
in a variety of topics of concern to the anthropology of consciousness—animism, anthropomorphism, totemism, and mimetic thinking.
These integrative processes utilize symbolic capacities in a presentational or imagetic modality that provides the basis for thought and
symbolization; they represent deep structures of knowledge operating independently of language and link somatosensory and metaphoric
processes in a system within which symbols affect physiological processes through an image-based presentational medium.

INTRODUCTION: ANTHROPOLOGY AND THE
STUDY OF CONSCIOUSNESS

Shamanism and similar practices for altering consciousness play a
crucial role in illustrating fundamental aspects of consciousness and
the relationship between physical and mental levels of reality. Alterations in consciousness induced by shamanistic practices constitute
an important contrastive perspective from ordinary waking consciousness and for understanding consciousness in general. The psychophysiological and experiential changes induced by shamanic activities help
elucidate the diverse subsystems that underlie ordinary consciousness.
The changes also provide data on a broader range of phenomenal
experiences that must be addressed in a comprehensive theory.
Transpersonal psychology and anthropology and contemplative and
Eastern psychologies provide data about forms of experience beyond
ordinary rational ego identity and consciousness. These experiences
reveal aspects of self and identity beyond that conventionally recognized in the individual personality. Anthropology's ethnographic
approach reveals a range of phenomena of consciousness, including
visions, possession, and other altered states of consciousness and spirit
world experiences. Although these experiences have often been treated

as ephemeral or pathological, their cross-cultural manifestations indicate that they reflect biological structures and functions.

Shamanism's practices for altering consciousness produce one pole in the various dualisms of human consciousness that contrast the experiences of ordinary waking consciousness and its intellectual, verbal, rational, externally oriented functioning with a transformed consciousness that is characterized by an internal orientation, intuition, and holistic, tacit, nonverbal perceptions and meanings. These perceptions and meanings have been known as "unconscious" and intuitive, as special forms of consciousness that are contrasted with the ordinary egoic waking modes of consciousness and are manifested in dreams, ASC, and transpersonal experiences. Some approaches use the term *consciousness* to refer to the specialized activities of the left hemisphere—the logical, rational, linear thinking processes—contrasted with mystical thinking, which is considered to be inferior. In the history of Western civilization, there are long-standing precedents that have excluded the intuitive perceptual mode from definitions of consciousness (Wautischier 1989). The traditions of European peoples and their New World descendants have tended to depreciate ASC in their emphasis on rational thought. This is manifested in diverse aspects of culture: Salem witch trials; pathological classifications in psychiatry of mystical states and ASC; mycophobia (exaggerated fear of mushrooms); the domination of secularly oriented religious organizations rather than ecstatic sects or cults; the dominance of behaviorist and materialist ideologies in science; and a drug-war mentality in government.

The failure to investigate these types of experiences in some cultures, and in science in general, is a consequence of what Laughlin, McManus, and d'Aquili (1992) called "monophasic consciousness," one that fails to consider other possible forms of consciousness. Because of this lack of direct consideration of the nature and role of consciousness within Western psychology, the well-developed traditions for understanding the nature of consciousness are largely what have been called the mystical, meditative, contemplative, and philosophical traditions of Asia. Learning about consciousness and its implications for understanding human nature requires that one direct attention to its study. But the meditative traditions that have studied these experiences have been viewed by some in science and medicine as engaged in ego regression to infantile states and as a befuddled way of thinking. The association with more primitive psychological functions and with the lower centers of the brain has undoubtedly contributed to pathological and inferior evaluations attributed to ASC. This misperception is based in the failure to recognize the contributions of the lower brain to higher cognitive processes and the systemic brain integration associated with these transformations of consciousness. But although characterized by the dominance of lower brain centers and the activation of delta, theta, and alpha waves, these shamanic ASC are not accompanied by the usual characteristics of "unconsciousness" but by self-awareness, intentionality, memory, and other faculties associated with the self-conscious rational mind. Furthermore, the ASC experiences are often associated with feelings of insight, understanding, integration, certainty, conviction, and truth, which surpass ordinary understandings and tend to persist long after the experience, often providing foundational insights for religious and cultural traditions.

Many of these models of consciousness have entered into Western discourse with the concepts, goals, and world views embedded in the language used by these philosophical traditions. Their association with religious systems has led to the perception that they are accepted on faith rather than as the result of critical analysis. However, these traditions are more appropriately characterized as contemplative practices or sciences of consciousness. They have developed procedures for the replicable observation of consciousness (Laughlin et al. 1992), based on systematic and rigorous procedures for examination, reporting, and verification of experiences (e.g., see Wilber 1990).

These Asian philosophical, mystical, or contemplative traditions have been central influences in the development of transpersonal psychology and the anthropology of consciousness. These investigations of consciousness have focused on altered states of consciousness and have provided data about a range of manifestations of consciousness that expand on the concepts and concerns central to Western psychology and philosophy. They also report fundamental similarities in ASC experiences across cultures, suggesting that they derive from biologically based neurognostic structures (cf. Forman 1998). The universality of aspects of transpersonal consciousness is also attested to in a perennial philosophy and psychology (Smith 1976; Wilber 1977). Similarities in steps, stages, and conditions recognized by philosophical and contemplative religious traditions, East and West, suggest biocognitive or neurognostic structures as the basis of these experiences.

The universal distribution of characteristics and phenomenon of

ASC reflects their biologically based structures. Anthropologists' work has revealed the universal use of ASC and their role in alterations in self, identity, and psychosocial relations as found in the context of shamanism, mediumship, possession, and related healing practices. This present work extends the understanding of these topics in addressing the psychophysiological basis of shamanic consciousness and its relationship to self, society, and healing. Consciousness is fundamental to anthropological concerns with trance, animism, shamanism, healing, and possession. The manifestations of consciousness in these contexts illustrate shamanism's fundamental role in culture and personal human evolution, particularly healing, self-transformation, and cognitive integration.

Neuropsychological Structures in Rock Art

The importance of neurological perspectives in interpretation of religious behavior is exemplified in recent examinations of universals in rock art (e.g., Lewis-Williams and Dowson 1988; Lewis-Williams and Clottes 1998; Whitley 1992, 1994a,b, 1998; Blundell 1998). These features have been attributed to neuropsychological structures experienced as a part of shamanistic ASC. A central theme of these approaches is that neuropsychology provides a basis for rock art motifs. Entoptic phenomena reflecting neurologically structured perceptual constants are the structural basis of rock art motifs, reflecting perceptions in shamanic ASC. The hardwired basis of hallucinatory experiences and their perceptual constants provides an iconographic system extended metaphorically in rock art representations.

Several putative universals of shamanism have been suggested as having their basis in natural models that reflect physical effects of ASC and their neuropsychological effects on mental imagery (Whitley 1994a,b,c). Constant human reactions to these underlying physical structures of consciousness produce universal forms of representation. The use of the animal world to represent shamanic ASC experiences contributes to cultural use of natural symbols and the "universal nature and neuropsychological basis of much of hunter-gatherer symbolism and iconography" (Whitley 1994a, 2).

Whitley's (1994c) work linking ancient rock art to culture through ethnography established the ubiquitous shamanic basis for these sites and activities. These were used both to induce ASC as a part of vision quests and to represent the experiences. His cross-cultural analyses bear out the original hypothesis of Lewis-Williams and Dowson that rock art represents neuropsychological structures revealed or elevated by ASC: "the ethnography universally and univocally supports a connection between rock art, ASC, and shamanistic belief and practice" (92). He further pointed out the cross-cultural use of similar metaphors for the visionary experiences of shamanism. Whitley analyzed recurrent shamanistic themes (death, flight, drowning, and sexual intercourse) as based on the use of neuropsychological models derived from somatic models and metaphors. Whitley also showed that frequently used animal symbols within shamanism are derived from natural symbols of power and behavioral/physiological analogies, reinforcing the importance of neurognostic perspectives in understanding shamanism and ASC.

Ecstasy—Altered States of Consciousness

The experiences produced within religious traditions were characterized by earlier anthropologists as awe, trance, or ecstasy; now these phenomena are referred to as altered states of consciousness (ASC) or transpersonal consciousness. Recognition of the powerful effects and the profound emotional and experiential transformations produced by shamanistic practices led to a characterization of ASC as fundamental to magico-religious practice. "Falling into a trance often constitutes the call to a religious vocation and . . . the ability to enter this state is a requirement for the specialist" (Norbeck 1961, 86). Possession is "one of the magician's professional qualifications . . . [and magic] requires and produces an alteration, a modification in one's state of mind" (Mauss [1906] 1972, 39, 128). Bourguignon's (1968) cross-cultural research illustrated the near universal role of institutionalized forms of ASC. This ASC aspect of magico-religious practice is most widely represented in the role of the shaman. "The first form of specialization of labor known to man was the performance of supernaturalistic rites" (Norbeck 1961, 101). This primordial role of the manipulation of consciousness was a function of the shaman. Cross-cultural research (Winkelman 1986a,b, 1990a,b, 1992) indicated the universality of shamans in hunter-gatherer societies, an ecologically specific adaptation to human psychobiological potentials derived from ASC. The shaman is a technician of consciousness who utilizes those potentials for healing and for personal and social transformations. Shamans' preeminent roles in hunter-gatherer societies as the principal political and religious functionary, the leader of hunting and group movement, and the bearer of cultural mythology underscore shamans' fundamental role in the evolution of human society and individual and collective consciousness.

The ubiquity of ASC and of their universal association with healing and spiritual experiences requires explanation. What is the reason for the alteration of consciousness and its association with religious, spiritual, and healing experiences? The answer proposed here is that shamanism and associated ASC constitute a normal alteration of human consciousness, providing an integration of cognitive, emotional, and behavioral capacities through psychophysiological manipulations of the human brain.

Evidence (cf. Weil 1972; Winkelman and Dobkin de Rios 1989; Winkelman 1996; Siegel 1990) indicates that the desire to alter consciousness is an innate, human, biologically based drive with adaptive significance. The ASC of shamanism are a manifestation of a fundamental homeostatic dynamic of the nervous system. These manifestations of consciousness involve a biologically based integrative mode of consciousness, replacing normal waking conditions—sympathetic dominance and desynchronized fast wave activity of the frontal cortex—with a parasympathetic dominant state characterized by high-voltage, slow-wave electroencephalogram (EEG) activity originating in the circuits linking the brain stem and the hippocampal-septal area of the limbic system with the frontal cortex (Mandell 1980; Winkelman 1986b, 1990b, 1992, 1996). This high-voltage, slow-wave EEG activity originates in the hippocampal-septal area and imposes a synchronous slow-wave pattern on the frontal lobes, producing interhemispheric synchronization and coherence, limbic-cortex integration, and integration across the neuraxis, a synthesis of behavior, emotion, and thought. The range of ASC induction procedures used cross-culturally reflects diverse means of evoking this natural potential of the human brain-mind, a psychophysiologically based integrative mode of consciousness.

This integrative mode of consciousness is a condition of homeostatic balance, a physiologically based mode of organismic functioning and integration. These conditions of systemic brain-mind integration provide different types of information processing than that associated with waking consciousness. Shamans represent the first people who learned to operate within and to utilize this integrative mode of consciousness, providing psychodynamic integration and transformation. Symbols, ritual, and myth, such as those referenced in the descent and ascent found in shamanic flight, represent these developmental transformations. These are exemplified in the death and rebirth experiences that represent the termination of one ego or identity and the birth of a new identity and sense of self. Hunt (1995a) analyzed these and other universal mystical experiences as presentational symbolic systems involving fundamental synesthetic structures of human information processing and consciousness. ASC utilize these imagetic structures of human conceptualization. Induction of integrative brain processing is achieved through rituals that manipulate biological functions through both physical activities and cognitive-emotional associations to produce transformations of consciousness, linking the individual with supraindividual and infrapersonal frames of reference.

These processes are found in a classic metaphor of ASC, enlightenment, which is found in esoteric traditions around the world. Enlightenment reflects the experience of being filled or illuminated with light, combined with insight and understanding. Enlightenment experiences are found not only in Eastern traditions, but also in Western traditions; for example, Saint Paul being blinded by the light of a vision; and Saint Augustine, Saint Theresa, and other saints overwhelmed with internal experiences characterized by blinding light. The structural features of the experiences show fundamental similarities, illustrating a common neurological basis.

Analytical systems developed in Buddhist and other Asian philosophies have provided extensive knowledge of the nature of consciousness, but the understandings of these analytical systems have seldom been incorporated into Western science (but see Walsh 1980, 1988; Wilber, 1977, 1979, 1980). Laughlin, McManus, and d'Aquili (1992) suggested that non-Western descriptions of consciousness have congruencies with neuropsychology's views of how the brain and the nervous system work as a complex of hierarchically functioning levels that progressively model and test models of reality. They suggested that analytical mystical systems characterize human consciousness in ways equivalent to the neurological perspectives on consciousness, as involving entrainment of circuits and networks, regulation of sensory input, information processing, and determination of adaptive action. The integration of the phenomenological descriptions with neurological ones provides a means for determining transcendent aspects of consciousness.

Shamanic and mystical traditions foster development of a different mode of perception involving deliberate cultivation of an internal visionary or imagetic world, a neurologically based symbolic system traditionally represented by spirits and other powers. The neuro-phenomenological perspective illustrates universal shamanic constructs to be neurognostic structures that are mentally and emotionally trans-acted in ritual, cognitive evolution, and psychological growth. The mystical traditions are "state specific sciences" that examine the attentional, perceptual, and cognitive processes underlying conscious-ness and that provide for further development of the human intellec-tual capacity within presentational (Hunt 1995a) and epistemologi-cal frameworks. This book explains these universal ASC by integrating the perspectives of perennial traditions of consciousness with the modern neurobiological science of the brain. This neurophenome-nological approach to the nature of consciousness requires a systems perspective.

THE NATURE OF CONSCIOUSNESS

A framework characterizing the nature of consciousness is neces-sary for addressing its relationships to shamanism. Human conscious-ness encompasses a broad spectrum of capabilities based on the in-teraction of biological capacities and symbolic representations acquired through learning. Linguistic analyses indicate that conscious-ness includes a wide range of meanings: conditions of being awake and having awareness; feelings and thoughts; self-awareness; inter-nal knowledge and conviction; communal knowledge and social awareness; conscience; the ability to know and learn; skills and ca-pacities; and the ability to teach and share knowledge and understand-ing (Winkelman 1994). Although some have insisted on conceptual-izing consciousness as a reflexive self-consciousness, reflexive consciousness itself has been characterized as a nonunitary phenomenom. Consciousness is used to refer to common capabilities of humans and other animals, as well as to differentiate between them, designating uniquely human linguistic, rational, and abstract capa-bilities. Consciousness also includes a range of functions that esoteric traditions claim supersede rational and egoic forms of consciousness, representing the evolution of what is conceptualized as spirit, soul, mind, self, and transcendental human capabilities. The diverse ap-proaches illustrate many different forms and manifestations of con-sciousness, as illustrated in Gennaro's model:

1. Phenomenal States, such as conscious bodily sensations and world-di-rected perceptual states

2. Non-perceptual Intentional States (e.g., world-directed desires and thoughts)
3. Self-Consciousness
   a. Non-reflective Self-Consciousness, i.e., Nonconscious Meta-psychological Thought Awareness
   b. Momentary Focused Introspection
   c. Deliberate Introspection (Gennaro 1995, 31)

Gennaro suggested an explicit hierarchy in considering bodily states to be the most primitive and in seeing nonreflective self-consciousness as less complex than introspection. The notion of a hierarchy of consciousness is a central feature of many mystical systems. In synthesizing the meditative traditions' views of consciousness, Wilber (1977, 1980) suggested a series of primary functional structures of consciousness involving different forms of the self and producing different levels of consciousness (see chapter 3 this volume). The commonality underlying this diversity in denotations of consciousness is revealed by etymological and epistemological approaches.

Etymological Roots of Consciousness

Linguistic perspectives (e.g., Winkelman 1994; Natsoulas 1983, 1991, 1991–1992, 1992) illustrate that consciousness is used to refer to a wide range of phenomena. The *American Heritage Dictionary (AHD)* definitions of *conscious* are: not asleep; awake; awareness of one's own existence, sensations, thoughts and environment; subjectively known; capable of complex response to the environment; intentionally conceived or done; and deliberate. The meanings of *consciousness* are prominently based on *conscious*, which has a Latin origin (*conscius*) meaning "knowing with others, participating in knowledge, aware of" (Morris 1981, 283; cf. Barnhart 1988). A communality underlying diverse usages of "consciousness" involves it constituting a "knowing system." This is explicit in the etymology of consciousness found in *com* (with) and *scire* (to know). The communal dimension of consciousness is also illustrated in the alternate form *conscience*, which shares a common Indo-European root with conscious (*skei*) (Morris 1981). Although often neglected in considerations of the meaning of consciousness, the form "conscience" is central, referring not only to the essence or totality of attitudes, opinions, and sensitivities held by an individual or a group, but also to the social context that creates and evaluates consciousness. The communal dimension of consciousness as socially shared knowledge is also reflected in the primary definition of *conscious* in the *Oxford English Dictionary (OED)*: "knowing something with others, . . . knowing, or sharing the knowledge of anything, together with another" (*Oxford English Dictionary*, 1989, 756). This communal dimension frames the meaning of consciousness in the relationship between individual and community. The interrelationship of social factors in the development of consciousness is illustrated in evolutionary perspectives. The intensive social behavior required for human survival necessitated the ability to attribute meaning and intentionality to others, to be able to predict their mental states and future behavior, and to roleplay in order to coordinate group behavior. Consciousness involves using awareness of "other" to model self.

The meanings associated with the linguistic roots of *consciousness* represent a range of denotations from biologically based organismic capabilities to culturally derived reference, learning and experience that provide for awareness and complex intentional responses (Winkelman 1994). Similarly, uses of the term "consciousness" in the cognitive, artificial intelligence, philosophical, and other scientific traditions indicate that consciousness refers to a number of interrelated behaviors characteristic of complex systems that respond to their environment. There is not one but many kinds of consciousness. Etymological analyses and multidisciplinary approaches indicate that the many meanings of consciousness are all fundamentally concerned with an informational relationship between an organism and its environment, the processes and properties of "knowing" systems.

Consciousness as a System

The dependence of consciousness on both the brain and the socially constructed experiences requires a systems approach to articulate their interrelations. Because consciousness operates in the organism's adaptation to the environment and to changing situations, it involves many different processes that sustain goal-directed behavior. Consciousness is based in internal processes and their relationships with the external environment. Variation in processes and interrelated structures that produce consciousness provide the basis for differences among the many different forms of consciousness.

A systems perspective is exemplified in many conceptualizations of consciousness. As described in the "Three Worlds" view of Popper and Eccles (1977), consciousness functions to couple the individual organism, its social group, and the environment. Understanding consciousness requires linking distinct phenomena, including: World 1—physical things; World 2—subjective experiences; and World 3—culture, objective knowledge, and products of the mind. Current theories (e.g., Baars 1997; Ellis 1995) characterize consciousness in terms of interacting components of a system.

Baars's (1997) global workspace theory illustrated that consciousness is based on widely distributed capabilities of the brain and is used for interpretation of, learning about, and action on the world, particularly in novel circumstances. There are many kinds of contents of consciousness, including both the external world and internal imagery, a sense of presence, bodily sensations, personal memories, intentions, expectations, and beliefs about oneself and the world. These conscious contents are made available for what Baars called the "unconscious audience," including memory systems, automatisms, motivational systems, and the interpretation or meaning systems. Key elements of consciousness include: (1) working memory, which provides the workspace for conscious experience; (2) "context operators," including the "director" (self), the environment, and attention, which selects among competing sources; (3) competing sources of information (representations, images, and perception); and (4) a variety of unconscious factors including memory, automatisms (behavior), motivational systems (emotions), and interpretive/meaning systems.

Ellis (1986, 1995) similarly emphasized that consciousness involves interaction of many factors, including representation of a context, internal conflict, how the context contributes to the conflict, and how to change the context to resolve it. This interaction is based on the interrelations of lower-order processes, including imagination, memory, representation, emotions, and desires. Ellis (1995, 3) suggested that conscious processes are characterized by the presence of emotional intensity and processing in which an imaginative act based on memory and desire precedes the perceptual, playing a fundamental role in eliciting arousal and attentional mechanisms Motivational processes based on judgments about what is important for the organism are crucial to the selection of perceptual elements for conscious attention. Conscious information processing uses a concept or an image of what might be, with the efferent imaginative production preceding the afferent perceptual consciousness. What determines the direction of attention is meaning, rather than sensory input; a predisposition to see occurs prior to perception.

The cornerstone of the human intellect and consciousness is the ability to conceptualize and manipulate subjunctives—the ability to imagine what it would be like if things were different than the way they are. Consciousness provides its substratum through a symbolization process that represents memories and their images and associations. The generalized or generic image has elementary cognitive functions that constitute a form of behavior. The formulation of mental images involves perceptual and somatic images of what it is like to move one's own body. This imagetic process is based in desire, a process motivated toward reproducing a representation of missing elements (Ellis 1995, 7). Representation involves looking for what is important to the organism and depends on the motivation to be aware of something, a general desire to know (Ellis 1995, 28, 128, 138).

Baars's and Ellis's models emphasize the relationships among a range of functions in producing consciousness. Consciousness reflects systemic properties of organismic functioning involving an ability to maintain adaptive interaction between internal and external environments. Consciousness begins with a question, the need to assess and to analyze incoming information in relation to existing conceptual frameworks. Consciousness uses this information to formulate goal-oriented behaviors, which reflect communal dimensions—priorities defined by awarenesses shared with others. Consciousness mediates the organism's adaptation to the environment through modulation of a range of capabilities, including attention, representation, memory, learning, desires, planning, and behavior. It couples the organism with its environment and social group to make decisions regarding changing situations. Relating to the environment in meaningful ways requires use of information in reference to previous experiences to address motivations and goals. Memory links sensations and perceptions, constituting the template for sensations and entailing a judgment about the relationship of present stimuli to past experience. A goal orientation cannot be based exclusively on reflexes; rather it requires an intelligent selection among behavioral options based on memory and judgment. Consciousness allocates attention in prioritizing biological, social, and personal goals. Goal orientation requires selection among options, based in memory, judgment, and abilities of discrimination. Goal-oriented actions are based on judgments of symbolic information derived from past experience (memory) and from perception and judgment of situations in light of current motivations.

The conceptualization of consciousness as a framework for processing information to guide behavior in adaptive and meaningful ways makes the interpretations used to construct meaning central to consciousness. The management of diverse inputs requires a concept of self as agent and the social other as context for self and situational evaluation. Consciousness and self are necessarily linked; because consciousness involves relationships between knower and known, it requires a knower with some sense of entityhood (self representation) and for whom priorities are weighed. Selves operate as subsystems that selectively modulate an organism's behavior in relationship to a changing hierarchy of environmental demands.

Explication of consciousness requires examination of the interacting subsystems that produce consciousness. These subsystems are exemplified in the common elements found in the models of Baars (1997), Ellis (1995), and others (e.g., Piaget 1969). Their overlap indicates the fundamental properties of conscious systems and provides a structure for analyzing different types of consciousness. These properties include: attention; representations of information, including external perceptions and internal images; learning and memory; pattern recognition and judgment; motivation and emotions; meaning; behavior; and self. Central to conscious systems are:

> *Awareness*, a capacity to handle many different forms of
> > *Representation* or *Information*—sensations, perceptions, images, and language—which depend on,
> > > *Pattern recognition*, evaluation and judgment motivated by
> > > > *Desires*, emotions and meanings attributed by the organism to manage
> > > > > *Relations* to the environment and goals, involving others and conflict, and based on experiences for the
> > > > > > *Knower* or *Self*.

Variations in specific aspects of each of these components provide the basis for a variety of forms, levels, and types of consciousness. Different forms of consciousness can be characterized in terms of the system that the subject utilizes and through which the world is known. These include different forms of attention (e.g., arousal, orienting, awareness); representation (e.g., iconic, symbolic, social, language);

memory (instinctual, perceptual, motor, episodic, semantic) and learning (e.g., reflex, associational, conditioning, reversal); motivations/emotions (e.g., desire, questioning, attachment, various affects); and self (e.g., somatic, social, egoic/mental, reflexive).

These subsystem elements help in illustrating the specific nature of shamanic ASC, which emphasize: (1) awareness of internal representations based in perceptual images rather than in the sensory world; (2) elicitation of emotions related to aspects of self, particularly repressed complexes and identities; (3) evaluation of these experiences within mythological contexts and systems of meaning for interpretation of self; and (4) activation of memories, particularly those of central emotional significance to self, motivational systems, and social dynamics. This management of diverse inputs requires mediation through symbolic processes involving self and social relations, which provide the concept of agent, and the social other as context for self and situational evaluation. These systematically interrelated processes that are central features of contemporary theories of consciousness correspond directly to Piaget's ([1966] 1973, 1971) epistemological approach to consciousness.

Genetic Epistemology and Consciousness

Consciousness is produced by the structures that mediate interaction between knower and known, making an epistemological approach to consciousness essential. The epistemological approach helps illustrate how consciousness involves the relations within a system. Genetic epistemology, exemplified in Piaget's work,[1] is concerned with the nature, origin, evolution, and validation of knowing, cognition, and consciousness. Piaget proposed that cognitive development and consciousness are epistemic,[2] based in the relationships constructed by the knower with the known. Knowledge, cognition, and consciousness are possible because of the necessary epistemic structures that the subject constructs. Piaget's epistemic stages or mental constructs underlying knowledge and consciousness proceed through fixed stages of development that represent different degrees of equilibration—adaptation of the organism to the environment. Piaget characterized consciousness as being constructed in the interaction between subject and object, a relationship between the knowing subject and what is known through the intervening cognitive (epistemic) structures that contribute to the nature of what is known. Consciousness requires a conceptualization or representation and is always mediated by a structure of interrelated concepts operating on a higher level than the experience.

Consciousness and its development are based in a number of processes that mediate the organism's relationship to the environment. The stages of cognitive development proposed by Piaget have a fixed structure, reflecting the possibilities and the limitations provided by biological structures. Development also depends on learning opportunities and the maturation of brain processing areas necessary to handle forms and combinations of information, as well as on environmental contexts. The social dimension and action on the environment provide essential input into the developmental process, constituting the context within which a frustration of desires motivates the construction of more encompassing models. Piaget characterized cognitive development as involving a shift from judgments based on appearances, naive perception, and empiricism to a critical rationalism. The development of consciousness proceeds from the external objects to the internal mental mechanisms and the cognitive unconscious, a shift from the level of action to the level of thought. This development enables the thinker to transcend strictly biological processes through the structures and the norms of the psychological and social levels. Genetic epistemology can be extended to an analysis of contemplative consciousness. Hunt (1995a) provided perspectives for assessing these conditions of consciousness as involving complex visual-kinesthetic synesthesias—multimodal integration of information—and development in an affective line of reasoning. Contemplative consciousness can be interpreted as superseding the naive, habitual, epistemic assumptions made about the nature of knowing and the relationship between knower and known, modifying epistemic constructs utilized at earlier levels (cf. chapter 3 this volume). Principal aspects of this epistemic change involve suspension of previous epistemic constructs provided by enhanced attention and by recognition of the role of habitualized symbols mediating perception, cognition, affect, behavior, and sense of self.

Central to Piaget's perspective is the role of reflective abstraction,[3] involving processes of operation on and differentiation from the preceding level, providing for the emergence of a higher-order stage that is more complex and unified than the previous. The emergence of the higher level is mediated (or assisted) by symbolic structures. The emergence of symbols into consciousness transforms the mode of consciousness at that level into the next higher level. The self plays a central role in this process, identifying with that new emergent form of consciousness and its structures, along with a disidentification with the previous structure. This permits transcendence of the structure and the ability to operate on it with the newly emergent structure. These different selves are mediated through the epistemic relationships that the knower constructs between the organism and the reality known, including physical, psychological, emotional, and social dimensions.

A neuroepistemological foundation for consciousness requires investigation of (1) the central role of activity—praxis—especially the participation in various socially constructed states of consciousness, as central to the construction of models of consciousness; and (2) cross-species commonalities in the development of the information processing functions of the brain[4] (Winkelman 1997a). This perspective provides the basis for characterizing different forms of consciousness in terms of epistemic structures and the physical components of the information-processing systems, which mediate the system of schemes, concepts, relations, operations, and forms of self that the subject utilizes. These are based on both brain function and cultural construction, which interact through the self.

The Social Dimension: Self, Other, and Consciousness

Baars (1997) characterized self and consciousness as standing in relationship to one another as context and content. The concept of *self* has an indispensable role in consciousness. Consciousness is "for something," and that is a self. Self is the organism's autorepresentation of the organism for the organism. Roles of self in conscious experiences include perceiver, actor, narrator, and the context for the long-term stability of identity. The self has basic access to the elements necessary for consciousness, including sensory experience, memory, and personal facts, as well as future intentions. The self provides the most basic expectations about the organism, its world, and a goal hierarchy to differentiate the priorities encountered. The self serves as a pattern recognizer, based on the brain system's ability to observe the output of other brain systems and to modify behavior to meet a hierarchy of goals. Baars pointed out that a "sensory motor self," based on the sensory motor mapping, provides a basic self/other differentiation, which is necessary for any kind of sensor system. This sensory self is different from the "narrative self," the interpreter engaged in providing stability and continuity in explaining to oneself what it is that one is experiencing. This function is manifested in "self/

alien" syndromes, as well as in brain pathologies. When brain dys-function creates gaps and discontinuities, the self provides a narra-tive that maintains the illusion of continuity, even compensating for gross violations of the self. Baars illustrated the existence of multiple selves within the organism and their adaptive functions in dealing with stress (cf. material in chapter 5, this volume, regarding the mul-tiple personality disorder).

The fundamental role of the self in consciousness is illustrated by Waller (1996) and Scheff (1993). Waller suggested that organizational theory and findings reveal that consciousness has been selected for problem solving under novel conditions. The solution of nonroutine problems requires a mental capacity to manipulate one's self to the task of problem solution. Waller concluded that the sense of self has evolved to maintain the appropriate problem-solving and task orien-tation.

Scheff combined the work of George Herbert Mead and Marvin Minsky to illustrate the fundamental and necessary role of self in consciousness. Minsky's (1985) contribution to a theory of mind was in an expansion of the role of agent. Scheff emphasized at least three different forms of agents: (1) instinctive, (2) learned skill sequences, and (3) command-control. Whereas instinctive and learned sequences agents become stereotyped and constant, command-control agents are variable in order to detect conflict and to serve as a mediator in making decisions. These three agents provide the basis for behavior sequences. Some of these are genetically inherited patterns; most end up being developed later in life through learning. These agents provide a basis for the development of ego and self. This self develops in response to the need for mediation of conflict between the different agents. Ini-tial conflicts to be resolved by ego involve those between different instinctive agents. Self and ego mediate among the demands of differ-ent agents through serving as a higher order agent within a hierarchy of goals.

Minsky characterized the ego as the highest-level command-con-trol agent, with control over a large number of lower-level agents. But the ego is not always in control of what the body does, with lower-level command-control agents potentially able to circumvent the goals of the ego. Scheff (1993) suggested that the self be viewed as a multilevel structure or process of agents. These may be expanded laterally at the same level or vertically across a number of levels of command-control. He suggested that the self is infinitely expandable and that intelligence is directly related to the number of levels that an agent controls. Although proliferation of agents increases the likelihood of conflict, a larger number of levels permits the more effective management of conflict. Selves provide for the hierarchy of levels of control necessary to deal with a variety of different kinds of internal conflicts. Agents may act in a number of different relations to one another, including serial and parallel or simultaneous actions. The simultaneous processing by many different agents provides a complexity and a speed of processing and the basis for intuitive solutions to problems. These agents also need to be combined through associative processes. Intelligent[5] behavior depends on combination of the serial analytical processes and the intuitive parallel ones.

Shamanism developed as a tradition for constructing, manipulating, and using a variety of selves for psychological and social integration. Although the self has seemed a relatively unproblematic concept to many, the nature of personal identity is much more complex when examined in cross-cultural context, particularly in the context of shamanism, possession, and the mythological systems within which they are interpreted. The numerous forms of self-referential systems found in mythology provide for polysemic representation. The process of mirroring plays a fundamental role in utilizing these systems to provide the template for self from these systems. This is based in a common auto symbolic, or self-specifying system, and is manifested in the sense of recognition of other, a presence. This notion of felt presence, the sense of self in the unknown other, is a manifestation of the plural symbolic capabilities of the creature in an attitude of openness toward the environment (Hunt 1995a). This is the basis for the concept of animism, the spirit entities widely viewed as a primitive of religion. This sense of "self in other" is manifested in the use of the disembodied self as a model of the unknown other, providing a basis for relations with the spirit world and others.

Self and Others.   Fundamental aspects of the nature of the self and consciousness are derived from social relations and their symbolic bases. Hunt (1995a) illustrated this with Mead's (1934) perspectives on the capacity of humans to "take the role of the other," based on internalizing and imagining the expressions of others toward self. The self and ego depend on models and conflict for their development. This is provided by social relations, where others frustrate goals and desires and provide norms for self characteristics. Mead emphasized the central role of the group in understanding the individual, who depends on the incorporation of others to coordinate his or her own behavior and development. This is Mead's concept of the generalized other, involving the internalization of the roles and knowledge of others in society. The self thus incorporates knowledge of the structure and the content of society. The use of others/society as a model for self entails a form of metaphoric understanding, using one modality (others) to elucidate another (self). These representations provide the locus of reference (self) and context (other) that makes consciousness possible through communicative interactions. Consciousness is further structured through internal conversations based on the contents of social life and the presumed perspectives of others. In this sense, consciousness is dialogic.

This dialogue, however, need not be based in verbal language but may be based in visual kinesthetic imagery. Although this capacity for ongoing self-reference is most obvious in speech and verbal thought, Hunt (1995a) suggested that it also involves nonverbal symbolic thought processes that he labeled "presentational." This recombinatory symbolic capability is first manifested in facial mirroring in infancy, providing the basis for learning how to take the role of the other, and consequently, to produce self awareness. "Social mirroring—as incipient 'taking the role of the other'—and cross-modal translations—as the core of the symbolic capacity—are coemergent and inseparable. Human cognition is, from the beginning, structured in the form of dialogue" (Hunt 1995c, 88). The cross-translation found in the "taking the role of the other" has its first manifestations in mirroring capabilities, which are present from birth. These are based in cross-modal translations between visual image (mother's face) and the kinesthetically felt face of the infant. These first manifestations of symbolic communication show the inseparability of cross-modal translation and the ability to take the role of the other. This mother-infant exchange enables the infant to discover its own face through the return of mirrored expressions and to take on the role of the other in mirroring the mother's facial expressions. This mirroring constitutes the first form of symbolic expression. The other as image and physical object subsequently emerges as the model for understanding of one's own unseen physical self, making the social foundation essential for self-consciousness.

Self-Referential Awareness.   The aspects of consciousness referred to as *reflexive awareness* involve the capacity to direct awareness at one's own ongoing subjective experiences. Hunt (1995a) contended that it is the cross-flow, or cross-modal translation, between different modalities that provides the basis for self-referential awareness. Hunt viewed self-referential consciousness as emerging from the integration of different modalities that provides a sentience of sentience. Although self-referential consciousness has been associated with language functions, self-referential functions arise from a more basic self-reflexive capacity that is intrinsic to the use of symbolic communication, but that may be expressed in modalities other than language. This is an extension of the view of mind as a sense that emerges from the convergence of the other perceptual modalities. Hunt characterized self-consciousness as based on the structure of self-referential metaphor that nonetheless involves the other. "Reflexive awareness of immediate subjective state is a special consequence of our capacity to 'take the role of the other' toward ourselves as personal awareness" (Hunt 1995c, 17). This self-awareness is not only reflexive but also evaluative, derived from social engagement and using the other as the point of reference.

Social Intelligence: Other and Mind

Mithen (1996) emphasized two central aspects to social intelligence, one based on social knowledge about conspecifics and the other based on an ability to infer the mental states of the conspecifics. The apes manifest social behavior that is more complex than in any other area of activity, suggesting that monkeys and apes also have a specialized social intelligence. This social intelligence has been referred to as Machiavellian, reflecting the "cunning, deception and the construction of alliances and friendships pervasive in the life of many primates" (Mithen 1996, 81). This social intelligence reflects the specific social processes that group living creates for primates. These social processes include a balance of competitive and cooperative relations; mate and food competition; and a wide range of alliance, play, and grooming behaviors. This produces a need for cognitive skills for cooperation and successful competition within one's social group. The social intelligence facilitates group interaction with a new level of mental processing that enables individuals to predict others' behavior based on hypothesis building and testing. This intuitive psychology domain provides the basis for attribution of mental states to others. This intuitive psychology, or a belief-desire psychology, entails a theory of mind, manifested in the ability to intuit the mental processes of others, or "mind reading." This is based on the use of the organism's own mind, as well as its feelings and behaviors in similar contexts, to provide a model of a mind of others and the behaviors the others would likely produce. This cognitive capability had social function—providing individuals with adaptive skills for group living through the ability to predict others' behavior. This also entailed social forethought and understanding, what Humphrey (1984) referred to as social intelligence. Mithen argued that these social behaviors constitute the biological function of consciousness, with the evolution of reflective consciousness derived from these social behaviors. The ability to read others' minds constituted an essential basis for the maintenance of social cohesion and enhanced the transmission of knowledge. This constituted a basis for consciousness, the foundation for a primordial aspect of consciousness as "knowing with" and knowing self through others.

The Sacred Self.   Shamanistic entities and processes, particularly animism, the guardian spirit complex, and possession, provide mechanisms and symbolic systems within which the self develops in interactional symbolic relationships with others. The most important representations in shamanistic thought are in the spirit world of "sacred others" (Pandian 1997), who operate in the spiritual and human social worlds. Pandian showed these religious phenomena to involve processes for identification of the cultural locus of the symbolic self. These systems also serve other cognitive and social functions, including the resolution of contradictions between the reality of suffering and broader systems of cultural meaning. These religious-meaning systems include models for the representation and, hence, the development of the self. The beliefs of these systems constitute the projective systems and norms for psychosocial relations that structure individual psychodynamics and collective patterns of behavior. Pandian characterized the "shamanistic sacred self" as involving processes that provide protection through a psychocultural therapeutic communication system that produces and maintains the symbolic self and culture. These shamanistic practices have particular relevance in social crises, where they provide the processes for reestablishing personal and cultural equilibrium through the introduction of new or modified symbolic forms of the sacred (social) self. The phenomena of animism and the spiritual worlds constitute models for self and society. These phenomena, their nature and functions in the self, and their forms of reference for characterizing ourselves, others, and the world are fundamental to consciousness. Concepts of self and agency (intentional actors) are central to shamanistic consciousness, especially as manifested in concerns with animism, totemism, guardian spirit quests, anthropomorphism, and possession. These "spiritual" concepts represent fundamental aspects of the organism's consciousness.

A NEUROPHENOMENOLOGICAL APPROACH TO CONSCIOUSNESS

The nature of consciousness is central to long-standing questions regarding the relationships of mind and body and the mental and material properties of humans. The neurophenomenological perspective used here provides a unitary approach to consciousness, deliberately integrating material and mental perspectives rather than reducing consciousness to one or the other. Examining the relationship between the physiofunctional organization of the brain and phenomenal experiences provides the basis for an integrated framework for understanding the interaction of biological and mental mechanisms in the production of consciousness.

The neurophenomenological or biogenetic structuralist approach (e.g., Laughlin, McManus, and d'Aquili 1992) provides a common approach for addressing the role of both neurobiology and phenomenal experience in the manifestations of consciousness. Recognizing the common basis in constructed precepts for our knowledge of both the physical world and internal experience enables consideration of the relationship between the classic dichotomies of objectivity and subjectivity, brain and mind, without creating an inseparable gap between the two. To overcome dualistic perspectives, we need a characterization of consciousness within a common framework for characterizing experience, neurobiology, and behavior that can address the mechanisms that produce consciousness. The neurophenomenological approach is not reductionistic to either materialism or mentalism; it recognizes that the physical world is a transcendent reality and that our knowledge and experience of it is through mediating constructs. It recognizes that mental and phenomenological levels have systematic principles and properties (e.g., symbolic cultural meanings) that, although dependent on the physical and biological levels for their manifestation, are nonetheless different from them. Conversely, the physical levels have their own inherent properties, but knowledge of them also reflects the structuring principles of the mental (epistemic) levels. These include the features derived from mental filtering, as well as the mental imposition of patterning on the physical (e.g., intentionality causing variation in physiological functioning). The properties of consciousness are not just the properties provided by brain structures; they are derived from interrelations of systemic properties of the brain with symbolic information and meanings provided by learning and culture. This interaction of biology and culture in production of consciousness necessitates a neurophenomenological approach that directly relates phenomenal experience to neurological structures and processes.

Human consciousness and phenomena associated with its manifestations—organismic control, self-knowledge, experience, information processing, planning, and the experiences of ASC—occur in the interaction of biological and symbolic systems. A range of biological manipulations of the body, including drugs, sensory stimulation and deprivation, and physical activities, can dramatically alter consciousness and the individual's experience of self and world. Conversely, voluntary control of mental process and attention to symbols can yoke experience and body physiology, forcing dramatic alterations in consciousness and organic responses. This illustrates the biocultural and psychophysiological nature of human consciousness and its production through interrelated biological and informational systems. Understanding human consciousness requires that we address both the biological basis that produces a substrate for consciousness and the phenomenological structures through which humans know and report their consciousness.

The neurophenomenological approach examines biology and experience within a common framework based in a recognition of the symbolic basis in epistemic structures of both subjective experience and knowledge of the physical world. If we fail to recognize that observations, whether of the physical world or of subjective experience, are based in symbolic models, then we unnecessarily dichotomize the world into separate spheres that are by definition irreconcilable. By recognizing the subjective and symbolic foundation of what we know of material reality, we obtain a common foundation for integrating what we experience as the division between the objective and the subjective worlds (a hypothetical materialism and an idealist epistemology [Winkelman 1997a]).

To distinguish the transcendent reality from our models, Laughlin et al. (1992) employed the terms *operational* environment and *cognized* environment, respectively. The operational environment is the world independent of human knowledge or representation of it (Kantian noumena). We do not perceive this external or operational world, reality as it is. Rather we experience symbols in the patterns of neural activity, which depend on the interaction of physiological systems with the cultural programs and epistemic assumptions acquired for processing the external world. What we know of the operational world is a cognized environment or model, a consequence of enculturated processing of the operational world. We ordinarily experience our models, not the environment itself; our perceptions are generally limited to our culturally cognized environments; and these models are necessarily incomplete and contain systematic biases and errors. Consciousness is what is represented to the organism, its cognized environments, both explicit and implicit, external and internal.

Because what we know of physical reality is a cognized environment, we derive a nondualistic perspective by recognizing that all domains of knowledge (e.g., physical science, philosophy, religion, metaphysics) are based in culturally programmed biocognitive potentials. But understanding this constructed nature of perception of reality also requires learning about the operations of the human brain—a part of the operational environment and a physical structure of the organism responsible for producing the behaviors and experiences that constitute evidence of consciousness.

The neurophenomenological approach provides a unified basis for addressing consciousness. The neurophenomenological approach adopts a structural monist perspective that accepts both mind and brain as manifestations of the structures of the human organism, comprising two different views of the same reality: "[M]ind is how brain experiences its own functioning, and brain provides the structure of the mind. . . ." " '[S]piritual' awareness is one way of knowing the being; 'physical' awareness is another way of knowing the being" (Laughlin et al. 1992, 13, 11). Neither the physical sciences nor the "spiritual" disciplines alone provide a complete explanation or representation of reality. A neurophenomenological approach is an integrative perspective for understanding consciousness in the recognition of the primacy of cognized models, as well as the roles of biology in structuring experience and consciousness.

Mental Effects on the Organism

A new paradigm is necessary to explain the ways in which language and symbolic actions cause physiological responses and other interrelationships of sociocultural and psychophysiological domains. The causal effects of mental and ideological levels often have been discounted in the materialist paradigms that have dominated Western science. The causal effects of the level of mind must be delineated for an understanding of the mechanisms of symbolic healing and other shamanistic treatment procedures, how our thoughts, expectations, and social and interpersonal dynamics affect our biology. Mental levels may create a "downward causation," with the biological and physical levels manifesting structuring by the mental levels (e.g., symbols or intentionality causing variation in biological functioning).

These causative factors are recognized as central in the cognitive revolution of psychology that replaced the bottom-up determinism of positivist materialist science with a recognition of the causal effects found in subjective mental processes. The cognitive revolution in psychology emphasizes an emergent interactionist perspective in "reciprocal causation" and "downward causation," where higher mental levels have effects upon the physical foundations from which they emerge (Sperry 1993). These causative principles are fundamental to shamanism, which uses ritual to restructure consciousness to produce an integration of individual and collective consciousness. Shamanism evolved as a system designed to enhance the development and the manipulation of these cognized environments and their interface with human emotions, beliefs, and physiological processes. The practices of shamanistic healing reflect the effects of beliefs, ritual, culture, mental phenomena, and meaning on physiological responses and health. The use of rituals to affect well-being and other symbolic effects on physiology represents some of the most far-reaching implications of these perspectives for the physicalist paradigms of Western science and biomedicine. These effects of mind on body, the causal relationships of the cultural on biological levels of human existence, are manifested in the general stress-and-adaptation syndrome, sociophysiology, hex death, psychoneuroimmunology, placebo effects, and total drug responses. Explicating the semantic sociopsychophysiological linkages underlying these phenomena requires a neurophenomenological approach to link meaning to psychobiological functioning. The underlying processes are revealed through the neurophenomenological approach, which illustrates that socialization processes canalize physiological development by habitualizing and automatizing physiological responses to symbolic meanings.

The effects of meaning—the interpretation of events—on physiological processes have been a long-standing realization from studies of stress. The stress-induced general adaptation syndrome and its psychophysiological effects provide a basis for elucidation of the symbolic model of healing. Research in sociophysiology illustrates the potent effects that social relations exert on health, morbidity, and mortality. The psychocultural and social effects on physiological processes are illustrated in ordinary and unusual physiological and behavioral responses (e.g., hex death, spontaneous remission of disease, symbolically timed deaths, mourning deaths, extraordinary healing, and conscious control of the autonomic nervous system and other physiological processes). The field of psychoneuroimmunology provides examples of powerful mental effects on physiological processes. These phenomena require a major reconceptualization of traditional views of causation. This shift in attention to the causal effects of consciousness reflects a revolution in science in which meaning has emerged with a central causal role. There are a number of different kinds or levels of meaning, different procedures and mechanisms underlying mental construction of the models that mediate our knowledge of the material world. These are evidenced in the distinct aspects of the brain, their information-processing capacities, and their relationships to self and consciousness. Shamanism and other consciousness traditions utilize these biologically based processes and representations, which constitute the foundation for shamanic universals.

Neurognostic Structures: Innate Modules for Consciousness

The biological structures of the organism play a fundamental role in the construction of consciousness. Universal phenomena of shamanism and mystical traditions reflect these biologically based structures of consciousness. The universality of basic experiences related to shamanism (e.g., soul flight) illustrates that these practices are not strictly cultural but are structured by underlying psychobiological features. Universal shamanic practices must be understood in terms of similar adaptations to a common underlying psychobiology. Their biological basis makes them *neurognostic* structures, reflecting biological structures of knowing. Laughlin, McManus, and d'Aquili (1992) referred to neurognosis[6] as the initial organization of the neural network that provides the basis for the universal aspects of mind. Neurognostic structures are the inherent knowledge structures of the organism, predisposing the structure of experiences and the cognized world. Universal shamanic characteristics reflect these neurognostic structures, as do archetypes, the primordial organizing principles structuring the basic patterns of the collective unconscious.

The concept of neurognosis is reflected in inborn modules for organizing knowledge, which are used by several researchers to explain the evolution of the human mind in terms of specific specialized programs. These ideas are exemplified by Fodor (1983) (e.g., *The Modularity of the Mind*), who proposes that there are hardwired input systems that provide for automatic information-processing systems. A similar model of human cognition is provided by Gardener's[7] *Frames of Mind: The Theory of Multiple Intelligences*. Gardener (1983) postulated that human capabilities are based on seven different types of relatively autonomous intelligences: bodily-kinesthetic, spatial, one for looking in at one's own mind, a module for understanding others, linguistic, musical, and logical-mathematical.

Mithen (1996) suggested that the evolution of the human mind involved development of specialized brain modules that provide the basis for abilities such as complex social interaction, "mind reading" of others' intentions, natural history knowledge, tool-using abilities, and language. Evidence for the existence of these modules comes from findings in developmental psychology that indicate that children are born with content-rich intuitive knowledge modules in physics (tool use), biology (animal behavior), psychology (social relations and mind), and language acquisition (Mithen 1996). These modules supported specialized skills for manipulation of physical objects; natural history, especially animal behavior; social relations (internalization of other); and mind (self and other awareness). The inevitability of language acquisition in normal cultural context and the normal attribution of beliefs and desires to others reflect the operation of these modular units of the brain. Mithen suggested that the capabilities of young children to understand the rules governing physical objects and their differences from mental concepts and living things involve similar specialized mental modules. This intuitive knowledge about the physical world was selected because it facilitated cultural transmission related to the production of tools.

The origin of religious thought in innate modules or neurognostic structures has been suggested by several authors (e.g., Boyer 1992; Mithen 1996; Laughlin et al. 1992). Boyer characterized religious notions as based on counterintuitive contradictions to the dispositions of innate modules, characterizing the supernatural as involving concepts that violate intuitive knowledge provided by the different specialized intelligences. But as Mithen pointed out, ethnographic evidence indicates that intuitive religious ideas are the norm rather than counterintuitive exceptions. Mithen proposed that the integration of innate modules, rather than their counterintuitive violations, provides the basis for religious ideas. Features of supernatural beings involve a "mixing up of knowledge about different types of entities in the real world" (Mithen 1996, 177), an integration of the multiple specialized intelligences of the early human mind. These concepts of supernatural beings, which mix properties of the social and the natural worlds or physical and social worlds, can only be achieved with a degree of cognitive fluidity between these distinct intelligences. Mithen's perspectives suggest that supernatural and religious ideologies reflect a cognitive fluidity that permitted the integration or synthesis of perspectives and operations from different cognitive modules.

I propose that shamanism utilizes, through metaphoric extension, the modules for social perceptions of "others," their intentionalities (mind reading), and animal behavior to represent spirits, animal familiars, and totemism. This extends Mithen's ideas by showing how the integration of basic modular functions—social other, mind reading, and natural history knowledge (animal behavior)—provided the cross-modal metaphoric foundation for fundamental concepts associated with shamanism. The psychophysiologically induced integrative brain states produced by shamanic ASC contributed to the integration of modular brain units and their functions. The practices of shamanism provided a physical basis for cross-modular integration of these innate capacities, producing the cognitive foundations for universal features of shamanistic thought. These are manifested in ritual; in concepts of animism and the spirit world and their relations to human communities; and in the role of animal spirits in shamanic practice, identification, and thought. Concepts of mind and social others and the use of metaphoric models foundational to consciousness are based in the neurognostic structures and processes of the paleomammalian brain.

BRAIN STRUCTURES AND CONSCIOUSNESS: THE TRIUNE BRAIN

A basis for different forms of consciousness underlying shamanic phenomena is found in the major architectural and functional strata of the brain and their different information processes. Although human consciousness is not specific to any single particular function or system of the brain, different modalities of consciousness are associated with different systemic information-processing functions, integration of brain processes, and patterns of homeostasis. All of the major systems of the brain participate in complex human behavior, but specific systemic patterns of brain functioning are associated with distinct experiential states and modes of consciousness. Recognition that consciousness is tied to the functioning of a biological system does not require reduction of consciousness solely to functions of the biological system. A neurophenomenological approach illustrates that both epistemic constructs and physiological patterns of brain operation contribute to consciousness. The relationship of brain physiology to consciousness is illustrated through an examination of how the physical structures of the brain and their associated activities relate to patterns of consciousness.

Explaining the relationships of physiological levels of the organism to consciousness requires a model of brain systems and their functions and interactions. MacLean (1973, 1990, 1993) proposed that the brain be viewed as involving three anatomically distinct systems that are integrated to provide a range of behavioral, emotional, and informational functions. MacLean's model has its limitations, but it is widely recognized that humans' motor patterns, emotional states, and advanced cognitive and linguistic capabilities are primarily managed by brain systems that emerged sequentially in evolution. This triune brain model provides a framework for explicating the relationship between systemic brain activities and consciousness, relating both to lower brain systems common with other animals and to the unique aspects of the human brain.

MacLean (1973, 1990, 1993) proposed a hierarchical tripartite model of the brain, a "triune brain," based on neuroanatomical, structural, and functional divisions into three strata: (1) reptilian/ organic brain (R-complex); (2) paleomammalian brain; and (3) neomammalian brain. The three formations have different anatomical structures that mediate different psychological and behavioral functions, with their own forms of subjectivity, intelligence, time and space sense, memory capabilities, and motor functions (MacLean 1990). Although the three segments are integrated, they provide the bases for different capacities and represent a functional hierarchy of information-processing capabilities that provide the basis for distinct forms of consciousness.

The *reptilian brain*, or R-complex, is composed of the upper spinal cord, portions of mesencephalon (midbrain), diencephalon (thalamus-hypothalamus), and basal ganglia. The reptilian brain regulates organic functions such as metabolism, digestion, and respiration; and it is also responsible for wakefulness, attentional mechanisms, and the regulation and coordination of behavior. The *paleomammalian brain* is based on evolutionary developments in the limbic system, which provided for the distinctions between reptiles and the mammals. This structure provides the basis for social behavior and non-verbal, emotional, and analogical information processing, and it functions as an "emotional brain," mediating affect; sex; fighting/ self-defense; social relations, bonding, and attachment; and the sense of self that provides the basis for beliefs, certainty, and convictions. The *neomammalian brain* (telencephalon or neocortical structures) resulted from hominid encephalization. The neomammalian brain provides the basis for advanced symbolic processes, culture, language, logic, rational thought, analytical processes, and complex problem solving.

MacLean proposed that these three anatomical structures of the brain provide the basis for different behavioral, psychological, and mental functions. The reptilian, paleomammalian, and neomammalian brains have distinctive mentalities, which he labeled protomentation, emotiomentation, and ratiomentation, respectively (MacLean 1993, 39). He used the terms "paleoneurognosis" and "paleomentation" to refer to cognitive functions of the reptilian and paleomammalian brain and the term "neoneurognosis" for functions of the neomammalian brain. The reptilian brain provides the basic plots and actions of the body. The paleomammalian brain provides the emotional influences on thoughts and behavior. The neomammalian brain uses enhanced symbolic capacities in elaborating on the basic plots and emotions and integrating them with higher-level information processing.

The Brain and Levels of Consciousness

The brain levels described by MacLean have homologies with major forms of consciousness described by Oakley (1983) and Hunt (1995a). Hunt suggested that properties of consciousness related to neural structures derive from "zones of convergence," with capacities for synthesis or "polymodal information integration" of many different processes represented in the different evolutionary levels of the brain. He specifically pointed to the thalamic structures of the brain stem; the limbic system; and the tertiary neocortical area, particularly the right hemisphere. These different brain structures' information-processing capacities contribute to widely recognized basic levels or forms of consciousness (e.g., Oakley's simple awareness, consciousness, and self-awareness).

Hunt suggested that the first of these areas provides the organism with primary awareness, or what Oakley referred to as "simple awareness—adaptation to the environment through reflexes, conditioned responses, and habituation, as well as through instrumental learning. This is common to all vertebrates, based in the confluence of peripheral sensory information in the reticular formation of the upper brain stem. This aspect of consciousness is mediated by the thalamic structures, which are basic for waking consciousness, constituting "a mini brain within the brain" (Baars 1997, 28). Central bases of the thalamic contributions to consciousness are derived from the activities of the intralaminar nuclei, which project to the cortical areas and trigger cortical arousal characteristic of waking consciousness. Baars suggested that the reticular formation and the thalamus are the only parts of the brain indispensable for waking consciousness. These brain stem centers central to the sleep and the wakefulness cycles are very similar to those found in reptiles and other animals, reflecting the basis for common aspects of consciousness across vertebrate species.

The second zone of convergence, based in the limbic system, provides the basis for more developed memory, derived from the coordination of different modalities involved in associational learning. This is based on the mammalian hippocampal and amygdala areas within the limbic system and on extended consciousness through imagery of anticipation and recall. This is Oakley's "consciousness"—information managed through cognitive integration of modeling of the external environment. The second zone provides for qualities of consciousness enriched by self, other (society), and emotions.

The third zone of convergence is the tertiary neocortical area and, in particular, the right hemisphere; these are involved in cross-integration and reorganization of perceptual modalities and are basic to symbolic cognition and self-awareness (paraphrase Hunt 1995a, 74–75). The third zone of convergence provides the basis for the recombination potentials characteristic of human thought, as well as Oakley's "self-awareness"—subjective experiences in which the knower focuses attention on representations of the self as an object in the world. Neocortical capabilities provide the basis for self-referential capabilities and cross-modal matching in preverbal humans and chimpanzees.

The emergence of consciousness in the interaction between different systems is illustrated in Hunt's (1995a) characterizations of consciousness as involving cross-modal synesthesias. Synesthesias entail subjective experiences of one sensory modality in terms of another sensory modality (e.g., the experience of color or somatic sensations from music). Hunt proposed that thought is based in emergent synesthesias, a transformation across the modalities of vision, kinesthesis, and vocalization. These synesthesias provide the basis for the symbolic capacity, the mind of the organism, and consciousness in cross-modal synthesis, a mediation and translation across different modalities.

The neomammalian brain (neocortex and connecting thalamic structures) represents the most dramatic evolution of the brain. The expanded neocortex's functions are based on extensive connections with the visual, auditory, and somatic systems, indicating the primary orientation of the neocortex to the external world. The neocortex also provides the neural networks for the portrayal of language and other symbolic activities, such as writing and arithmetic. Although these mental representations are salient aspects of self-awareness, the cognitive processes based in lower-brain structures persist because they are essential for human behavior.

The modern brain operates through the interconnection of the instinctual responses of the reptilian brain, the autonomic emotional states of the paleomammalian brain, and the cognitive processes of the neomammalian brain, integrating the features of these three functional systems. These relationships are mediated physiologically and symbolically, with many effects on consciousness and health. Interactions among levels of the brain are primarily based not on verbal language, but on other forms of mentation, social representation, and information processing, which utilize social, affective, and symbolic information to mediate, evoke, and channel physiological processes. The processes that present and integrate different sources of information to assess their significance for the organism's well-being provide the physiological basis for shamanistic healing effects on the organism. The relationship of innate drives and needs, social influences, and the representational systems constitutes the matrix for many different kinds of health problems—chronic anxiety and fears, behavioral disorders, conflicts, excessive emotionality or desires, obsessions and compulsions, dissociations, repression, and so forth. These problems are dependent on meaning, which is construed by processes that are subneocortical and based in information processing provided by prelinguistic symbolic modalities, affective associations, and self and social decisions constructed by the right hemisphere and the paleomammalian limbic system, all of which play a crucial role in providing the sense of unity to experience and the sense of assurance and conviction vital for self and species survival (Ashbrook 1993).

The functions of these brain structures that humans share with other animals typically operate outside the grasp and awareness of the left-hemisphere-based linguistic modes of representation. These levels of the brain and their functions nonetheless provide the basis for a complex information and intrapsychic communication system that subserves human experience and action. These brain processes have been referred to as "subsymbolic" and nonverbal, referring to their operation through nonlanguage symbols. The reptilian and the paleomammalian brains are fundamental to these aspects of mentation and representation. MacLean (1990) suggested that their functions include responsibility for behavior routines, basic personality, and the sense of self that permits social interaction and meaning, fundamental features of consciousness.

Paleomentation: Protomentation and Emotiomentation

MacLean (1993, 35) used paleomentation and paleopsychic processes to refer to two main types of mentation: (1) protomentation and (2) emotiomentation (emotional mentation), which are primarily based in the reptilian and the paleomammalian brains, respectively. These forms of communication utilize a variety of mediums (vocal, bodily, behavioral, chemical), which may be active and intentional or passive and unintentional. MacLean suggested that these nonverbal communication processes have the equivalence of syntax (orderly sequences) and semantics (meaning) and are found in animal behavioral patterns and humans' primary processing.

The R-Complex and Protomentation.   *Protomentation* refers to rudimentary cerebration involved in regulating the master routines underlying daily activities and the expression of the major behavioral displays used in social communication (MacLean 1990, 12). In addition to the rudimentary mental processes underlying prototypical forms of behavior, protomentation provides the basis for "propensions"—"drives, impulses, compulsions, and obsessions" (MacLean 1993, 35). MacLean suggested that the R-complex plays a fundamental role in species-typical communicative behavior, such as isopraxic and other "natural forms of imitation," and in the regulation of the animals' daily master routines and subroutines, integrating the movements and the total reactions of the organism. MacLean characterized the functions of the R-complex as the integration of somatic and autonomic components used in prosematic social communication and factors underlying evocation of displays. Although the R-complex "has a mind of its own" (MacLean 1990, 567), it does not have the apparatus for dealing effectively with the need to learn how to cope with new situations, nor does it have a role in the knowledge of the subjective self. The R-complex is directly related to pathology and ritual (see chapter 5 this volume), with this level of the brain isomorphically representing and entraining from lowest levels of the brain the interrelated social, behavioral, and physiological patterns of activity and meaning.

The Paleomammalian Brain and Emotiomentation.   *Emotiomentation* (or emotional mentation) involves brain and mental processes underlying affects; it involves subjective information derived from associations with feelings. Emotiomentation influences behavior, particularly that pertinent to self-preservation, procreation, and other socioemotional dynamics. The primary brain system underlying emotiomentation is the paleomammalian brain. The limbic system, specifically the hippocampus, is the source of convergence of exteroceptive and interoceptive neurotransmission, synthesizing internal and external sensory information and influencing the hypothalamus and other brain structures responsible for memory, emotions, self-representation, and social behavior. The paleomammalian brain provides the basis for the three cardinal behavioral developments in the evolution from reptiles to mammals: (1) nursing and maternal care; (2) audiovocal contact developed from maintaining maternal-offspring contact; and (3) play (MacLean 1990, 16). These set the basis for the family, social attachments, enactments, and symbolic meaning. The limbic system expanded considerably in higher mammals, meeting the primary functions of the modulation of affect to guide behavior; it also has an important role in dreaming. Limbic functions are "essential for a sense of personal identity and reality that have far-reaching implications for ontology and epistemology" (248).

MacLean (1990) suggested that the paleomammalian brain is not unconscious, but rather outside the grasp of the intellect. Nonetheless, this limbic brain plays a vital role in higher cognitive functions, including manifestations of the basic social personality. The limbic system plays a vital role in subjective apperception and rational thought, using feelings to guide self- and species-preservation behavior. The limbic system and its control of the autonomic nervous system play an important role in eliciting emotional mentation and in transforming it into physiological effects on the organism. This affective and symbolic manipulation of these physiological processes can have profound effects on the organism, for example, provoking physiological changes when the organism is confronted with situations that threaten or affront fundamental aspects of self-survival and interpersonal attachments. "[T]he housekeeping part of the nervous system involved in assimilation and elimination is called symbolically into play in prosematic communication involved in social assimilative and eliminative functions" (MacLean 1990:24). "Short of inducing physical exercise, emotional mentation represents the only form of psychological information that may provoke marked, and often prolonged, physiological changes *within* the organism" (23). Both physical exercise (e.g., dancing, clapping) and manipulation of emotions are fundamental to shaman healing and ASC.

Emotions affect others' behaviors through the activity of their minds and the interpretations modeled. Emotional functions of the paleomammalian brain are directly tied to fundamental aspects of bodily maintenance, including monitoring, reproduction, sensory systems, vital bodily functions, and the balance in the autonomic nervous system. The fundamental roles of emotions in human learning and development are revealed in the dynamics of child-mother/caretaker interactions. Empathic caring is an evolutionary adaptation, a manifestation of the coevolution of the paleomammalian brain and of family and social relations. The long-term dependence of infants on adults for survival required adaptations, such as the development of attachment behaviors as well as smiles, kissing, caressing, and other intimate social behaviors. Feelings of attachment, emotional security, and identity with family provided the basis for extension of such relations to nonkin, strangers, and the broader social and religious realms. These relations and sense of self also provide the basis for a variety of health problems derived from emotions elicited in social interaction. Shamanistic healing practices are centrally concerned with the management of these emotions, sense of self, and social relations, utilizing mechanisms for therapeutic interventions in the processes of the paleomammalian brain.

The limbic system produces an integrated sense of self and identity, the basis for ongoing experience and feelings regarding what is true or false (MacLean 1990, 578). Personal well-being is deeply intertwined with a sense of "communitas"/community, a social identity in which the empathy with other humans provides the basis for self and security. The paleomammalian brain mediates social signaling, which promotes a sense of community and provides for cooperation—physically, socially, and mentally—in ways that enhance human adaptation and survival. The paleomammalian brain produces and uses expressions of the face, vocalizations, actions, and gestures that provide information about minds and their motives and internal states. These communicative behaviors evoke similar experiences in others, creating a common or collective awareness, which is the basis of consciousness.

These communicative behaviors and processes have been referred to as kinisetic and paralanguage systems; they have not become obsolete in humans, but rather have been elaborated along with the development of verbal language (Bateson 1972). The earlier communication behaviors are still manifested in art, music, theater dance, facial expressions, and poetry, which reflects their continued importance in human communication, providing a mechanism for communicative functions not easily met by verbal language. The discourse of this nonverbal communication is "precisely concerned with matters of relationship—love, hate, respect, fear, dependency, etc.—between self and vis-à-vis or between self and environment" (Bateson 1972, 412–13). This fundamental discourse about self and relationships is relatively nonconscious and not subject to perfect voluntary control. Bateson suggested that dreams are a context in which these earlier forms of mimetic representation persist, depicting the relationship of the dreamer to his or her world. But although dreams operate in metaphor, he suggested that they do not provide the material to transform metaphor or mechanisms that signal the presence of metaphoric representation. This lack of metacommunication reflects the lack of self and social context in dreams. But the utilization of dreams for representation in shamanic ASC supersedes these limitations. This superseding is achieved through many forms of symbolic information managed through analogical and metaphoric representation, or trophes, based in presentational knowledge and mimesis, and manifested in animistic representations.

SYMBOLIC CONSCIOUSNESS: PRESENTATIONAL AND REPRESENTATIONAL MODALITIES

The contents of consciousness are manifested through different modalities, which are all fundamentally symbolic in nature. Laughlin, McManus, and d'Aquili (1992) illustrated this in a neurophenomenological or biogenetic structuralist approach to understanding the relationships among perception, symbols, and consciousness. The content of experience is a construct resulting from interaction of the nervous system with the enculturated mind and self. External perceptions and their interpretation are linked through symbolic processes, reflecting the brain's preeminent function in the construction of models of the environment that mediate input. There is an intimate integration of the systems mediating perception and cognition through the symbolic process's central role in the neural organization of experience and production of the cognized environment. The symbolic process emerged over phylogenetic evolution, constituting a nervous system function in which neural networks are entrained by partial information.

Any stimulus that elicits a model functions as a symbol, which evokes knowledge based on the relationship between the symbol and the meaning. "[A] minimal symbol [is] any stimulus that provides sufficient patterning for entree into a model that contains more information than that provided by the stimulus" (Laughlin et al. 1992, 165). The symbolic process operates on the principle of topographic projection, "the point-to-point conduction of abstracted pattern about a stimulus from the periphery into central cognitive models" (164), which provides for reproduction of spatial patterns, frequencies, and physical relationships of the environment in the cortex. The symbolic process is a fundamental principle involved in the development, elaboration, and maintenance of neural organization and the construction of conscious experience. This symbolic basis of thought is derived from embodied images operating independent of language.

Presentational Symbolism: Imagery and Action

Hunt (1995a,b,c) distinguished two fundamental modalities of symbolic cognition involving a self-referential capacity, which he referred to as representational symbolism and presentational symbolism. In contrast to linguistically based forms of representation, Hunt characterized a presentational line of development. Hunt built on

Geschwind's (1965) view of symbolic thought, describing it as being derived from cross-modal translation, and expanded the mainstream cognitive approaches in recognizing the emotional domain as one of multiple frames for symbolic intelligence. The original form of symbolic communication manifested through visual kinesthetic mirrorings is later subordinated to speech, but it continues to develop apart from it. Hunt characterized presentational modalities as based on symbolic arrangement of perceptual structures. The structures of this nonverbal symbolic intelligence are inherent physiognomies, entoptic structures (genetically based visual geometric design patterns), and microgenetic structures of perception, which Hunt suggested provide a universal grammar or deep structure analogous to that of spoken language. Hunt (1995a, 47) called these "the maximum experiential expressions of a conscious awareness system." This language of the psyche provides a basis for expression of a range of meanings derived from metaphoric polysemys, constituting a "nonverbal symbolic intelligence."

This presentational modality is examined by Newton as a sensorimotor and image-based theory of consciousness. Newton suggested that consciousness and intentionality are based in "nonintentional sensorimotor states associated with the basic goal-directed action abilities that humans share with simpler organisms" (Newton 1996, 3). Understanding meaning involves being able to think of something in terms of sensorimotor experiences, a "knowing how" to in terms of sensory motor experiences and actions. Newton pointed to support for the sensorimotor theory of cognition in the findings of "cross-field generalizations," where all fields of knowledge, including abstract ones, are based in spatial, kinetic, and kinematic terminology. The sensorimotor theory of cognition is also supported by phenomenological studies of intentionality, which show human experience to require embodiment, without which we cannot explain human activity, including cognition and language.

Werner and Kaplan (1952), McNeil (1979), Johnson (1987), and Newton (1996) illustrated that physical experiences and sensorimotor ideas and representations derived from memory traces of sensory and motor experiences provide the basic patterns and vehicles for signs that are used by semiotic extension to provide the media used to organize all abstract thought and cognitive structures. In both abstract and concrete domains, bodily and spatial systems are the ubiquitous system of reference, providing a sensorimotor basis for all of cognition. Johnson (1987) examined how conceptual activities are understood in terms of basic sensory motor experiences. Metaphors of embodiment used in descriptions of mental states have their basis in the construction of images or memories of previously performed sensorimotor activities, that is, imaging and remembering how it feels to use our bodies in particular ways. Abstract symbol structures are isomorphic with sensorimotor structures, which are represented through combinatorial arrangements of sensorimotor representations (Newton 1996, 23). The use of these sensorimotor structures as a medium for representing the conceptually more abstract relations is based on analogical reasoning. This is necessary because central to any mental activity is the use of structures of reasoning from familiar domains to understand novel domains. Cognition depends on metaphor, beginning with others serving as the basis for representing our own self (e.g., "mirroring") and continuing with the use of one's own state of mind and emotions to interpret other minds. Newton suggested that sensorimotor structures use analog models to provide the level of representation at the basis of ordinary consciousness—perception of self, environment, intentionality, and all higher cognitive activity.

This sensorimotor-imagetic basis for symbolic cognition is illustrated in the role of synesthesias in consciousness. Hunt (1995a) integrated and extended Geschwind's (1965) work on symbolic cognition and its basis in capacities for cross-modal translation across perceptual modalities, combining it with Mead's (1934) ideas about the roles of self and other in reflexive consciousness. Neurologist Geschwind argued "that the potentiality for the symbolic rests in a capacity for neocortical cross-modal translations between the structures of vision, kinesthesis, and audition" (Hunt 1995c, 410). It is "emergent out of cross-modal fusions and transformations between the different simultaneity-sequentiality ratios of the separate cortical 'analysers' for vision, hearing, and touch-movement" (416).

Understandings of objects are based on these integrations, how it feels to use them. Objects do not have an inherent symbolic quality but are understood in terms of their use; likewise, Newton argued, intentional mental states are better understood in terms of actions. Both physical and mental actions share a common structure of intentionality in reactivated traces of sensorimotor experience, which are the basis for planning of action and the construction of mental representations. Both ways of understanding involve use and are derived from past experiences.

These perceptual structures also constitute the basic form for awareness within nonsymbolic organisms. Nonetheless, Hunt (1995a) stated that neither representational nor presentational symbolism can be considered more primitive or advanced; however, immediate awareness plays a different role in each of these symbolic systems. Hunt contrasted representational and presentational symbolism in terms of the relation to conscious and unconscious processes. With representational symbolism, a highly automatized communication code is employed. Consequently, awareness of the expressive medium is subordinated. With presentational symbolism, the medium and its intentionality are focal, and a polysemic meaning emerges out of the unconscious. Representational symbolism is typified in ordinary language where the medium of expression is automatized and largely unconscious. Because the signification of language is arbitrary, consciousness enters representational thought as felt meanings.

The meaning of presentational symbolism appears to emerge directly and spontaneously as a consequence of an experiential immersion in the symbolic medium. This form of symbolism is exemplified in the expressive arts, in which an open-ended, unpredictable meaning emerges from the form of semblances that are sensed. Images provide knowledge beyond that embedded in propositional knowledge, particularly as illustrated in dream imagery, which has meaning beyond that found within waking symbolic consciousness. Imagery represents abstract information and cross-modal synesthesia. The generic image serves the cognitive or semiotic function of portraying some relationship of a concept or an object to the percipient, providing the underlying conceptual structure found in language.

Hunt utilized the perspectives of Arnheim (1969), Lakoff (1987), and Johnson (1987) in demonstrating that images and visual spatial metaphors are not developmental primitives but provide the basis for all symbolic cognition. Conceptual structures are meaningful because they kinesthetically embody abstract spatial metaphors. Hunt pointed out the symbolic structures found in basic perception are derived through cross-modal convergence and integration of perception, body movement forms, and imagery capabilities. These imaginal capacities operate independently of linguistic networks, using reorganized and recombinant visual perception to present meaning. Hunt's perspective is based on work of Gibson (1979), who viewed the perceptual template of imaginal self-presentation as derived from the motile creature's sense of position within the ecological array. Natural physiognomies reflect back to the percipient information used for symbolic self-reference based on how it is for the organism to act on that environment, providing a body-based template for representational symbolism. The most basic image is a proprioceptive image of what it is like to move one's own body. This conceptualization of image as behavior, a "truncated efferent response" (Ellis 1995), bases images in the most fundamental modalities of organismic awareness derived from the integration of spatial and visual images with bodily awareness.

Newton similarly contended that this sensorimotor basis for cognition is primarily visual.

[T]here is a precise overlap between the visual experiences traditionally referred to by the term "images" and the experiences, *in the visual modality*, that I believe constitutes understanding {that] . . . an "image" is not an objective entity functioning like a picture or other symbol, but instead is an *experience* generated in response to external events. The experience may be purely visual or it may include elements from various nonvisual modalities. (Newton 1996, 51).

The mechanisms of the conscious understanding of actions, objects, and persons all centrally involve imagery: the reactivation of past sensorimotor experiences of the subject, blended with current sensory and proprioceptive input in response to novel stimuli. (19)

Consciousness depends on an organism attending to sensory input and looking for patterns in that data (cf. Ellis 1995). The focusing of attention, looking for a form, produces an image. This imaginal consciousness is necessary for perceptual consciousness, which results from the match of a mental image with a pattern of sensory input. Newton (1996, 17) concluded that "imagery is thus essential to perceptual consciousness." The combination of activated imagery with current sensory input, a combination of the view of the world with our embodied selves, is consciousness. Newton argued that there is a sense in which all consciousness is self-consciousness, that the embodied perceiving self is part of the content of awareness. Awareness of one's self is based on ordinary perceptual awareness combined with somatic data. Self-awareness is in essence awareness of bodily responses to sensory input. The sense of reflexivity associated with conscious perception is due to the addition of proprioceptive and somatically generated input. This somatically generated input is the basis for the perception of the externality of perceptual objects. Perceptions of objects are dependent on our sense of bodily awareness and the external orientation of the objects to our bodies.

These perspectives are consistent with Piaget's approaches to cognitive development. Piaget characterized the initial interaction with the world as occurring through *schemes*, forms or structures of knowledge based on coherent, orderly, organized patterns of behavior. The sensorimotor scheme is an action scheme involving behavioral dispositions based on internal movements and acting like what is symbolized (or acting out the visual scanning of its form and dimensions). This development is based on the coordination of the senses and different perceptual schemes, centered on the infant's own body. In the final sensorimotor stage, the child acquires the ability to mentally represent objects and actions not immediately present. This deferred imitation is based on internal symbolic forms that are represented in visual images, which set the stage for transition to symbolic thought. Piaget's second major epistemic stage of development of cognition and consciousness is that of preoperational thought, semiotic function, which Kitchener (1986, 18) characterized as involving "the ability to represent or symbolize by means of imitation, play, signs, and symbols." This representation is initially visual and derived from the sensorimotor representation through imitation. This mimetic symbolic ability is primarily stored in images, not words, with thinking largely limited to the external sphere of motor behavior.

The work of Lakoff (1987) and Johnson (1987) illustrated that even language understanding is based in these experiences of embodiment. More-complex abstract forms are derived from bodily and spatial experience represented in image schemas. Image schemas provide the basis for all logical relationships, with perceptions providing the template that permits the operation of propositional logic. Newton argued that both conceptual and nonconceptual understandings derive from the agent's experience of its own basic voluntary actions. Newton considered the comprehension of natural language to be based in the analogical representational structures. Human response to linguistic material involves creation of mental models in images or unconscious structures based in sensorimotor representations constructed through those same mechanisms that underlie perception and action.

Newton (1996, 29) posited a central representational system for all modalities, including the visual, primary and secondary cortical association areas, somatosensory information, and emotional information. The common brain mechanisms for movement, language, and cognition indicate that cognition is based in the use of common sensorimotor representations that underlie nonverbal communication and spoken language systems. This is substantiated by Baars's review of experimental research illustrating that the physical-visual field and the mental-imagery field have substantial resemblances, not only in eliciting the same parts of the cortex, but also in terms of having the same properties as an experiential space. Baars suggested that simulated inner sensations provide our most detailed conscious information. Baars (1997, 64) characterized the image as a form of consciousness, suggesting that "[p]erception of the physical world may be the most ancient mode of consciousness." This provides a structure for knowledge through formulation of generic images of perceptual experiences, the iconic visuo-spatial representations that preserve information in forms similar to perception. Images are used to transform representations in an isomorphic relationship to the represented objects, serving as an analogue representation of an object.

Hunt (1995a) illustrated that image schemas provide the basis for both self-referential conceptualization and representation of external-world structures (cf. Lakoff 1987). This is manifested in the use of physical terms for psychological states, representing the metaphoric employment of the physical patterns of the world for structuring our recognition of human experience. Images manifested in the experiences of shamanic and meditative consciousness are structured through cross–modally based physical metaphors. Hunt (1995a) suggested that symbolic processes found in imagetic or presentational modalities, and the socially based reflexive self, provide a foundation for these phenomena.

Cognition through analogical processing within this bodily sensorimotor foundation and expressed through the visual modality is a core aspect of shamanism exemplified in the out-of-body experience or soul flight and its visionary presentations. Hunt characterized the classic phenomena of shamanism as involving the use of the presentational imagetic mode to reflect the structures of abstract intelligence. The shaman's soul journey is based in a self-referential capacity embodied in an imagetic expression of Mead's (1934) "taking the role of the other" toward self. These perspectives illustrate that shamanism and the mystical traditions involve ritual and symbolic technologies for the construction and the manipulation of forms of consciousness and experiences of self. These include capabilities for representing and transforming self, other, society, morality, and cosmology. These perspectives reflect a recognition that our knowing is indirect, based on consideration of one set of circumstances through the means provided by the use of another set to represent them. These metaphoric vehicles establish a cross-reference, a cross-modal linking, of symbol and referent through an inner kinesthetic embodiment that fuses visual spatial dynamics in meaningful patterns. These are exemplified in social life, self, consciousness, and analogical reasoning processes.

Mimesis and Cognition

Arnheim's (1969) *Visual Thinking* illustrated forms of uniquely human symbolic cognitive abilities operating independent of language skills and based in a generative module that is manifested in individuals with both hearing and speech impairments, in individuals with language-debilitating brain lesions or pathologies, and in children prior to language acquisition (Donald 1991). Uniquely human cognitive competence independent of language is manifested in "intentional communication, mimetic and gestural representation, categorical perception, various generative patterns of action, and above all the comprehension of social relationships, which implies a capacity for social attribution and considerable communicative ability" (Donald 1991, 167). Other contexts in which humans without language manifest advanced cognitive capabilities include games, sports, arts, crafts, emotional responses, work—and shamanistic experiences.

This language-independent symbolic representation is manifested through mimesis. "Mimetic skill or mimesis rests on the ability to produce conscious, self-initiated, representational acts that are intentional but not linguistic" (Donald 1991, 168). The intention of mimesis is to represent the structure of events through their reenactment and imitation. It is the *intentional* representation that distinguishes mimetic representation from mimicry. Mimesis operates on the principle of metaphorical similarity based on perceptual resemblance, providing a representation of the relationship between the self and the external world through movement. Mimetic expression is based on inputs of self-representation and episodic memory, encompassing and superseding the episodic memory system. The inherently cross-modal nature of mimetic representation and its ability to move across sensory and somatic modalities provided the basis for a uniquely human but prelinguistic level of symbolization and culture. Mimesis has properties that preceded speech and are necessary for it.

These "include intentionality, generativity, communicativity, reference, autocueing, and the ability to model an unlimited number of objects" (171).

Mimesis is an episode-bound and concrete form of representation, but it provides a medium for the expression of complex social interactions. The visuomotor domain, including facial expressions, gestures, postures, and movements, provides the principal means through which mimesis is expressed. It is based on activities integrated at a supramodal level through manual dexterity and highly developed hand-eye coordination. Mime provides the basis for the acquisition of many aspects of behavior, including mannerisms, body postures, social behavior forms, communicative gestures, and many skills for the construction of cultural artifacts. Mimesis plays a central role in artistic representation and provides a means of modeling and rehearsing others' social roles—in essence, expressing the social structure, social relations, social roles, and other social activities.

Emotional expression is a part of mimetic social adaptation that combines vocal and facial expression. Human facial emotional expressions have less of a voluntary character than other mimetic acts—they are not regularly self-observed, yet they are manifested in reciprocal exchanges through mimesis. This use of controlled expression of emotions was a part of early human evolution of social and communication skills and continues to be central to mimetic expression in human society today. The mimetic expressions found in basic emotions are universal (Eibl-Eibesfeldt 1989) and constitute the most basic common aspect of human nonverbal communication. In addition to facial expressions, these universal emotional mimetic expressions include "stroking, embracing, cuddling, and hand touching" (Donald 1991, 188), tongue displays, eyebrow movements, pointing, strutting, and other expressive patterns of behavior. Humans use these for representational purposes that constitute "the core of an ancient root-culture that is distinctly human . . . [and] still form[s] the expressive heart of human social interchange" (189). Mimetic skills are represented in a wide range of performance systems, including gestures, physical (manual) signals, postures, and rhythm.

These rhythmic behaviors of humans interrelate different parts of the body in a way that evidences the operation of a central mimetic controller. This mimetic controller is an "unencapsulated central system" that was the dominant representational device until the evolution of language. "Mime, play, games, tool making, skilled rehearsal, and reproductive memory are thus manifestations of the same

superordinate mimetic controller" (Donald 1991, 190). The generative skills and capabilities of the nonlanguage areas of the brain for
comprehension of social behavior and thought illustrate that the
unique intellectual skills of humans are independent of language,[8]
including planning, semantic representation, and most of the cognitive activities considered to be uniquely human. The language independence of this central system with higher cognitive functions is
manifested in semantic memory, propositional knowledge, planning
skills, social interaction, and evaluation skills that persist in the absence of language.[9] Donald suggested an independent generative system, an unbounded central system (or systems) with generative capabilities responsible for analysis and production of discourse and
narrative, formation of plans and scripts, conscious awareness, and
many other forms of generativity: "visual decomposition, perceptual
recombination, phonetic segmentation, verbal invention, tool making, parsing, and grammar" (92).

The mimetic skills required highly specific brain adaptations that
are apparently distributed across a number of brain systems. Some
aspects, such as emotional expression, prosody, and rhythm, are
apparently right-hemisphere controlled, whereas others, such as visual manual skills, are apparently left-hemisphere based. Donald
suggested that the mimetic controller is not localized but depends on
systemic functions with a widespread and complex anatomical basis
because mimesis is so rarely absent in humans. Human mimetic cognitive capabilities, including gesture, tool making, praxis, emotional
expression, social intelligence, social roles, and behavior, represent a
prelinguistic level of cognitive development. While functioning independently of language, these human capabilities are as complex as
language production. Mimesis is more restricted than language and
ambiguous in its representation. But mimesis provided the basis for
the later evolution of language by laying the groundwork of basic
social and semantic structures. Mimesis persists today as a superior
form of representation of certain forms of knowledge: "modeling
social roles, communicating emotions, and transmitting rudimentary
skills" (Donald 1991, 198).

Mimesis is also fundamental to shamanic thought and practice.
Donald suggested that mimetic skills of generative, recursive, intentional representations performed in a public or a group context provided the basis for primitive ritual. Group ritual and ritual dance were
among the basic social forms in which reciprocal mimetic enactments
were first performed. These collective social activities are dependent

on common cognitive models shared by the actors and the audience alike. In mimetic displays, vocalization generally plays a role only in communicating emotion. This is reflected in shamanic practices in the use of archaic language, which is unintelligible to members of the shaman's group, and manifestations in chanting and singing. The shamanic core of drumming and dancing involves mimesis manifested in rhythmic abilities. These are uniquely human supramodal capabilities representing the integration of vocal, visual, and motor components (Donald 1991).

Metaphor and Analogical Thought

Three basic innate human mental models or forms of representations were proposed by Johnson-Laird (1983). These include propositional models based on analytical logic, and images and mental models based on analogical representation. The mental models represent structural analogues of the world, with images as their perceptual correlates. Pattern mapping provides the basis for recognition, completion, and transformation of associations in pattern-recognition processes that form the basis for all forms of reasoning, from primitive categorization through logical inference. This construction of meaning is based on nonanalytical models, particularly analogue processes that map relations between systems through metaphoric processes. Shore (1996) proposed that there are four levels of analogy formation: (1) primary analogies based on direct perceptual analogies and involving pattern-seeking and recognition behavior; (2) cross-modality sensorimotor associations based on attribute similarity, relational similarity, synesthesia, and iconicity; (3) relationships based on self-conscious associations; and (4) structural metaphor isomorphic with content or thought that schematizes relationships between complex models. Friedrich (1991) placed analogy and metaphor in the broader context of the concepts of tropes, where something "stands for" something else. He characterized the different types of macrotropes (imagetic, modal, contiguity-based, formal, and analogical) as constituting independent and nonhierarchical systems.[10]

Analogical tropes are based on the ability of anything to be used to resemble something else. Analogical tropes are not, however, used to refer to just anything, but rather to things within the cultural context of meanings. Research on metaphor illustrates that culture plays the fundamental role in the formation of metaphoric models (e.g., see Fernandez 1991). Like formal tropes, analogical tropes are tied to traditions that provide their meanings and functions. Consequently, formal tropes have considerable differences across cultures. Shamanic systems' universals are not derived from culturally unique interpretations but reflect underlying psychobiological structures. These other basic tropes are well represented in the shamanic world view and practices. Contiguity tropes are found throughout shamanic ritual and thought, exemplified in sympathetic magic. The shaman's visionary experience exemplifies the use of imagery tropes, whereas the modal tropes are the underlying basis for the matrix of emotions that are at the basis of shamanic ritual.

Contiguity tropes utilize contiguity or juxtaposition along many dimensions—time, space, social, and contextual factors. The contiguity tropes based on the human body and animals are central features of shamanic thought. Contiguity tropes are manifested in the out-of-body experience of soul flight and the animal identity and transformations. Meaning construction typically utilizes previously stored foundational schemata as a point of comparison for analogically mapping novel information. Anatomical relations constitute a variety of contiguity tropes that utilize analogy between body parts and other contexts to create an imaginative pattern. Friedrich considers this projection of anatomical relations to be one of the most powerful and universal forms of metaphor based in part/whole relations (e.g., traditional synecdoche). These innate forms of representation were incorporated in a variety of animistic and shamanistic assumptions. Image tropes "represent various kinds of perceptual images that 'stand for themselves.' Epistemologically, these tropes depend on the experience or feeling of qualities that are in some sense primary or irreducible" (Friedrich 1991, 27). The emphasis on image tropes as involving the monadic aspects of qualities suggests that image tropes represent qualia. Image tropes are omnipresent in language use because of their pervasive presence in mimesis (29). Modal tropes are concerned with expressions of mood, as well as with the combination and interaction of moods. Modal tropes function as deep, organizing principles "rooted in a speaker's underlying emotions, affects, and feelings" (30–31). Friedrich considered irony to be the most intriguing of all modal tropes in that "what is said is not what is meant" (31).

Innate models are used in cultural-meaning construction, which involves analogical processing linking socially derived conventional models to experiences organized in relationship to these models (Shore 1996). Shore used "analogical schematization" to refer to processes of translation between inner models and outer models, which provide the basis for the construction of meaning. Analogical schematization occurs at a number of different cognitive levels, ranging from neural network behavior to microanalogies and complex structured macroprocesses. Schema induction is the most important process facilitating analogical transfer. The body and its ability to act are the most fundamental of these schema and manifest analogical process in mimesis.

Animism and Analogical Processes

Processes of metaphoric thinking in shamanic thought are found in animism, the belief in spirit beings. Tylor (1871) suggested that animism was the basis of religion and that it derived from the primitive philosopher's attempts to explain the differences between alive and dead, awake and asleep, and the meaning of dreams—phenomena that are fundamental to distinctions related to consciousness. Tylor viewed the belief in animism as reflecting a cognitive development that constituted a mistaken or false science. Tylor hypothesized that primitive philosophers reasoned that a spirit, an animating principle separable from the body, was responsible for the differences between life and death, waking and sleeping, and for the content of dreams. The presence of a spirit in the body explained life and waking consciousness, whereas its absence caused sleep, death, and dream experiences. However, *experiences* derived from interactions with culturally defined spirit worlds are more compelling reasons for acceptance of animism than are Tylor's rationalizations (Winkelman 1982). Nonetheless, animism has important cognitive implications.

Guthrie (1993) identified anthropomorphism, involving attribution of human characteristics to nonhuman objects, as the basis of religion. Religion provides explainations through anthropomorphizing—offering the concept of humanlike beings who provide the design and the purpose to the observed phenomena of the universe. Animism, attributing an intentional spirit essence with mind qualities like those of humans to the unknown and natural phenomena, is exemplified in anthropomorphic attribution of humanlike "mind" characteristics to gods, spirits, and nonhuman entities, particularly animals. The attribution of human characteristics to animals is a ubiquitous magico-religious practice, manifested in animal familiars and transformation, totemism, and the guardian spirit complex. These animistic relationships are based on metaphoric symbolic attributions.

Guthrie (1997, 489) suggested that the causes of animistic beliefs lie in "perceptual uncertainty and the gaming strategy with which we meet it." Guthrie pointed to a universal tendency for humans to conceive of other beings and objects as being like themselves and, consequently, to attribute to other things and events the characteristics humans share. Humans' attribution of humanlike characteristics to the unknown is not based on a desire to find comfort, but on an effort to make sure that they do not fail to respond to a humanlike actor if necessary. An error in falsely attributing human characteristics is less dangerous than failing to appropriately attribute characteristics of a live humanlike entity. Hence, humans attribute animistic anthropomorphic qualities to the unknown to make sure they are dealing with the most important contingencies. This attribution is based in human capabilities of mind and intentionality.

Bird-David (1999) reframed Guthrie's position, suggesting that the human tendency to animate things is engendered by socially based cognitive skills. Rejecting the standard assumptions that animism is a mistaken or failed epistemology or primitive level of development, Bird-David proposed an interpretation of animism from the perspectives of environmental and personhood theory that suggests it be seen as a relational epistemology. It is found in hunter-gatherer cultures because people share with others and personify other entities because they socialize with them and share with them. Bird-David suggested the universality of this relational mode because perception requires that humans be situated in their world and environment. The animistic principles inherent in the concept of spirits are recharacterized as "super persons" who are constitutive of sharing relationships with the environment. This relationship is central to maintaining personhood and communal affairs and identity.

"Natural History Intelligence": The Animal World. The "intuitive biology" module, a specialized capacity for organizing knowledge about animals and animal behavior, is manifested in young children. They illustrate an inborn capability to understand the fundamental differences between animate and inanimate objects, to attribute essence to living things, and to recognize types or "species essence" that cannot be accounted for on the basis of their experiences. This ability and the worldwide manifestation of classification schemata for the natural world (see Atran 1990) can be "explained by a shared, content-rich mental module for 'intuitive biology' " (Mithen 1996, 53) or natural history knowledge, acquired through

selective pressures on prehistoric hunter-gatherers. Some humans with autism who have extensive understandings of animal behavior illustrate this specialized intuitive biology module for acquisition of knowledge about the natural world. This natural history module provided the basis for compulsive learning about animals and their behavior, an important adaptive capability in marginal environments. This ability to organize information about animals provides a universal analogical system for creation and extension of meaning through contiguity tropes.

The reciprocal of the processes of anthropomorphism is found in totemism, the attribution of animal characteristics to humans and their groups. One of the most prevalent aspects of totemic thought is found in shamanistic activities, in which the shaman incorporates animal spirits and their abilities and populates the world with animal spirit powers. Typically, the totem is an animal that has a personal spiritual relationship to an individual or a collective relationship to the group. Although many nonanthropological critiques of totemism have mischaracterized it as evidence of faulty mental processes, more astute perspectives have understood it as a form of cognition. Levi-Strauss (1962) provided a synthesis of anthropological studies illustrating that totemism constitutes a system for differentiating societies by means of analogy. His analyses showed that totemic practices function as an analogical mode of thought, which involve the same processes and levels of mental functioning as those that underly scientific thought. Totemic thought involves processes by which a homology is postulated between the differential features existing among species and the differences among human groups; as animal species differ, so do human groups. Differences among human groups are represented through the differences recognized among animals. This use of the animal world constitutes one of the most fundamental aspects of analogical thought, reflecting the metaphoric utilization of an innate module for "natural history intelligence." This specialized capacity for organizing information about animals and their behavior and relationships provides a universal analogical system for creation, expression, and extension of meaning.

SUMMARY

Shamanism's relations to the animal world and to generic others constitute the natural ecology of human consciousness. Shamanic traditions involve modes of knowing that provide an extension of representation through metaphorical predication. The neurophenomenological approach illustrates that shamanic, religious and mystical thought play important roles in representing human perceptual and conceptual structures and in producing a variety of individual and collective effects that are central to human social life, self, consciousness, and healing. These potentials, first institutionalized in shamanism, represented an evolution to a more inclusive and integrative consciousness. This book demonstrates that shamanistic healing activities and ASC are primarily based in elicitation of integrative processes, particularly those related to the paleomammalian brain. These integrative operations of consciousness reflect homeostatic physiological responses produced through shamanistic activities. Emotional and psychosocial functions of the brain are principal processes through which meaning stimulates the nervous system. Self, social attachment, and bonding represent important mediating concepts in these neurophenomenological relations and the shaman's traditions.

NOTES

1. I have relied primarily on Kitchener's (1986) extensive analysis of Piaget's epistemology as the basis for this characterization.
2. Piaget's (1969, 1971) stages of development are cognitive in an epistemic sense, that is to say, concerned with issues of evidence, justification, and questions of truth.

> Most cognitive concepts—belief, memory, information, problem solving, pattern recognition, imagination, consciousness, judgment, hypothesis, representation, reasoning, thinking, and skills—are epistemic in nature. (Kitchener 1986, 25–26).

> These [epistemic] concepts include sensorimotor schemes, operations, "real" categories (space, time, causality, and object permanence), "formal" categories (classification, number, and quantity), perceptions, concepts, semiotic categories (ideas, images, symbols, signs), moral, emotional, and social categories, and so forth. (41)

Piaget's epistemology is Kantian, combining both empirical and developmental elements in extending Kant's perspective through constructivism, the epistemic subjects' construction of their knowledge. Piaget emphasizes "the active cognitive role of the epistemological subject in interpreting, categorizing, and structuring experience" (75) and constructing knowledge and objects. Piaget's conceptions of reality and knowledge correspond to Kantian notions of noumena and phenomena. He maintains a distinction between metaphysics and epistemology, differentiating epistemological issues of what is known from metaphysical questions of what really exists. This distinction is made by Kant between the metaphysical object (the thing-in-itself, or *noumenon*) and the epistemological object (the thing-as-known, or *phenomenon*) (paraphrase from Kitchener 1986, 104). Piaget also incorporates the Kantian notion that there are certain concepts and categories that are necessary for knowledge, including the formal laws of logic; concepts of space and time; and ideas such as cause, quantity, and classification that are imposed on experience. He also adds additional concepts and categories not considered essential by Kant. Piaget's difference with the Kantian formulation is in that he claims that there is a developmental process underlying those structures, rather than representing fixed (transcendental) categories. Piaget's theories involve an "interactionism" in which the subject's interaction with the environment through the epistemic structures employed in the processes of assimilation and accommodation is essential for knowledge.

3. Reflective abstraction is characteristic of each stage of epistemic development, involving the abstraction of elements from an earlier stage and their reflection onto a higher stage where they are restructured. Reflective abstraction consists in the transposition of properties from actions on the object onto a higher plane, where the structure of a lower level becomes the content of a higher level and subject to logical coordination by the epistemic subject's actions. Reflective abstraction involves two aspects: (1) reflecting as a projection from a lower plane to a higher plane, and (2) reflecting as a process of cognitive reorganization of the projected material. Reflective abstraction involves a creative reconstruction, operations on operations. Reflective abstraction is an unconscious process, but it can lead to both conscious products and formulations, as well as to unconscious results, especially when the phenomena cannot be incorporated into the conscious system of concepts.

4. Laughlin, McManus, and d'Aquili (1992) suggested that a neuro-phenomenological epistemology needs to address three epistemic processes or aspects: (1) phylogenetic encephalization; (2) invariant patterns of ontogenetic neuropsychological development; and (3) the sociogenetic, the societal conditioning of paradigmatic views of the operational environment. Piaget suggested that genetic epistemology requires consideration of (1) mental anatomy or structures; (2) comparative mental anatomy to determine the commonality in and diversity of mental structures; and (3) mental physiology, the study of mental functions.

5. Scheff suggested that intelligent behavior requires the use of a wide range of associations that are contingent, providing the basis for the mind. This contingency provides the base for total association, moving from a closed to an open system. Humans require an open system because

human interaction and interrelationships are inherently ambiguous, with meaning contextually dependent. Words always have multiple meanings, contingent on the context in which utterances occur; and concepts can be expressed through multiple modalities. This ambiguity requires an interpretive decipherment, a complex problem of interpretation. Humans seem to be particularly good at this interpretation, something of which computer programs are incapable. Scheff suggested that this interpretation and understanding are based on participants' ability to decode complex and ambiguous messages through using part/whole thinking. Meaning is derived by relating elements to a vast amount of knowledge and information available in a variety of local contexts, including biographical knowledge, the physical surroundings, earlier conversation, and a semantic and cultural network of relevant meanings. Culture and language are the most extensive context within which human meaning is constructed and derived; they play a crucial role in the development of human consciousness.

6. "[N]eurognosis canalizes the processes of perceptual discrimination, motor activity, and conceptual and symbolic differentiation and association [and] . . . the type and complexity of cognition of which the individual or the species is capable" (Laughlin, McManus, and d'Aquili. 1992, 61). Neurognosis refers to both structure and function, reflecting the physiological perspective where structure implies function: "Neurognosis consists of prepared pathways of neural connections specializing in sensory input, information storage, association and retrieval, and motor output, as well as systemic maintenance and many other functions" (73).

7. Gardner's approach also emphasized developmental history for these different intelligences, the cultural influences on their nature, and the interaction among the different intelligences.

8. Donald illustrated this in a review of the case of "Brother John," a paroxysmal aphasic who suffered from epileptic seizures that "selectively shut down language processing, while he remained conscious and able to remember what he was experiencing" (Donald 1991, 83). Although the individual's language skills, including speech comprehension, were impaired so as to be completely absent during the seizures, he was nonetheless aware of complex events, capable of participation in complex, goal-directed social interaction, and able to remember seizure activities after the seizures and to relate them coherently and correctly to others. He was able to carry out previously assigned tasks during the seizures, including complex mathematical problems, while still unable to speak. Communicative skills based on gestures remained, as did practical knowledge and the ability to think about things and to remember them, even though he could not find the words for them. His behavior

indicated that his basic aspects of mechanical intelligence were unimpaired, even to the point of being able to perform all normal tasks not dependent on language. "Gnosis and praxis were intact, as were episodic storage, self-representation, working memory, social intelligence, and scripts and schemas for action. Despite the loss of speech, he was able to cope with a variety of complex, uniquely human situations and problems" (86).

9. Similar functions are illustrated in the behaviors of the congenitally hearing impaired who lack sign language. The behavior of hearing-impaired people prior to the development of sign language illustrates that although their intellectual development was impaired by the absence of symbolic communication systems, they were nonetheless capable of complex uniquely human cognitive skills, problem solving and adaptations, episodic memory, and conscious awareness. Theories that left-hemisphere language skills are the basis of these capabilities are inconsistent with the persistence of generative skills in other aspects of thought in the absence of language, as well as the language skills of the right hemisphere. Donald concluded that the persistence of higher cognitive functions in the absence of access to language strongly supports a modular theory of mimetic expression.

10. Friedrich emphasized that the different types of macrotropes do not constitute a hierarchy for a number of reasons: the tropes cannot be derived from one another nor from a more comprehensive or basic subtrope; they cannot be ordered along an explicit dimension; the different macrotropes are not related to one another; and finally, the different macrotropes are not exclusive to one another; that is to say, they depend on collaboration and synergistic interaction in expressions. "All language is necessarily modal, formal, imagetic, and implicated in tropes of contiguity and analogy" (Friedrich 1991, 24).

2

～

The Nature and Basis of Shamanism: Cross-Cultural and Neurophenomenological Perspectives

CHAPTER OVERVIEW

The shaman is the primordial human specialist, a skilled manager of consciousness, emotions, social relations, health, and interaction with the natural and supernatural or symbolic domains. Shamanism is found throughout the world and across time. Although conceptualizations and manifestations of shamanism differ, it nonetheless reflects a transcendent reality based in human neurophenomenology and constitutes an etic phenomenon. A brief overview of the historical development of Western knowledge and literature on the shaman establishes the context for early-twentieth-century perspectives. Eliade's (1964) synthesis of the cross-cultural data on shamanism set the stage for contemporary considerations of the universals of shamanism and its cultural functions. As anthropological studies of shamanistic phenomena were extended in the twentieth century, debates arose as to the definition of *shamanism*.

Empirical answers to questions about the characteristics of shamans are provided by a study utilizing formal analysis of cross-cultural data (Winkelman 1984, 1986a,b, 1990a,b, 1992). This study illustrated that shamanism is a worldwide phenomenon of hunting-gathering societies. Shamanism involves cultural adaptations to psychosociobiological potentials through traditions for altering consciousness to provide access to integrative brain-mind states and to the structural foundations of consciousness. These universal shamanistic potentials show cultural variation, reflecting ecological and social adaptations to these potentials to meet human needs. Cross-cultural research suggests that applications of the term *shaman* be restricted to practitioners found primarily in nomadic hunting-gathering societies and sharing specific empirically derived characteristics. The term *shamanistic healer* can be applied to an expanded group of healing professionals who utilize altered states of consciousness (ASC).

Cross-cultural similarities in the form of shamanic experiences and practices indicate the necessity of neurognostic or neurophenomenological perspectives for understanding the bases of the experiences and practices. The shaman's activities and experiences are examined from a neurophenomenological perspective, assessing recurrent themes in terms of their neurological and biocognitive bases. Shamans' experiences, such as the soul flight, death and rebirth, and the guardian spirit quest, are analyzed as neurognostic structures and processes that represent the shaman's psychodynamics and self-transformation. Shamanic practice based in integrative brain states and psychobiological processes played a major role in human cognitive evolution. Shamanism is proposed as the mechanism by which the distinct modules for human thought were integrated, producing the basis for animism, totemism, and guardian spirit beliefs by integrating separate representational systems.

THE PHENOMENA OF SHAMANISM

The central role of the shaman as a primordial spiritual and religious leader is indicated in the prominent role of shamanic representations found worldwide in art, cosmology, and religious artifacts (Emboden 1989; Stahl 1989). The preeminent importance of shamanism in small-scale societies is also widely attested to in numerous ethnographic sources. But although its presence in human societies across time is evidenced in a number of sources of information, shamanism was not known in the indigenous cultural practices of post-Renaissance European societies. The modern introduction of shamanism to Western science and culture was through exposure to it in other cultures.

Historical Contact with Shamanism

Although evidence of shamanic practices is found across history and pre-history, the modern impact of shamanism on Western societies and science began only a few centuries ago. The conventional explanation (Flaherty 1992) of the origin of the term *shaman* in the English language is that it was borrowed from German. German scientific explorations brought the term and the concept (*saman*) from the Tungus of Siberia via Russian. Etymologically similar terms are widely dispersed in the Siberian region, Asia, and Europe. Shamanistic phenomena are recounted in literature as early as the fifth century B.C., while linguistic reconstructions, mythology, and archaeological findings provide evidence of shamanism of even greater antiquity. The Russian contact with shamanic phenomena and literary accountings began much earlier than the modern impact on Europe and scientific circles. In 1253, a Franciscan monk, Vilhelm av Ruysbroeck of France, returned from an expedition to outer Mongolia and reported his observations of what he labeled "devil worship" (Siikala 1978). With the Siberian migrations of Russians and scientific expeditions into Siberia in the seventeenth and eighteenth centuries, there were increasing encounters with shamanic activities. As a consequence, knowledge of shamanistic practices was increasingly brought to the attention of the intelligensia of Russia and, through them, to the rest of Europe. Shamanism impacted Western scientific, academic, and social spheres in the seventeenth century as reports from the non-Western world became an increasing part of the literary and cultural life of Europe (Flaherty 1992). In the context of the Enlightenment and the revolutionary changes wrought in thought and society, shamanistic practices came to represent an irrational side of human nature. This was contrasted with rationalism, which was dominating the emerging ethos of Europe.

The reports of explorers, traders, missionaries, colonists, military, and other representatives of Western culture in contact with these foreign practices provided a body of knowledge about what came to be known as "the shaman." The reports wove together a series of ideas that were loosely connected and observations that were typically rather poor and unsystematic, conditions that were elevated by filtration, cribbing and sensationalism (Flaherty 1992). The sensationalistic yet disbelieving perspectives of European investigators contributed to a pattern of observation and reporting of shamanistic phenomena that focused on incredulous and outlandish claims. This pattern contributed to a view of the shamanistic phenomena as representative of the irrationality of the non-Western other. Western perspectives also emphasized what was considered to be the deceitful and fraudulent nature of the shaman's activities. The shaman was viewed as a clever fraud, a "mad" theatrical performer, who by deceit and guile held sway over the simpleminded community.

Whereas most descriptions were fragmentary, a somewhat complete description of shamanic practices emerged on the Yakut, Evenks, Buryats, and other Siberian groups. The role of trance or ecstasy was widely recognized as a central tool of the shaman; it was used in self-healing, training, healing patients, divination, and the multitude of other tasks that shamans were called on to perform. In the late nineteenth and early twentieth centuries, more systematic and informed perspectives on the shaman emerged from systematic observation and from efforts to relate shamanism to a variety of ancient literary and mythological phenomena of classic antiquity (Flaherty 1992). Knowledge about shamanism impacted theology, medicine, mythology, literature, and finally anthropology and the social sciences. However, the trained ethnographic observations at the end of the nineteenth and the beginning of the twentieth centuries largely followed the political and societal reforms that had crushed or radically transformed Siberian shamanistic practices (Siikala 1978). Many ethnographies that appeared in that period were by political prisoners who described transformed practices of people integrated to varying degrees into more complex societies. It was not until Czaplicka's publication of *Aboriginal Siberia* in 1914, which compiled and analyzed many of these earlier sources, that appreciable amounts of this earlier material were available in English. Studies on shamanistic practices in Finnish, Hungarian, and Turkish peoples soon followed, although many of these were not available in English until the past several decades. Although the Siberian, Russian, and other Eurasian materials provided the primary focus for what was recognized as shamanism, reports from around the world contributed to a growing body of knowledge on shamanistic practices.

The Classic Shaman

A synthesis of a wide range of cross-cultural material on shamanistic practices was provided by the seminal and classic work of Mircea Eliade (1964) *Shamanism: Archaic Techniques of Ecstasy*. Eliade summarized the core of shamanism as involving the use of "techniques of ecstasy" (ASC) in interaction with the spirit world on behalf of the community. The shaman's activities involved healing, divination, and protection and finding game animals. The shaman's ecstatic state was characterized as a magical flight, "a trance during which his soul is believed to leave his body and ascend to the sky or descend to the underworld" (Eliade 1964, 5). The shaman was not *possessed* by spirits, but rather was in control of spirits and demons, through which many tasks were accomplished: healing, dream interpretation, divination, clairvoyance (clear seeing), handling of fire, communication with spirits of the dead, recovery of lost souls, mediation between gods and people, and protection against spirits and malevolent magical practitioners.

The shaman's classic flight may take other forms, including the vision quest experience and the soul journey, when some aspect of the practitioner—called the soul, spirit, or animal familiar—enters into an experiential world and interacts with spirit entities. The shaman's flight may be in corporeal form or in the transformed guise of animals or spirit allies. The shaman's spirit may enter into any of three classic worlds (lower, middle, and upper) during flight. The interactions in the spirit world typically involved psychodramatic struggles to recover the patient's soul. This soul loss could be caused by spirits' aggression or by theft by other shamans. The soul journey may also be used for other forms of healing, learning, combatting spiritual forces, acquiring needed information, helping others determine distant conditions or the fate of separated family members, finding lost objects, acquiring information for hunting, and escorting souls of the dead.

The shamanic ritual was a social activity of unparalleled importance in hunting-gathering societies, a "*spectacle* unequaled in the world of daily experience" (Eliade 1964, 511). It was the context for construction and performance of the basic cosmological, spiritual, religious, social, ecological, intercommunity, and healing activities in those societies. The shaman's curing ceremony was the most important group event and the basic means of structuring the relationship of the individual to the collectivity and cosmos. The shaman's community healing rituals played an essential role in the defense of the psychic integrity of the community. Shamans were antidemonic champions who fought spirits and disease and who defended "life, health, fertility, the world of light, against death, diseases, sterility, disaster, and the world of darkness" (509). The shaman brought the local community into interaction with the spirit world in a ritual charged with fear, awe, and other powerful emotional experiences. In a night-

time ceremony attended by all of the local group, the shaman enacted struggles and battles of animals and spirits, summoning spirit
allies while beating drums, singing, chanting, and dancing violently
and excitedly. Finally the shaman collapsed exhausted and, through
magical flight, entered into the spirit world, ascending to the upper
world and descending to the lower one to communicate with the spirits
and to obtain their cooperation.

At the basis of shamanistic practice and its assumptions is an
animistic system, a belief in a cosmos populated by spiritual entities
that had effects on all aspects of human life and nature. The spiritual
entities had roles in the essence of nature and natural forces, as well
as of humans and other animals. Spirits were central to shamanistic
healing, and communication with them was used to determine the
causes of illness, which was generally attributed to the influences and
actions of spiritual entities and personified natural forces. Learning
the language of the animals is central to this shamanic practice. The
shaman develops relationships with animal spirit helpers, especially
birds, which symbolize the magical flight. The animal spirits are
controlled by the shaman and are the vehicle through which the
shaman carries out a variety of activities. Animal transformation or
soul flight takes the shaman into an ascent into the sky, movement
through the earth, and a descent to the lower world, frequently
through "tree- or pole-climbing rites." The birch, post, or pillar symbolizes the Cosmic Tree, Sacred Tree, or World Tree, the vehicle of
ascension, which interpenetrates and connects the shaman's three
worlds—sky, earth, and lower world. Another mythical image of this
movement across worlds is the Cosmic Mountain or a ladder, which
the shaman ascends. The shamanic movement through these worlds
involves the *axis mundi*, the "center," "opening," or "hole" through
which the shamans, spirits, and gods descend and ascend. These
activities were typically concerned with health. They evoked beliefs
and practices that were at the center of cosmological and religious
belief systems of the cultures and their engagement with spiritual and
mystical experience. The theories of illness employed typically considered people to have lost their souls or to be plagued by witches,
ghosts, spirits, or the malevolent action of other shamans. These beliefs
represented basic psychocultural dynamics, with the spirit world interaction via the shaman's activities evoking powerful emotional
experiences and healing. In addition to socio- and psychotherapeutic
functions, healing ceremonies also incorporated empirical medicine.

Eliade's summary suggested that the shaman was a worldwide

phenomenon, with practitioners in diverse cultures sharing common characteristics and functions. Authorities on shamanism (e.g., Eliade 1964; Hultkrantz 1966, 1973, 1978; Harner 1982; Halifax 1979; Siikala 1978) have considered the universals to include an ecstatic state of communication with the spirit world on behalf of the community. Other universals ascribed to the shaman also include being found in hunting-gathering societies, selection for the position through an illness or a calling of the spirits, a vision quest, a death/rebirth experience, the capacity to fly, the ability to transform oneself into an animal, use of spirits as assistants, and the potential to be a witch or a wizard with negative use of power. Most also consider an essential aspect of the shaman's ecstatic states to involve, at least on some occasions, an experience labeled as soul flight. Soul flight is an experience in which the shaman's soul or spirit, along with some sense of self, is thought to depart the body and travel to a spirit world.

But some investigators disagree as to these and other characteristics, in particular the nature of the shamanic ASC. Some (e.g., Findeisen 1957) have argued that possession, when a spirit is believed to take over and control the individual, is also a characteristic of shamans. Many types of individuals and practices have been referred to as shaman and shamanism, respectively, including those also called witch doctor, medicine man, healer, medium, soothsayer, diviner, warlock, wizard, and others. There are numerous characteristics, activities, and roles ascribed to a shaman—an ecstatic practitioner, a healer, a psychopomp, a religious practitioner, a political ruler, a curer, a prophesier, and one involved in life-cycle rituals, the death transition, hunting magic, political ordeals, healing and depossession, physical and spiritual protection, sacrifice, contact with the spiritual world, art, mythology, religion, and animism. Of these many characteristics and descriptions, investigators wonder what can validly be attributed to a universally distributed phenomenon appropriately labeled "shamanism." One reason for this uncertainty and the inconclusive characterization of the shaman is the relative recency of systematic cross-cultural studies of these phenomena that can provide empirical answers to these long-standing questions.

THE SHAMAN AS AN ETIC PHENOMENON

Although shamans, mediums, and other magico-religious healers have been of long-standing concern to anthropologists, there have been few empirical cross-cultural assessments of the nature of shamanism and related magico-religious healing practices that utilize ASC. Generally, there is acceptance that practices related to shamanism are cross-cultural, or universal, but no clear explication of the commonalities nor establishment of an empirical basis for claims to universals. Some reject universals of shamanism, arguing that the term shaman should be restricted to Siberian and sub-Arctic practitioners (Siikala 1978). Others use the term shaman more broadly to refer to anyone who voluntarily uses ASC (Peters and Price-Williams 1981). Heinze (1991) exemplifies these definitional approaches, considering shamans to be those individuals who fulfill community needs by mediating between the profane and the sacred through accessing ASC. But she arbitrarily rejected other characteristics mentioned by Eliade and others (e.g., power over animals, fire immunity, and dismemberment experiences) because those characteristics are not associated with some practitioners she wishes to call shamans. While including Asian trance mediums within the denotation of shaman, she rejects the extension of the term shaman to similar practitioners in the United States. Arbitrary definitional approaches cannot establish what to call a shaman, nor can they elucidate cross-cultural similarities and differences among shamanistic healers. Establishing shamanism as an etic phenomenon (or transcendental noumena) requires cross-cultural research.

A Cross-Cultural Study of Magico-Religious Practitioners

Determining what is a shaman has been addressed by an empirical cross-cultural research project on magico-religious practitioners and shamanistic healers that utilized formal analysis of descriptive cross-cultural data (Winkelman 1984, 1986a, 1990a, 1992). This analysis permitted an empirical determination of the characteristics associated with shamans and the distribution of the characteristics, as well as relationships with other types of magico-religious practitioners and healers utilizing ASC. This study utilized a forty-seven-society stratified subsample of the Standard Cross-Cultural Sample (SCCS) (Murdock and White 1969; see Winkelman [1984, 1992] and Winkelman and White [1987] for data and methods). These societies cover a time span ranging from 1750 B.C. (Babylonians) to the twentieth century and provide worldwide coverage of the major geographic regions.

Determination of the possible etic status and cross-cultural characteristics of the shaman was based on coding of data from ethnographies and formal mathematical analysis of the data. The unit of analysis was each culturally recognized magico-religious practitioner status, social positions based on interaction with supernatural entities or power. These practitioners were individually assessed through the available ethnographic literature. The variables used to characterize the practitioners were developed from an emic perspective, based on the cultural perceptions of the nature of practitioner activities and characteristics as described in the ethnographic literature. Each culturally recognized status (practitioner type) was individually assessed with respect to more than two hundred variables evaluating a wide range of characteristics, including selection criteria; training conditions and procedures; ASC induction techniques, characteristics, and labeling; sources of power and relationships to spirit entities; magico-religious activities; types of healing and divination techniques employed; context and motives for professional activities; and sociopolitical powers and activities (original variables in Winkelman 1984; an updated/revised variable and data set is available on computer disk in Winkelman and White 1987; cf. Winkelman 1992). Evaluation of types of and relationships among these practitioners was based on mathematical assessment of the quantity of shared characteristics. Summation of shared characteristics provided the basis for determination of different types of magico-religious practitioners, based on the groupings determined by cluster-analysis procedures (see Winkelman 1984, 1986a, 1992 for methods and analysis).

These *types of magico-religious practitioners* are the groups revealed by cluster analyses, all of which include healing practitioners found in different regions of the world. These empirically derived groups of practitioners from different regions (e.g., Africa, Asia, and the Americas) share more characteristics in common than they do with other magico-religious practitioners in their own geographic regions. The empirical similarity in practitioners is more relevant than a priori definitions or geographical location. This suggests that the term shaman should be restricted to those magico-religious practitioners empirically sharing similar characteristics, including their principal presence in hunting-gathering societies, where their activities first arose in sociocultural evolution. The different types of empirically determined magico-religious practitioners have been labeled with terms frequently employed by anthropologists: shaman, shaman/healer, healer, medium, priest, and sorcerer/witch. These practitioner types differ in terms of central characteristics, as well as in the social complexity of their respective societies. The primary contrasts among these different magico-religious practitioners and shamanistic healers are provided in table 2.1 (adapted from Winkelman 1992).

Table 2.1
Magico-Religious Practitioner Types' Principal Characteristics

Characteristics	Shaman
Societal Conditions	Hunting and gathering, nomadic. No local political integration. No social classes.
Magico-Religious Activity	Healing and divination. Protection from spirits and malevolent magic. Hunting magic. Malevolent acts.
Sociopolitical Power	Charismatic leader, communal and war leader.
Social Characteristics	Predominantly male, female secondary. High social status. Ambiguous moral status.
Professional Characteristics	Part-time. No group—individual practice.
Selection and Training	Vision quests, dreams, illness, and spirit's request. ASC and spirit training or individual practitioner. Status recognized by clients.
Motive and Context	Acts at client request for client, local community.
Supernatural Power	Animal spirits, spirit allies. Spirit power usually controlled.
Special Abilities	Weather control, flying, fire immunity, death and rebirth, transformation into animal.
Techniques	Spirit control. Physical and empirical medicine. Massaging and plants.
ASC Conditions and Spirit Relations	ASC training and practice. Shamanic soul flight/journey. Isolation, austerities, fasting, hallucinogens, chanting and singing, extensive drumming and percussion, and, frequently, collapse and unconsciousness.

Shaman/Healer	Healer
Agricultural subsistence. Sedentary.	Agricultural subsistence. Sedentary. Political integration.
Healing and divination. Protection against spirits and malevolent magic. Hunting magic and agricultural rites. Minor malevolent acts.	Healing and divination. Agricultural and socioeconomic rites. Propitiation.
Informal political power. Moderate judiciary decisions.	Judicial, legislative, and economic power. Life-cycle rituals.
Predominantly male. Moderate socioeconomic status. Predominantly moral status.	Predominantly male, female rare. High socioeconomic status. Predominantly moral.
Part-time. Collective/group practice. Specialized role.	Full-time. Collective/group practice. Highly specialized role.
Vision quests, dreams, illness and spirit requests. ASC and ritual training by group. Ceremony recognizes status.	Voluntary selection, payment to trainer. Learn rituals and techniques. Ceremony recognizes status.
Acts at client request in client group.	Acts at client request in client group. Performs at public collective rituals.
Spirits' allies and impersonal power (mana). Power controlled.	Superior gods and impersonal power (mana). Ritual techniques and formulas. Power under control.
Occasional flight, animal transformation.	Prevent future illness.
Physical and empirical medicine. Massaging, herbal, cleanse wounds. Charms, spells, exorcisms, and rituals. Spirit control and propitiation.	Charms, spells, exorcisms, rituals, and sacrifice. Propitiation and command of spirits.
ASC training and practice. Shamanic/mystical ASC. Isolation, austerities, fasting, hallucinogens, chanting and singing, extensive percussion, and, frequently, collapse/unconsciousness.	ASC limited or absent. Social isolation; fasting; minor austerities; limited singing, chanting, or percussion.

Table 2.1 (continued)
Magico-Religious Practitioner Types' Principal Characteristics

Characteristics	Medium
Societal Conditions	Agricultural subsistence. Sedentary. Political integration.
Magico-Religious Activity	Healing and divination. Protection from spirits and malevolent magic. Agricultural magic. Propitiation.
Sociopolitical Power	Informal political power. Moderate judiciary decisions.
Social Characteristics	Predominantly female, male secondary/rare. Low socioeconomic status. Exclusively moral.
Professional Characteristics	Part-time. Collective/group practice. Temporal lobe syndrome.
Selection and Training	Spontaneous possession by spirit. Training in practitioner group. Ceremony recognizes status.
Motive and Context	Acts primarily for clients. Performs public ceremonies.
Supernatural Power	Possessing spirits dominate. Power out of control, unconscious.
Special Abilities	None.
Techniques	Propitiation and spirit control. Exorcisms and sacrifices.
ASC Conditions and Spirit Relations	ASC—Possession. Spontaneous onset, tremors, convulsions, seizures, compulsive motor behavior, amnesia, temporal lobe discharge.

Table 2.1 (continued)
Magico-Religious Practitioner Types' Principal Characteristics

Priest	Sorcerer/Witch
Agriculture. Semisedentary or permanent residency. Political integration.	Agriculture and sedentary. Political integration. Social stratification.
Protection and purification. Agricultural and socioeconomic rites. Propitiation and worship.	Malevolent acts. Kill kin, cause death, economic destruction.
Political, legislative, judicial, economic, and military power.	None.
Exclusively male. High social and economic status. Exclusively moral.	Male and female. Low social and economic status. Exclusively immoral.
Full-time. Organized practitioner group. Hierarchically ranked roles.	Part-time. Little or no professional organization. Killed.
Social inheritance or succession. Political action.	Social labeling, biological inheritance. Innate abilities, self-taught or learned.
Acts to fulfill public social functions. Calendrical rites.	Acts at client request or for personal reasons. Practices in secrecy.
Power from superior spirits or gods. Has no control over spirit power.	Power from spirits and ritual knowledge. Has control of spirit power. Power may operate unconsciously or out of control.
Affect weather.	Animal transformation, fly.
Propitiation and collective rites. Sacrifice and consumption.	Spirit control, ritual techniques.
Generally no ASC or very limited. Occasionally alcohol consumption, sexual abstinence, social isolation, sleep deprivation.	Indirect evidence of ASC. Flight and animal transformation.

The Cross-Cultural Characteristics of Shamans

The practitioners empirically clustered in the group labeled "shaman" conform to many of the general characterizations found in the classic descriptions of shamanism. Cross-cultural research indicates that shamans are the charismatic religious and political leaders in hunting-gathering societies (or slightly more complex societies with limited agriculture) where political integration and leadership are limited to the level of the local community. The shaman's involvement with political power is generally informal, indicated by high social status, by position of leadership in war or raiding parties, and by organizing communal hunts and deciding group movement. Shamans engage in activities on behalf of a client group or the entire local community, most frequently healing and divination; however, they all also (are thought to) engage in malevolent magical acts designed to harm others, normally enemies of the group. They may also be accused of sorcery by their own group. Shamans utilize ASC activities as the basis for their training and professional service. The shamans are selected and trained through a variety of auguries and procedures that involve ASC. These auguries and procedures may include having had involuntary visions; receiving signs from spirits; having experienced serious illness; deliberately undertaking vision quests; and the induction of ASC through a variety of procedures, including the use of hallucinogens, fasting and water deprivation, exposure to temperature extremes, extensive exercise (such as prolonged dancing), various austerities, sleep deprivation, auditory stimuli (such as drumming and chanting), and social and sensory deprivation. Their ASC are generally labeled as involving soul flight, journeys to the lower world, and/or transformation into animals (but not possession). Typical of shamans are the capacity to fly; a death and rebirth experience; relationships with and control of spirits, particularly animal spirits; and provision of hunting magic. The shaman's ecstatic visionary states, soul journey or flight, widely considered to be an essential feature of shamanism, are validated as a universal of shamanism by this cross-cultural research. However, not all professional ASC activities of shamans involve soul flight; and when soul flight does occur, it is only one phase of the shaman's ASC activities. Shaman ASC may take other forms, including vision quest experiences.

The !Kung Num Master: Contemporary Shaman.   Included in the formal sample used in this cross-cultural study were the !Kung Bushmen of southwest Africa. Their shamanistic healer (the Num master) was classified as a shaman with selection, training, and healing activities corresponding to the classic phenomena of shamanism. The medicine dance of the Num master and the !Kung Bushmen (the topic of articles [Marshall 1962, 1969] and a book [Katz 1982]) occurs in the context of their communal healing activities, which involve all-night sessions in which the men as healers dance to the incessant singing and clapping accompaniment provided by women. The extensive dancing is thought to activate an energy source that is then transferred to patients. Spirits are pleaded with or commanded in an effort to obtain their assistance in the cure of illness. These ceremonies occur on an irregular weekly basis. Although the more recent reports of the healing ceremony (Katz 1982) suggested that it does not involve drug ingestion, earlier observations (Marshall 1962, 1969; cf. film) showed the use of psychoactive substances, particularly for healers in training. Assessment of published data on pharmacological properties of the !Kung Bushmen medicine plants showed that the vast majority have evidence of being psychoactive (Winkelman and Dobkin deRios 1989). The characteristics of the !Kung Bushman Num master in twentieth-century Africa are strikingly similar to the characteristics of the classic descriptions of the Siberian shaman. This similarity cannot be explained by diffusion. The fundamental similarity across time, space, and cultures in the phenomena of shamanism indicates that these traditions develop from a common psychobiological basis. The cross-cultural distribution of fundamental aspects of shamanism reflects an underlying psychobiological basis and its adaptive consequences. These universal and cross-cultural characteristics of shamans reflect biosocial and neurophenomenological structures that constitute the primordial basis for religion.

Shamanistic Healers.   The practitioners labeled shaman, shaman/healers, mediums, and many healers shared the core characteristics of shamanism suggested by Eliade (1964): the use of ASC for their communities and in interaction with spiritual entities. However, they did not all share other characteristics attributed to shamans (e.g., soul flight, animal transformation, animal spirits, death and rebirth, hunting magic). Shamanistic healers represent the universal institutionalization of practices derived from psychobiological mechanisms for altering consciousness (cf. chapter 3 this volume). Because transformation of consciousness is central to the classic description and activities of shamans, all magico-religious practitioners utilizing ASC

in training and healing are referred to here as "shamanistic healers."
Shamanistic healers represent diverse cultural developments of the
psychobiological potentials at the basis of shamanism in the process
of the evolution of human social organization from the local communities of hunter-gatherer societies into agricultural societies with
hierarchical political organization and social stratification with classes.
Shamanistic healers share other characteristics: spiritual interpretations of therapy; utilization of spirit entities as projective mechanisms;
psycholinguistic programming through spells; symbolic ritual manipulations; restoration of social relations; and removal of illness attributed to spirits or other humans. Shamanistic practices have important therapeutic functions through affecting psychosocial processes
and as culturally relevant therapies that provide physical treatments
and community and intrapsychic integration (Winkelman and
Winkelman 1990). The different types of shamanistic healers differed
with respect to socioeconomic characteristics of their societies, their
socioeconomic and political status, their selection and training procedures, the specific characteristics of their ASC, the sources of their
power, and additional magico-religious activities, as indicated in table
2.1. These differences among magico-religious healers illustrate the
unique characteristics of the shamans as opposed to the other magico-
religious practitioners; and they reflect changes in the manifestation
of psychobiological potentials occurring as a consequence of sociocultural evolution.

The Evolution of the Shaman

The biological foundations in ASC provided the basis for universally distributed shamanistic healing practices. The origin of shamanism in psychobiological structures implies the persistence of these
structures in more complex societies. A broader group of practitioners—shamanistic healers—manifests these potentials, reflecting their
adaptation to different ecological, subsistence and social conditions.
Cross-cultural analyses (Winkelman 1986a, 1990, 1992) illustrate this
evolution in the systematic relationships of shamanistic healers and
other magico-religious practitioners to subsistence conditions and
social complexity variables. The relevant socioeconomic variables
underlying the evolution of shamanism were identified by Winkelman
(1986a, 1990a, 1992) as: (1) the absence/presence of hunting and
gathering versus agriculture as the major source of subsistence; (2)
fixity of residence (nomadic versus sedentary lifestyle); (3) political

integration beyond the level of the local community; and (4) social stratification (classes and castes or hereditary slavery). These relationships of socioeconomic conditions to forms of magico-religious practice were established as being independent of diffusion through use of autocorrelation multiple-regression procedures (Dow, Burton, White, and Reitz 1984; see Winkelman 1992).

Shaman. Practitioners classified as shamans were found throughout the world, except in the Circum-Mediterranean and Insular Pacific regions, where their absence reflects the lack of hunter-gatherer societies in these regions in the sample studied. Most shamans were found in societies with hunting, gathering, or fishing as the primary mode of subsistence; however, several were also found in pastoral societies of Eurasia and in four Amerindian societies with some reliance on agriculture. The shamans were found in societies without formal classes and mostly in societies lacking an administrative political organization beyond the local community; none of the shamans were found in sedentary societies. Independently significant contributions to the explanation of societal variance in the incidence of the shamans were found in the negative correlations of both political integration and fixity of residence with the presence of shamans. Increases in sedentary lifestyles and the development of more complex forms of political integration that followed the adoption of agriculture led to the disappearance of shamans and the transformation of their potentials and functions.

Shaman/Healers. The shaman/healers occurred primarily in sedentary societies with a major reliance on agriculture as a food source, which is positively correlated with their presence. This indicates that adoption of agriculture is a fundamental cause of the transformations of shamans into shaman/healers. The fundamental role of agriculture in this transformation of shamanism is further attested to by the significant association of agriculture with priests.

Healers. The presence of healers is significantly predicted by the presence of political integration beyond the level of the local community. Almost all healers also were found in societies with a reliance on agriculture as a primary food source.

Mediums. Although mediums are found in societies with subsistence based on agriculture (or occasionally pastoralism), agriculture does not predict the incidence of the mediums; many agricultural societies are without a medium present. The presence of mediums is significantly correlated with both the presence of political integration beyond the level of the local community and by social stratification, but only political integration is an independently significant predictor.

Priests.   The priests were generally found in sedentary agricultural societies or pastoral societies with political integration beyond the local community. Independently significant predictions of priests were found with agriculture and political integration. This illustrates the evolution of priests under conditions of agriculture and their emergence as sociopolitical leaders as societies increased in political integration.

Sorcerer/Witch.   The sorcerer/witch is found in societies with agriculture or pastoral subsistence patterns, but the social conditions significantly and independently predicting the sorcerer/witch are the presence of political integration and social stratification. Evidence suggests that these conditions produce the sorcerer/witch in the persecution of shamanistic healers (Winkelman 1992).

Biosocial Bases of Religious Practice.   These associations of shamanistic healers and other magico-religious practitioners with social complexity conditions suggest that macro- or general evolutionary processes are responsible for the disappearance of the shaman and the emergence of other types of shamanistic healers. Several lines of analysis (Winkelman 1986a, 1992) confirm that agriculture, political integration, and social stratification, conditions that predict the different societal configurations of magico-religious practitioners, led to the transformation of the shaman. Based on an integration of information about the relations of practitioner selection procedures and professional functions, Winkelman (1992) proposed a model of the evolution of magico-religious functions, which involve the psychobiological ASC basis, the role of social leadership, and the conflict between these two dimensions. These foundations and the relationships of socioeconomic conditions to societal configurations of magico-religious practitioners are illustrated in figure 2.1 (adapted from figure 11.1, Winkelman 1992, 41).

Figure 2.1
Practitioner Types, Biosocial Bases, and Socioeconomic Conditions

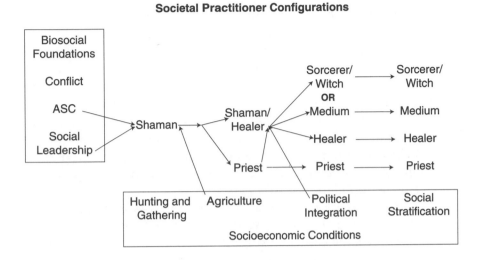

Explaining Universals of Shamanism: Neurognostic Bases

The role of the shaman, with a similar complex of characteristics, activities, and beliefs, is found in widely separated societies. The universality of the basic experiences related to shamanism is substantiated by the convergence of the formal findings of this study with other work on shamanistic practices. Specific universals include those emphasized by Eliade (1964): ASC (ecstatic) experiences; an interaction with the spiritual world; and relations on behalf of a community. These and other universal features of shamanism (visionary experience, soul journey, death-rebirth experience) reflect the neurological structuring of practices and consciousness. Neurognostic perspectives can explain interrelated findings about shamans, specifically: (1) the worldwide distribution of a specific constellation of characteristics found in the role of shamans in hunting-gathering societies; (2) the fundamental role of ASC in shamanistic practices; and (3) the universality of shamanistic healers and their use of ASC in healing and divination.

Universal patterns of shamanism could have resulted from diffusion of a single tradition (e.g., as La Barre [1970] and Furst [1976] suggested with respect to the Eurasian origins of North American shamanism) or from the independent invention of essentially the same institution. The worldwide presence of shamans in this sample in such widely varying linguistic groups as the Click (!Kung), Paleosiberian (Samoyed), Mon-Khmer (Semang), and the diverse North American Indian languages indicates that the diffusion hypothesis would have to postulate a very ancient common group. However, explanation of the distribution of shamanism through the processes of diffusion is rejected by autocorrelation analysis (Winkelman 1986a); the absence of shamans in some regions of the worldwide sample is related to the absence of nomadic hunting-gathering societies without political integration. Independent invention must be considered in the origin and the worldwide distribution of shamanism, which is derived from psychobiological potentials that constituted an adaptive response and provided the foundation for its persistence.

Shamans' presence in hunting-gathering societies with no political integration beyond the local level illustrates that shamanism corresponds to an ecologically and socially determined "type of religion" (Hultkrantz 1966). Hultkrantz modeled this "type of religion" on Steward's (1955) notion of "types of culture," reflecting the basic stages of sociocultural evolution (bands, tribes, cheifdoms, states). A type of religion "contains those religious patterns and features which belong to or are intimately associated with the cultural core and therefore arise out of environmental adaptations" (Hultkrantz 1966, 146). Hultkrantz also suggested that shamanistic phenomena derived from the psychological makeup of humans; these phenomena correspond to the functions and effects of ASC. The worldwide similarity in shamans derives from the common psychobiological bases of human consciousness and its adaptation to social and ecological conditions of hunting-gathering societies. These brain-mind conditions or states of consciousness at the basis of shamanism and related practices involve an alteration in the psychophysiology of consciousness and interaction among structural/functional units of the brain (see chapter 3 this volume). The ASC basis of shamanism is a manifestation of one of the fundamental homeostatic dynamics of the nervous system and human consciousness. This mode of consciousness involves replacement of the normal waking conditions—sympathetic dominance and desynchronized fast-wave activity of the frontal cortex—with a parasympathetic dominant state that is characterized by high-voltage, slow-wave electroencephalogram (EEG) activity originating in the circuits linking the brain stem and the hippocampal-septal area of the limbic system (Winkelman 1986b, 1991a, 1992, 1996). This high-voltage, slow-wave EEG activity imposes a synchronous slow-wave pattern on the frontal lobes, resulting in interhemispheric synchronization and coherence and producing a synthesis of behavior, emotion, and thought.

Shamanistic traditions have arisen throughout the world because of the interaction of innate structures of the human brain-mind with the ecological and social conditions of hunter-gatherer societies. This is possible because this ASC basic to selection, training, and professional activities occurs spontaneously under a wide variety of circumstances. These ASC experiences can be induced naturally as a consequence of injury, extreme fatigue, near starvation, ingestion of hallucinogens, perceptions of natural phenomena, bioelectric discharges, or as a consequence of a wide variety of deliberate procedures that induce these conditions (see chapter 3). Consequently, shamanism was reinvented or rediscovered in diverse cultures as a result of those experiences and because the experiences provide important adaptive capabilities. These are illustrated in a functional relationship of ASC procedures to shamanistic activities. This is derived from their usefulness in meeting challenges to survival, including healing through ASC-induced stress reduction and other physiological changes that enhance systemic integration of the information-processing strata of the brain (see Winkelman 1986b, 1992, and chapters 3, 4, and 5 this volume). The functional relationships of ASC to the shamanistic abilities of healing and divination derive from their psychophysiological effects on biological processes and social psychology. The uniformities in these practices worldwide are a result of the interaction of the psychobiological mental potentials with similar social conditions and human needs. Evidence that shamans derive from an ecological adaptation of biologically based ASC potentials includes (1) the universal distribution of similarly characterized shamans in hunting-gathering societies; (2) the lack of evidence of diffusion; (3) the evolutionary model explaining social processes transforming shamanism; (4) the biological basis of their integrative conditions of consciousness; and (5) their functional characteristics.

The shaman's role in the evolution of human consciousness derives from adaptive potentials of ASC, animistic beliefs, visionary perceptions, soul flight, and death-rebirth experience. These universal adaptations to biocognitive potentials derived from systemic integration of brain functions. Their biological structuring makes them *neurognostic* structures, reflecting their biological contribution to the bases of knowing. The neurognostic structures provide experiences that facilitate adaptation to the operational environment. These neurognostic or archetypal structures are experienced in the sensorium as real, representing a homeomorphogenetic symbolization of both structure and process, a consequence of the confluence of the restructuring process of the ego and the cognized environment (Laughlin, McManus, and d'Aquili 1992). This combination of archetypal and culturally specific elements found in the visionary soul journey and in the themes of death and rebirth involves the symbolic transformation of self and ego. These aspects of the shaman's experience and cosmology are used for psychodynamic transformation and growth. The following section addresses neurognostic aspects of shamanism that have important implications for the understanding of the psychology of their practices—the initiatory crises; the visionary experience and soul flight; guardian spirit relations; and death-rebirth experiences.

THE SHAMAN'S INITIATORY CRISIS

Eliade (1964) pointed out that selection for the role of the shaman may be derived from a crisis, a period of illness or insanity characterized as a spirit affliction and sickness, a consequence of a divine being choosing the individual for the shamanic role. This initiation crisis typically involved (1) an experience of suffering, followed by death, dismemberment, and rebirth; (2) an ascent to the sky and descent to the lower world; and (3) conversations with spirits and souls. The development of a dialogue with spirits is a sign of the improving condition of the initiates as they engage in and imitate conversations with the spirits, invoking them through chanting and singing. During this period the spirits gave the initiates new rules for life.

Characterizations of shamans' initiatory experiences as pathological largely reflects misunderstandings of the shamans' actual situation and an ethnocentric attribution reflecting cultural values that assume ASCs to be inherently pathological. The general Western tendency to consider as pathological those conditions that deviate from the ordinary state of awareness is reflected in the widespread characterizations of shamanic states as involving nervous disorders, neurosis, psychosis, hysteria, and epilepsy. Cognicentric assumptions, which view normalcy in reference to the rationality of ordinary consciousness, make shamanic conditions appear inherently pathological.

However, there are good grounds to assess the relationship between shamanic experiences and psychopathological processes because in some cultures the shaman's call to the profession is conceptualized as a form of illness. But even when shamanic initiatory experiences are culturally viewed as having pathological implications, portraying the shaman as a victim of spirit afflictions, the expectation is that the shaman will use these experiences for important developments. This contrasts with the inherent pathogenic interpretation of schizophrenic and psychotic experiences. The shaman's response may involve solitude and social isolation, but this severing of social ties is not pathological—it should be viewed as providing the focus necessary for learning from the spirits.

In spite of the similarity of shamanistic ASC with some pathological states (e.g., see Ackerknecht 1943, Silverman 1967, Noll 1983, Siikala 1978, Hultkrantz 1978), there is good evidence that these shamanic experiences are not pathological from their own culture's point of view, nor from that of psychiatry. Shamans are generally among the healthiest and best adjusted members of their culture. Assessment of the relationship of shamanic practice to psychopathology requires differentiation of the initial call or predisposing conditions leading to shamanism from the conditions of professional practice. A central differentiation of shamanic activities from psychopathology lies in the voluntary nature of the quest for the shamanic state of consciousness, a deliberate action distinctly different from the involuntary condition experienced by the person suffering from psychopathology.

Noll (1983) analyzed the relationship between shamanic states and schizophrenia, refuting arguments that the pathogenic personality traits of acute schizophrenia are the same underlying conditions that produce shamanic states of consciousness. Noll's state-specific approach to shamanism and schizophrenia provided an assessment of their respective phenomenologies that refuted their equivalence, showing they represent very different kinds of experiences and phenomena. Noll's comparison of the shamanic state of consciousness with schizophrenic states as described in the *Diagnostic and Statistical Manual* (*DSM*III) showed specific differences, including volition, the form and contents of thought, the nature of perceptions, and the nature of affect and sense of self. The willful entry into the ASC characteristic of shamanism provides an important distinction from schizophrenia. The shaman's social functions and deliberate communication during ASC illustrate the distinctiveness from the socially dysfunctional conditions of the schizophrenic. Shamans also illustrate an ability to discriminate between the experiences of everyday life and those of the shamanic world, a discrimination absent in the schizophrenic. The experiential qualities of shamanic states of consciousness and those of schizophrenia also differ sharply, even including those that constitute the hallucinatory experiences. The shaman's experiences are primarily of a visual nature, whereas schizophrenics typically have auditory experiences. Even when the shaman's experiences include auditory components, these tend to be of a helpful and healing nature rather than the accusatory, intrusive, and paranoia-inducing auditory experiences that are characteristic of schizophrenia. In contrast to the schizophrenic's emotional flattening, the shamanic state of consciousness is characterized by the expression of positive affective experiences, as well as by an intensification of emotion. The shaman also exhibits considerable skill in manipulating the emotions of the patient, a condition in direct contrast with the schizophrenic's sense of loss of control.

One pathological characteristic often attributed to shamanic ASC is epilepsy, because of convulsive shaking behaviors, tremors, and seizures. *Epilepsy* is a term used to refer to a wide variety of symptoms and disorders associated with disinhibition or electrical discharge patterns of any of the lobes of the cortex, most frequently the temporal lobe. Epilepsy is a generalized symptom of many different factors leading to the brain's failure to inhibit normal patterns of discharge, which then spread to all regions of the brain. Because these conditions occur only during the shamanic ASC and not at other times, this rejects an organic explanation of their basis for shamanism.

Dissociative disorders, particularly hysteria and hysterical neurosis, are often attributed to shamanism. However, their clinical characteristics do not correspond to shamanic ASC. A key characteristic of dissociative hysterical neurosis includes the loss of mental processes and conscious awareness. Even though the shaman may lose external perception during ASC, a continuity of conscious awareness is required for communication with the audience. The lack of amnesia and the persistence of self-awareness during shamanic ASC are quite distinct from hysterical disorders and their defense mechanisms designed to block awareness of particular conflicts. Shamanic activities have different goals, using ASC as a mechanism for attaining symbolic knowledge about the nature of the patient's psychological conflicts.

But Noll's (1983) assessment of the lack of congruence between shamanic states of consciousness and those of schizophrenia did not address a related issue—the nature of the shaman's initiatory experience. However, when the initiatory experiences are examined, they also show important distinctions from that of schizophrenia. Nonetheless, Walsh (1990) indicated that although pathological attributions to the shaman are inappropriate, the emotional turmoil and distress associated with the shamanic call in many cultures suggest that the shaman may undergo an initial crisis that entails a temporary form of psychosis. But again it appears that this initiatory crisis is not a universal feature of shamanism and therefore cannot be considered fundamental to the shaman. In some cultures the initiatory illness is absent, with all men engaging in the shamanic vision quest as a normal part of adult development. Walsh suggested that some initiatory crises may constitute a brief reactive psychosis, atypical psychosis, or schizophrenia or schizophren-form disorders. However, such interpretations require that the shaman's condition be examined from the perspective of psychopathology rather than as a form of psychological deconstruction designed to permit the manifestation of other neurognostic symbols and forms of self-reference. Walsh suggested that linkages between initiatory psychological disturbances and the widely reputed exceptional health of shamans may reflect a widely recognized phenomena. Psychological disturbances are often followed by increased mental health, a consequence of the growth experiences that they provoke. These kinds of crises are associated with phenomena labeled as divine illness and spiritual emergencies (see chapter 5 this volume), experiences that may provide the basis for development through the processes of individuation and self-actualization, as exemplified in the death-rebirth motif.

Death and Rebirth: Perinatal Experiences and Ego Transformation

The shamanic phenomenon of death and rebirth reflects fundamental processes of transformation of self. The motif of death and rebirth is manifested cross-culturally because it is derived from neurognostic bases that reflect structures of human consciousness. Central to the shaman's development is an illness or a spirit attack that leads to experiences interpreted as death. These illness experiences are thrust on the shaman from a variety of causes, both physical (illness) and cultural (stress and crises interpreted as spirit's torment or insistence). This experience of death is generally followed by descent to the lower world, in which the shaman is tormented by spirits. These entities may attack the initiate, slashing the body or devouring it piece by piece. A recurrent motif is the removal of the eyes and their strategic placement for the observation of the total dismemberment and destruction of the body. The skeleton may be stripped of all flesh and cleaned, while flesh and organs are consumed by various mythological parties. The body of the initiate is then re-membered, or reconstructed, a process that imbues the shaman with power and spirit allies.

The shaman's initiatory sickness involving personal death reflects the fragmentation of the conscious ego. Walsh (1990) suggested that these experiences represent a psychological transformation process, which tends to occur at times of overwhelming stress, resulting from the intrusion of unassimilated neural structures. The cross-culturally recurrent aspects of death, dismemberment, and rebirth represent deep archetypal or neurognostic processes of the human psyche. Walsh analyzed them as transformative processes occurring in response to the inability of the psyche to maintain balance. The death-rebirth experiences reflect the death of one identity in development of another. The underlying conflicts lead to a destructuring of egoic consciousness. As a consequence of the inability of the existing psychological structures to manage the stress, the organization of the psyche—identity, beliefs, habits, and conditioning—collapses, resulting in a period of introversion and reduction of intentionality. Laughlin, McManus, and d'Aquili (1992) suggested that this collapse of internal structures is experienced homeomorphogenetically as dismemberment, "autosymbolic images" of one's own breakdown.

Following the collapse of the psyche, experienced as dismemberment and destruction, a psychological reorganization follows, guided by an archetypal drive toward holism or holotropism. Walsh (1990) suggested that the spontaneously occurring threatening images symbolize the shadow, aspects of the self and the psyche that are disowned and repressed because they are considered to be bad and evil. When these structures are forcibly reelevated into consciousness in distressing symbolic forms, they may be perceived as threatening external entities. The spiritual world provides a conceptual domain for organizing the experiences of these structures, whose locus of intentionality is dissociated from the conscious neural networks of the ego. The symbolic manipulation of these spiritual constructs and their relationships to the ego can produce changes in affect and other psychodynamic processes. As one becomes more accustomed to the experiences, and as they are associated with symbols with positive affect, they lose their terrifying nature as representatives of death and become objects of exploration. The progressive development of the shaman requires that the ego have sufficient strength to reciprocally assimilate conflicting structures through transformations that can resolve the discrepant internal models. The shaman's experiences are structured by the cultural conventions and beliefs and, in some cases, by the tutelage of more experienced practitioners. This leads the shaman to transcendence at a new level. The universal experience of magical flight symbolizes this transformative experience. These are homeomorphogenetic transformations in structures of consciousness, a consequence of the restructuring process of the ego produced by the symbolic models, and the holistic imperatives toward psycho-integration. The death-rebirth experiences frequently result in dramatic alleviation of psychosomatic, emotional, and interpersonal problems resistant to previous psychotherapy, with reorganization guided by archetypal drives toward wholeness (holotropism) (Walsh 1990). This reflects the integration of the individual sense of self and experience within neurognostic structures of the organism.

Shamanic Structures of Consciousness

The universally attested-to shamanic experiences of death and re-birth represent structures of the collective unconscious produced in the interaction between neurognostic structures of the brain and the intrauterine processes and experiences associated with birth (Grof 1992). These shamanic structures have been examined by Grof, based on his decades of supervising more than twenty thousand shamanis-tic sessions with people from diverse cultures using holotrophic breath work and psychedelics. This provides an empirical basis for charac-terizing structures of consciousness that fall outside of those conven-tionally recognized in Western psychology. In addition to the tradi-tional biographical level of consciousness created in a person's experiences from infancy onward, there are two other major levels of consciousness—the perinatal and the transpersonal. The *perinatal* level reflects birth trauma experiences; while the *transpersonal* levels re-flect dimensions of consciousness that extend beyond a person's body and ego. Both of these levels of consciousness are central to death-rebirth experiences and other aspects of shamanic practices. In comparing his findings with those of shamanistic systems, Grof (1992, 17) concluded that "the ancient spiritual systems had actually charted with amazing accuracy different levels and types of experiences that occur in non-ordinary states of consciousness." Shamanistic techniques for altering consciousness reveal aspects of the deep structures of human consciousness and psyche, providing the organism with mechanisms "to free the bonds of various traumatic imprints and limitations, heal itself, and reach a more harmonious way of functioning" (19).

Grof described these structures as organizing the psyche and the unconscious with themes fundamental to both positive and negative emotional experiences of life, particularly anxiety, fury, pain, and suffocation. Grof analyzed perinatal phenomena as involving four distinct experiential phases or Basic Perinatal Matrices (BPMs):[1] (1) the amniotic universe, (2) cosmic engulfment, (3) the death-rebirth struggle, and (4) death and rebirth. These four perinatal matrices are aspects of the structures of the unconscious. The first is a reflection of the natural symbiosis based on the intimate physical and emotional connections of the organism with the mother. These experiences have strong sacred and mystical overtones, a sense of unity of one's self with god and the cosmos, an "oceanic ecstasy" similar to the "peak experiences" described by Abraham Maslow (1971). These experiences, attested to across time and cultures, reflect the basic global state of positive affect of the entire organism and its cognitive, emotional, and nervous systems.

Grof (1992) referred to structures formed around the experiences of agony and ecstasy of birth as "volcanic" or "Dionysian" ecstasy. This is a combination of the polar opposite experiences of pain and pleasure and is induced in shamanic rituals through painful induction procedures. The death-rebirth experience's culmination is the struggle of " 'ego death,' an experience of total annihilation on all levels—physical, emotional, intellectual, and spiritual" (73). Although this loss of the ego and the sense of ability to operate on the world are often experienced threateningly, Grof characterized this loss as the death of one's paranoid aspects, one's false egos that view the world as dangerous and that feel the need to be in control to guard against danger. The sense of rebirth that follows this release from fear produces a sense of great energy, which may be interpreted as light, pure god, or unitive feeling of reunion with the true self.

VISIONARY EXPERIENCE: SOUL FLIGHT AND THE GUARDIAN SPIRIT QUEST

A central aspect of shamans' activities for their communities is creating a relationship to a dimension of experience and reality known as religious, spiritual, numinous, and so on. The shaman's role in human consciousness reflects the functional nature of the perceptions of the spirit world in visionary experiences—the internal imagetic flow, which provides the basis of shamanic diagnosis, journeying, healing, and other activities. The communality underlying the spirit world and visionary perceptions is in their role in construction of meaning for individual and collectivity and in their psychosociophysiological representations and implications. Visions represent development of skills in using the presentational modality; spirits constitute a symbolic system for representing other, self, and internal differentiations.

Whether thrust on the shaman as a consequence of illness or sought through deliberately induced procedures, visionary experiences are a central tool of the shaman's development and interaction with the spiritual domain. These experiences may occur spontaneously, but the shaman's training involves the deliberate cultivation of this internal visionary state within the context of a cultural tradition that provides the content to experiences and guides their development. Noll (1985, 445) characterized "mental imagery cultivation," the deliberate development of enhanced mental imagery, as the central feature of shamanism, "an ecstatic healing tradition which at its core is concerned with the techniques for inducing, maintaining and interpreting the experience of enhanced visual mental imagery." Visionary experiences are a natural phenomenon of the central nervous system, resulting from disinhibition of the regulation of the visual cortex. This disinhibition results in hyperactivity of the visual regions, which are experienced as ongoing visual panoramas. This entry into the visionary world is a central part of the shaman's cognitive potentials, which constitute a human cultural evolution through their adaptive advantages. Their skills lie in being able to stabilize this internal world and utilize its images for a variety of purposes, including divination, diagnosis, healing, and psychodramatic social manipulation.

Noll (1985) suggested that the shaman's cultivation of visions involves two phases of training. First, the shaman learns to increase this internal imagery, enhancing its vividness through a variety of procedures. A focus on internal visual imagery provides an internal experiential focus, a figure-ground cognitive reversal that enhances the primacy of the internal imagetic reality to the degree that it provides an alternate experience to the external world. Second, the shaman develops increased control over the internal images, known as the inner-sight or inner-vision.

Shamanistic traditions exploit internal imagery as an innate human capability that plays a fundamental role in human cognition. This imagery reflects the mind's capability for producing representations from its own materials and through its own agency. This imagetic capability has important commonalities with perception, depending on the same brain capabilities and systems reflecting levels of information within the visual system (Baars 1997). The roles of internal imagery in cognition involve "metaphoric predication" between domains of experience and other forms of information processing. "[M]ental imagery activates 'unconscious' . . . nonvolitional levels of the psychophysiological apparatus . . . and increases the *affective acceptance* of visionary experiences . . . on a deep psychophysiological level" (Noll 1985, 446). Visual images link the somatic and the cognitive levels through analogical processes. The inner images attune both shaman and patient to the levels of psychobiological communication manifested in presentational aspects of the mind. The shaman's ability to heal derives in part from the use of this visionary ability to operate on neurognostic structures. The shaman's visions reflect the basic principles of neural organization of humans and their knowledge.

Achterberg (1985) provided analysis of the shaman's use of imagery to impact health. One such use is "pre-verbal imagery," in which imagination acts directly on the physical substrate, including tissues, organs, and cells. This type of communication may occur outside of deliberation and consciousness. She suggested that it evolved prior to language and utilized different neuro-pathways than those underlying spoken language (e.g., the presentational modality). Achterberg also identified a second type of healing imagery, which she calls transpersonal, utilizing symbols that are universal and reflect the action on the collective unconscious (or neurognostic structures). The symbolic encounter in visionary experiences involves linking the mundane world with the unconscious and transcendent aspects of consciousness. In linking together symbols of the cosmological order, the mind, the unconscious, and the social world, shamanic activities provide a means for manipulation of and integration of the psyche and the bodies of the clients. Images play a central role in muscular control, reflecting the widely distributed effects of conscious images throughout the brain, which enables them to drive the unconscious control centers of muscles (Baars 1997). Images represent goals that recruit and coordinate a wide range of unconscious systems and plans of action to achieve the goals desired. Images can play a fundamental role in providing for voluntary influence over the autonomic nervous system, with threatening images evoking the fight-or-flight response (sympathetic activation) and with pleasant images stimulating the parasympathetic system's relaxation response. "Imagery seems to be the only conscious modality that can trigger autonomic process" (Baars 1997, 141).

This internal visionary world includes the spiritual beings that Noll (1985) suggested have always been part of human consciousness and often constitute the spirit guides and teachers that train shamanic practitioners. These spirit experiences are found universally and must be considered an experienced reality, independent of their ultimate ontological status. In shamanism, the spirits play a fundamental role in representing the shaman's power, the illnesses from which the shaman's patients suffer, and the processes used to heal the patients. These spirits represent social and psychological processes operating on the individual.

This visionary world of the shaman is a representation of the group's psychodynamics, which are transformed through the shaman's activities. Although the shaman plays an active role in the construction of these experiences, the cross-culturally common structures that these experiences exhibit indicate that they represent fundamental aspects of human consciousness that reflect neurognostic structuring. These and other aspects of the shaman's world may still be accessed by those who submit to or spontaneously undergo the experiences that characterize the shaman's training (see Harner 1982). These visionary experiences involve the engagement with neurognostic representations of the fundamental forces of life and death, self and others, and the cosmos and of the most pressing concerns of the individual relevant to self, significant others, and the emotional and social dynamics of life. This dimension of reality is ritually manipulated to dramatically engage the patient and the community in a manner that transforms their experiences and well-being.

Laughlin, McManus, and d'Aquili (1992) suggested that the shaman's learning of the spirit world involves the organization of a cognized environment just as does our construction of our perceptions and beliefs about the operationalized (external) environment. The symbols and interrelationships represent the transformative process and can accelerate it by homeomorphogenetically entraining the neurocognitive structures with external symbols. This aspect of imaging involves the integration of a variety of physiological, psychosocial, and psychophysiological processes. Repeated elicitation of these patterns of entrainment leads to a restructuring at levels below that of conceptual and operational thought. The differentiation and reintegration of these lower structures have consequences that penetrate homeomorphogenetically upward, improving adaptation by integrating conceptual structures. The shaman links experience, feeling, intuition, and reason through myth, symbol, and ritual to achieve this integration of experience. The ritual evokes the experiences, with the symbols providing access to the mythology that provides interpretation for and shapes experience. Myth serves as a bridge between the iconic and the verbal rational levels by including elements of both domains. Reciprocal assimilation then permits the integration of the ego into wider structures of social consciousness, as well as into ritually elevated neurognostic structures (Laughlin et al. 1992). This is based in the integration of the internal cognized environment with the shaman's cosmology and mythology. The visionary level of shamanic experience provides access to some of the fundamental levels of the construction of consciousness, the manipulation of which enables the shaman to transform both individual and social states of consciousness and experiences. Visionary experience and capabilities play an important role in the induction of ASC, in healing, and in producing psychosocial effects, as illustrated in the phenomena of soul flight, vision questing, and the guardian spirit complex.

Shamanic Flight: The Out-of-Body Experience

Several terms—soul flight, soul journey, out-of-body experience, and astral projection—refer to a universal and essential feature of shamanism: the experiences of traveling to and encountering entities in the spiritual or supernatural world. The neurognostic basis of the shamanic soul flight is indicated by the cross-cultural distribution of experiences sharing a common structure: the out-of-body experience (Shields 1978); near-death or clinical death experiences (Moody 1975; Ring 1981, 1986; Sabom 1982; Schoonmaker 1979); and "astral projection" experiences (Green 1968; McIntosh 1980; Irwin 1985; Blackmore 1982). Although there are important distinctions among these experiences and shamanistic visionary experiences found cross-culturally, they share some basic experiential features and structures.

These homologies indicate that the core shamanic experience—soul flight—is an innate psychophysiological structure reflecting neuro-gnostic structures and psychosocial processes.

Shields's (1978) cross-cultural study of belief in the out-of-body experience, the core element of the shamanic soul flight or journey, found it to be reported nearly universally. Contemporary research indicates that phenomena that share many fundamental experiential similarities with shamanistic soul journey occur both spontaneously and deliberately among modern populations (Green 1968; McIntosh 1980; Blackmore 1982). The availability of these experiences is widely attested to in contemporary cultures by individuals who seek out the shamanic path (Harner 1982). These individuals report experiences similar to those of shamans—flying through diverse worlds, interact-ing with spirit beings, and acquiring information about both the ordinary and nonordinary realities. Laughlin, McManus, and d'Aquili (1992) suggested that experience of soul flight is a symbolization of the shaman's transformative experiences and experience of transcen-dence. The ascension metaphorically reflects the movement of the shaman's consciousness upward through the levels of consciousness.

Studies of near-death or clinical death experiences (e.g., Moody 1975; Sabom 1982; Schoonmaker 1979; Ring 1981, 1986; Blackmore 1982) reflect patterns similar to shamanic flight. In the near-death experiences, individuals come close to physical death from accident or trauma or may be clinically dead for some period of time. A set of core experiences emerges in the most complete cases that mirror the shamanic soul journey. The individual experiences some aspect of the self floating out of the body, with a continued awareness of the cir-cumstances surrounding the physical body. This is followed by move-ment away from the body and down a hole or a tunnel into another world, which is characterized by intense light, god, or deceased rela-tives. The individual is told to return to the physical world and may reenter the tunnel and their bodies. The near-death experiences have profound psychological consequences, leading to changes in person-ality, which include increases in religiosity, an enhanced importance of personal relations, increases in self-less behavior, and changes in values and beliefs about the afterlife, personal psychology, and spiri-tuality (Ring 1986).

Laughlin's (1997) biogenetic structuralist assessment of body im-age suggested that use of the body as a symbol system is universal and at the center of all shamanic cultures, constituting a somatocentric cosmology. The body image provides a neurocognitive model that humans use for organizing internal and external experiences. This body image is a construct of the nervous system, incorporating sensory, somatic, and skeletal information, as well as memory. Although the model of the body develops under socio-cultural influences, it begins as a largely hardwired program that constitutes a neurognostic foundation for human experience. These organizational principles are largely genetically determined, providing universal patterns of neural activity, specific behavioral and experiential components, and phenomenal body attributes central to the organism's "conceptual, imaginal, affective, metabolic, and motor operations" (Laughlin 1997, 52). Body image is "composed of symbolic transformations of meaning at various levels of organization, from primitive arousal, vestibular, postural, metabolic interoception, and affect to more advanced conceptual and imaginal functions" (52), particularly the organism's view of itself. These body images combine memory and perception, which can "evoke constitutive cognition, affect, autonomic, somaesthetic, and other models via body image entrainments" (59). Laughlin (1997) reviewed neuropsychological research literature indicating that there is a distinct independent mode for representing image (as opposed to verbal) information, which is predominantly dependent on right-hemisphere processing of nonverbal imagery. There also appears to be a right-hemisphere specialization for the association between faces and emotions and handling abstract meaning associated with imagery. The shamanic practices integrate these imagetic, emotional systems of personal significance.

Although the body as metaphor is central to the major ASC of shamanism, often referred to as an "out-of-body" experience, it is primarily visual. Hunt (1995a) characterized the out-of-body experience as a synesthesia based on visual images of the body and bodily sensations. Hunt reviewed a range of materials that substantiate that "body as container" as a presentational metaphor is at the basis of the cross-cultural similarity of accounts regarding out-of-body experiences and similar phenomena. The experiences of the soul journey (out-of-body experience) involve complex synesthesias based in this capacity for cross-modal translation in the perceptual modalities. Central to Hunt's perspectives is Mead's (1934) work on the capacity of humans to "take the role of the other"—communicative interactions in which one monitors messages from others to construct their model of the social perceptions regarding one's self and personal characteristics. The prototype of soul journey is derived from "taking the role of the other" in using visual imagery to represent one's own body as it would appear from others' perspectives. The taking of the role of the other toward one's self provides a form of self-awareness or consciousness derived from imagining and internalizing the expressions of others toward self. This capacity for self-reference is most obvious in speech and verbal thought. Out-of-body experiences involve manifestations of this self-referential capacity in a visual spatial mode operating independent of the constraints of everyday life and the verbal cognitive mode. This reflexive self-awareness provides the capacity to direct awareness at one's own ongoing subjective experiences. This reflexive self-awareness is changed in contemplative traditions, with ASC used to develop the detached observational attitude necessary to suspend the socially engaged evaluative process underlying reflexive awareness.

Hunt (1995a, 157) analyzed "white light" experiences as cross-modal synesthesias, "a cross-translation and transformation between the modality-specific properties of the tactile-kinesthetic body image and the visual field." Hunt suggested that the vortex tunnel and "hollow body" experiences found in many mystical traditions "can be understood as a complex synesthesia between this 'hollow' tactile structure and the symmetrical funnel or cone of the visual field itself" (158). Their widespread presence in shamanic, mystical, near-death, and other experiences reflects their natural self-referential presentational foundation (253) and structures of abstract intelligence in the imagetic mode. "[W]e have geometries and luminosities as metaphors for an encompassing totality, . . . an extremely pervasive self-referential capacity that synthesizes [the] . . . cross-modal translation capacity basic to all symbolic operations" (255). This presentational mode of symbolic cognition exceeds the verbal-analytic modality because of the more immediate nature of imagery and its emphasis on the wholes instead of the parts. These experiences exceed humans' ordinary verbal conceptual ability and force the self-referential capacity to maximal levels of operation in the imagetic-intuitive mode (paraphrase from Hunt 1995a, 255).

The communality in experiences across diverse cultures suggests that the shaman's soul flight derives from an "archetypal" or neurognostic structure. This experience in which some aspect of the person—soul, spirit, or perceptual capacities—is thought to travel to or to be projected to another place is not an exclusive property of shamanism. Rather, it is a potential available to people who avail themselves of the experiences that evoke these innate structures, as indicated by the near universality of reports of these experiences

(Shields 1978). Although the ASC of mystics, mediums, and other shamanistic practitioners are not typically soul journey or flight, similar experiences may occur in the meditative traditions and can be developed as *siddhis* (Eliade 1969). Because sedentary lifestyles and political integration result in declines in shamanism, these trends must also be seen as central to the decline in the centrality of the soul flight. Participation in the vision quest declined as a function of organizational complexity, through which it tended to become the exclusive domain of the professional shaman (Jorgenson 1980). These changes reflect the intimate interaction between forms of consciousness, spirit concepts, self, and social relations.

The Guardian Spirit Quest

The vision quest, or guardian spirit quest, whether individualistic or as a form of shamanic training, was the most fundamental and widespread religious complex found in Native American cultures (Benedict 1923). It had its parallels in shamanistic practices around the world. Central to the vision quest and the guardian spirit quest were efforts that exemplify the shaman's seeking of an ASC and a relationship with the spiritual world as central to training and development. The vision quest activities were conceptualized as involving the individual development of a special relation with the spirit world based on seeking a personal relation with spirit allies or guardian spirits. The guardian spirit encounter was often seen as central to the development of one's special skills and competencies as an adult. In some cultures, it was central to religious activities for all men, as well as for women in some cases.

A person's training for the vision quest began as young as six or seven years old, when instruction was provided in how to attract guardian spirits and how to behave with respect to them. The process for producing the experiences of contact with the spirit world involved submission to conditions requiring considerable personal endurance, sometimes withstanding extreme pain for extended periods of time. This included the use of purgatives, prolonged fasting, self-imposed isolation, exposure to temperature extremes, exercise to exhaustion, extreme physical punishments like whipping and scourging the body, and other austerities, including extensive self-inflicted wounds in some cases. If these procedures were successful, they produced experiences that were interpreted as a vision or a visitation from the spirit world. The spirit allies encountered in the vision ex-

perience provided powers, strength, fortitude, or good fortune represented in an object that symbolized and served as a source of power.

Swanson's (1963) in-depth analysis of the psychosocial functions
of the guardian spirit quest indicated that they gave many different
kinds of power and advantages—endurance and strength, luck in
hunting, protection in battle, assistance in love, protection or restoration of one's health, and the power to cure others. The guardian
spirit enabled people to do things, providing possibilities that people
could use or reject. Guardian spirits were viewed as distinct from the
person's soul, spirit, and vital force. The guardian spirits did not take
over the person, nor were they viewed as part of the individual's own
personality. Guardian spirits were the spirits of specific plants, animals, or other natural phenomena. The guardian spirits had selected
the individual with whom they were exclusively associated; the relationship was viewed as a gift bestowed on the recipient—it was freely
given, although often with conditions, and it could be withdrawn.

These experiences were part of the process through which a person engaged the transition from childhood into full adulthood.
Swanson suggested that the guardian spirit quest is a search for the
charisma that will enable the person to perform as a competent adult.
The guardian spirit complex meets the individual's need for empowerment and guides the individual in the personal and social choices
from among the options available for adult development and specialization. The guardian spirit quest serves as a means of self-assess-
ment and examination of the commitment to pursue a specific interest in life. This perspective illustrates the role of spirits not as external
supernatural agents, but as aspects of one's self and individual identity.

SHAMANIC SPIRIT RELATIONS AND
SELF-TRANSFORMATION

The shaman's visionary experiences are within an experiential world
or nonordinary reality known as the spiritual. This spiritual world is
a universal aspect of religion that is manifested in the concept of
animism—the postulation of intentional causal abilities to nonphysical entities (animatism) and similar spiritual entities to physical beings. Key to the shaman's capabilities of creating an alternative experiential reality are the psychodramatic aspects of the practices (Siikala
1978), an interaction with the spirit world within which the shaman
manipulates the patient's consciousness, self, and emotions. This spirit

domain is crucial to the shaman's ability to evoke transformations of consciousness inducing experiences, in personal and social worlds.

The conceptual framework provided by spirits involves aspects of the person that are conceptualized in psychology and psychiatry as personality, self, id, ego, complexes, motivation, obsession and other psychodynamic processes, and experiential phenomena not well understood within the frameworks of Western science. Spirit illnesses, possession, and illness due to malevolent action of spirits can be viewed in psychological terms as a negative introject, a negative self-belief that the person has internalized. These unconsciously internalized ideas may have major impacts on individual psychodynamics and physiological processes. Spirits are experientially real and representations of the fundamental cognitive structures constituting knowledge of self, others, and nature. These psychodynamic functions of spirit concepts are illustrated by their role in the guardian spirit complex as representations of idealized self and goals of self-development. Spirit concepts play a fundamental role in representing the social world, the individual's social relations, and conceptions of self.

Social anthropology has viewed the concept of spirits in terms of their symbolic relationships to norms for social behavior and as representations of social forces (Skorupski 1976). Swanson (1960), basing himself in Durkheim's (1915) ideas about the elementary forms of religious life, suggested that spirits and supernatural beings be viewed as personifications of sovereign groups, in essence, the persistent superorganic organizational features of society. Spirits represent social attitudes (e.g., morality), social relations (ancestors, guardians), social experiences (possession, loss), and social purposes (motivations, goals), particularly those of sovereign groups and those that persist across generations.

Spirits and their characteristics and effects provide an externalization of meanings produced by social processes at nonverbal and unconscious levels of the organism. These levels of primary meaning are nonverbal (or presentational) aspects of the community's understanding of the fundamental aspects of the individual and social group. At this level, the difference between self and other, between ego and body, are not dissociated. ASC and the mythic world are mechanisms that enable both the shaman and the patient to engage in this primordial level of experience and communication that affects personal physiology and social relations.

This view of the spirit world as symbolically representing aspects of the social world, individual psychodynamics, and their interrelationships permits an understanding of the psychotherapeutic functions of shamanistic systems. The relations of the spirit world to the self and the ego are symbolic, with both the supernatural domain and the domain of the self entrained with common neural networks via symbolic systems (Laughlin, McManus, and d'Aquili 1992). These symbolic systems simultaneously differentiate and integrate the self and self-organization in adaptation to the cognized social and natural environments. In addition to the ego structures that mediate consciousness, the organism also produces a variety of other neural networks that are outside of the ego's experiences. These structures from earlier development have been automatized, and repressed, or have remained at levels ordinarily not entrained with the conscious ego. These structures represented in the concept of the spirit world can affect the conscious ego and the body while operating through processes outside of the direct grasp of consciousness. The ego tends to deny its relationship to these structures, which predominantly function outside of consciousness as dissociated complexes. The spirit world is a phenomenological symbol system representing these internal complexes and their relationships. Their manipulation permits the shaman to transcend the current levels and structures through presentational symbolic processes to produce experiences that psychologically and emotionally transform the individual. Manipulations of consciousness induced by ritual lead to reduction in egoic repression, with unconscious material emerging, guided by cultural expectations, in combination with integrative processes.

Jung regarded shamanic imagery to be confrontation with complexes, a process of individuation. Complexes represent similar phenomena conceptualized in both psychiatric and spiritualist terms. Complexes are an organized dynamic of perception and behavior that are split off or dissociated from aspects of one's normal personality and social identity, such as manifested in multiple personality disorders. These "splintered off" or dissociated aspects of the personality are mechanisms that allow for the functioning of disowned aspects of one's own capabilities and characteristics or for the projection and manifestation of one's unconscious potentials. Shamanic practices symbolically induce therapeutic transformations by using the spirit world concepts to structure interactions among dissociated complexes of the individual and to integrate them within collective patterns and dynamics. These dramatic social interactions involve psychodramatic transactions (e.g., see Jelik 1982) that restructure psychodynamics, ranging from individual psychobiological homeostasis to psychosocial relations between individuals and their community.

Constructs of the spirit world play many important roles in representing and evoking experiences; in mediating between body, psyche, and society; and in managing intrapsychic and psychosocial dynamics. Siikala (1978) analyzed shamanic ritual as involving a form of role-taking in interaction with the spirit world, producing self-transformation for the patient. The shaman's manipulation of roles includes adopting various personalities of the spirits, as well as providing new roles for the patient to enact. This role enactment in communication with the spirit world reflects and affects the psychodynamics of the patient. The spirits are representations of many aspects of the personal psychodynamics—emotional processes and attachments, social forces, repressed complexes, and other split-off aspects of the patient's own identity and consciousness, including aspects of personal and collective consciousness. In ritual manipulation of the spirit world, the shaman symbolically transforms individual psychophysiological processes, particularly emotions. Shamanistic healing integrates the physical, psychological, emotional, and social, using symbols that crosscut these levels and enabling symbolic process to affect physiological conditions. The shaman's role-taking models a transformation of social roles. Communication with the spirit world involves intrapsychic and psychosocial communication through symbolic processes that alter the relationship between the self and world to achieve a psychological balance, catharsis, and integration. Shamanistic practices manipulate neurognostic structures to evoke processes for achieving a systemic psychophysiological integration of emotions and attachments of self with others.

Ritual Transformation of Social Experience

Shamanistic ritual activities have properties that alter consciousness. Laughlin et al. (1986, 120) suggested that this universal drive to alter consciousness is a manifestation of a "structural drive toward differentiation and reorganization of neural systems mediating consciousness." Shamanistic practices use ritual to shape and to direct experiences that help people enter into other states and modes of consciousness. These practices evoke cognitive and emotional responses that cause physiological changes. Ritual also affects the nervous system by the manipulation of cultural symbols and natural symbols, as well as through direct physiological manipulations (forced immobility, control of food, sleep, attention, etc.). The shaman's ritual alteration of consciousness has numerous functions based in activation of neurological structures and their effects on individual and social consciousness.

The shaman's ritual drama includes dramatization of social roles, enactment and resolution of threats and conflict, and the depiction of processes of social life and the natural environment. One of the most important functions of ritual is expressing social relations and cosmology. Dramatic enactments and the symbolic portrayal of these relations in the context of shamanic rituals serve numerous social purposes. Ritual manipulation of symbols provides a context for conditioning of the orientation response toward cultural symbols of importance and salience. Ritual procedures associate the participant's identity and social self with elements represented in cosmology and society. Van Gennep ([1909] 1960) discussed this in his classic formulation of the ritual passages of separation, transformation, and incorporation. Rituals connect previously developed (socialized) intentionalities with symbols, eliciting conditioned responses that can transform structures of consciousness. Participation in ritual drama evokes and programs experiences, activating developmental sequences for the individual. Ritual has expanded functions in directing attention toward culturally significant events; verification of cosmology and social relations; modeling cognitive development; interpreting transpersonal experience; and symbolic penetration, the symbolic evocation of neurophysiological structures mediating consciousness (Laughlin et al. 1986; cf. chapter 5 this volume).

The relationship of the dramatic social activities of ritual to the neuropsychology of the participants derives from the biocognitive foundations of symbolic activity. An essential function of ritual is to both produce and control human experience. The neurophenomenological perspectives of Laughlin, McManus, and d'Aquili (1992) characterized ritual as a "theater of the mind," procedures in which the experience of the participants is manipulated by cultural and natural symbols. Ritually induced states of consciousness contrast with the normally static and stable social life by providing a period of fluidity for transformation of social status and self-experience through liminal or transitional states. The ritual then resolves status ambiguity by marking the social transition and by producing feelings of unity or community with the social group. The need for ritual mediation of social relations provides shamanism with many roles.

Community Relations, Coordination, and Opioid Bonding

Eliade's (1964) characterization of the shaman emphasized that the ecstatic interaction with the spirit world was on behalf of the *community*. The reasons for the community orientation of shamanic practice are suggested by research that illustrates the effects of social relations on psychophysiology. A central function of shamanistic ritual is the production of integrative social relations through multiple interrelated mechanisms. Intensification of social relations is an inherent aspect of the shamanic activities. Shamanic activities are the most central and most important of public events, and typically they demand the participation of all members of the local community. Shamanistic healing ceremonies function to enhance health and well-being through heightening group identity, strengthening community cohesion and commitment to the ill person, reintegrating them into the social group, and resolving difficulties among members of the community.

In contrast to the individualistic view of sociobiological evolution that has been predominant, Caporael (1996) provided a perspective on the factors involved in social interdependence that contribute to reproduction and survival. These illustrate the fundamental social functions of shamanism. Rather than viewing human sociality as a by-product of individualism, Caporael viewed the evolution of sociability as central to human survival. Without structural features that help create and maintain interdependence, individual reproduction is reduced.

Caporael proposed an expanded evolutionary theory based on hierarchical and multiple levels of nested organization, a theory that makes the interaction between levels, in essence coordination, an essential aspect of the evolutionary forces acting on the human gene pool. "A central requirement is a view of the ecological niche as the reciprocal construction of the organism and environment" (1996, 263). For humans this environment is not merely the physical environment but also the social environment of conspecifics. The evolution of coordination is a central problem addressed through face-to-face social interaction that constituted a "repeated assembly," part of the mind's natural environment. " 'Repeated assemblies' are recurrent entity-environment relations composed of hierarchically organized, heterogeneous components having differing frequencies and scales of replication. . . . Thus, (human) phenotypic nature is repeatedly assembled, generation-to-generation, and interacts with the repeated assembly of different group structures" (64). The human species has had the social group as a principle component of the repeated assemblies that affect human adaptation. Group living was crucial in human evolution, functioning in the interface of the individual with the habitat. "[F]itness should have been correlated with the evolution of perceptual, affective, and cognitive processes that support the development and the maintenance of group membership" (266).

The group as a part of the repeated assembly that relates humans to their environment provides values, the medium through which coordination is achieved. This value orientation shared by members coordinates their responses at an automatic level. Rather than contemplating action, values provide for automatic coordination of behavior. Caporael (1996, 266) pointed out that "mental systems specialized for face-to-face interdependency in evolutionary time must be 'reweavable' for the production of large-scale social coordination." Caporael detailed core configurations of situated face-to-face activity. However, her perspective does not address the potential role of shamanic practices in these core configurations or in the production of social coordination. Ethnographic research indicates that shamanic practices are central to the coordination that occurs within bands and macro-band levels that Caporael specified as part of the core configuration.

Hayden (1987) pointed out that linkages among resource stress, community, and intercommunity alliances enabled shamanistic rituals to contribute to human survival. Shamanistic rituals contributed to intensification and enhancement of interpersonal bonding, within-group cohesion, and interband alliances. The sense of unity and pan-human identity associated with ASC experiences contributed to the development of strong emotional bonds between bands of people who shared shamanistic rituals. Such interband alliances were vital to survival in times of resource scarcity, and the intense emotional bonding during ASC strengthened the commitment to help other individuals and groups in times of need. The bonding was enhanced by specific physiological changes induced by shamanic activities.

The fundamental function of shamanic practices in enhancing social cohesion is mediated by psychosociophysiological mechanisms. In addition to the general ASC mechanisms' production of positive social affect and bonding, there is the release of endogenous opiates produced by a variety of shamanistic procedures (Winkelman 1986b,

1992). There are a variety of shamanic activities that have been shown to elicit endogenous opioid mechanisms (see chapter 3 this volume): prolonged rhythmic exercise, high-intensity exhaustive exercise, anaerobic exercise, nighttime activities, the stressful procedures used to induce ASC, and the elicitation of hope and positive expectations. There is also opioid release by cultural symbols that have been cross-conditioned with physiological, emotional, and cognitive responses and that can consequently elicit the endocrine and immunological systems (Frecska and Kulcsar 1989). The central role of community relations in shamanistic healing reflects their role in evocation of endogenous opioid mechanisms and consequently psychoneuroimmunological responses and synchronization of individuals within a group.

Frecska and Kulcsar reviewed research that illustrated that brain opioid systems provide neurochemical mediation of social bonding. They pointed out that the endogenous opioid system and social symbols become cross-conditioned in early development. This is based on the co-incidence of opioid release in contact with mother, which is provided by breast-feeding. This association of the basic social attachment symbol/figure (mother) and the experiences of well-being enhanced by opioid substances creates a cross-conditioning of social symbols and physiological responses. This provides a basis for the reciprocal and coactivation of the opioid system and subsequent social attachments. Endogenous opioids facilitate social attachment and bonding through opioid action on psychological processes, promoting regression and enhancing bonding through reducing ego boundaries. This involves "neurobiologically mediated, complex forms of attachment . . . which result in deep psychobiological synchrony between adults" (Frecksa and Kulcsar 1989, 71). Frecksa and Kulcsar suggested that these socially and ritually manipulated opioid mechanisms constitute a means of coordinating core biological functions. They pointed out that the cortical areas (orbital frontal cortex, the temporal lobe, and the amygdala) that are involved in affiliative interactions, social bonds, multimodal sensory information processing, selective attention, and top-down physiological regulation are also the areas with the highest density of opioid receptors.

Shamanistic healing rituals enhance social attachments through symbolically elicited physiological responses. The psychosocial manipulations of these personal and social relations in small close-knit societies induce a synchrony among individuals at psychobiological levels, enhancing group commitment and bonding among members. Opioids also have a wide range of therapeutic effects, being central to the functioning of the immune system and playing important roles in recognition of novelty, environmental adaptation and habituation, and memory (see chapter 3 this volume). A significant feature of the social impacts of opioid-mediated social relations is enhanced attachment to others and the consequent internalization of those others as significant relations for modeling self.

Caporael pointed out that the definition of *self* is in relationship to shared group membership, which is constructed in a nested hierarchical organization that plays a fundamental role in in-group/out-group relations. The membership in different groups creates different social identities and potentially creates both conflicts and synergisms.

> The topography or 'evolutionary landscape' for the evolution of human relations and practice is simultaneously social-organizational and cognitive. Dynamic psychological shifts in level of identity (which can result from various conditions including group size, shared fate or outcomes, and salient group boundaries . . .) are hypothesized to maintain core configurations. . . . Personal identity, the locus of conscious awareness of goals, plans, and beliefs, is the product of multiple interacting and dynamic selves." (Caporael 1996, 268)

This creates a person characterized by multiple selves. Caporael, however, did not explicate the mechanisms by which these multiple personal identities and multiple group identities are mediated and integrated. Clearly, the practices of shamanism, which require the participation of all band members and which provide the context for the expression of multiple identities, were the preeminent social activities that provided the basis for this personal integration.

SHAMANISM AND PSYCHOCOGNITIVE INTEGRATION

A natural result of the evolution of the human brain is the fragmentation of consciousness (Laughlin, McManus, and d'Aquili 1992), reflecting both the increasing modularity of consciousness and the diversification of self into more statuses. Shamanic traditions institutionalized procedures to overcome this fragmentation of consciousness by synchronizing this divergent human cognition through traditions using ASC to induce integrative brain processes. The shaman's use of external symbols and the relationships of the symbols to cultural psychodynamics engage transformative process through entraining neurocognitive structures, provoking a restructuring of the self at levels below conceptual and operational thought. Laughlin et al. (1992) suggested that shamanic healing practices involve two basic principles: (1) a holistic imperative, a drive toward more integrated levels of consciousness; and (2) shamanic projection, a positive projection of a more advanced state of development into another person, based on the unconscious transference of control of the individual's intentional processes to a powerful individual or "master." This shamanic projection underlies the patient's transference during therapeutic processes. The neurophenomenological perspective of Laughlin et al. (1992) showed that the shaman's practices represent an evolution through the "holistic imperative," a drive toward wholeness, or a more integrated levels of consciousness.

The need for shamanic activities in the form of psycho-social integration in early human communities is illustrated in Mithen's (1996) considerations of human cognitive evolution through specific neurognostic features, or specialized processing modules, of the brain. How integration of distinct modules occurred to produce cognitive fluidity remains an unresolved problem. I propose that shamanism contributed to this integrative cognition through the systemic neurophysiological, psychophysiological, psychosocial, and symbolic effects of ASC, which produce integrative brain states. The cognitive aspects of shamanic practices reflect the metaphoric integration of specialized brain modules through psychobiological processes. The integrative potentials of shamanism help explain the rapid rise of culture in modern Homo sapiens sapiens and the origin of shamanistic and religious features—animism, animatism, and totemism—from the cross-modal analogic and psychophysiological integration of processes from different innate modules.

Cross-Modular Integration in Early Human Cognition

Mithen (1996) pointed out that in the period from 60,000 to 100,000 years ago, Homo sapiens sapiens initially showed few departures from the early toolmaking traditions of ancient Homo sapiens and Neanderthals. But significant departures from these earlier traditions are found in practices such as burying the dead; making grave offerings, which included animal parts; and utilizing tools made from materials besides wood and stone, which began around 100,000 years before present (YBP) with modern Homo sapiens sapiens. Between 30,000 and 60,000 YBP, this new mentality is manifested in the carving of many kinds of figures, the use of jewelry, and the dramatic evolution of art and culture. This involved a cognitive fluidity in which knowledge produced by the different modules could be integrated through forms of metarepresentation—the ability to combine thought and knowledge produced by these specialized modules. This integration provided the basis for new ways of thinking and behaving based on metaphor, providing for an enormously expanded capacity for imagination and analogical reasoning.

How the different specialized modules were integrated to produce complex behaviors is problematic because this cross-modular integration is relatively recent (40,000 to 50,000 YBP), long after the emergence of anatomically modern humans. The major transition in human evolution around 40,000 YBP has no associated changes in brain size. Neanderthals were quite similar to *early* modern humans in terms of technical skills but did not show comparable levels of cultural achievement. Mithen (1996) suggested that this provides a fundamental clue to understanding the nature of the modern mind. Archaic Homo sapiens sapiens and Neanderthals had specialized skills for tool use, animal exploitation, and social behavior, but these modules were not capable of integrated functioning to produce more complex behaviors such as art.[2] The early artifacts often referred to as art were also tools,[3] providing storage of important information, particularly that relevant to long-term and seasonal variations in animal behavior and hunting plans. The modern human's cognitive fluidity also provided the basis for integrating technical intelligence and social intelligence in the production of artifacts that were designed to send social messages regarding status, group affiliation, and relationships through the use of personal decoration and adornment.

A key feature of the modern mind was the capability for production of art based on a visual representation, a symbolic code. These early representations of animals illustrated the ability to integrate a high degree of technical expertise with a highly developed and intricate knowledge of the natural world, specifically animal anatomies. Visual symbols reflect an evolution of thought. Mithen (1996) pointed out that visual symbols have specific properties (e.g., execution of preconceived mental template, intentional communication, and meaning attribution) that were present in early humans; however, the early humans did not produce art with these capabilities because these distinctive cognitive domains were not integrated. Early humans manifested cognitive abilities to create preconceived mental images in their working of stone artifacts; they had a social intelligence that depended on use and interpretation of intentional communication; and they had a capacity for attributing meaning to "inanimate objects or marks displaced from their reference" (Mithen 1996, 161), as manifested in their use of natural history intelligence to find animals. The interpretation of animal marks as a basis for inference about behavior indicated the presence of cognitive processes similar to those by which modern humans interpret meaning from other humans' signals or marks. However, early humans did not use this capability for the same kinds of symbolic processes involved in the art of modern humans. The cultural explosion circa 40,000 YBP involved integrated functioning of different mental modules and provided the basis for producing and interpreting visual symbols.

This crossing of information between cognitive domains is not what evolutionary psychology predicts. Cosmides and Tooby (1992) have argued that this kind of process should not have occurred because it would lead to behavioral mistakes. Mithen (1996) pointed out that the capacity to cross domains, to develop concepts about concepts, is the normal condition of human thought. Normal human thought involves various forms of synthesis, in which natural and social domains, the physical environment and social acts, and virtually every aspect of behavior involve the use of modules that link together diverse domains of reasoning. Hunter-gatherers think of the world in a highly integrated fashion, with an interpenetration of natural world modules and social world modules manifested in an ideology and metaphysics that there is a single environment that encompasses humans, animals, and plants in a living nature. Typical of hunter-gatherers is the application of modules across domains, exemplified in the interactions of mental and social modules with those for animal behavior. This produces (1) anthropomorphic thinking, attributing human mental and social characteristics to animals, including animism, and applying mental models of intentional agents to the unknown; (2) totemism, applying natural history models to the social domain; and (3) the guardian spirits, applying animal and natural history models to differentiation and interpretation of self and others.

Mithen (1996) suggested that the explanation of the Middle/Upper Paleolithic transition and the capabilities for combining these specialized intelligences is in the ability of the modern mind to integrate the modules of the different forms of intelligence. This integration involves analogical thinking and metarepresentational thinking, processes for representing knowledge between and across different domains. The ability to map across domains is a fundamental feature of human symbolic capacities (see Hunt 1995a). This analogical predication provides the basis for creative thought. It does so either by introducing new knowledge into domains or by providing new ways of processing existing knowledge of a specific domain, integrating it in different cognitive domains. This process of the modules working together, a "representational redescription," provides multiple representations of knowledge, making it applicable beyond the special module-specific goals for which it is normally used (Mithen 1996, 58). This metarepresentation capability to represent knowledge across domains can be used to form representations of concepts and beliefs across conceptual domains that the modules cannot form on their own (188).

Mithen (1996) suggested that these changes leading to the modern human mind derived from the impacts of language on consciousness. This involved a transformation of the *social* language of early humans as language use about the nonsocial world began to infiltrate social discourse. This transference of the original function of language for social relations to other domains reflects processes of metaphorical extension of the social world to discourse about physical objects. This introduction of nonsocial information into social intelligence provided selective advantages for those who could make use of this information (e.g., in enhanced toolmaking, hunting, mate competition, and care of offspring). The adaptive advantages of utilizing this information led to a rapid evolution from a specialized social language to a general-purpose language. This expansion of language provided a system for integrating these different modules within the mind.

Mithen (1996) proposed that these language-based multiple representations of knowledge from distinct areas of the brain provided the basis for cognitive fluidity and representations of art that could not be produced by any single intelligence. But artistic depiction is not dependent on language or on ideas requiring expression based in spoken language (see Humphrey 1998). Rather, art involves an imagetic, presentational, analogical modality that necessarily predated spoken language. Thus, language, spoken or otherwise, cannot explain the evolution of artistic representations based in this modality. Extension of the social language module to other domains of intelligence played a role in the cross-modular integration, but it is inadequate to explain the emergence of art and religious behavior tens of thousands of years prior to the hypothesized language induced cultural explosion around 40,000 YBP. Language integration across modules cannot have produced religious behavior and art, which depend on imagetic and mimetic modes that persisted as predominant forms of self-presentation of information even following the emergence of language as a general communication tool (Donald 1991). Shore (1996, 320) suggested a direct relationship between "meaning construction" and mimetic representation, with both being based in analogical processing; this capacity is a central aspect of hominid cognition. The integration and expression of imagetic information in art and religion, in particular in shamanism, preceded the integration by linguistic representations.

The production of early art images combining animal and human references depended on the capability to integrate the processes of the social intelligence and the natural history intelligence. The integration of these modules produced anthropomorphic and animistic thinking. The metaphoric relationship between the social and the history domains is also found in totemism, in which human members and groups are attributed characteristics derived from the natural world. The processes of totemic thinking involve human thought about its place in nature and a means of conceptualizing human intergroup relations in terms of the models provided by the natural world (Levi-Strauss 1962, 1967). Related to these universal human tendencies of anthropomorphism and totemism are those of animism—applying human mental and social characteristics to the natural world. Animism is pervasive in hunter-gatherer thought, the natural world and the social world of persons constituting a single integrated environment in which spirits imbue not only the human world and actors, but also the animal and plant actors of the natural world. The reversal of this attribution is found in the guardian spirit complex, in which the natural history domain is applied to the interpretation of self and the mental domains. These concepts—animism, anthropomorphism, and totemism—are central features of shamanic thought. The early presence of these concepts as evidence of cross-modular integration and religious practices prior to the Middle/Upper Paleolithic transition indicates the presence of the foundations of shamanism. Shamanism enhanced these integrative thought processes through practices involving mimesis, which provided the basis for analogical thought through metaphoric predication.

Shamanism is universal in hunter-gatherer societies because it reflects an ecological adaptation to psychobiological potentials. The biological basis made shamanism a fundamental institution of early modern human societies. Integrative brain conditions produced by the hominid "mimetic controller" (Donald 1991) and shamanic ritual alterations of consciousness produced universals of shamanic thought and practice and mechanisms for cognitive and social integration. The cross-modal integration of innate modules for knowledge about mind, social relations, and the animal world constituted a basis for metaphoric predications about the nature of self and others, manifested in animism, animal spirits, totemism, the guardian spirit complex, and soul journey. These metaphoric cross-modal integrations of representations from the innate modules of the brain produced fundamental forms of trope (metaphor) underlying analogical representation and a major cultural and cognitive evolution.

Shamanic practices enhanced integration of the different cognitive modules because shamanism accessed a biologically based mode of consciousness, producing a variety of integrative brain conditions. These are discussed in chapter 3 as involving interhemispheric integration; frontal-limbic integration; brain stem-limbic-frontal integration; and integration across the neuraxis. These brain wave patterns are found in a wide variety of ASC induction conditions, in temporal lobe syndromes, and in hypnosis (see chapter 3 this volume). Shamanism emerged because of numerous adaptive consequences of its practices, including enhancement of representation, healing, stress reduction, and information integration. The shaman's reliance on visionary experience as a foundation for training and practice attests to the role of shamanism in the primordial development of imagery manipulation. The shaman also had excellent skills in three other innate module domains: in language, being the holder of the first or ancient sacred languages; in natural history, being the master of the animals and often guiding hunting; and in social intelligence, being the leader of the group.

Linguistic Roots and Survivals of Shamanism

Shamanic practices were so fundamental to diverse aspects of hunting-gathering societies that multiple referents to the shaman remained embedded in language after shamanism disappeared. Etymological inquiry into the Indo-European (I-E) term for "shaman" has been inconclusive,[4] but a range of mythological sources attest to the presence of ancient shamanic activities (Eliade 1964). Cognates with the term "shaman" are found in many I-E languages, exemplified in the ancient Sanskrit (Pali) word for a religious specialist—*samana* (Wayman 1969–71).

The lack of more substantial linguistic evidence of shamanism in I-E is a consequence of the ancient repression of shamanic practices by more complex religions, as indicated by the sociocultural evolutionary model of magico-religious summarized in the section "The Evolution of the Shaman" earlier in this chapter. Ancient (and historical) I-E repressions of shamanic practices and the subsequent evolution of new religious forms are reflected in the lack of a common root for the sacred in I-E languages. "[D]esignation of the 'sacred' confronts us with a strange linguistic situation: the absence of any specific term in common Indo-European. . . . [There is] no common term to designate religion itself, or cult, or the priest, not even one of the personal gods" (Benveniste 1973, 445–46). Morris (1981) pointed out that *sak-*, with meanings of "sanctify" and "sacred," is a widespread and ancient I-E root pertaining solely to religion. Reference to shamanic practices are found in meanings of the I-E roots with the prefix *sa-*, virtually all of which have magico-religious implications,[5] suggesting it reflects a preproto I-E root for *shaman*.

Benveniste (1973, 448) offered a reconstruction of the I-E prototype of sacred in the root *$*k^1wen$ (*$*k^1eu-$), which is expressed in the adjectival form as *kailos* in the Slavic, Germanic, and Celtic. The concept of "holy" expressed in the I-E root *kailo-* means "whole, uninjured, or good omen" (Morris 1981, 1,520). The I-E root of *kailo-* is *ka-*, meaning "to like, desire." It is attested to in Old English derivative forms including *holy* and *hallowed*. Its suffixed forms (e.g., *kan*) have shamanic and magico-religious meanings including to sing, to cast a spell, to enchant, to charm, incantation (Shipley 1984).

Weik- is an I-E root with widespread use as a referent to magico-religious practice, but it is not generally considered in the context of the sacred and religious. This reflects its representation of the negative and devalued aspects of the supernatural. The I-E root *weik-* is the source of witchcraft, wizard, (sacrificial) victim, and other magico-religious terms. The etymology and use of the term "witch" in I-E cultures illustrate the direct relations of witch to the earlier traditions of shamanism. The I-E root *weik-* has five general meanings (Morris 1981, 1,548):

1. clan (social unit above the household). The zero-grade form *wik-* in Sanskrit *vis*, dwelling, house, with derivative *vaisya*, settler;
2. words connected with magic and religious notions [such as divination, wizard, bewitch, and the Latin *victima*, and animals used as sacrificial victims];
3. to be like . . . likeness, image, icon;
4. to bend, wind . . . turn;
5. to conquer.

These roots of *witch* have little association with the contemporary or historical meanings of the word. They do, however, have substantial relations to shamanistic activities and to related magico-religious practices. The shaman is the group (clan) leader, reflecting the social foundations of shamanism and the shaman's preeminent role in the collective functions of hunting-gathering societies. Concepts of magic, religion, divination, and images are more directly related to shamanistic activities than those typically attributed to witchcraft. Meanings "likeness" and "image" reflect the magical use of enactment and imitation (e.g., Frazer's [1890] Law of Similarity or Imitation) and reflect the shaman's use of visionary experience as the basis of shamanic practice. The meanings "bend" and "wind" have direct connections with the roots of I-E shamanism, as identified by Eliade [1964] in Varuna, the master of magic, who was known as the "Great Binder." The meaning "conquer" is related to the shaman's battle with spirits and the hunter/warrior role of the shaman, reflecting a meaning also found in the root *ka*.

Ancient I-E terms used to refer to shamanistic activities coalesce around three primary sets of consonants and their alternate forms: *w (v)*, *k (c)*, and *s (sh)*. These similarities suggest that the radical root referring to the shaman provided a basis for diverse developments as societies evolved from hunting and gathering to more complex subsistence and social patterns. Parallels to the shamanic referents in the *w, k,* and *s* sounds are also found in the basic tripartite division of Proto-Indo-European society (e.g., India) into the warrior (*ksatriyas*), farmer or clansman (*vaisya*), and priest/hermit (*bhraman/samana*). The linkages to shamanic bases are directly manifested in the relationships of the primary meanings of roots of *weik* to the tripartite structure of I-E society:

Social Institution	Meaning of *weik-*
Vaisya (settler, farmer)	clan
Ksatriya (warriors)	conquer
Bhraman/samana	religion and magic

The shamanic terms associated with the sounds of *w* (or *v*) are found in examples such as witch, wizard, wisdom, wise, vision, aware, awake, will, and the Teutonic god woden (odin). The shamanic survivals associated with the *ka* sound may be found in cant, cantor, chant, knowledge, consciousness, gnosis, kannabis, and others. Combinations of the *s* and *k* sounds may also reflect shamanic connections (e.g., scalpumancy, skeleton). The shamanic roots associated with the *s* sound are manifested in other contemporary English terms such as sage, saint, satan, sacred, sacerdotal, sacrifice, savant, and sapient. Other possible shaman related *sh* words include: sham and shame; shade (as in ghost, spirit); shammatize (excommunication, to destroy and curse); and shamade (drum beat for a parley). *Shamble* has old meanings of "a table or counter for sale of goods or meat," "a place where animals are killed," and "to cut up or slaughter and dispose of a corpse." Most of these meanings have to do with animals, a core concern of the shaman who is a hunter par excellence. The implications of dismemberment also have direct relationship to the shamanic archetypal processes of death and rebirth. *Shamble* also means "an ungainly awkward or unsteady walk, an irregular gait or motion," an analogy to the shaman's dance.

The wide range of shamanic associations with the roots for sacred (*sak*), holy (*kwen-*) and witchcraft (*weik-*) suggests that the original root for *shaman* in pre-Proto-Indo-European provided the basis for a wide range of derivative meanings and activities. Cognates of *shaman* survived into modern English in terms that reflect both original meanings and the changes in meaning that occurred as a consequence of the transformation of shamanism under socioeconomic evolution.

SUMMARY

Shamanism constitutes a primordial cultural evolution based on the utilization of diverse physical and metaphoric processes for psychophysiological and cognitive integration. Shamanism developed in hunter-gatherer societies worldwide because it was based on neurognostic potentials. These potentials were utilized to extend understanding through metaphoric predication and cross-modular integration of cognitive modules. The spirit world of shamanism provided models for conceptualizing self and other and their interrelationships, playing a fundamental role in self development and transformation. Shamanic healing used these self/other models in the therapeutic processes and in social integration.

NOTES

1. "There is an important spiritual aspect of BPM1, often associated with a profound feeling of cosmic unity and ecstasy, closely associated with experiences we might have in a good womb—peace, tranquility, serenity, joy, and bliss. Our everyday perceptions of space and time seem to fade away and we become 'pure being.' Language fails to convey the essence of this state, prompting most to remark only that it is 'indescribable' or 'ineffable" (Grof 1992, 39).

2. One characteristic of early humans was their failure to produce in a medium other than stone (e.g., bone, antler, or ivory) the same type of highly technical artifacts found in stone tools. Mithen (1996) suggested that early moderns were not capable of thinking of animal materials as suitable for tools because they thought of them as animals—part of the domain of natural history intelligence. They were not capable of thinking about animal parts as objects for manipulation with the skills of technical intelligence. Moreover, the stone artifacts produced by early humans were general-purpose tools rather than specialized tools for specific types of tasks. Social strategies did not integrate tool use, nor was social information integrated into toolmaking.

3. "Many of the art objects can indeed be thought of as a brand new type of tool: a tool for storing information and for helping to retrieve information stored in the mind" (Mithen 1996, 170). Art artifacts, therefore, served as a form of recording environmental events, particularly serving as mnemonics. Mithen suggests that these art forms may have served as a form of "tribal encyclopedia," with the representation serving as a way of storing information about animal behavior. "But they are carefully arranged to act as a mental map for the surrounding environment to facilitate the recall of information about that environment and animal behavior. They thus play an important role in decision-making about use of resources and improving the predictions about animal location and behavior" (173).

4. The term *shaman* was not part of historical English but was borrowed from the Tungus of Siberia. Such derivation suggests that there could be no cognates of the shaman in contemporary English and other I-E languages. But evidence of such cognates exists in many I-E languages. A

pre-Proto-Indo-European root for *shaman* is suggested by the ancient Sanskrit (Pali) words for a religious specialist, *samana*; and for a hermit and divine being with supernatural power, referred to as *yaksha* (Fischer-Schreiber, Ehrhard, and Diener 1991). The religion of ancient India was generally subsumed by the frequently compounded words *samana-brāhmana* (Pali) or *śramana-brāhmana* (Sanskrit) (Wayman, 1969–71). The *brāhmana* represented the institutionalized form present in the bureaucratic and political aspects of the religious practice, and the *śramana* reflected the shamanic basis.

5. All twelve of the Indo-European roots beginning with *sa-* and listed by Morris (1981) and their associated meanings are provided below, along with parenthetical reference to their shamanic implications where they are not apparent.

   sā-   to satisfy; sad, sufficient (wholeness, completeness).

   sab-   juice, fluid; a beer (ASC).

   sag-   to seek out; to seek, to know; keen perception; a seeking; taking possession of; laying claim; seek, quarrel (divination, spirit relations, knowledge).

   sai-   suffering; sore, suffering mentally (needing healing).

   sak-   to sanctify; holy, sacred; performer of sacred rites; sacerdotal, saint.

   sal-   salt, dirty gray (relation to shamanism unknown).

   salam (slm)-   to be whole; safe, peace, completeness (healing).

   salik-   willow, salicin (tree as axis mundi, salicin as medicine).

   sānos-   healthy; sane.

   sap-   to taste, perceive; to be wise, sage, savant.

   saus-   dry; withered, harsh, austere (cf. Sanskrit *sram*, to practice austerities, the root of *samana*).

   sā wel-   the sun (symbol of ascent, magical flight, enlightenment).

3

~

Physiological and Phenomenological Bases of Altered States of Consciousness

CHAPTER OVERVIEW

Institutionalized procedures for inducing altered states of consciousness (ASCs) have been documented in virtually all societies of the world, reflecting a universal of culture and religious behavior. This usage of ASCs reflects a psychophysiological basis derived from activities and functions of basic brain structures and their homeostatic balance and integration. ASCs reflect the operation of a *mode* of consciousness, a fundamental aspect of human nature. The nature of this mode of consciousness is illustrated by its relationships to brain structures and functions. A neurophenomenological approach identifies the four major modes of consciousness—deep sleep, dreaming, waking, and integrative (or "transpersonal"). These different modes of consciousness reflect cyclic systemic operations of brain structures, in adaptation to external and internal environments.

Societies have a number of adaptations to the integrative mode of consciousness, which is manifested in conditions labeled soul flight, possession, obsession, vision quests, enlightenment, samadhi, and others. Cultures relate to ASCs in different ways, some deliberately either enhancing or blocking access and either extolling or vilifying these experiences. Cross-cultural research illustrates patterning in the characteristics and the interpretations of ASCs (Winkelman 1986b, 1992), manifested in three major types of ASC-induction-procedure profiles and phenomenological manifestations: (1) shamanic soul flight, (2) mediumistic/possession, and (3) mystical/meditative ASCs. The differences among these ASC traditions include cultural beliefs regarding them; phenomenologically different experiences (e.g., flight, external domination, void, etc.); physiological and behavioral conditions (e.g., amnesia, convulsions, unconsciousness, contentless experience, dissociation, etc.); and the types of societies in which they typically occur. Sociocultural evolution, specifically political integration, has led to transformations in the culturally specific forms of ASCs (Winkelman 1990b) as exemplified in the distinction between soul flight and possession ASC.

The different ASCs found cross-culturally involve similar integrative brain wave patterns across the neuraxis. A wide variety of techniques produce a parasympathetic dominant state characterized by entrainment of the frontal cortex by highly coherent and synchronized slow-wave discharges emanating from the limbic system and related lower-brain structures. These procedures and conditions produce an integration of information processing between the R-complex and the limbic system, between the limbic system and the frontal cortex, and between the hemispheres of the cortex. Evidence for the biological basis of this mode of consciousness is found in cross-cultural studies, in the psychobiological effects of various ASC agents and procedures, and in several common phenomena that manifest this general pattern of interrelationships among brain systems. The physiological basis for the effects of hypnosis involves similar brain mechanisms—an enhanced transfer of internally derived information between the limbic system and frontal cortex. This is also exemplified in the dream processes, particularly those dreams characterized by cross-modal transfer between dream and waking consciousness. Conditions producing temporal lobe discharges also predispose individuals to enter ASCs, functioning as tuning procedures acting on the autonomic nervous system to facilitate ASC induction. Examination of brain patterns of ASCs from the perspectives of MacLean's (1990) model of the triune brain illustrates the elicitation of the paleomentation and the emotiomentation processes of lower brain structures (R-complex and limbic brain) and their management of emotions, attachment, social relations and bonding, sense of self, and convictions about beliefs.

Three different principal forms of ASCs—shamanic soul flight, mediumistic possession, and meditative—are examined in terms of physiological, emotional, self, and social parameters. The experiential, physiological, and social concomitants of these different experiences suggest that although they involve important commonalities in inducing integrative brain-mind conditions, they also involve differences between them that may warrant characterizing them as different modes of consciousness. Different forms of integrative consciousness are examined from an epistemological perspective that links their characteristics to functions of brain subsystems.

CULTURAL AND ALTERED STATES OF CONSCIOUSNESS

A (near) universal of human culture is the existence of institutionalized procedures for altering consciousness. This chapter identifies both the common biological bases underlying ASCs and a possible basis for distinguishing among a range of ASCs. Not all ASCs involve integrative or transcendent forms of consciousness, but they generally reflect the consequences of destabilization of the waking mode of consciousness in ways that permit the manifestation of integrative potentials and experiences. This occurs because an attenuation of the waking mode of consciousness and its primary faculties and functions permits the emergence of integrative symbolic and cognitive processes normally repressed by waking consciousness. Most activities that destabilize the baseline state (Tart 1977) or waking mode of consciousness produce manifestations that reflect this integrative mode of consciousness and its principles and structures. The disruption of waking consciousness may be achieved in numerous ways, including pushing psychological functions beyond their limits, disrupting subsystems by sensory overload or deprivation, manipulating the autonomic nervous system balance, or focusing or withdrawing attention. Repeated destructuralization, combined with patterning forces that redirect psychological functioning toward culturally desired patterns of experience, leads to a new, stable, discrete ASC.

Cultures differ in how they relate institutionally and personally to the experiences and potentials of ASCs. Most cultures have traditions designed to enhance the availability of ASCs. In contrast to cultures characterized by an ethos based on the shamanic or meditative technologies, the dominant cultural ethos of Indo-European societies generally ignores these forms of consciousness or subjects those who seek them to pathologization, social marginalization, or persecution. There are widespread biases against ASCs and cultural resistance to ASC experiences in Western society and cultures (Grinspoon and Bakalar 1979). Historically, manifestations of ASCs were persecuted by the dominant political structures through witchcraft accusations (Harner 1973b). Western psychology has tended to consider shamanic type experiences to be pathological (Noll 1983) or "primitive," manifested in the perspectives that meditative states are regressions to infantile levels (see Wilber [1980] for discussion and critique). Hostile attitudes toward most drug-induced ASCs are reflected in severe restrictions (medical prescription) or legal prohibition of the use of major psychoactive substances.

A contrastive perspective on ASCs is found in the view that many cultures have of hallucinogens as sacred plants (e.g., see Schultes and Hofmann 1979; Winkelman and Andritzky 1996). Contemplative traditions indicate that altering consciousness provides a variety of adaptive advantages through development of a more objective perception of the external world. Rather than being bound up in a habitualized subjectivity, altering consciousness is viewed as a means of recognizing the illusory and constructed nature of ordinary perception. This provides the basis for greater awareness.

Even when there is cultural repression of ASCs, they continue to be manifested because they reflect a biological basis and its inevitable expression in human experience. The classic mediator of these ASCs was the shaman; whereas today it is the mediums, meditators, and others. Although contemporary Indo-European societies lack legitimate institutionalized procedures for accessing ASCs, nonetheless, many forms of ASC are sought and utilized—alcohol, tobacco, marijuana, opiates, sedatives, caffeine and other stimulants, mood enhancers, and so forth. Even though many of these are viewed as counter-cultural, deviant, pathological, or even criminal, the positive use of ASCs has been explored by some segments of modern Indo-European societies in hypnosis and spiritualism; has been institutionalized in psychotherapy by Freud; has been linked to means of transcendence and universal archetypal structures by Jung; and has been taken as foundational by transpersonal psychologists.

Cultures differ considerably in the attention that they give to ASCs, but all cultures have practices that support the ability to consciously function in this mode (Winkelman 1986a; Laughlin, McManus, and d'Aquili 1992). This is because these structures of consciousness are a part of human biological potentials, a manifestation of "fixed structures" of consciousness that reflect latent human potentials. This pan-human psychobiological foundation provides the basis for the claims of universal religious truths and the perennial philosophy and psychology. But there are cultural differences in relating to ASCs, which are represented in Laughlin et al.'s (1992) model as degrees of knowledge of "dream culture" or ASCs and normative encouragement to explore these aspects of consciousness. These degrees of knowledge range from "monophasic" cultures, which institutionally value only waking consciousness, through "polyphasic void" cultures, which encourage exploration of phases of consciousness beyond phenomenal reality. The societies that do emphasize a polyphasic approach to consciousness have a number of interpretations. Different approaches reflect the effects of cultural traditions and social conditions on psychophysiological processes, but the underlying biological bases for ASCs are attested to in their universal manifestations.

The universality of ASCs is strongly supported by cross-cultural research. Bourguignon (1968) found that approximately 90 percent of the societies in a worldwide sample had institutionalized ASCs. ASC induction procedures were found in all forty-seven societies of another cross-cultural study (Winkelman 1986a, 1992); even societies lacking institutionalized shamanistic healers have ASCs involved in nonprofessional community healing practices. This universal distribution of ASCs supports the hypothesis of a biologically based mode of consciousness, which provided the basis for universal manifestations. Analysis of cross-cultural data on the ASC induction procedures and characteristics associated with training for shamanistic healers (Winkelman 1984, 1986b) also found evidence for this biological basis in the continuity[1] among different ASC induction procedures, such evidence supporting the hypothesis of a common, underlying, biologically based mode of consciousness.

MODES, STATES, PHASES, AND WARPS
OF CONSCIOUSNESS

The universality of shamanistic practices reflects underlying biological structures. This biological basis is illustrated by a neurophenomenological approach that reveals the congruencies of the biological functions of the brain with phenomenal experience. There is a wide range of formulations of the different types of consciousness. The focus of this section is on the patterned variability in manifestations of consciousness that are biologically structured. Without denying the legitimacy of more extensive differentiations, the purpose here is to identify a basis in the systemic organization of the brain that can provide a structure for explaining the similarities underlying the diversity of forms of consciousness. These biologically structured foundations are discussed as *modes* of consciousness.

The different biologically based modes of consciousness are revealed in the homologies of the recurrent patterns of systemic neurophysiological functioning with the major differences in experience. The mediating physiological systems and the associated functions and processes provide the structure for the nature of and differences among modes of consciousness. The transcendent nature of these modes is indicated by the congruence of the biophysiological and mystical approaches, which concur in a recognition of four fundamental conditions or modes of consciousness: (1) waking consciousness, (2) deep sleep, (3) REM (rapid eye movement) sleep (dreaming), and (4) transpersonal, mystical, or transcendental consciousness (which I will refer to as "integrative consciousness"). These four modes of human consciousness reflect fundamental aspects of systemic organismic function and balance. The next sections integrate this perspective of biologically based modes of consciousness with previous frameworks for description of consciousness provided by Tart's (1975, 1977) models of states of consciousness and by Laughlin et al.'s (1992) neurophenomenological perspectives on the phases and warps of consciousness.

Modes of Consciousness

A *mode of consciousness* is a biologically based functional system of organismic operation that reflects conditions of homeostatic balance among brain subsystems to meet global organismic needs. The different modes of consciousness are based on the differential activation and integration of different functional systems and information-processing capabilities of the organism. Different modes of consciousness differentially entrain biological, personal, social, and cultural information-processing functions. Different modes of consciousness are revealed in the congruencies and the interrelationships of (1) the biophysiological structures and functions of the brain with (2) the primary daily patterns of variation in behavior and experiences of humans and other animals. The relationship of the recurrent patterns of systemic neurophysiological functioning to recurrent structural variations in behavior and experience indicates the biological and the functional bases. The mediating physiological systems, their patterns of homeostatic balance, and the associated functions provide the structure and the nature of the different modes of consciousness. Although modes manifest some variance in their patterns as a consequence of learning and cultural factors, they reflect underlying biological commonalities and specificity of function in terms of organismic needs. Individuals are bound to certain cycles of biologically based alteration in consciousness, but cultures produce variability in terms of the specific states and contents of consciousness within modes.

The four different modes of consciousness—waking, sleep, dream, and integrative consciousness—reflect fundamental aspects of systemic functioning of the human organism that meet the following system functions and needs, respectively: learning, adaptation, and survival needs (waking); recuperative functions, regeneration, and growth (deep sleep); memory integration and consolidation and psychosocial adaptation (dreaming); and psychodynamic growth and social and psychological integration (integrative). These and other aspects of the different modes of human consciousness are illustrated in table 3.1 in terms of a range of biologically and phenomenologically based systems, which include the following: arousal—the ergotropic-trophotropic (or sympathetic-parasympathetic) divisions of the autonomic nervous system; the skeletal and somatic muscular system; sensory and motor processing; attention/awareness; egoic functions and personal identity; learning and memory consolidation; left- and right-hemisphere elicitation and integration; and differential utilization of the triune brain.

The biological basis and functional necessity of these modes of consciousness are reflected in cross-species commonalities in waking, deep sleep, and dreams and in cross-cultural commonalities in ASCs. The roles of different areas of the brain in each of the different modes of consciousness illustrate that there is no *single* functional or anatomical basis of the brain that is solely responsible for the elicitation and maintenance of these different modes. Excising the reputed centers for sleep, dreaming, and waking typically shows the reemergence of these modes of consciousness in the absence of the proposed control centers.[2] The lack of a single specific anatomical center for the initiation, maintenance, and termination of modes of consciousness reflects their systemic functional nature. Similarly, the multiple

Table 3.1
Basic Modes of Consciousness

System	Deep Sleep	Dream Sleep	Waking	Integrative
Autonomic Nervous System	Parasympathetic activation Sympathetic deactivation	Parasympathetic activation Sympathetic activation	Parasympathetic deactivation Sympathetic activation	Parasympathetic activation Sympathetic activation
Skeletal/ Somatic	Weak active Muscle tone	Inhibited	Strong	Variable/ inhibited
Brain Wave	Delta	Theta and mixed wave	Beta and mixed waves	Theta and alpha
Sensory Input	Weak monitoring	Weak monitoring	Strong external	Variable/ internal
Perception	Absent	Vivid internal	Vivid external	Variable/ internal
Motor Output	Involuntary	Inhibited	Strong voluntary	Inhibited/ variable
Attention/ Awareness	Absent	Weak	Moderate/ habituated	High
Ego Functions	Absent	Weak/ repressed	Present/ dominant	Present/ variable
Identity	Weak	Repressed	Dominant	Transpersonal
Freudian Unconscious	Absent	Present	Repressed	Present/ integrated
Hemisphere Activity	Synchrony Frontal absent	Desynchrony Right dominant	Desynchrony Left dominant	Synchrony Right and left
Programming	Absent	Absent	Present	Present
Learning	Absent	Present	Present	Present/ variable

Table 3.1 (continued)
Basic Modes of Consciousness

System	Deep Sleep	Dream Sleep	Waking	Integrative
Memory	Absent	Present/ limited	Present	Present/ variable
Thought	Absent	Analogical	Rational/ intuitive	Integrative/ relativistic
Reptilian Brain	Dominant deactivated	Organismic control	Initiates awareness	Consciously controlled
Limbic Brain	Systemic involve- ment	Learning, memory, emotions	Emotions, social communi- cation	Self-integra- tion/higher emotions
Neocortex	Maximal inactivation	Relative inactivity info processing	Language problem solving intentional- ity	Interhemi- spheric synchroni- zation
Functions	Recuperation Growth Healing	Info process- ing Learning Integration	External adaption Learning Cognition	Integration Psychological growth Flexibility
Neuro- transmis- sion	Cholinergic serotonin	Cholinergic	Noradrener- gic	Serotonin/ variable

mechanisms for inducing ASCs attest to their systemic functional nature as a mode of consciousness fundamental to human nature. The multiple methods for inducing modal operations are exemplified in the sleep-waking control apparatus—a systemic processes of the organism in which regulatory functions are capable of responding to a variety of inputs, outputs, and conditions (Koella 1985). The input channels of this regulatory system are "heteroreceptive," utilizing and responding to multiple sources, and are capable of input to maintain homeostasis. Koella's model of the control of sleep and waking cycles through a general purpose "vigilance-controlling apparatus" shows that sleep and waking modes differ not by the involvement of distinct systems, but by the nature of these systems during the different modes of consciousness. The vigilance-controlling apparatus utilizes all of the major strata of the brain: higher mental functions primarily organized by the neocortex; lower functions primarily organized through the brain stem, striatal structures, and limbic system; and motor functions (Koella 1985). This total utilization illustrates the systemic involvement of the brain in all modes of consciousness. The modes of consciousness reflect systemic interaction across the different levels of the brain, with different modes emphasizing different patterns within and across systems (e.g., see Parmeggiani 1985) and different neurotransmitter systems (e.g., see Hobson 1992).

States of Consciousness

Tart (1977) distinguished the following: state of consciousness (SoC); discrete states of consciousness (d-SoC); baseline state of consciousness (b-SoC); and altered states of consciousness (a-SoC or ASC). Although baseline and altered states of consciousness are conditions characterized here as modes of consciousness, Tart's other states of consciousness are conditions that vary within modes of consciousness. Tart defined *states of consciousness* as conditions that differ qualitatively from others by the presence of conditions or characteristics that are absent in other states. States of consciousness represent how people judge usual alterations in experience and are identified by the individual's assessment of patterns of experience. *Discrete states of consciousness* are unique dynamic patterns, configurations, or systems of psychological structures or subsystems that, in interaction, stabilize each other's functioning and actively maintain a constant overall pattern of functioning and identity within varying environments. Different states may involve different biological responses, but the characteristics are determined by personal significance. Because d-SoCs differ in terms of personal significance or psychological subsystems, they are a subsidiary level of analysis to that of modes, which are derived from physiological differences. Different states of consciousness are found within the sleep, dreaming, waking, and integrative modes of consciousness.

Tart's (1977, 192) baseline state of consciousness (b-SoC) "is an active stable overall patterning of psychological functions that, via multiple (feedback) stabilization relationships among the parts making it up, maintains its identity in spite of environmental changes."

The waking mode of consciousness is the biological frame of reference for relating to the world and the system within which organisms function behaviorally and humans function egoically. Differences in the level of organization of modes and states are illustrated by the number of discrete states of consciousness within the waking mode of consciousness. For example, during the waking mode of consciousness, a person may experience qualitatively different states of consciousness: driving a car, reading a book, eating, having sex, and daydreaming. The sleep and dream modes of consciousness also include different SoC within them. These have been referred to as "stages" in the context of recursive variations in the activities occurring during sleep (Dement and Mitler 1974). During the mode of deep sleep, certain pathological states of consciousness may emerge, including nightmares, somnambulism and nocturnal automatisms, and sleep drunkenness. Similarly, the dream mode of consciousness includes states of consciousness exemplified in the dysfunctions found in sleep terrors and hypnagogic states, as well as in lucid dreams. The integrative mode of consciousness also has a number of states of consciousness (e.g., soul flight, possession, samadhi) that are referred to collectively as ASCs.

Phases and Warps in Consciousness

Phases and warps of consciousness represent distinct cognized episodes of experience and the transition between them, respectively (Laughlin, McManus, and d'Aquili 1992). *Phases* reflect a more-detailed differentiation of the internal variation within specific modes and states of consciousness, what Laughlin et al. (1992) characterized as discrete continuities in the overall fragmentation of consciousness. The attentional and psychophysiological structures that produce waking consciousness are programmed by culture, socializing members to a selective range of potential experiences. Personal consciousness is produced through cultural programming of the development, automatization, and inhibition of awareness/attention. This results in a series of overall stable organizations of the psyche—discrete states and phases within the waking mode of consciousness. Phases reflect cyclic and sequential coordination of neural network activity and cognized episodes of experience and involve recursive patterns of reentrainments of neural systems into the conscious network.

Warps are experiential and neural transformations (Laughlin et al. 1992, 141) that produce the transition between two different modes or states of consciousness. The hypnagogic warp occurs between the waking phase and the sleep phase. The hypnopompic warp occurs between the dream phase and the waking phase. Warps normally pass so quickly that they are usually unconscious to the subject (e.g., one is seldom aware of the point of falling asleep). One may control or enhance consciousness by directing attention to the previous warp, but the shift through the sleep-dream-waking cycle or modes involves a series of warps that operate largely outside of consciousness.

Control of phases, states, and modes of consciousness can be achieved by exercising control over warps and by entraining structural aspects of neural functioning normally outside of awareness. Ritual is one way used to exercise control over the operating structures of consciousness (Laughlin et al. 1992). Shamanism uses technologies to induce warps in consciousness to access different modes and states. Shamanistic practices utilize nighttime ritual activities and dream incubation to reduce the barriers to awareness of ASC experiences on return to the waking mode of consciousness.

Modes, states, and phases of consciousness are nested levels of analysis for the bioorganismic structural, phenomenological, and cognized aspects of consciousness. Modes include several states of consciousness, which are characterized by cyclic phases.

Although some of Tart's (1977) states of consciousness correspond to modes (e.g., b-SoC), there are important conceptual differences. Modes of consciousness are biologically based, and their functions are related to organismic needs and homeostatic balance. States of consciousness reflect sociocultural learning and psychosocial needs. States operate within modes, and states' functions are determined by the social, cultural, and psychological functions rather than by the strictly biological needs. Production of warps in consciousness is central to shamanic practices and access to the integrative mode of consciousness. Different cultures produce different types of stable states of consciousness within the integrative mode of consciousness; these are referred to here as ASCs.

DIFFERENT ASCs IN THE INTEGRATIVE MODE OF CONSCIOUSNESS

Terms such as *shamanic journey, possession, vision quest, soul flight, mystical union,* and others have been used to refer to a range of ASCs. A determination of which of these correspond to unique physiological conditions, phenomenologically different experiences, and cross-culturally valid types of ASCs was derived from analysis of shaman-istic healers (Winkelman 1986b, 1990b, 1992). The use of entailment analysis[3] permitted determination of which variables (ASC charac-teristics and induction procedures) occur together and which have exclusion relations (do not co-occur), identifying three main types of ASCs. The first involves association of excessive motor behavior (e.g., dancing), sleep states and a period of apparent unconsciousness, and the interpretation of the experience as involving soul flight. The sec-ond shows the empirical association of sleep deprivation, auditory driving (e.g., chanting and drumming), fasting, sensory deprivation, and austerities, which correspond to conditions typical of meditative practices. The third involves the association of amnesia, convulsions, and spontaneous seizures with possession. These three entailment chains correspond to three major types of ASC traditions. The first, with soul flight, corresponds to the shamanic tradition. The second represents the yogic and meditative traditions. The third corresponds to mediumistic or possession-trance traditions. These different types of ASCs are manifested in the different types of magico-religious prac-titioners—shamans, shamanistic healers, and mediums, respectively.

Types of ASCs

Shamanic Soul Journey.   The shaman's ASC is characterized as a flight, soul journey, or out-of-body experience during which the shaman's soul or spirit is believed to leave the body and travel into other worlds. The shaman's classic flight may take other forms, in-cluding the vision quest experience and an animal transformation during which some aspect of the practitioner becomes an animal and enters into nonordinary experiential worlds and engages in interac-tion with spirit entities. Procedures used by shamans to induce an ASC—chanting, dancing, fasting, austerities, and hallucinogens—manipulate the sympathetic nervous system to the point of exhaus-tion and collapse into a parasympathetic dominant state with visions.

Mediumistic Possession.   Bourguignon (1976a,b) established the importance of the distinction between possession ASC and other types of ASCs. Possession ASC is distinct from shaman's ASC because it is largely auditory, in contrast to the shaman's visionary experience, and because it involves a domination of the person by spirit entities. Cross-cultural analyses indicate that possession ASC is significantly associ-ated with symptoms of temporal lobe discharge and with the presence of political integration beyond the local community (Winkelman 1986b, 1990b, 1992). Possession also involves a variety of different forms, ranging from pathology to mechanisms for communication, expression, political action, and transformation of self and other.

Meditation. Walsh (1990) illustrated the differences between shamanic ASC and meditative ASC in a phenomenological mapping and comparison of the raw experiences of shamans with those of yogis and Buddhists. Shamans show changes in highly emotionally charged identities, in a sustained communicative interaction with an audience, and in a focus on out-of-body experiences and the content of inner experiences interpreted as nonordinary realities. Buddhists contrast with shamans in terms of more self-control and concentration, lower arousal, a sense of calm and emotional detachment, a loss of sense of self, a greater awareness, and contentless experience. Although there are differences in meditative approaches and traditions, there are important similarities at psychophysiological, cognitive, and conceptual levels.

Societal Conditions and ASC Induction Procedures

There are cross-cultural patterns of relationships between social conditions and ASC induction procedures and characteristics that reflect societal effects on the use of ASCs. The differential use of and access to procedures for the alteration of consciousness have been noted (Jorgensen 1980; Winkelman 1990b). Dobkin de Rios and Smith (1977) pointed out that as societies grow in structural complexity, plant hallucinogens are eliminated from widespread use and are usurped by the elite segments. Winkelman (1990b) found the use of hallucinogens to be significantly related only to the absence of political integration. This finding indicates, as predicted by other researchers, that the use of hallucinogenic drugs in ASC-induction procedures declines with increasing political integration of the society. Ritualized societal use of alcohol was found to be positively and significantly correlated with agriculture, social stratification, political integration, and technical specialization; but none of these variables contributed significantly to explanation of variance beyond the others. Alcohol use occurs in societies that are more complex than those with hallucinogenic drugs. The use of any drugs at all was not significantly related to any social complexity variables, with both drug and nondrug ASCs found in both simple and complex societies.

There are general sequences in development of ASC-induction procedures, as seen in the contrast of the soul flight of the shaman with the possession of the medium. The shamanic soul flight or journey is found as the predominant ASC among only the shamans of hunting-gathering societies. The archetypal motif of the shamanic flight might be found almost universally, but it is not the predominant explanatory model for institutionalized ASC experiences in complex societies. Instead, other interpretations (e.g., possession, mysticism, void) become more prevalent. Political integration is directly related to the formation of possession ASC experiences. Distinctions between different types of drug-induced ASCs and nondrug ASCs were used in an evolutionary model to represent different types of societies in terms of ASC-induction procedures (Winkelman 1990b). Social complexity variables (Murdock and Provost 1973) are positively correlated with this variable, with the strongest correlations found for political integration and social stratification (Winkelman 1990b). These correlations partially support an evolutionary model of the forms of ASCs, with political integration as a principal cause of change; however, other social or cultural variables must be investigated to determine the causes of the remaining 50 percent variation in the nature of ASCs. There is no single simple evolutionary process underlying the procedures for inducing ASCs.

THE BIOLOGICAL BASIS OF THE INTEGRATIVE MODE OF CONSCIOUSNESS

Although many anthropologists have assumed an underlying communality to trance, shamanism, mediumship, possession, and other ecstatic religious practices, the physiological basis for ASCs or their communality has seldom been addressed (but see Laughlin, McManus, and d'Aquili 1992; Lex 1979; Prince 1982a,b; Winkelman 1986b, 1992, 1996, 1997b). The present work extends these perspectives in illustrating that different ASCs are similar in their physiological concomitants.

The assumption of a fundamental physiological similarity underlying different ASCs might seem groundless because they are induced through diverse means, including drumming, chanting, singing, dancing, stimulants, hallucinogens, alcohol, sensory stimulation and deprivation, fasting, temperature extremes, fatigue, emotional manipulations, and physiological sensitivities. In spite of varied agents and procedures, fundamental psychobiological similarities exist in ASC effects on functional systems of the brain and constitute different means of evoking a basic mode of organismic functioning. The variety of conditions that produce similar ASCs illustrates a ubiquitous response of the brain. A wide variety of procedures and agents will evoke limbic-system slow-wave discharges that synchronize and dominate the frontal cortex (Mandell 1980; Winkelman 1986b, 1992). The universal manifestation of ASC experiences (Bourguignon 1968; Winkelman 1986b, 1992) reflects activation of this biologically based mode of organismic operation, which provides psychosocial and psychocognitive integration.

The nature of this integrative mode of consciousness is illustrated by contrast with waking consciousness. Many procedures alter waking consciousness and produce conditions diametrically opposed to the waking conditions dominated by the frontal cortex, the left hemisphere, and logical, rational, verbal experiences. Because of the use of information modalities normally repressed or ignored in the waking mode, ASCs provide new means of integration of symbolic and physiological systems.

Meditative traditions have referred to these forms of consciousness as transcendental or transpersonal. "Trans" qualifies these conditions as representing factors that go beyond individual personal characteristics, implying that these structures are "beyond" or outside the individual. The perspective presented here is that these experiences are better understood as "infrapersonal," being found within all individuals, representing psychobiological factors that structure human experience. These internal structures can be activated by a variety of mechanisms. ASCs within the integrative modes of consciousness share characteristics in their deliberate elicitation, manipulation, and integration of these structures by the physiological, psychodynamic, and socioemotional mechanisms of the nervous system.

Key physiological mechanisms underlying ASCs and integrative forms of consciousness are found in activation of the paleomammalian brain, specifically the hippocampal-septal circuits, the hypothalamus, and related areas that regulate emotions and the balance in the autonomic nervous system (ANS). The ability of diverse procedures to induce common changes in consciousness reflects activation of the parasympathetic nervous system by a variety of inputs (Leukel 1972). The parasympathetic state, slow-wave synchronization of the frontal cortex, and interhemispheric integration reflect activation of basic aspects of brain operation related to sensory and physiological integration; mental and emotional integration; insight and transcendence; and interhemispheric integration.

There are three primary characteristics of integrative ASCs or modes of consciousness: The first characteristic is the integration of information across different functional systems of the brain; the second is the ability to act on structures of consciousness as content rather than self; and the third involves a greater degree of flexibility and conscious control of biological and mental systems.

A primary characteristic of integrative consciousness involves hierarchical integration of brain mechanisms, especially as manifested in limbic-system driving of the frontal cortex through serotonergic-induced integration across the neuraxis. This represents the integration of preconscious or unconscious functions and material into self-conscious awareness. This involves hemispheric synchronization, an increased coherence between the two frontal hemispheres. Research on the specific effects of hallucinogens and meditation (and ASCs in general) illustrates that many conditions produce interhemispheric fusion, a coherence and synchronization within the brain reflecting a greater integration of distinct brain processes.

A second characteristic of integrative forms of consciousness is the ability to act on the structures of previous levels of consciousness. This ability enables observation of previous operational structures of the unconscious, the self, the ego, and other aspects of the psyche and their manipulation from a higher level of awareness and self-organization. This observational ability produces changes in the processes supporting consciousness and self (e.g., the integration of unconscious or repressed material).

Operation on the structures of consciousness produces a third characteristic of integrative forms of consciousness. This involves great variability in the options available in physical and mental system activations. The autonomic nervous system may show activation or deactivation of either subsystem; somatic and skeletal muscles may be inactive or highly active; brain wave patterns may assume a number of parameters (but particularly in alpha and theta ranges); attention and awareness may range from omnisentience to total void; aspects of conscious and unconscious identity may be manifested or repressed; programming and learning may be accelerated; and different brain systems may be activated or deactivated. Integrative forms of consciousness increasingly subjugate the organism's experiences and functioning to conscious and deliberate control.

The adaptiveness of these conditions is illustrated by the relationship of brain functions to cognitive and emotional processes. Consciousness is manipulated in shamanistic practices to produce psychodynamic integration through the elicitation of functions derived from components of waking and dreaming modes of consciousness and through the use of ritual to control consciousness. Shamanic states of consciousness constitute conditions akin to a "waking dream," derived from coactivation of processes normally associated only with the dream mode (e.g., vivid internal imagery) or waking mode (e.g., ego functions, voluntary focus of attention). These potentials are subsequently developed in an enhanced understanding of the nature of human consciousness, knowledge and awareness, and the ability to selectively and deliberately access a greater range of aspects of consciousness as needed.

This universal, biologically based, integrative mode of consciousness is substantiated by diverse forms of evidence, including cross-cultural data; a general psychophysiological model of brain dynamics of ASCs; effects of ASC induction procedures; the psychophysiology of hypnosis; and the psychophysiological concomitants of dreaming. Manifestations of similar ASCs cross-culturally reflect the wide variety of procedures and conditions that contribute to the induction of common psychophysiological changes involving activation of the limbic system and induction of a slow-wave synchronization of the frontal cortex by slow-wave discharges that stimulate integrative processing across the neuraxis. The basic similarity of neurophysiological conditions induced through a wide variety of techniques and those resulting from predispositions caused by central nervous system conditions supports the hypothesis of a biologically structured integrative mode of consciousness. Selection for a biological disposition to these highly focused internal states of awareness is illustrated by the genetic basis for hypnotic susceptibility. That this integrative mode of consciousness involves cross-modal integration of waking and dream capabilities is illustrated by dream characteristics and by the basic rest-and-activity cycle, in which periodic penetration of dreamlike mentation occurs during waking consciousness.

A Physiological Model of Integrative Consciousness

The functional basis for the shamanistic ASC is exemplified by common physiological effects of many ASC induction procedures. Davidson (1976) suggested that common physiological mechanisms underlying ASCs involved extensive ergotropic (sympathetic) activation leading to trophotropic (parasympathetic) collapse. Lex (1979) suggested that ritually induced ASCs share common physiological features of right-hemisphere dominance, cortical synchronization, and a dominant trophotropic (parasympathetic) state. A wide range of ASC-induction procedures results in a trophotropic pattern—parasympathetic discharges, relaxed skeletal muscles, and synchronized cortical rhythms—and creates a state of right-hemisphere dominance. Right-hemispheric activation typical of ASC reflects its mediation of lower structures, particularly the limbic system.

Mandell (1980) suggested that physiological mechanisms underlying regularities in ASCs or "transcendent states" are based in a common underlying neurobiochemical pathway involving the temporal lobe. Transcendent states of consciousness result from the loss of serotonin inhibition to the hippocampal CA_3 cells, which produces an increase in the cells' activity and the manifestation of hippocampal-septal slow waves. This activity may manifest itself in a range of effects, from the slowing of the EEG, as in a relaxed state, to the strongly driven hypersynchronous hippocampal-septal seizures. This manifestation of high-voltage, slow-wave EEG activity (alpha, theta, and delta, especially 3 to 6 cycles per second [cps]) imposes a synchronous slow-wave pattern on the frontal lobes. Mandell suggested that the neurobiological basis underlying ecstatic and transcendent feelings, including their ineffable and religious components, involves a "biogenic amine-temporal-lobe limbic neurology" (Mandell 1980, 381) based in the "mesolimbic serotonergic pathway that extends from the median raphe nucleus in the mesencephalon, coexistent with part of the mesencephalic reticular formation regulating arousal . . . to the septum and hippocampus" (390). This produces slow-wave hypersynchronous discharges across the hippocampal-septal-reticular-raphe circuit. Agents and procedures that invoke this pattern include hallucinogens, amphetamines, cocaine, marijuana, polypeptide opiates, long-distance running, hunger, thirst, sleep loss, auditory stimuli such as drumming and chanting, sensory deprivation, dream states, meditation, and a variety of psychophysiological imbalances or sensitivities resulting from injury, trauma, disease, or hereditarily transmitted nervous system conditions (Winkelman 1992).

Diverse classes of drugs (e.g., amphetamines, cocaine, and hallucinogens), as well as activity, stress, and sensory stimulation, affect serotonergic mechanisms, disinhibiting temporal lobes structures and producing synchronous discharges (Mandell 1980). Similar inductions of hippocampal-septal slow waves can be produced by alterations in septal-hippocampal relations that are caused by anticholinergic drugs and by the action on hippocampal pyramidal cells by polypeptide transmitters (Mandell 1980, 408–9), releasing ecstatic, affectual, and cognitive processes. The loss of inhibitory regulation by serotonin results in hyperexcitability of the CA_3 cells and reduction or loss of the cells' role in the "gating" of emotional response. This loss of gating or associative matching between external events and the internal emotional stimuli represented within the temporal lobe limbic system, combined with the hippocampal-septal synchronous discharges, results in an emotional flooding—ecstasy (paraphrase, Mandell 1980, 400). The loss of hippocampal CA_3 modulation removes regulatory input, leaving the "inside world" dominant.

Mandell (1980) suggested two bases for transcendent states in the hypersynchronous temporal lobe activities: the hippocampal-septal system and the amygdala. Spontaneous discharges in the hippocampal-septal system are referred to in psychiatric nomenclature as "interictal attacks." Spontaneous synchronous discharges originating in the amygdala are generally labeled as temporal lobe epilepsy, or, mistakenly, schizophrenia.

The hippocampal-septal circuits involved in the production of theta activity are central aspects of the limbic system, a central processor of the brain integrating emotion and memory. The hippocampal-septal region receives the terminal projections from the somatic and the autonomic nervous systems, forming part of an extensive system of innervation connecting areas of the brain, in particular linking the frontal cortex and the limbic system. The limbic cortex receives all interoceptive and exteroceptive information, with the hippocampus, the amygdala, and related structures serving as the point of information convergence en route to the frontal cortex. Mandell indicated that the hippocampus is the focal point for the activities producing transcendent consciousness through the mechanisms that reduce the inhibitory serotonin regulation of temporal lobe limbic function. The hippocampal-septal system is an association area involved in the formation and the mediation of memory and emotions. The hippocampal formation influences the hypothalamus and other brain structures responsible for self-preservation, family-related behavior (MacLean 1990), and the management of novel sensory information.

The amygdala processes emotional information and transmits it to various areas, including the hippocampus. The amygdala also serves as a system of brain innervation, particularly to the frontotemporal region of the cortex and the forebrain. The hippocampal-septal system and the amygdala receive input from and exert control over the hypothalamus. The hypothalamus has direct control over the pituitary, which releases a wide range of neural transmitter substances, including those similar to hallucinogens and opiates. The pituitary also releases substances that act on the reticular activating system and regulate the sleeping and waking cycles.

The hypothalamus regulates the balance between the sympathetic and the parasympathetic divisions of the autonomic nervous system (ANS), maintaining body functions in an interactive balance of activation and deactivation. The sympathetic nervous system is the activating system, responsible for the stimulation of the adrenal medulla and the release of hormones. Activation of the sympathetic nervous system results in diffuse cortical excitation, desynchronization of the EEG, and increased skeletal tone, as manifested in the orienting response and the waking mode of consciousness. Sympathetic activation prepares the body for action. Activation of the parasympathetic system leads to decreased cortical excitation, an increase in hemispheric synchronization, and the restorative functions of the organism; it is evoked by a number of chemical, hormonal, temperature, and other influences, including direct stimulation in the range of 3 to 8 cycles per second. Parasympathetic activity increases by closing one's eyes and leads to an increase in synchronous alpha patterns in the EEG. Increases in parasympathetic dominance lead to the relaxation response and ultimately to sleep, coma, and death. Parasympathetic dominant states normally occur only during sleep, but ASCs generally involve phases with a parasympathetic dominant state, as evidenced in collapse and apparent unconsciousness. But in contrast to the lack of awareness typical of unconsciousness, the parasympathetic dominant ASCs are generally characterized by continued self-awareness. A wide variety of conditions will evoke this sequence of excitation and collapse (Gellhorn 1969). The fact that a wide variety of conditions evokes this pattern illustrates the normal biological basis of the integrative mode of consciousness, a parasympathetic dominant state with EEG slow-wave discharges, particularly in the theta range.

Hypnosis

McClenon (1997) suggested that shamanism utilized hypnotizability, which also reflects limbic-frontal integration characterized by theta wave discharge patterns. Crawford (1994) reviewed research illustrating the neurophysiological basis for hypnosis. Highly hypnotizable people have attentional filtering mechanisms that function more strongly, enabling them to sustain attention with better focus and to ignore irrelevant environmental stimuli. Their ability to focus on an internally generated environment is renowned and reflects a fundamental characteristic of the shaman's visionary experience.

Crawford proposed that hypnosis and its enhanced attention reflect an interaction between subcortical and cortical brain mechanisms that enable highly hypnotizable people to sustain attention as well as disattention. Crawford suggested that concentration and suppression are two aspects of the same cognitive processes involving the willful direction of attention. The attentional mechanisms involved in extreme focus of attention and hypnotizability are those related to the far frontal cortex's regulation of limbic system activity and gating for incoming sensory stimuli. A consequence of the highly hypnotizable individual's more efficient far frontal limbic attentional systems is the ability to disattend to extraneous stimuli, known as cognitive inhibition. This fronto-limbic attentional system also plays a role in the modulation of emotions and in comfort and discomfort.

Crawford (1994, 210) related hypnotizability and inhibition associated with theta-wave production to class II inhibition, which is associated with "efficient and attentive performance." Crawford reviewed research that indicated a relationship between enhanced theta power and hypnotic suggestibility. This enhanced theta is associated with right-hemisphere activity among highly hypnotizable individuals, as well as with the quiescent periods of meditation. Enhanced limbic frontal interaction characteristic of highly hypnotizable individuals is a pattern of brain functioning that typifies the broader model of ASCs presented here. Both ASCs in general and hypnosis in particular involve enhanced interaction between the limbic and the frontal brain, an increase in coherence and integration across the neuraxis. Like other ASCs, hypnosis minimizes the importance of the external environment. Of significance to the broader model of ASCs presented here is the flexibility of outcomes at both experiential and physiological levels that is associated with highly hypnotizable persons, particularly their cognitive flexibility and their ability to shift awareness and cognitive strategies. Highly hypnotizable individuals also show other specific information-processing abilities: to become deeply engrossed in imaginative activities; to produce vivid imagery; and to engage in "holistic information-processing styles" (paraphrase Crawford 1994, 223). These abilities are also characteristic of dreams.

Dreams and Integrative ASCs

Deliberate induction of sleep or dreams in shamanistic ritual reflects the physiological and systemic effects of sleep and/or dreams. Sleep involves the basic shift to parasympathetic dominance and shares characteristics with meditative states (Davidson 1976; Schuman 1980). There are substantial parallels of REM sleep (dreaming) with yoga ecstasy in terms of cortical and visceral arousal, inhibition of skeletal muscle tone, loss of distinctiveness in sense of time, vivid perceptual imagery, and parasympathetic dominance (Gellhorn and Kiely 1972). REM sleep patterns are very similar to those of hallucinogens, evoking visual imagery and hippocampal-septal slow waves (Mandell 1980). Dreams involve forms of information processing that are central to ASCs (Hunt 1995c). Laughlin, McManus, and d'Aquili (1992) characterized dreams as the aspect of the unconscious in closest contact with ego awareness and as a manifestation of the operational infrastructure that provides the basis for ego consciousness.

Shamanism explicitly sought to integrate dream consciousness within waking consciousness. I propose (cf. Peters 1989) that shamanic consciousness uses an integration of the potentials of dreaming and waking consciousness. Shamanism sought this integration through a ritual, typically lasting throughout the night. The integration of dream cognition with shamanic activities was inevitable, given the normal cycles of dream mentation and the typical periods of "unconsciousness" for the soul journey. The importance of dreams for the general model of the integrative mode of consciousness is examined in this section, which considers the evolutionary role of dreams, the physiology of dreams, and the nature of dream cognition and experiences.

Comparative Perspectives on Dreams. The periods of sleep involve equilibrium conditions that allow for modulation of the fundamental cyclicities that synchronize biological periodicity of cells and coordinate physiological adaptations to inner rather than outer needs. The physiological patterns of sleep found in humans are shared with other animals, reflecting the patterns' neurophysiological functions and structures and their importance as organismic activities. Sleep of a generalized form is found in fish, amphibians, and reptiles; but the differentiation of sleep into NREM (deep sleep) and REM (dreams) does not appear evolutionarily until the birds and mammals (Graham 1990). Evolutionary changes in mammals' brain function, which emerged about 140 million years ago in the ancestor of the marsupial and placental mammals, provided the basis for the distinction of REM sleep within the sleep cycle (Winson 1985). Both REM and NREM sleep have remarkably similar characteristics across marsupials and humans (Sterman and Clemente 1974). These homologies reflect the systemic nature of brain involvement in sleep phenomena and the status of deep sleep and dreams as functional modes of consciousness. The ubiquity of dream sleep in mammals and the drive to recoup lost dream time reflect the biological basis of this mode of consciousness and its necessity for normal functioning. Winson (1985) suggested that the mammalian adaptations involving extensive learning created the resultant need for integration of experience over time in order to guide future behavior. The mammalian adaptation or solution (except for monotremes and echidna) for achieving learning without a large prefrontal cortex was "off-line processing" or REM sleep, where association of recent memories was achieved during periods of sleep. This "off-line" processing facilitated use of the frontal cortex for advanced cognitive and perceptual activities (Winson 1990).

Evolutionary Functions of Dreams.   Winson (1985, 1990) suggested that REM sleep/dreams and the Freudian unconscious represent a phylogenetically ancient mechanism in which memories, associations, and strategies are formed, modified, or consulted. This neural system of information processing was functioning before rational consciousness arose in humans, and its types of information processing are distinct from the processes of the frontal cortex and associated structures (Winson 1985, 209). REM sleep is a basic mammalian memory process for evaluating experience and forming strategies. Dreams are a means of reviewing experiences and their transfer from short-term to long-term memory (Graham 1990). Winson (1985) showed the fundamental role of the hippocampus and amygdala structures in the dreams and memory. These limbic system components provide a core information-processing area, based on the organization of information derived from assessment of events and their emotional associations.

Hippocampal theta rhythm (3 to 6 cps brain waves) is an indicator of a special type of information processing in the hippocampus (Winson 1985). This hippocampus theta activity reflects processes during which the information from the primary sensory areas is integrated, processed, and transferred to the neocortex. There is variation in theta activation across species; but overall this activation appears in each species and is associated with behaviors that are central to survival for the species. The same neurons perform the task of synchronizing sensory information, species-specific survival activities, and REM sleep. The function of the theta waves in sensory information processing in the lower mammals suggests that a similar process occurs in REM sleep, but with information processing based on internal sensory input from memory reflecting the processing of previously acquired information.

REM Sleep/Dream Characteristics. REM (desynchronized) sleep is active sleep with desynchronized waves more characteristic of waking than deep sleep, ergo, "paradoxical sleep." During late phases of deep sleep, control of the autonomic system by the hypothalamus is reduced, allowing for a brain pattern similar to wakefulness. In contrast to deep sleep (characterized by depressed levels of cortical arousal, synchrony of the EEG, and continued behavioral muscle tone), REM sleep is characterized by[4] higher levels of CNS arousal, sympathetic system activation, desynchrony of the EEG, and loss of muscle tone.

During dream sleep, the nervous system behaves as if it were in a state of continual orientation, but with motor inhibition and suppression of homeostasis. Similarities of REM sleep physiology to the general orientation response include the involvement in the same areas of the brain stem in their initiation; motor paralysis with an activated cortex; hippocampal theta rhythms; and common neural systems involved in their control (Hunt 1989b).

REM sleep is not like deep sleep but more like a paralyzed hallucinatory state. The sensorial structures, functions, and activities operate according to similar principles during waking and dreaming, whereas the source of stimulation changes. This is possible because while the brain is actively processing dream information, centers in the lower brain stem inhibit the striate muscle system, preventing movement. Muscle inhibition during REM sleep allows for emotional reactions and intentional behavior to proceed without movement of the body. Hunt (1989b) suggested REM sleep is right-hemisphere predominant. The right-hemisphere role[5] in dreaming reflects a different symbolic form of presentation than that used in waking consciousness. The bizzareness of dreams reflects the imaginative and creative capacities of the presentational modality. Dreams appear bizarre and illogical from the point of view of waking consciousness because dreams involve a different system of information representation, processing, and consolidation.

Dream Cognition

Dream mentation differs from the typical mentation of the waking mode of consciousness (see Hunt 1989b; Broughton 1986; Hobson and Stickgold 1994), including cognitive processing and intense imagery and emotion that appear bizzare and delusional from the perspectives of waking consciousness. Although the psychoanalytic perspectives have emphasized the deficient character of dreams (e.g., repressed desires or compensatory mechanisms), these pathologization perspectives reflect the monophasic approach of Western culture attempting to make sense of other states of consciousness in terms of the waking ego. Dreaming is a specific type of mentation—a manifestation of a presentational or imagetic modality manifested in hallucinoid imagery. Whereas the body remains relaxed and generally unresponsive to the outer environment, the rapid eye movements reflect intense internal neurocognitive processing, and the activity of the lower brain suggests the active rehearsal or enactment of customary behavioral patterns. During dreams the information-processing characteristics of logic, rationality, and formal operations are replaced by a transductive or analogic reasoning organized on the basis of similarity in configuration or meaning.

Winson (1985, 1990) suggested that dream "distortion" is the normal associative processes involved in the information processing, interpretation, and integration of experience in the REM mode. Dream condensation functions not as a disguise or distortion, but as a symbol that expresses an unconscious concept for the person. The unconscious materials manifested in dreams include strategies for dealing with the external world that are organized and interrelated in a way that constitutes an "unconscious personality" (Winson 1985, 245). Laughlin, McManus, and d'Aquili (1992) illustrated that dreams subserve the experiential and emotional needs of both the conscious and the unconscious personalities. Dreams involve the interaction of the mediating and supporting structures of egoic consciousness with structures disentrained from egoic consciousness. Laughlin, McManus, and d'Aquili suggest that dreaming be viewed as a form of "homeomorphogenetic play" in which the neurocognitive systems operate independently of the outer environment.

Hunt (1989) characterized dreams as imagetic, affective, and presentational modalities that involve symbolic intelligence and an abstract line of cognitive and emotive development. This characterization is based on a cross-modal synesthetic fusion, involving imagery, imagination, and the use of metaphor. Hunt linked the function and bases of dream to the core of the human symbolic capacity derived from visual, spatial, and physiognomic expression. The visual imagery of dreams involves condensed patterns, a form of intentional communication that nonetheless requires an interpretation of meaning. Hunt suggested that dreams' largely visual (rather than verbal) nature reflects their bases in a visual-spatial imagetic intelligence, an abstract form of symbolic representation that requires interpretation.

The mental imagery of dreams constitutes a kind of surface structure expressing meaning of deeper syntax of a propositional knowledge base. Hunt (1989b) illustrated this syntaxical structure in a review of studies that indicated that dreams have a narrative structure, exemplified in a top-down control of the dream imagery. This visual-spatial system manifested in imagery provides a creative reorganization of past experiences. Evidence that the imagery of dreams is represented in a form distinct from that of language is found in the ability of the visual modality of dream imagery to present information not accessible to the linguistic system. This is exemplified in what Hunt referred to as archetypal-titanic dreams—the fusion of a number of different dimensions of experience is reflected in the visual-spatial imagery. This visual-spatial system of symbolic presentation is normally inhibited by the dominance of left-hemisphere verbal representational systems; conditions that attenuate the left hemisphere's verbal representational systems allow the expression of this presentational intelligence.

The complexity of information extracted from the dream images attests to the existence of a separate nonlanguage system of symbolism, construction, and meaning. The geometric images often found in these states are autosymbolic characters, an abstract-dynamic geometric imagery that has been considered the root of thought processes (Arnheim 1969). Hunt suggested that these geometric patterns manifest transformational operations that constitute the deep structure of intelligence but operate independently of the linguistic representational systems. These visual structures constitute a template for symbolic operations that provide the basis for cross-modal translations. It is this nonlinguistic template that provides the basis for symbolism and the ground from which cross-modal translations make language possible[6]. Hunt suggested that the visual kinesthetic felt meanings constitute "the deep structures of all representational (left hemisphere) symbolic intelligence" (Hunt 1989b, 207). "The bottom line here is that neurophysiological findings are congruent with phenomenological and cognitive-experimental evidence of two distinct cognitive processes in dreaming: a sequentially directed narrative component and a simultaneous visual-spatial component, each of which interacts with and may 'entrain' the other" (Hunt 1989b, 172). These two components, embodying representational and presentational symbolism, are normally in continuous interaction in the dream processes, with a relatively greater predominance of the right-hemisphere capacities. This may be due to the more restrictive functions of left-hemisphere capabilities caused by the loss of social context and interaction.

Dream "Deficits"

Dreams' roles as sources of creativity and insight that can be applied to solving everyday problems through accessing information not normally available have been long held. But Blagrove (1996) argued that there is a lack of evidence for claims to these cognitive functions of (ordinary) dreaming. Dreams reflect aspects of waking consciousness, but they do not have the same capabilities as waking consciousness. Dreams in general lack a self-reflective nature and normally do not manifest a sense of conscious control. Dream recall indicates a single-mindedness or an awareness and a single thematic track to dream content. Characteristic of REM sleep is the absence or impairment of attentional mechanisms, particularly the voluntary focus of attention. Dreams lack a self-reflective awareness that one is in the dream state. This lack is illustrated in the engagement with a train of thought for extended periods without reflection on one's situation. Situations that contradict waking knowledge of the world are accepted without critical reflection. The lack of intentionality and the single-minded character of dreams suggest that they cannot play a role in problem solving. The dreamer does not appear to have any perspective, but rather is completely engaged in the dream interaction without waking consciousness's ability to use reflection. In contrast to the daydreamer's engagement with fantasy, the REM dreamer usually is not capable of recognizing the delusional nature of experiences, nor of exercising conscious control or stopping to reconsider the possibilities. Although the experience of self in dreams is ordinarily tied to the identity one has in the waking mode, there are significant differences in that sense of identity in the dreamer's lack of any perspective other than the dream or in the dreamer's absense from the dream (Hunt 1989b).

Lucid dreams differ from ordinary dreams in the dreamer's conscious awareness of the ongoing dream (LaBerge 1985; Gackenbach and LaBerge 1988). Qualitative differences in lucid dreams include possession of waking faculties, such as reason, memory, reflection, and volition. The experiences of lucid dreams are subject to deliberate cultivation, as is evidenced in the reports of yogic traditions. Hunt (1989b) provided an overview of lucid dreams and related phenomena that showed that the physiological, phenomenological, and cognitive aspects confirm their nature as spontaneous meditative states. Similarities between dreams and meditative states are also found in common EEG and autonomic changes; in increased incidence of lucid dreams among long-term meditators; and in physical detachment, inactive conditions, social withdrawal, and enforced motionlessness. Their relationship to shamanic experiences is illustrated in the similarities Hunt detailed between lucid dreams and out-of-body experiences.

Consciousness of oneself dreaming is extremely rare (although cognitive training does increase self-reflectiveness during dreams). Recognition of dreaming (lucidity) generally leads to spontaneously awakening upon awareness of the dream state. LaBerge (1985) has also pointed to the difficulty of maintaining a sense of conscious awareness during the dream state even among those who practice lucid dreaming. Laberge has pointed out that the lack of intentionality during ordinary dreams is also manifested in lucid dreaming. Rather than intention determining lucid-dream outcomes, it is the power of expectation.

This sense that ordinary dreams have of occurring to us in an automatic fashion is quite different from what typically occurs during waking consciousness. Dreams' single-mindedness or mindless action is intensified as a consequence of isolation from the sensory data and social relationships that sustain waking consciousness. The altered sense of self also reflects the lack of frontally based systems of reference from which one ordinarily obtains an additional perspective from which to think reflexively about oneself, creating self-consciousness.

Although dreams may include material indicating goal-directed action, intentionality, or planning, Blagrove (1996) contended that dreams provide a passive representation of such activities: the dream symbolizes waking life's goal-directed action rather than an act of engagement typical of waking life. In waking consciousness and active daydreaming, we engage in rehearsal, imagining consequences and possible reactions, and exercise a degree of control over outcomes that is different from dreaming.

How can these cognitive limitations be reconciled with the widespread anecdotal reports of insightful dream cognition and processing? These contradictions can be resolved by recognizing that extraordinary dreams have unusual cross-mode integrative processing present. These dreams have a special integration between the dream and waking modes of consciousness. Dreams ordinarily studied in Western psychology reflect a deficit in comparison with waking consciousness. Most of psychiatry's and cognitive science's approaches to dreams have focused on a very narrow range of dream experiences (Hunt 1989b). Intuitive, archetypal, and other forms of dreams reflecting transpersonal and cross-modal potentials are a consequence of additional information provided through limbic-frontal integration. The rarity of such integrative experiences reflects the difficulties in cross-phasing, particularly in monophasic cultures. A typical and dominant characteristic of dreaming is amnesia and a failure of transfer or cross-phasing of most of the activity of dreams to waking consciousness.

Although dream experiences are not part of many people's conscious experiences, shamanic traditions extend the dream experiences into the waking mode to produce integrative consciousness. Dream incubation and other ASCs prior to or during sleep enhance cross-modal transfer between the two modes of consciousness. These deliberate cultural activities linking conscious awareness with the activities of the dream mode constitute a form of integrative consciousness. These activities integrate with the conscious self the unique presentational modality of the paleomammalian brain, its role in memory formation and consolidation, and its management of a significant aspect of emotions and self.

Hunt (1989b) suggested that dreaming may not have a fundamental function, but may be based on the use of a self-referential and self-transforming system that makes dream production open-ended.

The existence of relatively distinct types of dreaming is particularly well illustrated in cross-cultural review of dream use and experiences (Hunt 1989b). This multiplicity of dreaming reflects its operation through symbolic cognition. Shamanism used dreams to enhance information transfer to the waking mode and its application for healing.

The normal integration of the waking and the dream modes is illustrated in Rossi's (1986) research on the ultradian rhythms and the sleep-dream-waking cycles, which showed that dreamlike periods and mentation also occur during the waking mode. The information processing of dreams also occasionally intrudes on waking consciousness. Waking-consciousness episodes of external vigilance and maximal verbal, logical, and analytical mental activity are followed by periods of drowsiness, daydreaming, fantasy, and increases in alpha EEG waves. The finding that daydreams are indistinguishable from night dreams in content supports this contention that these involve periods during which the functions of the dream mode of consciousness intrude on the waking cycle (Broughton 1986). Rossi suggested that these ultradian rhythms are a psychophysiological basis for ASCs, involving the phase of extreme relaxation in the Basic Rest-Activity Cycle, originally discovered by Kleitman ([1960] 1972, 1970). This cycle involves regular fluctuations in brain wave activity—visceral, and somatic responses from upper to lower extremes of variation during the waking mode of consciousness. The cycle is also manifested in sleep in the alternation of phases of deep sleep (high-voltage, low-frequency) and REM sleep (low-voltage, mixed, faster frequencies).

The ultradian cycle has a wide range of characteristics (Rossi 1986), which include a periodicity of 90 to 120 minutes, a shift in hemispheric laterality to the right hemisphere, and activation of parasympathetic psychophysiological processes. Motor behavior shows a global decline, including increases in response latency, reduced muscle tonicity, and reduced bodily activity. Sensory perceptual behavior changes involve a range of sensory alterations, including after images and hallucinations. Cognitive behavior manifests regressions, dissociations, amnesia, confusion, autonomous ideation, a wandering of the mind, fantasy, and time lags in response. Social behavior is characterized by a "take a break" attitude, reduction in task focus, and social relaxation. Affective behavior includes a sense of comfort, relaxation, dissociation, and a perception of objectivity and impersonality. Transpersonal aspects, including blissful experiences and dissolution of the subject-object dichotomy, may emerge. Underlying the ultradian cycle is the relaxation response resulting in "a natural period of introversion" (Rossi 1986, 104). The "ultradian low" is a state of consciousness in the waking mode in which the parasympathetic activation is strongest; it represents penetration of the dream mode of consciousness into the waking mode.

But dreaming and waking modes of consciousness are normally exclusive. Ordinary dreaming has a distinct neurotransmitter profile from waking consciousness (Hobson 1992). The dream mode has a cessation of serotonin and norepinephrine activity. The cholinergic system is responsible for the REM sleep induction and maintenance system, whereas the serotonergic system has an inhibitory or gating role, suppressing intrinsic cholinergic neurons (Hobson 1992). The role of serotonergic pathways in integrative neuromodulation and ASCs suggests that the differences in dreams reflect the lack of integrative influences of serotonergic pathways linking cognitive appraisal and ego systems. Shamanic practices induce this integration.

Functional Aspects of Integrative Consciousness

The use of procedures to alter consciousness by shamanistic practitioners is universal and has functional relationships to shamanistic goals. A range of evidence indicates that ASCs are functionally related to healing and divination activities in that they facilitate the actual occurrence of healing and information acquisition (Winkelman 1984, 1990b, 1992 chapter 10, and chapters 4 and 5 this volume). Research reviews (e.g., Shapiro 1980; Walsh 1979, 1980; Taylor, Murphy, and Donovan 1997) indicate that meditative traditions improve physical and psychological well-being. Adaptive functions of altering consciousness are reflected in the ability of hypnotic suggestibility to reduce those aspects of pain related to emotions, motivation, and cognition—forms of psychological distress. Relief of distress and of the discomfort aspects of pain through hypnosis are associated with activity in the fronto-limbic attentional system.[7] Crawford (1994) proposed that hypnotic analgesia is achieved by frontal cortex determination that incoming stimuli are irrelevant and by actively inhibiting somatosensory information from the thalamus.

Other adaptive functions of the integrative mode of consciousness are illustrated by research indicating that the hippocampal slow-wave states are an optimal level of brain activity for energy, orienting, learning, memory, attention, and efficient cognitive performance (Mandell

1980). Although ASCs are characterized by the dominance of activity from evolutionarily earlier parts of the brain, this condition of consciousness is not inferior to rational thought or to the left hemisphere's logical, rational verbal modes of experience. The predominance of right-hemisphere functioning, in contrast to left-hemisphere dominance of waking consciousness, links ASCs to unconscious mental activities that provide the basis for higher cognitive processes.

The triune brain model of MacLean (1973, 1990, 1993) provides a framework for explicating the functional aspects of ASCs. A central feature involves the evocation of activities of the paleomammalian brain or limbic system. The theta and alpha wave production is focused in the limbic system, which plays a vital role in subjective apperception in both emotional mentation and rational thought, using feelings for guiding behavior. Limbic system activities are responsible for an integrated sense of self, which provides a locus for memory and self-realization, generating the feelings of conviction and a sense of authenticity that are used to substantiate mental ideas, concepts, beliefs, and theories (MacLean 1990). The paleomammalian brain mediates patterns of social signaling that promote a sense of community and provide for cooperation—physically, socially, and mentally—in ways that enhance self-security. These structures of the "emotional brain" mediate emotions, social relations, bonding and attachment, and the sense of self that provides the basis for beliefs, certainty, and convictions.

ASCs stimulate the integration of the interconnected heritages of the instinctual responses of the reptilian brain, the autonomic emotional states of the paleomammalian brain, and the cognitive processes of the neomammalian brain. Behavior, emotions, and reason are synthesized in the integration of these three functional systems of the brain. These relationships are mediated physiologically and through ASCs, symbols, social representations, and information processes, which utilize social, affective, and symbolic information to mediate, evoke, and channel physiological processes.

The paleomammalian brain produces and uses information through facial expressions, vocalizations, actions, and gestures, which provide information about other minds and their motives and internal states. These communicative behaviors evoke similar experiences in other individuals, creating a common or collective awareness and affecting others' behaviors through the interpretations modeled. Emotional mentation involves subjective information pertinent to self-preservation, procreation, and socioemotional dynamics. These processes fundamental to self and well-being are evoked by ASCs. MacLean (1990) suggested that the primary functions of the limbic system involve modulation of affect to guide behavior, playing an important role in transforming emotional mentation into physiological effects on the organism. Emotional mentation can provoke profound physiological changes when the organism is confronted with situations that threaten or affront fundamental aspects of self, survival, and interpersonal attachments.

The paleomammalian brain's functions are central to concerns with emotions, sense of self, and social relations. Emotional processes play an important role in illness. The relationship of innate drives and needs, physical and social influences, and the representational systems of the brain constitutes the matrix for many different kinds of health problems—chronic anxiety and fears, behavioral disorders, conflicts, excessive emotionality or desires, obsessions and compulsions, dissociations, repression, and so forth. Processes that integrate different sources of information and that reassess their significance for the organism provide a basis for shamanistic healing.

Summary

Psychophysiological effects of ASCs involve common biological changes in brain and ANS functioning. These changes lead to a state of parasympathetic dominance in which the frontal cortex is synchronized by slow-wave patterns originating in lower centers of the brain. These patterns are driven by several mechanisms that have effects manifested in theta and alpha EEG, reflecting an integration of information transfer across the neuraxis. However, the three major types of ASCs revealed by cross-cultural research—shamanistic, mediumistic, and meditative—also have evidence of variation in addition to these common psychobiological conditions. Evaluation of the nature of ASCs requires the combination of three types of information: behavioral, physiological, and phenomenological (Locke and Kelly 1985). The following sections integrate behavioral and phenomenological ASC data from cross-cultural research (Winkelman and White 1987) with research on ASCs' physiological effects.

PSYCHOPHYSIOLOGY OF THE SHAMAN'S ASC

The shaman's ASC has been characterized as a magical flight, a soul journey, or an out-of-body experience during which the shaman's soul or spirit is believed to leave the body and enter into other worlds (Eliade 1964, 5). This experience is not one in which the shaman is possessed by spirits, but rather one in which the shaman exercises a control over the spirits, a control through which many tasks can be accomplished. The shaman's ASC may take other forms, including the vision quest experience and an animal transformation in which the practitioner becomes an animal. All ASCs involve entering into a nonordinary experiential world and engaging in interaction with spirit entities. The shamans may be selected through spontaneous ASC experiences, such as involuntary visions or dreams interpreted as signs from spirits. But the shamans then deliberately undertake a variety of experiences, exemplified in vision quests, where they induce ASC through a variety of procedures, such as fasting and water deprivation, exposure to temperature extremes, and various austerities, including sleep deprivation. Other typical procedures include extensive monotonous auditory stimuli (such as drumming and chanting) and extensive exercise (such as prolonged dancing to the point of collapse). The shamans may also use hallucinogens or other psychoactive substances, particularly tobacco. During the soul journey (which characterizes all shamans but not all of shaman's ASC), the practitioner appears unconscious but is actually engaged in activities in an experiential realm, which can be recounted on return.

The typical procedures for inducing the soul journey have common physiological[8] concomitants that underlie and contribute to the experiences. The extensive dancing and percussive activity leading to collapse and unconsciousness indicate sympathetic system activation to the point of exhaustion, which leads to parasympathetic dominance. The subsequent reports of the visionary experience indicate that, although during the parasympathetic dominant state the shaman may appear unconscious, experientially the shaman is aware. Harner (1982) emphasized the shaman's remembering what happens during the soul journey as a characteristic of the shaman's ASC.

Laughlin, McManus, and d'Aquili (1992) suggested that the ergotropic-trophotropic (sympathetic-parasympathetic) system activation and manipulation are responsible for these and other invariant features of shamanic and mystical experience. Hunt (1995a) suggested that the very deep rest produced by the physiological states involves profound muscular relaxation and induces a kind of "letting go" feeling. This physiologically induced experience, similar to those of deep meditative states, provides a deep sense of calm and, consequently, detachment and acceptance. These characteristics also derive from

the common effects of a number of procedures that induce an alpha-
theta dominant brain wave pattern.

Shamanic Induction Procedures

Extensive Motor Behavior.   Extensive motor behavior (such as
dancing), exertion, and fatigue result in hyperventilation and in oxygen and blood sugar depletion. Together these can cause hypoglycemia, the appearance of slow wave activity, and hallucinatory experience (Prince 1966; Strauss, Ostow, and Greenstein 1952; Engel, Ferris,
and Logan 1947), as well as elevated carbon dioxide levels, which
produce 3 to 5 cps brainwave activity (Leukel 1972). Prolonged periods of stereotypy (repetition of an invariant patterns of movement
without an observable goal, such as in pacing, drumming) produce
an increased rhythmicity and a general slowing of the EEG pattern
(Antelman and Caggiula 1980). Extensive dancing and percussion
behavior produce a slow-wave parasympathetic dominant state, especially when resulting in collapse. Dancing and stimulation of the
extremities are likely to induce the release of endogenous opiates
because the central opioid systems are activated by prolonged rhythmic exercise (Thoren et al. 1990) and exhaustive anaerobic exercise
(Rahkila, et al. 1987), with high-intensity exercise stimulating the
release of opioid peptide beta-endorphin (Sforzo 1989; Mougin et al.
1987).

Auditory Driving.   A universal feature of shamanistic healing
practices is the use of drumming, other percussion, singing, or chanting. This rhythmic auditory stimulation imposes a pattern on the brain,
driving entrainment of both alpha and theta waves (Neher 1961,
1962). Auditory driving creates visual sensations of color, pattern,
and movement, and leads to organized hallucinations, seizures, and
general emotional and abstract experiences (Neher 1962). The driving effects of drumming show a predominate activation of the EEG
in the theta range (Maxfield 1990; Wright 1991 for review). Activities such as chanting and music making are also capable of producing a driving response in the brain. Chanting and music produce
widespread EEG coordination, with a high index of common activity
in theta and low alpha among the experienced chanters, and dominance in the alpha band for naive listeners (Rogers 1976; Rogers and
Walters 1981). Neher (1962) found that the responses to auditory
driving parallel those of photic driving, which include (1) driving at

the frequency of stimulation; and (2) driving at alpha regardless of the frequency of stimulation (Vogel, Broverman, Klaiber, and Kun 1969). These findings suggested that the cortex is easily set into oscillation at the alpha frequency or slower and that singing, chanting, and percussion procedures produce or enhance this state of dominance of slow-wave frequencies. Oubré (1997) reviewed evidence indicating that chanting is a vocal communication system predates speech and that has the functions of creating group solidarity. This limbic-based communication system provides information about visceral states linking members of the group.

Fasting and Nutritional Restrictions.   Fasting induces in the body a hypoglycemic state, which can cause seizures (Leukel 1972), and increases susceptibility to driving influences on the EEG (Strauss, Ostow, and Greenstein 1952). Food and water deprivation have a direct effect on the pituitary and adrenal glands, which stimulate the hypothalamus and hippocampal-septal systems. Wallace (1961) discussed research and studies linking calcium deficiency to conditions characterized by neurological symptoms ranging from muscular spasms to major convulsions and seizures. Kehoe and Giletti (1981) extended Wallace's calcium deficiency hypothesis, arguing that nutritional deficiencies can contribute to changes in central nervous system functioning that facilitate the induction of ASCs. Gussler (1973) reviewed a range of dietary factors that affect serotonin synthesis and result in emotional disturbances, hallucinations, changes in cognitive and emotional functioning, and, in some cases, convulsions.

Sensory Deprivation and Stimulation.   Social isolation and reduction of motor behavior lead to an increase in cortical synchronization, a greater sensitivity to parasympathetic stimulation and a slowing of the alpha band with the emergence of delta waves (Gellhorn and Kiely 1972). Reduction or elimination of proprioceptive discharges, or an increase in muscular relaxation, leads to a parasympathetic dominant state with an increase in cortical synchronization (Gellhorn 1969). Sensory deprivation research indicated that the prolonged absence of environmental stimulation leads to hallucinatory experiences (Zubec 1969; Keup 1970). Reduction of sensory stimuli can lead to a loss of serotonin inhibition similar to the interference of hallucinogens in the serotonin synthesis and release (Mandell 1980). Extensive, prolonged, and intense sensory stimulation can lead to the same effects as sensory deprivation through habituation and the complete blockage of perception of stimuli. Sensory stimulation of a distressing nature, both physical and psychological, can result in the induction of an ASC.

Austerities and Endogenous Opiate Releasers. A variety of stimuli (burns, extreme cold, pain, injury, and toxic substances) all lead to hypertropic activity of the adrenal cortex and the secretion of the hormone ACTH (adrenocorticotropic hormone), contributing to the stimulation of sympathetic nervous system to collapse and resulting in a parasympathetic dominant state. Extremely painful stimuli can result in the direct stimulation of the hypothalamus and hippocampal-septal area, resulting in the emergence of synchronized slow-wave potentials in the EEG (Gellhorn and Loofbourrow 1963). Gellhorn (1969) pointed out that emotional stress can provoke the release of endogenous opiates. Increases in stress lead both to increased activity of the brain stem reticular formation and to 3 to 5 cps activity (Leukel 1972). In general, extreme emotional stimulation leads to sympathetic activation, which, when prolonged, can then lead to a rebound parasympathetic collapse. Shamanistic practices also release endogenous opiates through a variety of stressors (e.g., pain, fasting, water restriction, strenuous exercise, hyperstress of emotions, etc.). Endorphin levels increase as a result of stimulation of sensory endings associated with muscles and joints (e.g., long distance running), conditions also produced by the extensive dancing typically associated with shamanic activities. Exercise can also overwhelm temperature-regulation mechanisms and can cause increased circulation of endogenous opioids (Appenzeller 1987). Exposure to extreme cold will elicit both opioid and nonopioid pain inhibitory systems (Bodnar 1990; Kiefel, Paul, and Bodnar 1989). Endorphin release is provoked by extreme physical trauma and prolonged periods of high levels of stress (see Henry 1982; Pomeranz 1982; Gambert et al. 1981; Madden et al. 1977). Opiates directly affect the hypothalamus, producing slow wave activity (Henricksenet al. 1977), particularly a rapid increase in delta/theta brain waves and a reduction of fast-wave frequencies (Fink 1978). Opiates' slow wave effects increase susceptibility to driving influences from other induction procedures and contribute to the activation of the hypothalamic area, which receives projections from the pain receptors. A number of typical shamanic procedures result in the release of endogenous opiates or endorphins (Prince 1982a; cf. chapter 4 this volume). Endorphin levels are highest at night (Henry 1982), a typical time for shamanic activities. Austerities such as flagellation, self-inflicted wounds, exposure to temperature extremes, and feats of endurance all result in the release of endogenous opiates. The social bonding associated with shamanic ritual also induces opioid release (see chapters 2 and 4 this volume).

Hallucinogens.   A wide variety of psychoactive plant substances are utilized in shamanistic traditions (e.g., see Dobkin de Rios 1984; Furst 1976; Schultes 1972; Schultes and Hofmann 1979; Winkelman and Andritzky 1996). Some produce ASCs through actions on specific centers of the brain, whereas others produce their effects through toxic interactions with the body. The psychophysiological model presented here suggests that in either case the overall psychophysiological effects are similar because toxic substances can produce hallucinations, visions, seizure-induced ASCs, and a parasympathetic collapse (see Freedman and Kaplan 1967; Forster and Booker 1975). Although characterized by a number of different chemical structures and modes of action, hallucinogens produce a number of common physiological effects (Aghajanian 1982; cf. chapter 4 this volume). The chemical structures of these substances are closely related to the neural transmitters and alter consciousness through intervention in normal functioning of the neural transmitters (Hoffmeister and Stille 1982). The major hallucinogens (e.g., mescaline, peyote, psilocybin mushrooms, LSD) contain phenylalkylamine and indole alkaloids similar in chemical structure to the neural transmitter serotonin (Mandell 1985). They release the inhibitory effects on the mesolimbic temporal lobe structures, leading to synchronous discharges in the temporal lobe limbic structures (Mandell 1980). The hallucinogens' effects on the serotonin mechanism lead to inhibition of raphe cell regulation of the visual cortex and, consequently, to hyperactivity of the visual regions and the experience of an ongoing visual panorama. Common effects include production of high-voltage synchronous activity in the hippocampus, which may be maintained for days or weeks (Mandell 1980), and an overall effect of synchronization of the cortex (Fairchild et al. 1967). Although hallucinogens cause both sympathetic and parasympathetic excitation (Gellhorn 1969), they generally lead to a state of parasympathetic dominance. It is likely that all hallucinogens, known as such for their effects in producing the vision experience, have similar physiological effects in producing a state of hippocampal-septal slow-wave dominance, although they may act through different mechanisms. Effects of hallucinogens in the alteration of consciousness, particularly therapeutic effects, are covered in chapter 4.

The Temporal Lobe Syndrome and ASCs

The similarity of the shaman's ASC and possession to pathological states has been noted (e.g., see Ackerknecht 1943; Silverman 1967; Noll 1983; Siikala 1978; Hultkrantz 1978). But there is abundant evidence to substantiate that shamans are not pathological from their own culture's point of view, nor from the perspective of descriptive clinical diagnostic criteria (Noll 1983). Anthropologists have recognized, however, the presence of symptomology readily labeled as reflecting psychological disruptions or a labile nervous system in shamanistic practitioners while explicitly rejecting a pathological interpretation of the shaman's condition. Siikala (1978) characterized shamans as having a nervous condition, and Hultkrantz (1978) suggested hysteroid or hysterical traits and a hereditarily transmitted labile nervous constitution. However, both reject interpretations of mental disorder, pointing to evidence that shamans are among the best-adjusted people in their communities.

The physiological basis for the association between shamanistic ASCs and pathological symptomology is illustrated in Mandell's (1980) model of transcendent states. The physiological changes that result from central nervous system dysinhibitions associated with epilepsy and other temporal lobe discharge phenomena, as well as from other central nervous system conditions associated with trauma, toxicity, and seizure, involve the same basic pattern of brain changes that Mandell calls "transcendent consciousness" (cf. Wright 1989). The similarities of ASCs with psychopathological conditions are based in the increased facility that psychopathological conditions provide for entering ASCs and the physiological structures and processes common to both.

The presumption of pathology in ASC conditions is often derived from the similarity of those conditions to characteristics of epilepsy. *Epilepsy*[9] refers to a range of dysinhibitions or electrical discharge patterns of any of the lobes of the cortex, most frequently the temporal lobe. Epileptic electrical discharges are characterized by the dominance of a slow-wave pattern in the EEG that reflects common synchronous entrainments across diverse areas of the brain. The temporal lobe epileptic may experience fear, panic, and terror or experiences interpreted as ecstatic or religious. Some temporal lobe seizures consist primarily of subjective experiences of visual, auditory, tactile, or olfactory hallucinations; a distorted sense of time; or feelings of intense emotion, such as fear or ecstasy (Adams and Victor 1977). These episodes are occasionally followed by a decrease in awareness, motor automatisms, agitation, amnesia, and a need to sleep. Neppe (1981, 1983) showed temporal lobe phenomena to be associated with deja vu and subjective paranormal experiences.

Temporal lobe discharges can be deliberately induced, as illustrated in research on the hot and cold water baths used in India as part of ritual (Subrahmanyam 1972; Mani, Gopalakrishnan, et al. 1968; Mani, Mani, et al. 1972). Those baths result in temporal and generalized seizures in individuals without evidence of neurological disorder. The stimulation of the temporal lobe produces two typical experiences relevant to shamanic ASC. Penfield's (1975) studies of temporal lobe stimulation provoked two forms of response—"experiential" and "interpretive"— involving a "split" consciousness and a reinterpretation or change in the meaning of the ongoing experience. Mandell (1980) concluded that these experiences are mediated by limbic connections that present interpretations of experience to consciousness through nonverbal concepts.

The link of temporal lobe syndromes with shamanic practices is suggested by studies showing consistent personality changes associated with the temporal lobe syndrome. A number of neuroscientists[10] have suggested that the temporal lobe syndrome is associated with a distinct personality and behavioral syndrome characterized by emotional deepening, preoccupation with philosophical and religious interests, hyposexuality, hypergraphia (automatic writing), and an increased need for social affiliation. Temporal lobe epilepsy results in changes in the personality: aggressiveness, changes in sexual behavior, religiosity, and a deepening of affective response with the preservation of intellectual function (Waxman and Geschwind 1974).

These psychological changes associated with the temporal lobe conditions indicate why they are used in selecting shamanistic healers. In many cultures, the tremors and epilepsy are interpreted as signs of divine favor and selection for religious and healing roles. These conditions have adaptive value and contribute to the professional functions of shamanistic healers through "kindling," a long-lasting or permanently reduced threshold for neural excitability and greater susceptibility for entrance into ASCs because of previous seizure or excitation (Mandell 1980). These conditions play a primary role in the selection of individuals for shamanistic roles as mediums.

THE MEDIUMS AND POSSESSION ASC

Mediums are a distinctive type of shamanistic healer found primarily in societies with two or more levels of political integration beyond the local community. Mediums are frequently referred to as shamans, but mediums are empirically clustered in a group with different characteristics[11] in formal quantitative analysis (cluster analysis) (Winkelman 1986a, 1992). This illustrates the importance of differentiating shamans and mediums, particularly the medium's experience of possession, in which a spirit takes over the person's behavior.

All shamans and mediums engage in the deliberate alteration of consciousness, often initiated by illness, involuntary dreams, or visions. Mediums are characterized as having experiences leading to training for the practitioner status that occur beyond their control or intention. These possession experiences are culturally conceptualized as the personality of the individual being replaced by a spirit entity. It is this possession, rather than soul flight, that characterizes mediums' ASC. Although the initial ASC of the medium occurs spontaneously, the neophyte medium then engages in deliberate ASC-induction procedures (e.g., dancing, chanting, fasting, and ingestion of alcohol[12]). Once the medium has undergone training, ASC episodes generally no longer occur spontaneously, but only when the medium intends to enter ASCs. Nonetheless, the characteristics of the mediums' professional ASC still involve possession, with the medium being controlled by the possessing spirit. The medium is believed to lack control of what happens during the ASC, often reporting amnesia for all that transpired during that time. Although shamans' spirits could act outside of their direct control, shamans were generally thought to control the spirits, whereas the mediums were thought to act under compulsions from the spirit world.

The relationships of shamans and mediums to the socioeconomic conditions indicate that mediums are the form that ASC potentials take in societies with political integration beyond the local community. Those societies with political integration beyond the local community, and no mediums present, have shaman/healers (or healers with extensive use of ASCs). Shaman/healers may have provided the origin of the medium's role, with processes of political integration and social stratification being responsible for the social changes that prompt the transformation of these shamanistic potentials. The medium's lack of active seeking of ASCs indicates a discontinuity from the shamans' traditions. Furthermore, the association of specific psychophysiological conditions with possession suggests that it involves an ASC distinct from shaman's soul journey. The possession ASC of mediums showed symptoms of lability in the central nervous system— compulsive motor behavior, tremors, convulsions, seizures, and amnesia—that have been linked to the temporal lobe discharges (Mandell 1980; Winkelman 1986b, Wright 1989).

Concepts of Possession

A classic cross-cultural review of possession phenomena was provided by Oesterreich ([1921] 1966) in his *Possession Demoniacal and Other among Primitive Races, in Antiquity, the Middle Ages, and Modern Times*. Oesterreich showed a common pattern of possession experiences across time and cultures. Possessed people generally undergo such a dramatic transformation that it appears that they have become other people, manifesting changes in behavior, voice, expressions, movements, physiognomy, or appearance and the presentation of an alternate personality or identity. The continuity with similar possession phenomena in the modern world is illustrated by Goodman (1988). Oesterreich's and Goodman's reviews illustrated nearly identical cross-cultural cases, suggesting a common psychophysiological basis for possession experiences. A closer examination of the phenomena grouped under the lable "possession" illustrates that it has been used to refer to a wide range of phenomena—ASC, trance, dissociation, hysteria, spirit domination, displacement of personality, obsession, mental illness, and a variety of other conditions. To facilitate research about the putative phenomena, the present work has followed Bourguignon's (1968, 1976a,b) precedents in using the term "possession" in a more restricted way. Bourguignon demonstrated the utility of this distinction by showing its relationship to social conditions. Bourguignon distinguished possession trances from other types of spirit relationships established during trance. Bourguignon (1976a, 8) defined *possession trances* as those involving "alterations or discontinuity in consciousness, awareness or personality or other aspects of psychological functioning" that are accounted for by possession, a belief that a "person is changed in some way through the presence in or on him of a spirit entity or power, other than his own personality, soul [or] self." Bourguignon has also defined possession trances in a stronger sense as cases "in which the altered state is explained as due to a takeover (possession) of the body by a spirit entity" (Bourguignon and Evascu 1977, 198). The distinction of possession from other forms of ASCs has not been emphasized by some researchers (e.g., Peters and Price-Williams 1981; Siikala 1978; Heinze 1991), who have subordinated the differences between possession and soul flight to their commonality as ASCs. There is some justification for this subordination in the similarities of possession and soul flight as ASCs; nonetheless there are good grounds for distinguishing ASCs characterized as possession from soul flight and other forms of ASCs.

Social and Physiological Correlates of Possession

The cross-cultural findings (Winkelman 1986a,b, 1992) reported in the next paragraph have utilized Bourguignon and Evascu's (1977) more restrictive definition of possession as involving the "takeover" of the person by what is presumed to be an external spiritual entity. The practitioners and societies with possession have been examined with respect to their psychophysiological and social conditions.

Possession ASC and Societal Complexity. Societal differences in the incidence of possession ASC are revealed by cross-cultural analyses (Bourguignon and Evascu, 1977) that reported significant positive relationships of possession ASC to stratification, jurisdictional hierarchy, food production, and agriculture. Winkelman's (1986b, 1992) replication found that possession correlated positively with all social complexity variables from Murdock and Provost (1973) and significantly with most, particularly political integration, population density, and social stratification. But political integration was the only variable that independently explained significant variance. These results refine previous hypotheses, indicating that development of possession beliefs is specifically associated with political integration. But these political conditions account for only half of the variation in the distribution of these practices.

Physiological Correlates of Possession. A difference between shamanic flight and spirit possession is found in the association of the latter with amnesia. Although memory does occur in some situations of possession, amnesia does not occur with soul flight, and all cases of ASCs with amnesia are associated with possession (Winkelman 1986b, 1992). The amnesic aspects of possession have frequently been suggested as fraudulent. Oesterreich ([1921] 1966) rejected the fraud hypothesis for amnesia and possession on the basis that the extreme agitation, contortions, and dislocations could not be due to voluntary actions. The organic basis of amnesia and possession beliefs is revealed by differential involvement of the structures of the limbic system in various emotional manifestations (Wright 1989). The occurrence of amnesia with epilepsy and the empirical association of amnesia and possession suggest a relationship of the physiology to the beliefs. Cross-cultural research (Winkelman 1992) showed variables reflecting the temporal lobe syndrome—amnesia, spontaneous seizures, the rapid onset of illness, compulsive motor behavior (excessive, agitated, violent, or uncontrolled motor behavior apparently beyond the control of the practitioner), and the presence of tremors, or convulsions—were all positively and significantly correlated with possession. A temporal lobe measure based on compulsive motor behavior, tremors, and convulsions accounts for substantial variance in the societal incidences of possession beliefs, suggesting organic contributions to the incidence of possession ASC. The empirical association of possession with amnesia, convulsions, and spontaneous seizures supports the contention that the conditions are not faked, but rather that temporal lobe conditions contribute to predispositions to an ASC interpreted as possession. The relationship of possession with social conditions provides insight into why such associations may occur.

Combined Physiological and Social Predictors of Possession. Physiological measures (temporal lobe conditions) and social conditions (political integration) have independently significant correlations with possession (combined 75 percent of variance). But the physiological measure (temporal lobe discharge) accounted for greater explained variance (58 percent) than did political integration (40 percent), suggesting that psychophysiological factors are central to the basis that motivates the development of beliefs in possession. But societal conditions and institutional practices can contribute to the production of temporal lobe symptoms. The incidence of temporal lobe discharge in ASCs is significantly predicted by social variables; the most significant social complexity variable was social stratification (Winkelman 1990b). Social stratification apparently promotes seizure disorders leading to ASCs. Previous analyses (Winkelman 1986b, 1992) showed that possession ASCs traditions occur in the lower classes of stratified societies, indicating that their deprived status and resultant experiences may contribute directly to the physiological conditions. The predominance of women in possession ASC cults often corresponds to geographical areas in which women lack adequate nutrition (Gussler 1973). Possession may result from dietary and nutritional deficiencies, which can cause behavioral symptoms (e.g., tremors) similar to the temporal lobe syndrome (Kehoe and Giletti 1981). Dietary deficiencies can contribute to changes in the central nervous system that result in emotional disturbances and seizures (Gussler 1973). Epilepsy and other temporal lobe syndromes may be acquired as a result of metabolic imbalances such as hypocalcemia and hypoglycemia (Forster and Booker 1975; Adams and Victor 1977). Thus social conditions creating dietary deficiencies may be responsible for physiological conditions that predispose individuals to seizures and the interpretations of their conditions as possession.

Active ASC Induction and Temporal Lobe Control. Possession conditions may also reflect the absence of cultural traditions that provide early direct training in ASCs. Training in ASCs may affect the manifestation of temporal lobe discharge conditions that contribute to possession interpretations. Although the shamans generally deliberately seek their ASCs, mediums typically have illness and seizures overwhelm them before seeking training. Shamans induce ASCs deliberately and seek their positions at earlier ages (childhood or puberty) than mediums (late adolescence and early adulthood). This appears related to the differences in the manifestation of seizure phenomena and possession interpretations. Active ASC induction may prevent involuntary induction of the physiologically triggered states by developing conscious or ritual control over these psychophysiological discharges. The shamans, like the mediums, may also have personality configurations disposing them to ASC experiences, exemplified in the involuntary visions and dreams indicating their selection. But the shamans are not possessed, nor do they suffer from seizures and amnesia. Through early involvement in ASC training, shamans may avoid such conditions. This notion that shamans' active ASC induction leads to control of physiological predispositions to spontaneous ASCs is supported by the finding that deliberate induction of ASCs may inhibit seizures (Mandell 1980).

Drug-Induced ASCs and Temporal Lobe Discharges. The relationship of drug induced ASCs to temporal lobe symptoms was examined at both the level of the individual practitioners and at the societal level (Winkelman 1990b, 1992). Among shamanistic healers with temporal lobe discharge symptoms or drug-induced ASCs, the use of hallucinogens has a strong negative correlation with temporal lobe discharge symptoms. A similar relationship is found at the societal level, with use of hallucinogens significantly and negatively correlated with temporal lobe discharges. These findings suggest that when societies use hallucinogens in their institutionalized ASC-induction procedures, this usage tends to preclude seizure disorders associated with their practitioners' ASC. This active versus passive approach may be responsible for the negative relationship of drug-induced ASC and seizures in that active ASC induction may prevent involuntary ASC and possession experiences. This prevention of seizure-induced ASC may be achieved by developing conscious or ritual control or release of these psychophysiological discharges through drug action. The lack of deliberate training early in life contributes to the involuntary aspects when internal physiological imbalances predispose individuals to spontaneous ASCs later in life. Political and religious hierarchies preempt the individual autonomy and control characteristic of hunter-gatherer societies, making possession and its claims of powerlessness adaptive for mediums.

Conceptualizations of Possession

The definition of *possession* proposed by Bourguignon (1976a,b) does not represent all emic perceptions of the phenomena. Uses of the term possession by anthropologists and others have often carried negative and pathological implications; cultural conceptions of the desirability of the phenomenon have often taken opposing stances. This is illustrated in Goodman's (1988, 2) definition of possession as a situation in which a "supplicant asks a being of the other, the alternate reality, who possesses no physical body of its own, to descend into his/her body for the duration of the ritual and to use it as it sees fit." This definition emphasizing possession as an invited phenomena is elaborated by Asante (1984), who argued that transcendent states of consciousness are found in African religions in the phenomenon of possession. The African traditions of transcendence do not emphasize the withdrawal characteristic of the ascetic traditions but embody enlightenment in possession as a " 'perfect harmony' with self, nature, and the universe" (Asante 1984, 173). In possession "it is not the person who is being possessed, but the gods and goddesses. Therefore, the act of possession always starts as an act of volition on the part of the person, not on the part of the gods. The person possesses the 'gods' through searching in the proper mode and finding harmony" (174-75).

Brazilian spiritists provide further differentiation of possession (Krippner 1987). "Grade One Possession" is "obsession," in which people feel under the control of an alien spirit but retain their basic sense of self and identity. This can be seen as corresponding to an obsessive-compulsive neurosis. "Grade Two Possession" involves cases interpreted as past-life personalities or splits within the individual's psyche. This can be viewed as a hysterical personality syndrome that results from the development of a negative alter personality. "Grade Three Possession" involves the control of the individual via the influence of another human, as is attempted in the practice of sorcery or witchcraft. "Grade Four Possession" and "Grade Five Possession" involve cases in which the individual is believed to be controlled by other spirits who may inhabit their bodies.

This discussion of the different spirit influences during possession illustrates that it involves a variety of relations, which is illustrated in Boddy's (1994) characterization of possession as involving relationships and boundaries that are flexible and negotiable. Typologies for classifying possession phenomena (e.g., Shekar 1989) illustrate that it cannot be reduced to a single conceptual entity. Possession involves a wide range of psychodynamics, psychosocial conditions, and therapeutic mechanisms, as well as variant degrees of influence (e.g., domination, influence, obsession). Even the pathological models of possession subsume a range of phenomena. Shekar grouped the different theories of possession into three categories—dissociation, communication, and expectation or sociocultural explanations—and these are concerned with pathology, communication, and self/social transformation.

Possession as Pathology. The pathological approaches have characterized possession as hysterical dissociation and a mechanism for dramatic symbolic enactments of conflictive situations, including the expression of repressed desires that are unacceptable to the ego or to social norms. Possession is often associated with "glazed eyes, psychomotor activity, change in facial expression and voice quality, and constricted attention, . . . sleep disturbances, depressed mood, psychosomatic ailments, anxiety, and panic attacks" (Ward 1989a, 29), conditions often associated with neurotic disorders, suggesting that some cases of possession involve pathological states. Indeed, possession experiences are often in response to traumatic, disturbing personal afflictions or adversities (Ward 1989b), and contemporary diagnoses of multiple personality disorder are similar to possession (cf. chapter 5 this volume).

Possession as Communication.   Shekar (1989) characterized possession enactments as an assumption of the sick role, which affects the action of socially significant others toward the possessed person, providing personal, emotional, social, and material benefits. Although this view may also be assimilated within the pathological models as a culturally specific form of expressing distress, the pathological models fail to consider the cultural interpretation of the events labeled as possession and their significance in reference to broader cultural norms (Ward 1989b). Crapanzano and Garrison (1977) (cf. Garrison and Crapanzano 1978) used contextual analysis of possession to show it to have multiple significance, serving as "an idiom for articulating a certain range of experience" (Crapanzano and Garrison 1977, 10). Explicating the communicational intent requires consideration of spirits' roles in the person's world, their effects on behavior, and their cultural meanings. Such analyses reveal the role of possession in shifting responsibility from self to other, objectifying emotions in terms and referents that transcend the other, and placing the locus of responsibility in the broader social order. These communication idioms may function even for those not suffering pathological distress (Lambeck 1989) and nonetheless contribute to health, modulating relationships in both public and private life and providing a social support network. Kinship terms extended in cult membership provide primary relations in the context of separation from natal kin. Possession plays a role in managing problems of everyday life and in changing relationships between wives and husbands, enabling women to indirectly make demands and to achieve catharsis of emotions. Possession experiences can also provide identity changes that alter power relations and interpersonal hierarchies. Possession provides women with a social resource for managing stress and exerting social power.

Possession as Normative Behavior.   The sociocultural explanations see possession as a phenomenon that people emulate because of repeated exposure to its normative manifestations across their development. Possession has adaptive functions, including political, theatrical, expressive, and therapeutic ones. "Possession cults are flexible and continuously transformative. . . . They have to do with one's relationship to the world, with selfhood—personal, ethnic, political, and moral identity" (Boddy 1994, 414). Possession plays a role in flexibly articulating relations between reference groups and in rendering benefits of group membership, particularly for women under conditions of patrilocal marital residence and class oppression. The possessing spirits provide ties of kinship and a "third party enabling them to negotiate their self-constitutive interaction" (423). Boddy (416) characterized possession as actively working on behalf of women and their families through channeling the assistance of spirits. These responsibilities are often confronted with dramatic changes that must be accommodated to traditional frameworks of interpretation. Possession consequently functions as both modes of cultural resistance and inspired change, constituting forms of identity formation and self-transformation.

Epistemological Perspectives. The importance of possession for understanding alternate views of reality is emphasized by Boddy (1994, 407): "Spirit possession rests on epistemic premises quite differently from the infinitely differentiating, rationalizing, and reifying thrust of global materialism." Possession has epistemological implications for the nature of knowledge, self as knower, and the process of learning. Epistemological concerns are primarily focused on the nature of the knower, on selfhood and identity, and on the nature of the other, including external powers. Possession provides a mechanism for the incorporation of various "others" in the development of self. Possession can be used to reformulate identity and to provide for other mechanisms of self-expression and knowledge. Possession involves forms of knowing, "epistemic states" based in a reciprocal and reversible relationship between knower and known, with the knower implicated in the knowledge by being bodily possessed by it (425). Csordas (1993) linked these knowledge processes to "somatic modes of attention," the basis through which our bodies objectify our knowledge and incorporate the presence of others. Interaction with these others is the basis for constructing our intersubjectivities through a body language. This knowing is an intimate corporeal act embodied in possession. "[T]he body is the ground for legitimating objective knowledge, internalizing it, and making it experientially real [or originating it]; objectification is the process of rendering embodied knowledge graspable by others through performance and conversation" (Boddy 1994, 425–26). These epistemological perspectives are central to meditative ASC.

MEDITATIVE ASC

Meditative traditions go back more than three thousand years (Walsh 1988) and have manifestations in cultures around the world. Meditation is traditionally associated with religious traditions of Asia (e.g., Hinduism, Buddhism, Taoism). Material from early Christian, Islamic, and Judaic religions illustrates a wider distribution of meditative traditions (West 1987a; Walsh 1983; Brown, B., 1974). Meditation practices are also found outside of religious traditions in secular meditation activities (West 1987a). Shamanistic healing traditions found cross-culturally (Winkelman 1984, 1986a, 1992) utilize many ASC procedures for both practitioners and clients that are common to those found in meditative practices, including repetitive chanting, percussion and music, fasting, sensory isolation and austerities, and ritual activities that focus and occupy attention. The shamanistic practitioners with meditative or yogic ASCs were not associated with any particular socioeconomic conditions besides their presence in agricultural rather than hunting-gathering societies. Some of the shamanistic healing practices identified in this cross-cultural study have obvious connections with the classic mystical traditions, such as the Japanese Buddhist ascetic and the Kurd dervishes. Other less obvious but perhaps more illuminating examples come from the Roman Eastern Cults, which were of Eastern or Oriental origin (Winkelman 1992; cf. Cumont 1956). Yet underlying the diversity of practices and traditions are fundamental commonalities that reflect the foundational neurognostic structures.

Although the meditative practices have many universal aspects, even those who claim universal features also point to a number of distinct forms of consciousness manifested in meditation. This diversity of forms illustrates the necessity of a neurophenomenological approach to examining meditative experience in terms of the relationships of physiological and phenomenological aspects of the practices to the intentionalities of the practitioners. This is exemplified by research on EEG patterns in meditators, which illustrates that physiological parameters vary between traditions but coincide with phenomenological descriptions of meditative conditions—control, focus, coordination, integration, and insight. Meditative traditions provide further evidence of neurognostic phenomena in commonalities among diverse meditative traditions, including agreements about the nature, processes, and stages of development of consciousness. Commonalities in meditation practices are addressed in terms of the physiology of meditation; the processes of contemplative development; the development of attention; the constructed nature of perception; the development of new senses of self and identity; and views of the levels of consciousness. The different senses of self are examined as a basis for constructing a neurologically based epistemological system that explains differences in the meditative ASCs and the integrative mode of consciousness.

Definitions of Meditation

Although *meditation* has a plethora of definitions, many agree about core concerns. Meditation traditions share the goal of changing attentional processes, turning consciousness upon itself to develop control of attention and the processes of consciousness (Pekala 1987; Goleman 1977). Shapiro (1990, 101) similarly suggested:

Meditation is a family of techniques which have in common a conscious attempt to focus attention in a nonanalytical way and an attempt not to dwell on discursive, ruminating thought . . . helping an individual feel a sense of alignment, harmony, non-duality with the deepest wisdom of the universe. As a result of this experience, a person "wakes up" and recognizes an interconnectedness with the universe, others, and one's self. . . . [A] second goal of the meditative traditions is how to utilize that altered states experience, not as an end in itself, but as a source of inspiration for subsequent lifestyle and behavioral change.

West (1987a, 10) defines meditation as "an exercise in which the individual turns attention or awareness to dwell upon a single object, concept, sound, image, or experience, with the intention of gaining greater spiritual or experiential and existential insight, or achieving improved psychological well-being." Walsh (1983, 19) offered a definition that synthesizes many of these perspectives:

The term "meditation" refers to a family of practices that train attention in order to heighten awareness and bring mental processes under greater voluntary control. The ultimate aims of these practices are the development of deep insight into the nature of mental processes, consciousness, identity and reality, and the development of optimal states of psychological well-being and consciousness. However, they can also be used for a variety of intermediate aims, such as psychotherapeutic and psychophysiological benefits.

Neurophenomenological Perspectives on Meditative Commonalities

Investigators of diverse meditation traditions have concluded that underlying the variety of cultural forms are common objectives, practices, processes, and stages of development (West 1987a; Walsh 1980, 1988; Wilber 1977, 1980). These commonalties constitute a perennial psychology (Wilber 1977) and perennial philosophy (Smith 1975). Consensus about the nature of consciousness, the functions of the human mind, the mind's construction of reality, and the varying forms of consciousness reflect their empirical experiential approach to the study of consciousness. Walsh refers to these meditative traditions as consciousness disciplines (Walsh1980) and as Asian psychologies (Walsh 1988), emphasizing their empirical approach to the nature of human psychology and consciousness. Laughlin et al. (1992) referred to these meditative traditions as contemplative traditions, reflecting their emphasis on examination of the nature of human consciousness and its operations. These traditions constitute "state specific sciences of consciousness" concerned with the nature and the development of consciousness, both ordinary and transcendental. Their focus on observation of subjective, or internal, experience and on reporting on its processes provides a basis for understanding consciousness.

These meditative traditions involve an examination of the relationship between the knower and the phenomena known through transcendental inquiry (Wilber 1979). This inquiry and validation are based on the mental processes of injunction to proceed in certain ways to produce observable experiences; the experience, apprehensions, and observations; and the subsequent mental and social verification or confirmation of the experience. The verification process occurs in a different mode and epistemic structure than does the observation, with language and social norms employed to verify perceptions derived from experiences that are transrational and transverbal.

Laughlin et al. (1992) characterized contemplative development as involving maturational processes that reflect the development of structural features of human neurophysiology through the conscious application of the individual to his or her own development. They characterized these developments as relatively rare because they require both considerable effort and the supportive social institutions and "technologies" to transform the relation of the physical substratum with the mental realm. The symbolic reorganization of the functioning of the neurobiological systems derives from the role of symbols in communication between the conscious and the unconscious aspects of the nervous system and in the ritual manipulation of neurognostic structures to activate specific patterns of response within the nervous system. Laughlin et al. (1992) propose that manipulations of the ANS (the ergotropic-trophotropic balance) are the basis for experiences of higher phases of consciousness. These experiences are characterized by homeomorphogenetic relationships of the ergotropic-trophotropic nervous system events with experiences of centering and movement of psychic energy, the result of proprioceptive sensing of ANS and endocrinal activities or those of the sympathetic plexus. The recurrent integration of cultural symbols with the evocation of sequences of ANS activation enables subsequent symbolic ritual evocation and manipulation of physiological processes, based on previous association and homeomorphogenenic recruitment and resonance (Laughlin et al. 1992).

The universal features of meditative traditions reflect the neurophysiological structures that produce the cross-cultural patterns. The recurrent features of contemplative traditions reflect awareness of neurognostic structures achieved through examination of attentional, perceptual, and conceptual processes, and through this examination, developing an ability to control physiological responses including EEG, respiration, pain, oxygen consumption, and bleeding (see Taylor, Donovon, and Murphy [1997] for review).

Meditation and the Brain

Different disciplines may produce different autonomic conditions and psychophysiological responses to stimuli while in the meditative state (e.g., see Kasamatsu and Hirai 1966; Anand, China, and Singh 1961). There are also some fundamental physiological similarities across disciplines: a shift toward parasympathetic dominance (e.g., reductions in cortical arousal, in muscle tension, in skin conductance, in cardiac function, and in respiration rate) (Gellhorn and Kiely 1972); an overall decrease in frequency of the brain wave pattern to alpha and theta ranges; and an increase in alpha and theta amplitude and regularity in the frontal and central regions of the brain (Wallace and Benson 1972; Davidson 1976; Kasamatsu and Hirai 1966). These similarities involve the same basic systemic physiological changes associated with the integrative mode of consciousness—a parasympathetic dominant state with enhanced theta and systemic neural integration.

Because meditation emphasizes an internally focused receptive mode, early investigators suggested that meditation was a right-hemisphere experience, in contrast to the external, active, logical, analytical, and verbal aspects of left-hemisphere mentation. However, the hypothesis of meditation as primarily a right-hemisphere phenomenon has not been supported by research. Meditation does apparently involve right-hemisphere activation, particularly as it involves an active effort to inhibit verbal-analytical thought, to control attention, and to focus on visual imagery. The early stages of meditation may involve a relative shift toward right-hemisphere mentation as habitual left-hemisphere activities (language, logic, etc.) are deliberately suspended and activities more characteristic of right-hemisphere mentation are then allowed to emerge (nonverbal, preverbal, and imagetic constructs). However, advanced states of meditation involve suspension of the activity of both frontal hemispheres.

Pagano and Warrenburg (1983) reported that long-term practice of transcendental meditation (TM) produces greater right-hemisphere involvement. But they concluded that "meditation does not appear to globally facilitate RH- [right-hemisphere] specialized task performance, nor to globally impair LH-specialized task performance" (Pagano and Warrenburg 1983, 187). Delmonte (1987b) reviewed research indicating that those who are inclined to adhere to meditative practice have a predisposition to nonverbal right-hemisphere absorption and activities. However, a predominance of right-hemisphere processes is not found at advanced stages of meditation, which inhibit cognitive functions and activity of both hemispheres (Delmonte 1987a). Advanced meditators are concerned with the automatized attentional processes of the lower brain centers, which meditators reelevate to conscious control. Rather than an increased right-hemisphere activation, the overall pattern is one of interhemispheric integration and synchronization, which reflect activation of lower brain structures. Stroebel and Glueck (1980) suggested that passive meditation leads to a reduction of affective outflow from the limbic structures and to enhanced interhemispheric transmission of signals. A range of studies indicated an increase in coherence, particularly in long-term meditators, which has been interpreted to mean that meditation creates spatial ordering of the central nervous system and a coherent ordering of brain function. Fenwick (1987, 109) questioned this interpretation but agreed that "there is synchronization and spreading out of spindling within the thalamic structures, thus causing an increased similarity of spectral frequencies in different cortical areas."

Evidence that meditation leads to an increase in slow-wave brain patterns has been available since the early 1960s (Kasamatsu and Hirai 1966). Kasamatsu and Hirai's research on Zen teachers and advanced students showed typical changes in brain waves involving an increase in alpha waves, which then decrease in frequency toward strong "frontally dominant theta rhythms (five to seven cycles per second), during which meditators report peaceful, drifting, and generally pleasant experiences" (Taylor, Murphy, and Donovon 1997, 58). Fast-wave beta activity has been reported among advanced meditators during deep meditative states involving yogic ecstasy and intense concentration; but in general the EEG during meditation shows an overall decrease in frequency of the brain wave pattern to alpha and theta ranges and an increase in alpha and theta amplitude and regularity in the frontal and central regions of the brain (Wallace and Benson 1972; Davidson 1976; Kasamatsu and Hirai 1966; Stroebel and Glueck 1980). An increased density of alpha rhythms, especially in the occipital areas, is followed by the alpha frequencies sweeping forward to the frontal areas, a slowing of the alpha rhythms, and appearance of theta, especially in the frontal areas (Stroebel and Glueck 1980).

Increased theta activity as a function of a meditator's competence substantiates attentional development because the sustained low-amplitude theta is associated with sustained attention. A range of studies showed that meditation produces a synchronization within the thalamic structures and a greater coherence across different cortical areas (Fenwick 1987), as reflected in experiences of harmony and integration. The similar effects of hallucinogens (Mandell 1985) suggest that increased interhemispheric coherence is a property sui generis of the integrative mode of consciousness.

The physiological findings of increased interhemispheric synchronization, a relative decline in left-hemisphere activation, and greater coherence or integration across cortical areas are consistent with what the contemplative disciplines themselves consider to be the consequences of meditation on the functioning of the human mind and consciousness. These neurophenomenological correspondences illustrate the importance and the value of seeking the concordance between physical and phenomenological data. Commonalities across meditative traditions that reflect these neurological processes include the nature of attentional processes; the operation of perception; the nature of human identity and self; and the different forms or levels of consciousness and their characteristics.

Attention.   One commonality in meditative traditions is retraining attention to induce ASC and greater concentration and awareness. A central objective in the retraining of attention is an enhancement of the ability to concentrate on specific ideas, objects, or tasks; to focus attention for an extended period of time; and to achieve awareness of pure attention (Odajnyk 1993). The focus on the intentional manipulation of attention and on the development of greater control results in an increased awareness of unconscious mental processes and in insight into the nature and process of mental operations. A common point of meditative traditions is that most human behavior is mindless and unconscious, a kind of culturally induced hypnosis in which people habitually identify with their ego, thoughts, and behaviors (Walsh 1983). Changes in attentional processing reverse habituation, increase perceptual awareness, and lead to a reduction in habituation to external stimuli (Taylor et al. 1997). Deautomatization of habitual mental processes and interference with the automatization process free up mental energy and affect the entire psychological structure (Odajnyk 1993). Meditation enhances preattentive processes, visual imagery ability, and internal locus of control (Taylor et al. 1997) This development of attention permits enhancement of awareness through disidentification with one's mental content. When concentration becomes habitual and automatized, it creates a complex that enables an autonomous and permanent process of meditation, enhancing all levels of awareness. Meditation literature (e.g., Shapiro 1990; Walsh 1983; Goleman 1977; Ornstein 1972) indicates two principal attentional strategies. The primary differences contrast: (1) awareness, mindfulness, or insight meditation, characterized by a focus on the field or on the contents of mind, consciousness, or awareness; and (2) concentrative meditation, characterized by a development of focus of attention on a specific object or activity (e.g., breath). Castillo (1991) described three stages in the development of attention in meditation in the Yoga-Sutra: (1) *dharana* (fixed attention); (2) *dhyana* (continuous attention); and (3) *samadhi* (coalescent attention). Fixed attention, holding the attention of personal consciousness on a specific object of meditation, is followed by continuous attention, the holding of attention on the object of fixed attention without a sense of self-consciousness. Coalescent attention becomes so concentrated that all awareness of the external world is lost, resulting in the experience of void or nothingness, in which all that exists for the meditator is attention. This extreme concentration of attention results in the loss of sense of self or personal consciousness.

Perception. Claxton (1987a) characterized Buddhist meditation as involving the analysis and understanding of perception. The awareness of the habitual perceptual and cognitive processes leads to a cessation of the ordinary unconscious projective and associative processes (Odajnyk 1993). Delmonte (1987b) characterized concentrative meditation techniques as constricting or shrinking the perceptual field to facilitate reorganization of the construct system. This focus facilitates grasping the constructed nature of perception. Examination of the construction of perception and experience provides awareness that the foundations of ordinary perceptions are based in unconscious and inaccurate assumptions (Claxton 1987a, 25–26). This awareness leads to the realization that the objects of the world of perception are interdependent characteristics derived from one's mental models. Meditative practices inhibit "all four psychological functions—sensation, thinking, feeling, and intuition" (Odajnyk 1993, 57). With the deautomization of the cognitive constructs habitually employed, one is then capable of observing them. Suspension of habitual constructs also permits awareness of the nonverbal, somatic, and imagetic processes.

Presentational Intelligence

Hunt (1995a,b,c) characterized meditative traditions as constructing systems of knowledge from microgenetic imagetic features of biologically based perceptual and conceptual systems. Hunt's perspective was derived from a synthesis of the perspectives of Heidegger, of Mahayana Buddhism, and of the ecology of perception. These cross-cultural and cross-disciplinary commonalities point to neurognostic structures of human perception, mind, and knowledge. Contemplative traditions involve cognitive processes based in presentational states "understood as a reconstitution on the level of symbolic cognition of presence-openness as the basic structure of perception in motile sentient creatures" (Hunt 1995c, 220). Hunt suggested that "these states manifest exactly the same cross-modal metaphoric processes as in all symbolic cognition. The difference is that transpersonal states show the structures of symbolic cognition unfolding presentationally, for their own sake" (199). Although these states are based on experiential capacities that are strictly human, they are derived from basic structures of perception shared by all motile organisms (200).

Mystical experiences focus on the microgenetic iconic stages of perception and geometric perceptual patterns that provide the basis for the more complex and abstract mental processes based on rearrangement of simpler schema through cross-modal synesthesia. The neurophysiological basis of these perceptions is indicated by the common forms and experiences reported by contemplatives cross-culturally and found in the phenomena of hallucinatory constants and entoptic phenomena. These structures are given cultural explanation, but they reflect an immediate perception of sensory events before interpretation, experiences that are universal because of their neurognostic basis. They provide a metaphoric vehicle for meaning, "as an abstract presentational metaphor also based on cross-modal synesthetic translation" (Hunt 1989, 191). These experiences include the "white light experiences" and the imagined body that are widely reported in mystic and shamanic traditions. Hunt characterized the "light-of-the-void" experience, a luminescent glow, as the most basic quality of the visual system and, through cross-modal translation, a metaphor for openness. The meditative traditions use these metaphors for expressing knowledge of consciousness itself, as embodied in the concept of "enlightenment." Light as the most basic quale provides an inclusive metaphor for the totality of consciousness. Contemplative traditions also employ darkness and concepts of body image, self, and other. Hunt (1995) suggested that luminosity involved at the basis of visual microgenesis provides the metaphor for the totality or absolute experience of light. These cross-modal translations provide the basis for the sense of presence and openness that underlies presentational capacities of human intelligence. The source of synesthesias is in the translations between different sensory modalities, which provide a basis for symbolic meanings. These meanings are felt meanings, reflecting "a cross-translation and transformation between the modality-specific properties of the tactile-kinesthetic body image and the visual field" (Hunt 1995b, 157). Hunt suggested that the vortex tunnel experiences found in many mystical traditions as well as the "hollow body" chakra experiences "can be understood as a complex synesthesia between this 'hollow' tactile structure and the symmetrical funnel or cone of the visual field itself" (158). Hunt also suggested that evidence that these mystical experiences derive from cross-modal integration is provided by introspective studies that illustrated phenomena similar to the "white light" experiences. Hunt reviewed research that suggested that advanced meditators have more direct access to the experiences provided by properties of their visual field and enhanced visual spatial intelligence (Hunt 1995a,b).

Hunt (1995b) characterized meditative development of the presentational symbolic capacity as involving a special form of self (witnessing consciousness) that "comes to observe its own developed forms as the immediate medium for presentational felt meanings—the more diffuse the patterns thereby synthesized (space, bodily presence, and holding), the more all-inclusive the felt significance" (Hunt 1995b, 131). Symbolic imagery accommodates to the self in meditation, allowing a development beyond concrete projective mechanisms through the utilization of abstract qualities found in the physical world (e.g., light, space, and energy) as abstract metaphors for consciousness and self (paraphrase Hunt 1995b, 119).

Self: Divided Consciousness and Enlightenment

A central consequence of the meditative traditions is a dramatic change in the nature of identity. The increased attention that an individual pays to internal experiences during meditation necessarily leads the individual to increases in self-conscious and self-evaluation (West 1987b), a greater psychological differentiation, and clearer understanding of one's own psychological needs and attributes (Carrington 1987). Walsh suggests that this examination leads to a deconstruction of the permanent sense of self. A commonality of meditative disciplines is their emphasis that individuals have false beliefs about the nature of the self, derived from mindless and unconscious automatic information processing. Unlearning conditioning and automatic processing leads to the realization that one's notion of self and individual identity is distorted and illusory, maintained by a lack of awareness of the unconscious processes that serve to construct the perception of continuity of identity (Walsh 1988). Meditation practices bring about a greater awareness by disrupting habitual conditioning and identification with thought and behavior. The development of greater attention and awareness and a dishabituation from one's habitual identifications and reactions reveal that the appearance of a continuous sense of self is a selective and arbitrary construction from fluctuating mental contents, and only one of many possible ideal selves that the individual presents to the social world.

Castillo (1991) analyzed Hindu yogis as involved in development of co-conscious selves and divided consciousness. The personal self, or *jiva*, participates in the world, in contrast to the uninvolved observing self, called witness and *atman*. Participating consciousness is "physical, impermanent, and engaged with the world, . . . performs actions in accordance with social norms, . . . [and] is comprised of the personal mind, thoughts, emotions, sensations, and memories" (Castillo 1991, 1–2). *Atman* or *purusha*,[13] observing consciousness or witnessing self, is "nonphysical, permanent (immortal), an uninvolved witness of the physical self and the world . . . and experiences those actions as if they were performed by someone else" (1). The goals of yoga are the separation of these two aspects of self and consciousness. The control of attention permits transcendence of the participating self through the development of attention to the point where only the experience of attention itself exists. Training of attention allows for a permanent meditational attention in addition to the habitual focus on everyday activities. Permanent development of this inner consciousness is referred to as *atman*, "True Self," Witness, or Looker (Castillo 1991). Meditators experience both aspects of consciousness simultaneously through restraining participating consciousness. The ultimate goal of yoga meditation, the separation of the observing self or true self (*atman*) from the participating self or false self (*jiva*) is referred to as *moksha*, meaning liberation. With liberation, the observing self only witnesses events (does not participate in them) and is therefore freed from the pain and suffering that come from an identification with the personal self. Castillo suggested that this split in consciousness is recognized within Western psychiatry as a state of depersonalization, the experience of being detached from one's own body or mental processes. In depersonalization, one is an uninvolved witness to one's own behavior, with the feeling that one's personality is unreal and not associated with one's identity; this is the essence of the observing self.

Contemplative Views of the Post-Formal Development of Consciousness

Disparate meditative traditions recognize similar features of consciousness, including specific layers or levels of the functioning of consciousness that correspond substantially with conceptual frameworks of Western science. Wilber contended that underlying the conceptual frameworks of different meditative traditions are the same deep structures of consciousness that are recognized in Western and Eastern psychologies and religious philosophies' views of cognitive, emotional, motivational, social, moral, physical, and cognitive evolution (e.g., Wilber 1977, 1980, 1986). Wilber characterized development of consciousness in terms of the evolution of the self, which proceeds through fixed ordered stages that constitute a universal hierarchy of development. These stages incorporate Piaget's four basic stages (sensorimotor, preoperational, concrete operational, and formal operational thought), but they extend beyond formal operational thought in a series of transpersonal stages of development (vision-logic, psychic, subtle, causal, and ultimate or absolute levels of consciousness).

Alexander, Davies, et al. (1990) and Alexander, Robinson, et al. (1994) analyzed the meditative system of Maharishi's Vedic psychology and suggested forms of consciousness both similar to and different from those of Wilber, even though Wilbur also uses Vedic perspectives. Vedic psychology views the development of the higher stages of consciousness as involving systems underlying all dimensions of human consciousness—perception, action, affect, self, cognition, and ethics (Alexander, Davies, et al. 1990, 52). But their states of consciousness begin with sleeping, dreaming, and waking, followed by transcendental, cosmic, glorified cosmic, and unity consciousness. Although these states address many of Wilber's stages, and even use the same terms, they do not correspond exactly. In particular they differ in not characterizing these states as having an inherent developmental sequence. "According to Vedic psychology, because all the fundamental structures or levels of mind are inherent, they can thus be experienced whenever awareness settles down to a sufficient degree" (56). The states emphasize the importance of a multidimensional approach; rather than a single domain of development, the transcendental developments involve integration of a number of different domains and specialized mental faculties.

Hunt (1995a) suggested that mystical experiences represent lines of intellectual and affective development not addressed by the cognitive emphasis of the Piagetian approach. But Hunt rejected the view that this development is post-formal or post-representational. Instead, he suggested that it involves achievement of formal capabilities within affective lines of development. "The affective schemata covers the side of cognition involving energetics, valuation, feeling, and the experience of self and other. They are most immediately reflected in dream symbolism" (Hunt 1995b, 118). Piaget suggested that affective development would lag behind intellectual development because it lacked a fixed point of accommodation, which the physical world provided for intellectual development. Hunt suggested that a framework for affective development is provided by the observing self, which generates a

> permanent sense of presence, openness, and compassion that constitutes "formal affective operations"—finally as reversible and decentered in their own fashion as logical intelligence. (Hunt 1995b, 118)
>
> Although self-referential presentational meaning is a fundamental potential of the human mind and appears cross-culturally as its own line of development in the various mysticisms and shamanisms, it is not the only such fundamental potential of mind, nor the inevitable formal or logical end of psychological development. In this regard, meditative realization is perhaps best seen in terms of Gardner's multiple frames of mind, as the abstract unfolding of one meta-frame. (132)

Alexander, Davies, et al. (1990 and Alexander, Robinson, et al. (1994) suggested that post-formal developments achieve autonomous integrated ego stages based on self-actualization and post-conventional moral reasoning and demonstrated that the higher states of consciousness proposed by Vedic psychology constitute a developmental achievement of the order of the different stages proposed by Piaget. The evidence includes entirely new modes of knowing, solution of problems inherent in prior developmental levels, increasing differentiation and hierarchical integration of cognitive structures, more veridical or invariant knowledge of objective reality, increasingly adaptive and effective thought and behavior, cross-cultural evidence for the universality of these stages, and major theological reorganization (paraphrase from Alexander, Davies, et al. 1990, 57–58). Central to these developments is achievement of a self-referral mode based on separation or differentiation of the self from other mental activities, "a new 'self-referral' mode of knowing that allows consciousness to know itself directly as Being without conceptual mediation"

(Alexander, Davies, et al. 1990, 53). These developments transcending representational thought do not eliminate it; rather they enable representational thought to occur effortlessly and with a liberation from the habitual domination of attention by the symbolic representations of language. This permits the integration of the affective and intellectual functions and the interpenetration of operations. This is exemplified in Wade's (1996) emphasis on an affective dimension in post-formal development.

Contemplative developments do involve changes superseding Piaget's formal operational thought. Piaget suggested there would be developments following formal operational thought as a consequence of the continuation of the process of equilibration. Other psychologists (e.g., Riegal 1973) have characterized post-formal developments as involving relativism, dialectical thought, and acceptance of contradiction. Post-formal thought overcomes concern with contradictions and the rejection of personal considerations and subjective feelings characteristic of the "objectivity" of formal operational thought. Post-formal thought is based on a relativistic logic that recognizes that different points of view are equally valid from their respective perspectives and that one's own view of reality is only one of many partially valid views. Post-formal thought recognizes that reality embodies many inconsistencies and integrates inconsistencies into a greater whole through their resolution within a broader context recognizing complementarity of perspectives.

Dialectical and relativistic thought within mysticism is discussed by Schoun (1975) as "speculative formulation." Schoun (1975, 5) characterized this approach as "comparable to the infinite series of possible views of the object, views that are realized through indefinitely multiple changes of point of view . . . so the different aspects of truth, however contradictory they may appear and notwithstanding their indefinite multiplicity, describe the Integral truth that surpasses and determines them." Speculative formulation accepts apparent contradictions because each statement is from a point of view and can only be part of the whole truth because expression assumes a specific form that cannot be the only possible expression of the truth (Winkelman 1993). This view entails a realization of cultural relativism in superseding the limitations of specific cultural perceptions to recognize universal truths (e.g., see Smith 1975, 1976). The recognition of cultural relativism entailed an evolution of consciousness, moving beyond culturally specific and limited frames of reference, a partial transcendence of cultural conditioning factors. The esoteric traditions' recognition of the relative truths of each individual tradition embodies a recognition that culture frames human knowledge and experience, a realization that there is no way to express an absolute objectivity, only relative objectivities created within cultural systems. These perspectives make epistemology a fundamental aspect of meditation in particular and of consciousness in general, as is exemplified in Piaget's genetic epistemology.

Contemplative Development from Epistemological Perspectives

Forms of meditative consciousness can be viewed as epistemological structures involved in the suspension of limiting epistemological assumptions made at earlier stages of development. Epistemic structures, which genetic epistemology proposes are adopted at early stages of cognitive development, are suspended in meditative development, permitting manifestation of presentational and affective modes of cognition. Suspension of automatization of perception, social evaluation, affect, and self permits utilization of nonlanguage imagetic symbolic structures. This epistemological approach to consciousness is justified by the nature of consciousness, as well as by the perspectives of many contemplative traditions. Consciousness shares commonalities with epistemology in being concerned with the nature, characteristics, and processes of knowing (Winkelman 1997a). Epistemology is concerned with the nature of knowing, making it a basis for understanding the essence of what is consciousness ("knowing with"). Piaget's genetic epistemology was specifically applied to the development of consciousness, providing a linkage of Western cognitive traditions and Eastern contemplative traditions through epistemological perspectives.

An epistemological approach to consciousness is also justified by the perspectives of meditative traditions. Claxton (1987a,b) provided an epistemological characterization of the central psychological doctrines of Buddhist meditation as constructivist and focusing on analysis and understanding of ordinary consciousness as a construction—a mental model that subserves and provides the basis for one's experiences and actions. The view of transcendental consciousness in Vedic psychology is explicitly epistemological, being concerned with the processes of knowing and the relationship between knower and

known. Flier (1995) used the theories of basic subject-object structures of consciousness proposed by Kegan (1982, 1994) to illustrate
developmental epistemic relationships in mysticism. Flier characterized mysticism as ways of knowing that involve the kinds of differences that Piaget posited as distinguishing levels of cognitive development. Similarly, d'Aquili (1982) analyzed mystical experiences as
epistemic states, outlining nine a priori primary epistemic states.

These confluences of epistemology and consciousness justify the
use of an epistemological perspective in examining meditation traditions and their stages of the development. I propose that meditative
development involves the suspension of assumptions and points of
reference that change understanding of the nature of self, reality, and
knowledge. Suspension of previous epistemic structures also permits
integration of previously repressed levels into a more complete experience of the self. Hunt (1995a,b,c) also implicated the role of "suspension" in meditative developments, with ASCs central to changes
in reflexive self-awareness, enabling development of the detached
observational attitude. Meditative approaches supersede previous
epistemic structures by interfering with the automatized structures
that organize experience of the world and the level of consciousness.
This permits reemergence of earlier symbolic forms, the presentational
modality.

The integration of these two epistemological actions—suspension
and reelevation—provides a basis for changes in the constructs used
to understand the nature of self and reality. The construction of
knowledge and experience requires epistemic structures, assumptions
about the nature of the knower and what is known. Although they
provide a fundamental basis of knowing, they also constrain what
can be known. Epistemic structures assimilate to their own principles
rather than accommodate to the nature of what one seeks to know.
Consequently, the suspension of epistemic structures can enhance
knowledge and experience by removing limitations. This leads to
recognition of several principal characteristics of meditative consciousness: the culturally relative nature of knowledge (cultural relativism)
and the adoption of universalistic perspectives; the constructed nature of human perception (suspending habitual cultural programming
of the structures of attention and perception) and the development of
an awareness of neurognostic structures; the false and incomplete
nature of one's sense of self (suspension of participating self as the
point of reference) and the liberation of the "observing self"; and
transverbal and transconceptual apperceptions (suspending language

descriptions and conceptual thought), which permit the manifestation of neurognostic structures of perception and awareness.

Meditative Consciousness and Epistemic Brain Systems

Conditions of meditative consciousness have similarities across traditions and relationships to the operations of the brain systems supporting consciousness. The relationship of brain development and functions to epistemic structures has been suggested by d'Aquili (1982), Adams (1993), and Winkelman (1997a). MacLean's (1990, 1993) model of the triune brain is used to illustrate the neuro-epistemological nature of consciousness, that is, the relationship of forms of meditative consciousness to the epistemic structures of the functional organization of the brain.

Psychic Consciousness.   Wilber (1980) characterized development into the transpersonal realms as beginning in self-integration of body, shadow, persona, and mind, which permits disindentification with the different persona and transcendence of the exclusive and restrictive identification with these structures. Wilber suggested "psychic consciousness" as based on suspension of some of the previous assumptions about the world, achieved through control of attention, leading to the suspension or deautomatization of the perceptual and cognitive constructs habitually employed. The application of attention to the processes of perception and interpretation makes the constructed nature of reality apparent. Also, it provides a deconstruction or substruction of perceptual and cognitive activities and an awareness of the neurognostic structures of human consciousness, providing an ability to act on physical levels with the intentions represented in the mind. Goleman (1977) suggested that insight meditation leads to a clarity of awareness and perception, producing a range of experiences. However, even more prevalent than perceptual characteristics (brilliant light, luminous forms, color perception) are a variety of emotional characteristics (rapturous feelings, tranquillity, devotional feelings, equanimity, and attachment). These characteristics together constitute what is often referred to as pseudo-nirvana, which must be overcome if the meditator is to continue to develop.

Subtle Consciousness.   Subtle consciousness involves what Wilber referred to as archetypal structures, illumination, and transcendental insight. These changes in awareness depend on the creation of co-conscious selves through the separation of the participating and observing selves. Self and individual identity change as a consequence of unlearning of automatized (habituated) information processing and conditioning of thought. The freedom from the pain and suffering comes from developments of self at this level, which depend on the ability to both suspend and elicit attachments and emotional processes. The experiences of nirvana and bliss are a reflection of this suspension of attachment and the ability to experience rapturous emotions independent of immediate stimuli for such pleasurable experiences.

But it is the Vedic cosmic consciousness that is described as based in the unbounded or nonattached self, no longer identified with thought but with an inner contentment reflecting a self not dependent on reinforcement from external sources. This state has significant similarities with the subtle stage described by Wilber (1980, 1986) in its concern with rapture, bliss, and overwhelming love and compassion. These characteristics of positive affect are associated with the state of refined or glorified cosmic consciousness in Vedic psychology, characterized as reflecting a unification of self and the world and enhanced feeling or affect, particularly love and devotion.

Vedic psychology characterizes feelings as having a role in interconnecting the different levels of the mind, particularly "the interface between mind and senses and between the intellect and ego" (Alexander, Davies, et al. 1990, 304). A fundamental role of feelings in early development is in their role in mediating social influences providing symbolic constructions of self and knowledge. Feelings provide the basis for attachments to others, which define the social group and moral definitions, and reciprocally, one's sense of self. In meditative development, emotional attachments are suspended to permit socially decontextualized evaluations (cultural relativism) and joy and bliss independent of surrounding circumstances. Feelings also link "the intellect back to the intrinsic evolutionary motivation of the ego and ultimately to the inner self" (304). Feelings play an important role in guiding decision-making processes, but in a more relaxed mode, being more flexible, relational, and sensitive to context. They also operate through the intuitive mode, which is holistic and more rapid.

A central aspect of d'Aquili's (1982) neuroepistemological perspective is the affect associated with epistemic states. Beliefs about a wholeness, goodness, and purpose to reality are attested to in the mystical experiences of many world religions, where it is interpreted as union with god. Meditative experiences labeled as cosmic consciousness and absolute unitary being are both tied to positive affect. D'Aquili linked these to right-hemisphere and limbic processes, which provide emotional coloring to experience. This illustrates the fundamental role of the limbic brain; first, its manipulation in achieving the ecstatic rapturous emotional states of the limbic brain; and second, the suspension of limbic processes in achieving equanimity, nonattachment, and other forms of emotional detachment. D'Aquili (1982, 374) suggested that biological bases for affective components associated with cosmic consciousness derive from connections of sensory association areas and the inferior parietal lobe with the limbic system.

Causal Consciousness. Wilber (1980) characterized the causal level as involving the unmanifest realm or void, manifested as consciousness without objects in the field of awareness and without the experience of the universal self. Void consciousness is achieved by completely cutting awareness off from the outer world, concentrating it under the complete control of the will. Wilber characterized this development as based on the subordination and abolition of the predominant centralizing tendencies of the ego sense, leading to the experience of the formless universal self (over mind) in which all manifest forms are radically transcended and no longer arise in consciousness. This development is recognized as an advanced state in many traditions and known by terms such as "the void" and "the void consciousness" (Goleman 1978; Wilber 1977, 1979). This final state is generally considered to be an experience beyond description and conceptual distinctions, permitting the development of a perception of reality beyond concepts. In this sense, voidness refers to the perception of reality without conceptualization—personal, cultural or linguistic. "It is the unconditioned state" (Goleman 1978, 210). This experience of voidness requires the obliteration of all conceptual distinctions and the development of a perception of reality beyond concepts. Although void consciousness is considered to be "beyond description," there are characterizations of this experience as reflecting a "seamless" universe (Wilber 1980), a universe void of boundaries (Wilber 1979). Reality involves a wholeness and a connectedness, an interdependent nature, where perceptions of separate self-identity and perception of isolated objects are an illusory imposition on the undifferentiated nature of ultimate reality.

Table 3.2
Hypothesized Relationships between Levels of Meditative Consciousness and Epistemic Constructs

Levels of Meditative Consciousness	Epistemic Constructs					
	Self	Environment	Emotions	Mind	Social Bonds	Language
Sensoriphysical	Subjective	Awareness Objective world	Survival Reflexes	Behavioral Schemes	Absent	Absent
Phantasmic-emotional	Biophysical body	Object constancy	Survival and pleasure	Image mind	Attachment	Absent
Representational mind	Egocentric Social	Concrete symbolic Social categories	Preconventional Social egoic	Mimetic, episodic Social rules	Egocentric Social roles	Behavior Iconic
Rule/role mind	Social	Cultural	Repressed	Concrete operations	Membership	Verbal
Formal-reflexive	Egoic Dissociated shadow	Verbal description	Repressed	Formal operations	Postconventional	Verbal
Vision-logic	Centaur Mind/body integration	Relationship Object suspended	Integrated	Dialectic/integrative	Relativist/ universal	Transcended

Psychic	Deconstructed	Deconstructed Subject-object suspended	Self-other integration	Transverbal	Suspended	Suspended
Subtle	Archetypal/ Suspend participating	Formless Preverbal	Activated bliss/ nonattachment	Suspended	Suspended	Suspended
Causal	All forms and interpretations of experience are suspended Archetypal overmind Universal self	Suspended/ Seamless void	Suspended	Suspended	Suspended	Suspended

Table 3.3
Levels of Consciousness/Forms of Self and Hypothesized Relationships to Triune Brain Systems

	Form of Self/ Consciousness	Mechanism
Sensoriphysical	Limited self-differentiation and self-awareness as a separate entity (vertebrate ego)	Reptilian brain developed through behavioral intentionality
Phantasmic-emotional	The sense of self developed in contrast to the physical environment and social others (sensorimotor intelligence)	Emergence of paleo-mammalian brain and socioemotional dynamics
Representational mind	Mythic group membership identity; preconceptual and preoperational thought	Emergence of the frontal cortex and symbolic representation
Rule/role mind	Conformist "superego" self and concrete operational thought	Frontal/mental subordinates paleomammalian brain and automizes reptilian brain
Formal-reflexive	Individualistic formal operational ego dominant sense of self	Frontal/mental suppresses/dissociates paleomammalian and reptilian brains
Vision/logic	Integrated body and mind, intuitive thinking, self-actualized self	Integration of frontal brain with paleomammalian and reptilian brains
Psychic	Culmination of vision logic in a pluralistic universalistic perspective that examines and deconstructs perceptual and cognitive activities	Frontal brain operates within and controls paleomammalian and reptilian brains
Subtle	Archetypal levels, collective unconscious and formless experience; the pseudonirvanic realm of illumination, transcendental insight, absorption, rapture, and bliss	Suspension of operations of frontal brain and activation of paleomammalian brain
Causal	The unmanifest realm or void, the transcendent ground of lower structures, manifested as consciousness without objects in awareness and a sense of the cosmic experience of the universal formless self (overmind)	Suspend frontal, paleo-mammalian, and reptilian brains' representational operations

The epistemological realizations of causal consciousness involve a recognition that the objects and the self known are the consequence of the separations, divisions, and distinctions that humans impose on the world, not something intrinsic to the world. These realizations provide the possibility for a nondual mode of knowing. Whereas thinking distorts ultimate reality in creating things, nondual awareness provides an understanding of perceiver and perceived as part of a system of mutually interdependent interactions. This realization provides the basis for recognition that objects are mental phenomena in the sense that they are created through habitual processes of constructing the perceived environment. This realization is explicitly epistemological. With this realization, seer and seen, or subject and object, are no longer considered to be separate and inseparable, but part of this ultimate level of reality.

Odajnyk (1993, 66–67) characterized meditative experiences as involving changes occurring as a consequence of meditation, pushing the reductive and selective operations of the brain and the nervous system to such a point that they essentially shut down the entire sensory apparatus. D'Aquili (1982, 375) suggested that there are neurophysiological mechanisms generating the epistemic states of absolute unitary being, involving "an extremely rare subjective state in which there is no perception of any discrete being and in which even the distinction between self and other is obliterated. All being is apprehended as unity." D'Aquili also suggested that the parietal lobe of the nondominant hemisphere is responsible for holistic perception and generates the subjective sense underlying the experience of absolute unity. This sense of an absolute unitary being may be manifested in either positive affect, which is usually referred to as god or, with neutral affect, referred to as the void.

This neuroepistemologically grounded neurophenomenological model of consciousness is outlined in tables 3.2 and 3.3. These tables identify the epistemic constructs associated with (1) the levels of consciousness proposed by Wilber (1980) (with modifications, particularly the social mimetic stage) and their relationship to (2) the evolutionary strata of the brain proposed by MacLean (1990). I hypothesize that the different levels of consciousness identified in the perennial psychology have underlying epistemic structures (table 3.2). Although the considerations here focus on the developments subsequent to formal operational thought, table 3.2 identifies the epistemic constructs of the full range of consciousness (including the first levels of consciousness documented by Piaget) in terms of the awareness of self, environment, emotions, mind, social relations, and language. These forms of consciousness represent the sequential development of different forms of information processing derived from the interaction between the different brain evolutions identified by MacLean (1990) and the intentionality of the organism, forms of the self (table 3.3).

These levels of consciousness do not strictly replace one another but emerge in an additive fashion through the prepersonal and personal levels. Some development involves an "add on" model, whereas other developmental sequences are based on repression of epistemic states to allow for the dominance of other states. It appears that personal-level development first involves repression of the functions and drives of the reptilian and mammalian brain and that the completion of the personal levels in the vision-logic developments involves a reintegration of capabilities from these phylogenetically earlier systems. What is added in the suspension of epistemological assumptions is a recognition of ordinary awareness as being based in a construction, a belief based in meditative experiences. This process is a central feature of Piaget's models of the development of consciousness embodied in the concept of reflective abstraction. Reflective abstraction is characteristic of each stage of epistemic development, involving the abstraction of elements from an earlier stage and their reflection onto a higher stage where they are restructured as content.

The meditative suspensions (habituated attention, emotional detachment, self-identity, conceptual structures) generally follow the sensorimotor through formal operations in the sequence of acquisition (attention to objects, emotional attachments, self, and cultural constructions). The initial suspension of the exclusive (ethnocentric) monocultural descriptions of the world leads to realization of cultural relativism. The psychic levels lead to the suspension of patterns of habituated perceptual habits and behaviors, followed by subtle level suspensions of emotional attachment and self-identity, and the causal level suspension of conceptual structures. This appears to generally follow the sequences of acquisition. Cultural descriptions, a late epistemic acquisition, are suspended first, followed by a suspension of constructs in the order acquired earlier (perceptual structures, emotional attachments, self, mind).

Determination of whether the epistemological sequencing proposed here reflects an arbitrary order of epistemic suspensions or whether this reflects necessary and fixed sequences determined by neuro-epistemic structures requires further study. First, there is a need to determine if the transpersonal experiences necessarily emerge in a fixed order. The differences between Wilber's (1980) account of hierarchical consciousness levels and other models of transpersonal consciousness (e.g., Vedic psychology of Maharishi Mahesh Yogi [Alexander, Davies, et al. 1990]) suggest that transpersonal states of consciousness may not occur in fixed sequences but emerge in different orders based on the intentionality of the specific traditions.

SUMMARY

The ontological and functional basis of shamanism and other shamanistic healers lies in the psychophysiological potentials provided by a particular pattern of biologically based organismic operation, the integrative mode of consciousness. The pattern of parasympathetic dominance, in which the frontal cortex is synchronized by slow wave patterns that originate in the limbic system and related lower brain projections into the frontal parts of the brain, creates an interaction, coordination, and increased coherence of the potentials of many parts of the brain. The diverse circumstances and procedures that evoke this condition indicate that it is a natural state of the human organism, a mode of consciousness. The independent discoveries of access to this mode of consciousness and its potentials has given rise to universal shamanistic practices. Human potentials manifested in ASCs are institutionalizationed to meet human needs in the activities of the different shamanistic healer types, which represent institutionalizations of ASC potentials under different social conditions. Primary differences among ASCs reflect the effects of society in structuring consciousness. The contemplative traditions' investigations of consciousness suggest that there are functionally and experientially distinct conditions with distinct psychobiological characteristics that constitute different integrative modes of consciousness. An integration of brain research with experiential reports will be necessary to determine which of these forms of consciousness have distinct physiological bases (modes) and which only reflect psychological differences (states).

NOTES

1. A biologically derived mode of consciousness suggests that diverse induction procedures represent different means of inducing a common set of changes in brain functioning and consciousness. Consequently, dif-

ferences in the use of these different ASC-induction characteristics should reflect continuous differences, rather than discrete types or clusters, because different induction procedures are functionally equivalent with respect to the underlying physiology of consciousness and their use should be interchangeable. On the other hand, if different ASCs do not involve a common biological mode of consciousness, the relationship among induction procedures should be best represented as distinct conditions. Formal comparisons (Winkelman 1986b) indicate that the differences in ASC-induction procedures and characteristics are best represented as continuous gradations rather than as discrete separations. This supports the hypothesis of a common biological mode of consciousness.

2. For example, although the center of sleep-waking control was originally thought to lie in the midbrain reticular formation, subsequent studies showed that the excision of most sites involved with sleep and dream function resulted in only partial or transient sleep disturbances and in the persistence of sleep and waking cycles in the absence of the proposed sleep sites and their particular functions (McGinty 1985). This systemic and multiply managed organization of modes of consciousness is also illustrated in the brain's control of dreaming. There have been considerable difficulties in implicating any single region of the brain as entirely responsible for the initiation of REM sleep; apparently there does not exist a "REM sleep center" (Graham 1990), but independently acting groups of cells are responsible for different specific aspects of REM sleep. REM sleep periods may begin as a consequence of a "committee" decision made by interconnected neural groups simultaneously reaching critical levels of activity, with a number of interlinked areas involved in REM production.

3. Entailment analysis determines which variables co-occur, or have implicative relationships (White, Burton, and Brunder 1977). Entailment analysis indicates that if one variable is present, another is necessarily present (logical entailment) or present with minimal exceptions (material entailment). Further details are provided in Winkelman (1986b, 1992).

4. Furthermore, REM sleep is characterized by eye movements and muscle twitches; low-voltage desynchronized EEG; increases in the rates of respiration, cardiac function, blood flow, and brain temperature; and muscle and reflex inhibition (Pivik 1991; Morrison and Reiner 1985). In addition to atonia and brain arousal, reduced sensory responsiveness and marked alteration of homeostatic control are unique features of the dream mode, manifested in skin temperature responding to ambient temperature rather than being maintained. Dream sleep is also characterized by suppression or depression of thermoregulatory sweating and vasomotion, thermal tachypnea, and shivering thermogenesis (Parmeggiani 1985).

5. Although dreaming is characterized by a greater predominance of right-hemisphere activity and activation, left-hemisphere contributions are also present. These are found not only in language expressions of the experience, but also in the persistence of dreaming in commiserated patients, even with the imagetic capabilities characteristic of dreams located bilaterally. The left hemisphere apparently plays a primary role in the voluntary generation of imagery, whereas the right hemisphere is engaged in a more holistic nonvoluntary function of intuitive understanding.

6. Hunt considered the representational and presentational processes to be interdependent in their common foundation in a human symbolic capacity. Expressions of language exemplify sequential organization, while the representations of the presentational mode exemplify the simultaneous expression of these capacities. Dreams manifest synesthetic functions underlying both of these symbolic processes. "We arrive then at a picture of two systems, both self-referential and creatively recombinatory expressions of the human symbolic capacity, interacting in different measures to produce both normative dreaming and its imagetically predominant variations" (Hunt 1989b, 168).

7. "Diverse physiological studies suggest that the frontal cortex and the cingulate mediate thalamic pain input from the spinothalamic tract" (Crawford 1994, 218). During hypnotic analgesia, the far frontal cortex appears to be involved in a topographically specific inhibitory feedback circuit that cooperates in the regulation of thalamocortical activities.

8. This information on the physiology of shaman's ASC is largely derived from Winkelman (1986b, 1992).

9. Epilepsy is not a disease in and of itself; rather it is a generalized symptom of the failure of the brain to inhibit normal patterns of discharge and the synchronized spread of the discharge pattern to the point where it takes over all regions of the brain. Epileptic manifestations range from the generalized seizures involving both hemispheres and resulting in convulsions and the loss of consciousness (e.g., grand mal seizures) through intermediate forms to the partial seizures, generally involving only one hemisphere and not resulting in impairment of consciousness. Epilepsy may result from fevers, injury, or disease, or it may be produced by metabolic imbalances, nutritional deficiencies, endocrine disorders, and many other diseases or traumas to the central nervous system (see Forster and Booker 1975; Adams and Victor 1977).

10. See Bear and Fedio 1977; Bear 1979a; Bear, Schenk, and Benson 1981; Schenk and Bear 1981; Bear, Levin, et al. 1982; Geschwind 1979; Geschwind et al. 1980; Sachdev and Waxman 1981.

11. The shaman's and medium's differences involve thematically related

characteristics reflecting the socioeconomic conditions under which each type of shamanistic healer is found. The shamans were associated with animal spirits and hunting magic, reflecting their subsistence patterns, while mediums were involved in agricultural rituals. Mediums had lower social and economic status than shamans, while shamans had high social esteem derived from their informal political power. Mediums are predominantly women, generally of low social status, whereas shamans are predominantly men and of high social status. Shamans were also involved in malevolent activities designed to magically harm their enemies, which were absent among mediums.

12. Although alcohol seems to produce a different type of ASC than the above-mentioned procedures, it also induces a slowing of the brain wave pattern and a state of parasympathetic dominance. Okamoto (1978) reviewed studies indicating that the most consistent effect of alcohol on the EEG is a slowing of the alpha frequencies. The appearance of slow-wave spindles of theta and delta has been interpreted as a reflection of ethanol action on the amygdala and the hippocampus. Chrusciel (1982) noted that a general effect of alcohol is an improvement in the synchronization of the cortical discharges, a decrease in beta EEG, and an increase in the alpha and theta waves. The effects of alcohol are mediated at least in part by an action on central opiate (endorphin) receptors (Chrusciel 1982; cf. Davis and Walsh 1970).

13. Taimni (1968) discussed the purusa as the essence of the substrate of the subjective: the power of consciousness to function through and in collaboration with vehicles of the mind, providing the connecting link of matter and energy. The purusa, along with all of the vehicles that have not been separated off from consciousness, constitutes the subjective part of this dual relationship. It is referred to as "Seer" (Taimni).

4

_Physiological Bases of
Shamanistic Therapies_

CHAPTER OVERVIEW

This chapter addresses the principal physiological processes that underlie the therapeutic bases for universal aspects of shamanistic healing—the use of a variety of procedures to induce altered states of consciousness (ASC) in community healing rituals and in interaction with a symbolically constituted spirit world. The universally distributed utilization of ASC in both the training of shamanistic healers and in the treatment of their patients derives from psychobiological potentials. The psychobiological changes caused by ASC produce a common alteration in human functioning, from neurophysiological through cognitive levels, which permits the emergence of a holotropic healing response and other integrative potentials. Chapter 3 illustrated that a wide variety of ASC-induction procedures create similar changes in brain functioning, inducing a parasympathetic dominant state characterized by slow wave discharges that synchronize the frontal cortex. This chapter extends this psychophysiological model of ASC, reviewing physiological and clinical literature that corroborates the therapeutic effectiveness of a variety of shamanistic healing techniques. The therapeutic aspects of ASC are addressed in the context of a general model of the psychophysiological effects of ASC in inducing the relaxation response and other physiological changes. The use of symbols in mediating the stress and adaptation syndromes and psychoneuroimmunological responses is a prominent feature of shamanistic healing. Some specific aspects of shamanistic activities receive corroboration of their therapeutic effectiveness from studies within Western science and medicine. Evidence of the therapeutic effectiveness of shamanistic activities is found in the general psychophysiological effects of ASC, in research on music therapy, in a variety of procedures that release endogenous opiates, in laboratory and clinical evidence on the effects and use of hallucinogens as therapeutic agents, and in clinical research on meditation's effectiveness as a therapeutic modality.

GENERAL PHYSIOLOGICAL BASES FOR SHAMANISTIC THERAPIES

That shamanistic healing practices should provide therapeutic relief is apparent from ethnographic research because the users often obtain symptomatic relief from such procedures. However, from the point of view of Western science and culture, such claims have generally been considered to be false. Westerners' accounts of shamanistic healing practices have frequently depicted them as fraud, deception, and chicanery; and Western psychology and culture have tended to consider shamanic experiences to be pathological. In contrast to this depreciation of shamanistic practices, the functions and the physiological bases of ASC indicate that they represent important human potentials. Meditative traditions show that ASC provide a basis for managing attention, attachments, and emotions, and other bodily processes.

More recent perspectives have presented the shaman as an individual of exceptional mental health, the community therapist, and the representation of an important stage in the evolution of human consciousness (Walsh 1990). Rejecting the pathological views of shamanism prevalent in the psychiatric literature, Walsh argued that the shaman is a model of health and psychological growth. He suggested that shamans were the first to engage in training and development involving the transformation of emotions, the reduction of fear and anger, and the development of love, joy, and compassion, factors central to the shaman's healing activities. These aspects of shamanic therapies involve several mechanisms for the transformation of the patient's health. Eliade's (1964) classic characterization of the shaman emphasized healing practices based in ecstatic states (ASC), in community relations, and in manipulation of spirit beliefs, factors that have mutually reinforcing effects in transforming consciousness to enhance health and well-being. ASC are a core element of the shaman's therapeutic repertoire and underlie many treatment effects.

ASC Bases of Shamanistic Therapies

The universal presence of shamanistic healing practices based in the alteration of consciousness reflects the functional relationships of the healing practices to the abilities of healing and divination (see Winkelman 1982, 1986b, 1991a,b, 1992, 1996; cf. chapter 3 this volume). When magico-religious practitioners have ASC induction as a part of their training, they also engage in healing and divination as a part of their professional roles. The alteration of consciousness in community healing practices is a fundamental therapeutic adaptation of human psychobiological potentials to psychosocial needs. Even those societies that lack formal shamanistic healers had collective ceremonial activities involving ASC and healing (Winkelman 1984, 1992).

The ASC-induced physiological changes facilitate shamanic healing by improving psychological and physiological well-being in a number of ways, including physiological relaxation; facilitating self-regulation of physiological processes; reducing tension, anxiety, and phobic reactions; inducing and eliminating psychosomatic effects; bypassing normal cognitive processes in accessing unconscious information; interhemispheric fusion and synchronization; limbic-frontal integration; cognitive-emotional integration; and social bonding and affiliation (Winkelman 1992). General physiological aspects of ASC—parasympathetic dominance, interhemispheric synchronization, and limbic-frontal integration—have inherent therapeutic effects. The effects reflect activation of aspects of the brain that are related to mental and emotional integration. The key physiological mechanisms of ASC and their therapeutic effects derive from activation of the paleomammalian brain, specifically the hippocampal-septal region, the hypothalamus, and related areas that regulate emotions, self and other perceptions, and the balance between the sympathetic and parasympathetic divisions of the autonomic nervous system (ANS).

Shamanistic healing practices are universal because their biological basis has enabled them to emerge either spontaneously from a wide variety of circumstances or as a consequence of deliberate ASC induction. Shamanism's potentials were institutionalization as basic therapeutic resources because of their implications for human adaptation and survival and because of the psychocognitive effects and powerful healing potentials of the ASC experiences. Shamanistic ASC involve physiological conditions with both general and specific adaptive consequences.

Understanding the therapeutic role of ASC requires recognition that both drug and nondrug procedures are used interchangeably to alter consciousness and to induce common physiological changes (Winkelman 1986b; Mandell 1980; chapter 3 this volume). These changes include cortical driving and synchronization, limbic-frontal and interhemispheric integration, and induction of a parasympathetic dominant state. Chapter 3 detailed shamanistic ASC-induction techniques that lead to this pattern of integration with a parasympathetic dominant. These conditions provide inherently therapeutic effects through evoking a general relaxation response by the body, a regenerative and recuperative state.

Budzynski (1986) reviewed therapeutic mechanisms associated with the ASC-induced activation of the brain-mind interface that permit regulation of typically unconscious processes. The integration facilitates resolution of conflicts by presenting to the conscious mind understandings of the unconscious mind. The unconscious mind is repressed by the dominant hemisphere, but its tendencies or scripts persist and affect behavior, emotions, and physiology. ASC induction enhances expression of repressed aspects of the self through activities that reduce critical screening processes of the left hemisphere. The ASC-induction procedures affect the left hemisphere, which fatigues more rapidly and which releases control and repression of the right hemisphere. This expression of the normally repressed side of the brain enables enhanced ritual reprogramming at these unconscious nonverbal levels. Increases in suggestibility from reduction in critical screening by the left hemisphere facilitate psychoemotional and mental reprogramming via the chants, songs, myths, psychodrama, and direct suggestion provided by the shaman, which elicit emotions and reprogram them through healing ritual.

ASC characteristics of dishabituation, increased suggestibility, and interhemispheric fusion and integration indicate that a therapeutic basis of ASC is in creating a labile system to be manipulated psychocognitively and emotionally by the healer utilizing a psychocultural symbolic system. Shamanistic healing practices utilize ASC to produce an alternative to the current personal state of consciousness, inducing changes in the individual's perception of self and social relations, mediated through emotions that affect physiological systems in ways that facilitate healing.

The parasympathetic dominant state of ASC reflects a basic relaxation response of the organism, the ultidian low state of waking consciousness. This wakeful hypometabolic state is characterized by a generalized decrease in the activation of the sympathetic nervous system and by an increase in alpha and theta wave activity. This is the basic body response to counteract excessive activity of the sympathetic nervous system. The relaxation response has preventive and therapeutic value in diseases characterized by increased sympathetic nervous system activity, particularly in lowering of blood pressure, control of hypertension, treatment of heart disease, and reduction of premature ventricular contractions (Benson, Kotch, et al. 1979).

Inducing parasympathetic dominance has therapeutic effectiveness against a range of stress-induced and exacerbated maladies by physiologically inducing relaxation. Progressive relaxation techniques (see Lehrer, Woolfolk, and Goldman 1986 for review) have therapeutic effectiveness. Negative emotions and maladaptive mental processes that cause physiological stress can be changed by focusing the patient's awareness of the use of the skeletal muscles. Lehrer et al. suggested that progressive relaxation therapy leads to decreases in psychophysiological reactivity in anxiety neurotics, with lasting somatic changes that indicate its usefulness in treatment of hypertension. Further effects of the general relaxation response are discussed at the end of chapter 4 (in section Reduction of Arousal, Stress, and Anxiety) in review of research on meditation's effects.

Therapeutic effects can be achieved by rapid collapse into a parasympathetic dominant state that can lead to erasure of previously conditioned responses, to changes of beliefs, to loss of memories, and to increased suggestibility (Sargant 1974). Sargant reviewed the classic research showing that induction of a parasympathetic collapse from stress and emotional excitement can abolish conditioned reflexes and can produce an ultraparadoxical phase in which the conditioned behavior and responses are reversed. Increased suggestibility can enhance placebo and other psychosomatic effects, resulting in physiological improvement.

Core Shamanic ASC Therapy: Music

Cross-cultural similarities in shamanic ASC include the use of singing. Shamanic healing involving music and song is based in effects of auditory driving (drumming, clapping, rattles, and other percussion) and linkages to ancient audio-vocal systems of the brain (Oubré 1997). Physiological effects of these procedures were detailed in chapter 3. The relationship of shamanism to music therapy has been explicitly made by individuals in the field (e.g., Winn, Crowe, and Moreno 1989); and numerous studies have suggested therapeutic effects from music (Hanser 1985; Rider 1985; Rider, Floyd, and Kirkpatrick 1985; Davis and Thaut 1989; cf. other articles in the *Journal of Music Therapy*).

Music can act therapeutically by counteracting effects of stress, with implications for a variety of illnesses and diseases, physical as well as psychological and psychosomatic. Music can counteract stress-related biological changes by producing significant improvements in galvanic skin response (GSR), muscle tension, heart rate and blood pressure, and mood and attitude (Hanser 1985). Music has a range of physiological effects on the body, beginning with the sensory neurological systems and including the involvement of glandular systems, the autonomic nervous system, involuntary muscular responses, and reflexes. Music can decrease electromyographic responses (EMG), affect brain wave responses, and reduce pain (Rider 1985). Music therapy has shown consistent decreases in verbal reports of state anxiety and increases in relaxation (Davis and Thaut 1989). Rider suggested that potential audioanalgesic mechanisms of music include endorphin production from thrill response, dissociation through distraction, and autogenic conditioning. Physiological mechanisms for the therapeutic results may include increased breathing and enhanced oxygen content created by singing and chanting.

Winn, Crowe, and Moreno suggested that the effectiveness of music therapy derives from ways in which music, singing, drumming, and related procedures affect access to unconscious information. Music enhances access to unconscious material in ways that facilitate its integration into consciousness. Health is enhanced by elevation, integration, and resolution of unconscious and repressed internal conflicts that create emotional illness and exacerbate physical problems. Other functions of songs in shamanistic therapy include their ability to elicit confidence and positive expectations.

Music's effects on the body reflect information processing in ways distinct from language. The localization of music abilities in the right hemisphere (for right-handed nonmusicians) is illustrated by its persistence in people who lose language abilities due to left-hemisphere trauma. The multitude of emotional and synthetic effects derived from music reflect its operation on right-hemisphere processes. The processing of music in the right hemisphere (versus the left hemisphere) implicates music's role in holistic brain processes and communication with subcortical areas of the brain. These processes include expressive capabilities that existed prior to spoken language (Oubré 1997). These expressive capacities, epitomized in song, are a primary medium for expression of emotions (Newham 1994).

The universal use of song and music in shamanistic healing also reflects their ability to affect humans through symbolic meaning. In addition to the physiological effects of music, shamanistic practices may use music as a psychological therapy. Music therapy utilizes the relationship between the meaning expressed and the patient's prior psychodynamic experiences and unconscious. Music may both stimulate unconscious material into consciousness and provide for emotional reprogramming through expression of cultural themes, psychodynamics, and motivations. Music may act at id, ego, and superego levels and produce a variety of experiences, including releasing emotions and satisfying desires. The development of "singing cures" and voice movement therapy (Newham 1994) attests to the persistent value of music as a therapeutic modality.

Physiology of Community Bonding: Endogenous Opioid Releasers

The biologically based ASC therapies of shamanistic healers are realized in collective community ceremonies. The participation of the local residential group (e.g., the entire band in hunting-gathering societies) is typically mandatory for shamanistic healing practices (Winkelman and Winkelman 1990). Collective social integration produced by shamanistic healing practices through the participation of the local community strengthens group identity. Ritual healing ceremonies are primarily oriented toward interpersonal and social processes, exerting an influence on well-being by enhancing community cohesion through reintegrating patients into the social group. The relationship of social support to morbidity, mortality, and recovery indicates that social relations can have prophylactic and therapeutic effects. Community participation and relationships have not only therapeutic roles derived from psychological and social influences (e.g., positive expectation, social support), but also physiological effects derived from the opioid-attachment, psychosociobiological interaction and psychoneuroimmunological responses.

Frecska and Kulcsar (1989) provided evidence that shamanic healing practices involve complex forms of psychobiologically mediated attachment that promote synchrony between individuals, reinforcing identification and internalization of social relations. This innate drive for affiliation and processes for evocation of opioid mechanisms are integrated through shamanistic practices. Opioid release is implicated in mother-infant attachment; social attachment; alleviating, mediating, and moderating separation distress; helping elaborate the positive affective states of social comfort; social play; and mediating the pleasurable qualities of social interaction (Frecska and Kulcsar 1989). Shamanistic healing evokes ceremonial opioid release, which emotionally charges cultural symbols and which cross-conditions cognitive and endocrine systems. This cross-conditioning permits later ritual symbolic evocation of the previously entrained physiological processes.

Frecska and Kulcsar (1989) reviewed findings that indicate that shamanic healing practices use a variety of procedures and mechanisms to release endogenous opiates (cf. chapter 3 this volume). This release is essential for integrated social functioning and internalization of social identification. This psychobiological synchrony is established during socialization through a cross-conditioning of cultural symbols and the activation of the endogenous opioid system. Ceremonial (shamanistic) opioid release is based in emotionally charged cultural symbols that are cross-conditioned to cognitive and endocrine systems during early socialization, linking mythological and somatic spheres. This association permits subsequent ritual elicitation of the opioid system through the coincidence of cultural symbols and social affiliation, producing a symbolic or placebo elicitation of opioid release through ritual influences and their social attachments.

In addition to the opioid elicitation effects of social relations, a wide variety of other shamanistic activities also stimulate release of endogenous opioids. An issue of *Ethos* (vol. 10, no. 4, 1982) focused on the numerous aspects of shamanistic healing activities associated with elicitation of endogenous opioids. Although some activities are more directly relevant to the healer than the patient, there are many activities that directly affect the patient and other participants. These activities include extensive dancing and other exhaustive rhythmic physical activities (e.g., clapping); temperature extremes (e.g., sweat lodges); stressors such as fasting, flagellation, and self-inflicted wounds; emotional manipulations, especially fear; and nighttime activities, when endogenous opioids are naturally highest (see chapter 3 this volume; Thoren et al. 1990; Rahkila et al. 1987; Sforzo 1989; Mougin et al. 1987; Appenzeller 1987; Kiefel, Paul, and Bodnar 1989; Bodnar 1990).

A fundamental mechanism of opioid elicitation found in shamanistic healing is the extensive dancing and clapping performed by healer and participants. The opioid mechanism triggered by the A-delta mechanosensitive afferent nerve fibers mediates the behavioral, analgesic, and cardiovascular effects of exercise (Thoren et al. 1990), which has widely recognized therapeutic effects. Thoren et al. indicated that disorders such as hypertension, anorexia nervosa, depression, and addictions may be therapeutically treated through exercise. Experimental studies show that endogenous opioids have an anticonvulsant and inhibitory action with respect to interictal and ictal discharges (Molaie and Kadzielawa 1989). Endogenous opioids have a role in environmental adaptation and memory, the recognition of novelty, and the interaction with and habituation to new environments (Netto, Dias, and Izquierdo 1986). The opioid neuropeptides are recognized for reduction of pain, as well as for enhancing tolerance of stress, improving adaptation, and globally stimulating immune system functioning.[1]

A common aspect of shamanistic ritual is the enactment of an encounter with powerful supernatural forces, especially those with control over the processes of nature, illness, and death. These symbolic "others" represented as spirits provide foci for enactments that produce emotional experiences considered to be the most profound known in these cultures (Eliade 1964). Opioids are specifically elicited by situations of helplessness (Maier 1986), which has survival value in improving endurance and conserving energy in emergencies. Ritually induced release of opioids is triggered by the terrifying experiences enacted by the shaman. Prince (1982b) reviewed evidence indicating that the experience of terror may also induce analgesia-euphoria through endorphin release. He formulated a mock hyperstress theory for the elicitation of endorphins by severe psychological threats, where the ego's involvement with highly personalized horror scenarios in alternate realities produces hormone release. Maier

(1986) similarly implicated experiences of "uncontrollability" and inescapable situations as inducing opioid release.

General characteristics of shamanistic healing rituals also include the elicitation of placebo responses through the use of trickery and slight-of-hand. Deception is deliberately perpetrated by the practitioner because it is known to produce a successful outcome at another level (e.g., see Levi-Strauss 1963). Trickery confirms belief and produces positive expectation, with direct implications manifested in the "biology of hope" and in psychosomatic and placebo effects. Placebo effects constitute *symbolic* manipulations in that the treatment procedure does not have the biological mechanisms to produce the physiological effects that are intended. But the presentation of a "mechanism" by which the desired physiological change could be effected (e.g., the placebo pill) elicits the desired condition in the body. Expectation that the placebo will have effects provides symptomatic relief for many, as well as biological consequences (e.g., those who show pain-reduction responses to placebos have elevated endogenous opioid levels).

Shamanistic healing practices share common therapeutic approaches in the use of spirit beliefs as symbolic representations that provide psychosocial, psychocognitive, emotional, and projective mechanisms, as well as manipulation of psychosocial relations and psychophysiological dynamics. These symbolic manipulations operate through psychobiological intervention in stress mechanisms and the general adaptation syndrome, as well as in elicitation of psychoneuroimmunological responses. Symbolic manipulations also play a central physiological role in another primary aspect of shamanistic healing rituals, the elicitation and manipulation of emotions and their physiological consequences. Pert (1986; Pert et al. 1985) suggested that neuropeptides and neuroreceptors function as an information network that links body and mind through the manifestation of the emotions by the limbic system, the focal point of neuropeptide receptors and the brain center for emotion. The opioids and emotions serve as an intercommunication system in which opioid release stimulates emotional experience and emotional experiences stimulate opioid release. These are mediated by meanings provided by spirit constructs. Spirit beliefs not only are symbolic explanatory models of the experiential components in psychocultural belief systems, but also act as psychocultural manipulators of the emotional-neurological and mind-body interface.

STRESS AND WELL-BEING: RITUAL EFFECTS ON THE AUTONOMIC NERVOUS SYSTEM

Evidence for the effects of the mental level on physical well-being is found in cases of spontaneous remission of disease—the rapid and inexplicable disappearance of documented medical conditions. This remission is often coincident with participation in religious activities. Similar effects are seen from being subject to hexes or from other magical or prophetic declarations about another's imminent death, some of which are followed with an individual's demise, even when under medical supervision (Cannon 1942). These effects of mind are not only in extraordinary phenomena; ordinary functions of consciousness have downward effects on the physical levels of the organism, as illustrated in the phenomena of stress and the general adaptation syndrome.

Stress is a challenging construct to define and operationalize because it is based in the personal response rather than just in external circumstances. Central to stress is how the organism perceives itself and the situation and responds in terms of those perceptions and assessments. Stress involves both psychological and biological dimensions and also complex emotional, cognitive, and behavioral responses to threats, strong environmental demands, or personal loss. Virtually anything, including both positive and negative events, could be stressful to an individual if it affected his or her personal life. Stress occurs as a consequence of rapid changes in major patterns of people's lives, changes that have important implications for their sense of self or that challenge central assumptions that people make about their world. Stress results from perceived inability to effectively adapt to anticipated circumstances. Stress produces a negative affective response and the resultant anxiety or fear experienced in response to frustration of or threats to one's desires, goals, and well-being. Stress occurs when modes of adaptation are not adequate, when one's assessment of external demands exceeds one's perceived abilities for meeting physical as well as personal and social needs. This inadequacy makes the causation of stress symbolic and related to one's sense of self and to one's perceptions of future actions of significant others.

Much stress is socially induced as the result of interpersonal interaction or cultural definitions of situations and expectations. Stress derives from the individual's interpretation of the situation, occurring when habitual behavior is disrupted and an adequate adaptation cannot be achieved. But the same situation does not affect all uniformly—people differ in their abilities to revise behavior or expectations. Stress lies in the interaction of the situation and the individual's perceived ability to meet it. Both the significance and symbolic meaning of the situation and the individual's repertoire of coping behaviors are crucial elements in the situation's effects on the individual. For humans, stress is predominantly social. Culture provides the basis from which small groups achieve a consensus on how to perceive events, helping to reduce individual uncertainty and anxiety. Disruption of the individual's social ties produces stress. Stress occurs when the person experiences information incongruities, a disconcordance between expectations and perceived reality. Human well-being is dependent on social relations of acceptance and affirmation, and negation of this social support induces physiological changes.

The body can adapt to chronic physical stressors, but it does not adapt to chronic emotional stress. Emotional stress must be dealt with through defensive reactions and coping responses. Central to human adaptive responses to stress are psychological or coping reactions and the effects of meaning on physiological responses. Beliefs manage the effects of stress on social relations, emotions, and the mind. The action of mental and symbolic levels on the physiological substratum is examined in psychosomatic medicine and sociophysiology, which examine how sociocultural and biological factors interact. Emotions are central to stress through the significance that the organism attaches to perceptions, attitudes, beliefs, and expectations and that is derived from personal needs, culture, and previous socialization. These emotional reactions effect changes in the autonomic nervous system, linking meaning and physiological responses.

The Autonomic Nervous System: The Anatomical Basis of Stress

Control of organic functions is maintained by the complementary activities of the ergotropic (sympathetic) and trophotropic (parasympathetic) divisions of the autonomic nervous system (ANS). The anatomical basis of the ANS includes the hypothalamus and portions of the endocrine system, the reticular activating system, the limbic system, and the frontal cortex. The ANS controls heart and gastrointestinal functions and mediates the balance between stimulation (activation of the sympathetic division) and relaxation (activation of the parasympathetic division). Sympathetic activation provides the energy for muscles through the stimulation of the ergotropic system and through activities in the posterior hypothalamus that mediate alertness, arousal, strength, and vitality. Parasympathetic activity is involved in storing sugar, fat, and protein through the trophotropic system and the activity of the anterior hypothalamus, which mediates rest, recuperation, and sleep.

The ergotropic system provides adaptive responses to the external environment, whereas the trophotropic system maintains a homeostatic balance. The ergotropic system functions periodically; the trophotropic system has continual functions. The cyclical patterns of consciousness reflect a balance between the needs for maximization of external orientation and adaptations and the needs for internal adaptation and homeostasis. The tuning or balance between the ergotropic system and the trophotropic system is created through conditioning, which sets the relationships that establish and maintain the rhythmic interactions between waking and sleeping modes of consciousness. The ergotropic system subserves the fight-or-flight response, providing a global activation of the body. It is responsible for mediation and control of short-term adaptation (rather than long-term development). Activation of the ergotropic system is associated with either positive or negative emotions, dependent on the interpretation made of the physiological changes and the immediate situation. The trophotropic system regulates the vegetative nervous system, from cellular activity through digestive functions and sleep; and it is responsible for synchronization of the cortical EEG patterns, for relaxation, and for control of somatic functions vital for long-term well-being of the organism. The primary function of the trophotropic system is the repair and development of the organism, especially during undisturbed sleep.

The ergotropic and trophotropic systems can be driven top down (from higher cognitive levels and intentional control) and bottom up (discharges in lower levels of the nervous system); in both cases they operate on the principle of homeomorphogenetic recruitment across different levels of the nervous system and body (Laughlin, McManus, and d'Aquili 1992). The complementary activation and balance provided by the ergotropic and the trophotropic systems provide for a hierarchical integration of the activities of the somatic, the autonomic, and the neural systems. This manipulation of ANS balance is a central mechanism of shamanistic healing, as are stress responses, psychosomatic reactions, and psychosocially induced diseases.

Stress and the General Adaptation Syndrome

Selye (1936) discovered the general systemic reaction to all different forms of stressors, which he labeled the general adaptation syndrome (GAS). The body's response to stress as manifested in the GAS
involves three main stages: (1) stress or alarm reaction of the body;
(2) resistance with a new adaptation at an increased level of pitu-
itary/adrenal activity; and (3) exhaustion that consumes body because
of the inability to maintain homeostasis. The GAS sequences—alarm,
resistance, exhaustion—are characterized by anxiety, followed by a
combination of anxiety and depression, and finally depression. These
physiological responses to stress are based in the ANS and the endocrine system and constitute distortions of normal adaptive mechanisms. Aversive stimuli provoke a state of hyperarousal in the ANS,
contributing to pathological conditions by causing increased cardiovascular function and disrupting the ANS balance. The psychophysiological responses involve an increase in sympathetic nervous system
activity, with prolonged activations causing physiological changes that
exhaust the body's resources and make it more susceptible to disease.
Prolonged activation of the sympathetic nervous system can cause
collapse and damage to organs and can lead to cardiac failure and
death.

The pituitary-adrenal cortex (more generally, the activity of the
hypothalamic-pituitary-adrenocortical system and the adrenal medulla) provides the mechanism mediating the GAS. The pituitary
secretes hormones that in turn stimulate release of hormones by other
endocrine glands and brain areas. These hormones produce a general, intense, undifferentiated arousal and activation of the sympathetic nervous system, which is basic to emotions, and a generalized
physiological response to the environment, which prepares the organism for action. Sustained stress results in increased peripheral and
brain activity, particularly central nervous system (CNS) noradrenergic neurons; but the long-term effects of stress are more complex (Gray
1982). Exhaustion leads to a fall in noradrenergic activity if the
stressor's demands on the noradrenergic impulses are too severe.
Synthesis then increases to restore noradrenaline levels, accompanied
by an increase in the turnover of noradrenaline. This does not ha-
bituate, with the release and synthesis of noradrenaline maintained
at a higher equilibrium when the adaptation to chronic stress is complete. The synaptic vesicles responsible for the synthesis, storage, and
release of noradrenaline have a limited lifespan and are replaced by

axoplasmic transport. The increase in brain noradrenaline levels can be maintained for only a limited time until the vesicles are depleted. Noradrenaline may also be replaced by new synthesis; but because of slow transport, it arrives at the nerve long after termination of the original stimuli, perhaps as long as six or seven days (Gray 1982). During the second stage of resistance, the prolonged activation can lead to an exhaustion of pituitary and adrenal defenses, as well as of other aspects of the endocrine system, leading to collapse. The response to stress is nonspecific in that stress affects the aspect of the system that is weakest.

The endocrine glands play an important role in the mediation of stress by the secretion of hormones, particularly from the pituitary and the adrenal glands. The hypothalamus stimulates the adrenal glands to release epinephrine, a vasodilator that accelerates the function of the heart and the CNS, and norepinephrine, a vasoconstrictor that increases cardiac activity and raises blood pressure. Norepinephrine and epinephrine act together to mobilize fatty acids for use as energy. Epinephrine, norepinephrine, and cortisol appear to have negative effects on the immune system, making the body more susceptible to infection. Stress can affect pathogenesis through the elicitation of activity in the sympathoadrenomedullary and the pituitary adrenocortical areas. Stress hormones link the psychological and the behavioral conditions to disease. Psychological, emotional, and environmental stress lead to elevated corticosteroid levels and may be considered necessary for the physical response (adrenal-pituitary) to occur. Emotional stress also elicits activity in the limbic system, particularly the hypothalamus, triggering the release of ACTH (adrenocorticotropic hormone) from the anterior pituitary. The adrenal cortex synthesizes and secretes corticosteroids in response to stress and stimulation by ACTH. Cortisol modulates the stress responses, but its overproduction can cause damage to organs. The glucocorticoids break down body proteins and hinder the action of the lymphocytes, causing immunosuppression. The disruption of cortisol regulation also contributes to many other diseases, as well as to depression and anxiety.

Symbolic Interaction and Stress

The elicitation of stress mechanisms by social situations and by symbolic meanings that do not permit a response leaves the body mobilized for actions it cannot undertake, contributing to the development of many conditions—ulcers, hypertension, cardiovascular problems, migraine headaches, and so on. These and many other problems are a consequence of the self's inability to manage social, psychological, and emotional aspects of life. Fear of or expectation of situations can produce the same psychophysiological responses as actual situations. Physically, socially, or symbolically threatening situations call forth physiological responses that are mediated by genes and their cultural conditioning and by associations with current context and needs.

The interactions between social and physiological conditions are addressed in the symbolic interactionist approach, which sees the individual as maintaining a self-concept as a result of social interaction, where a person acquires the meanings that other people attach to him or her as social objects. This definition of self by others mediates how events impact the individual. When face (social presentation of self) is inconsistent with self ideals, this produces stress.

Although the causes of stress are often social, cultural, and symbolic in nature, they nonetheless have physiological implications. Physiological reactions provoked by physical stimuli (attacker) may also be evoked by symbols or ideas (a shadow makes me think and feel that someone is going to attack me!). The body's homeostasis can be disrupted by symbolic threats to one's self, with the individual's subjective response of fear having powerful effects on physiological functioning. Humans respond emotionally to a wide variety of conditions—traffic, noise, competition, fear, not feeling wanted or loved. It is more the individual reaction than the situation itself that determines the body's physiological response.

The GAS activation and stress reactions evolved to deal with threats to physical survival; but today, people's responses result from forces involving interpersonal interaction, as well as the broader macrosocial context—economic and political processes that affect the individual and create conditions that are stressful. The human organism faces emotional threats with the same defense systems used to deal with physical enemies (the flight-or-fight system). But the symbolic threats do not permit a physical struggle, so the organism does not use up the chemicals generated by symbolic occurrences. The body mobilizes for action, stimulating the cardiac system and releasing energy for defense, which is not used but is deposited in arteries, causing arteriosclerosis and other conditions. Management of emotional effects on the organism's homeostatic balance is central to healing.

Psychoneuroimmunology

Psychoneuroimmunology illustrates that stress effects immune responses. Psychoneuroimmunology involves investigation of the interaction among the central nervous system (CNS), the endocrine system, and the immune system (Lyon 1993; Varela 1997). The interactions are not strictly material, but they involve the organism's adaptations. Psychoneuroimmunology shows that the immune system is affected by the interactions between psychological and physiological processes, particularly the ways in which thought, feeling, and behavior interact in disease processes (Lyon 1993, 77). The relationship between individual and social levels in the interaction of behavior factors with disease is not yet well understood. Lyon suggested that explaining that interaction requires an understanding of the relationship of biological processes to the subjective foundations of existence. Lack of consideration of these subjective foundations has limited medicine's ability to conceptualize the nature of this interrelationship.

The development of psychoneuroimmunology derived from findings that contradict conventional views of the autonomous, self-regulating immune system. Resolving these contradictions led to recognition of immune processes as a part of the responses of the organism in adaptation to the environment. The immune system mediates the effects of psychosocial dynamics and events on pathophysiological states. The psychoneuroimmunological perspective recognizes that all diseases are multifactorial, requiring a biopsychosocial perspective (e.g., Engle 1980) to explicate their diverse mechanisms of interaction. A systems perspective is necessary to understand how symbols bring about physiological changes in the body and how effects are communicated across different domains or levels of mind and body. The immune system can be conceptualized as a sensory system within which the white blood cells provide the "messenger molecules" mediating communication among the CNS, the immune system, and the endocrine system (Lyon 1993). The immune and neuroendocrine system peptides provide the basis for signaling the immune system in response to "noncognitive stimuli" (e.g., viruses and bacteria). This signaling enables the immune system to function as a sensory system and to relay information to the neuroendocrine system to initiate physiological changes.

Varela (1997) characterized the immune system's structure and

functions as a "second brain," providing a self-regulating control of
the body's responses to the environment. The immune system has
organs distributed throughout the body (lymphocytes, B-cells, T-cells
of the thymus, the spleen, and the lymphatic system). The immune
system adapts through learning and memory. The interaction of mind
with both the nervous system and the immune system enables emotions to exercise their influence on health. CNS responses to stress
release hormones (glucocorticoids) that interact with the lymphatic
system by action on their surface receptors. This interaction stimulates the immune system to release lymphocytes and immunotrans-
mitters that act directly on the neurons of the limbic system (Varela
1977). The ANS innervation of bone marrow can also affect the
immune system, particularly the T-cells, which cause further neurotransmitter production.

The sensory and the communicative functions of the immune system provide the basis for the reverse effects, when the activity in the
CNS allows for effects on hormones, lymphocytes, and the immune
system. These perspectives have been developed as "immuno-
semiotics," in which the parallels between the brain and the immune
system are used as a basis for examining the latter in terms of "biological meaning," "communication between lymphocytes," and the
"sign systems" perceived by the cells of the immune system (Lyon
1993). This model has been extended in the use of neural network
theory to address ways in which the immune systems function
"cognitively" in discrimination, inference, and memory and ways in
which these systemic activities provide the basis for an "immunological self." Varela suggested that the body's sense of self, with cognitive
properties involving learning and memory, functions through the
immune system. This sense of identity is based on the network of T-
and B-cells that move through the body, binding to it and each other.
These interactions constitute a molecular and cellular level of self,
with interactions with organs across the body providing extensive
linkages like the nervous system. This "immunosoma" or "immuno-
body" identity derives from the emergent property of these complex
interactions. The immunological response takes place within the larger
biological and social context, which raises questions of "the nature
and location of agency" (Lyon 1993, 91) and the relationship between biological and social dimensions of being.

Psychoneuroimmunology requires a simultaneous consideration of
the biophysiological and psychosocial bases of human experience and

functioning, the context of the relationship between the cellular level of organismic functions and the psychosocial environment of the organism. Lyon (1993) suggested that bodily (somatic) experience involves many levels but is necessarily social (involving interpersonal interaction). Lyon also suggested (1993, 92) that this resituating of the organism in context indicates a reconceptualization of human emotion, which necessarily incorporates the biological and the cognitive as a necessary part of "being in the world." "It is only through understanding emotion can we recontextualize and 'resocialize' discourse about disease and healing." This social experience is a necessary part of the body's immune response linked to emotion.

Emotions are the "intervening variables interposed between the meaning for the individual of the information . . . and somatic responses that follow" (Lyon 1993, 85). The CNS responds to emotional stimuli with changes in hormone and activity levels, affecting the immune system as "information molecules" that act on the immune system indirectly through hormones and directly through neurotransmitters. The psychoneuroimmunology research agenda requires establishing the links between cellular levels and behavioral levels, showing how the nervous, endocrine, and immune systems communicate through symbolically mediated physiological interactions. Social relations play a fundamental role in these processes.

THERAPEUTIC EFFECTS OF HALLUCINOGENS[2]

Shamanistic practices in many societies use substances referred to as hallucinogens, psychedelics, and "sacred plants" or "plants of the gods" (Harner 1973a; Schultes and Hofmann 1979; Dobkin de Rios 1984; Winkelman 1996; Schultes and Winkelman 1996). The predominant Western perspective that hallucinogens (or psychedelics) are dangerous drugs without social benefits is countered by evidence that these substances have therapeutic effects. Ethnographic studies in non-Western societies provide evidence of hallucinogens' therapeutic uses, with corroborative evidence of therapeutic effectiveness provided by biomedicine's clinical studies on the effects of LSD (Winkelman and Andritzky 1996). Laboratory studies of the physiological, sensory, emotional, behavioral, and cognitive effects of LSD illuminate the general psychophysiological effects of hallucinogens, their consciousness-altering properties, and their therapeutic mechanisms. Common physical effects underlie the cross-cultural similarities in their use.

Although hallucinogens differ in their chemical structures and mode of action on the brain and endogenous transmitter systems, they share some common effects (Aghajanian 1982; Mandell 1985; Winkelman 1996). LSD, phenylethylamines (e.g., mescaline), and indolealkylamines (e.g., psilocybin) are virtually identical in their clinical effects, with the major differences being in their potency (Hollister 1984). Hallucinogens have common effects in blocking serotonin reuptake, in disinhibiting mesolimbic temporal lobe structures, and in permitting the emergence of synchronous brain discharges. Hallucinogens also inhibit the regulation of the visual centers by the raphe cells, thereby producing visual hyperactivity or visions. Hallucinogens produce high-voltage synchronous activity in the hippocampus (Mandell 1980), synchronize the cortex, and induce a parasympathetic dominant state (Gellhorn 1969). The therapeutic effects of hallucinogens derive from both the general aspects of ASC and the associated psychophysiological effects and benefits, as well as from specific mechanisms related to their physiological effects on serotonergic transmission. There are also specific neurophysiological, sensory, behavioral, emotional, and cognitive effects of hallucinogens that provide mechanisms for their therapeutic potentials (Winkelman 1996).

The misconceptions implied by "hallucinogen" make a new terminology necessary to appropriately characterize the nature of these substances. An integration of (1) the patterns of use revealed in cross-cultural studies of traditions utilizing these substances as therapies and (2) neurobiological research on the mechanisms of action of LSD provides the basis for a neurophenomenological perspective on these substances as "psychointegrators" (mind, soul, and spirit integration) (Winkelman 1996). The term *psychointegrator* reflects the substances' systemic neurophenomenological effects, integrating brain processes and experiences. Psychointegrators stimulate mental and emotional processes, impelling the organism toward an integrative state. This systemic integration is derived from effects on the serotonergic system and its role in modulatory neurotransmission. Psychointegrators activate emotional and personal processes of the paleomammalian brain and stimulate memories and feelings underlying personal identity, attachment and social bonding, emotional stability, and convictions and beliefs. One emphasis of psychointegrators is on psyche, meaning not only mind but also the soul and the spirit. Psychointegrators stimulate the integration of behavior, protomentation, and socioemotional dynamics with language-based ratiomentation, egoic representations, and personal identity. These biochemically based physiological effects may force emotional awareness, recall of repressed memories, integration of emotional and rational processes, and the resolution of conflicts through stimulation and integration of different functional systems of the brain.

The following review illustrates these principles of action of psychointegrators. The term *psychointegrator* is employed in place of the terms *hallucinogen* and *psychedelic*. (Hallucinogen, psychedelic, and so forth, are still used, however, to represent the vocabulary and the ideas of others whose work is discussed.) This is not to preclude further terminological differentiation of the diverse substances characterized here as psychointegrators (e.g., see Naranjo [1996] on the distinctions of "fantasy enhancers" and "feeling enhancers" in contrast to LSD). Rather it is to call attention to their commonality in stimulating emotional, mental, and experiential transformations and integration.

The Cross-Cultural Use of Psychointegrators

A wide range of ethnographic literature attests to the traditional use of psychointegrator plants as therapeutic agents (e.g., see Aberle 1966; Anderson 1980; Andritzky 1989; Dobkin de Rios 1984; Furst 1976; Harner 1972; Schultes and Hofmann 1979; Schultes and Winkelman 1996; Wasson 1980; Wasson, Cowan, and Rhodes 1974). These traditions typically involve integrated magico-religious and therapeutic applications and interpretations, with ubiquitous mystical, spiritual, and medicinal uses (Schultes and Hofmann 1979; Dobkin de Rios 1984; Winkelman 1996).

Worldwide beliefs in spiritual effects of psychointegrators have suggested their prehistorical role as progenitors of religion (La Barre 1972). Many groups' names for these plants—"flesh of the gods," "voices of the gods," "the sacred language," "ancestors," "little saints," and other phrases—reflect the belief that religious practices were inspired by indwelling spiritual influences attributed to the plants. Many religions' rituals, sacraments, and deities reflect cases in which a universal human need for religious interpretation and transpersonal experience coalesced around the experiences induced by psychointegrative plants. La Barre suggested that the potentials of hallucinogens to stimulate the visions and supernatural experiences gave rise to new religious traditions, revealing the subconscious, represented in supernatural and spiritual beliefs. The psychointegrator-induced supernatural world reflects the subjective world of human experience and the basic aspects of human perception and consciousness. Psychointegrators can provide societal "defense mechanisms" (La Barre 1992) or psychosocial transformation processes, discussed by Wallace (1956) as "mazeway resynthesis."

Cross-cultural data indicate that these substances alter experience in a dramatic way, shifting awareness to an experiential domain interpreted as sacred. Patterns of psychointegrative plant use include their application in healing and their interpretation as leading to spiritual and mystical awareness. The apparent universal features of their use include establishing direct contact with the supernatural, a means of healing, relationships with animal powers, transformation into animals, establishing personal relationships with a spiritual reality, divination, promotion of social solidarity, and reinforcing interpersonal and community relations. The experiences include a personal relationship with mythical reality, identification with an animal spiritual realm, and the dissolution or death of the ego and its transformation (Winkelman 1996).

These substances shift self-awareness to an "other-worldly" domain interpreted as the sacred or spiritual. These experiences have important personal and social effects, with simultaneous therapeutic, religious, spiritual, and medicinal roles. This ubiquitous pattern of use has implications for understanding the nature of human consciousness and the spiritual because they uniformly evoke experiences interpreted as a spiritual aspect of collective human identity. These cross-cultural similarities in perception illustrate that a biological substratum is responsible for these experiences. The relation of the biochemical effects to the experiences and to the perceptual, cognitive, emotional, and behavioral changes induced has been detailed by Winkelman (1991b, 1996), who linked the neurophysiological effects to the cross-cultural similarities in psychocognitive experiences (cf. Grof 1975). The role of biological mechanisms in providing the basis for common effects is illustrated by the similarities in human and animal behavior under the influence of hallucinogens (e.g., see Jacobs 1984; Appel and Rosecrans 1984; Davis et al. 1984; Hollister 1984; Freedman 1984).

Nonetheless, these same studies indubitably implicated individual and environmental factors in the experiences. The "set" (individual characteristics and expectations including attitude, motivation, mood, and personality) and "setting" (the physical and social context of use) produce quite varied experiences under hallucinogens (Dobkin de Rios

1984; Bravo and Grob 1989; Yensen 1996). The shamanistic healers manipulate these personal and situational factors as an integral part of the therapeutic system employing these substances (Bravo and Grob 1989). The extensive role of the shamanistic healer in manipulating these set and setting factors before, during, and following treatment is based on knowledge of the client's personal situation. Therapeutic sessions are preceded by meetings of the healer with the patient and the patient's family or community and incorporate ritual procedures to guide expectations of the therapeutic outcome. The treatment session itself is usually implemented in the context of a traditional ritual procedure that guides the ingestion of the substances. Ritual procedures guide and shape the patient's experience, particularly through singing and chanting, which present mythological and symbolic elements to elicit and to shape the patient's emotions and experiences. The shamanistic healer guides the experiences both within the immediate context of the ritual therapy and following the treatment session to integrate experiences for the patient. The ability of these substances to mediate such powerful mental (set) and social (setting) effects is illustrated in clinical research and is a reflection of psychointegrators' neurophysiological properties.

Clinical Paradigms in the Study of LSD

The set and setting effects of psychointegrators are reflected in the various psychotherapeutic traditions in the clinical study of LSD (lysergic acid diethylamide). Clinical use and study of LSD in Western psychotherapy (e.g., see Grof 1975, 1980; Lukoff, Zanger and Lu 1990; Bliss 1988; Yensen 1985; Aaronson and Osmond 1970; Cohen 1968; Abramson 1967; and Bravo and Grob 1989 for reviews) has produced three different models of the nature of the effects: These three paradigms have been called psychotomimetic, psycholytic, and psychedelic (Yensen 1985, 1996; Bravo and Grob 1989). These different effects from the same substance reflect the interaction of the state of extreme activation and neurobiological flexibility produced by psychointegrators with the set and setting factors that shape the effects.

The Psychotomimetic Model.   Initial research on the effects of LSD viewed it as a substance that create or mimicked psychosis. LSD could produce psychoticlike reactions, and self-reports during an LSD experience were seen as evidence of disturbed cognitive functioning. But research showed the psychotomimetic model to be inadequate in that LSD could produce experiences quite distinct from those of a typical psychotic state. These qualitatively quite-different experiences were exemplified in what Cohen (1971) described as a typical "good trip." The positive LSD experience led to a change in the way in which one approached ordinary experience. The world was seen in a new light, "desymbolized." Dramatically changed meaning and new or increased significance was attributed to everyday objects. The individual became hypersensitive and hypersuggestible, and he or she reacted differently: thought became nonlogical, opposites were reconcilable, and there was an increased tolerance for ambiguity. The individual might experience an oceanic feeling, a dissolution of self into a mystical union, a feeling of being at one with the universe (Cohen 1971).

The Psycholytic Model.   The positive aspects of the LSD experience led to the psycholytic paradigm, based in recognition that LSD could aid psychotherapy. The term *psycholytic* means "mind-dissolving," reflecting the hallucinogen-induced relaxation of the ordinary sense of self, altering the relationship between the conscious and unconscious (Bliss 1988). LSD could ease memory blocks, promote catharsis, and shorten the course of therapy. The psycholytic approach employed a series of low doses of LSD in conjunction with therapy sessions. This led to a weakening of psychological defenses, heightened emotional responsiveness, elicited repressed memories, and released unconscious material. The ability to relive early life memories and to retain the memories in post-LSD sessions facilitated the progress of psychotherapy. Among those patients for whom psycholytic therapy has been recommended are those with psychosomatic problems and psychic rigidity; isolated individuals and those fixated at egocentric levels; concentration camp survivors with rigid defenses; patients with whom classic psychoanalysis has been unsuccessful; disorders rarely healed by psychotherapy, such as severe chronic compulsions and severe alcoholism; and severe character neuroses, depression, and compulsion (Zanger 1989).

The Psychedelic Model.   The subsequent LSD paradigm was referred to as *psychedelic therapy*, a term reflecting the "mind-manifesting" properties of the substances. The psychedelic model derived from studies on the effects of large doses of LSD, particularly on alcoholics (Osmond et al. 1967). These studies indicated that those who benefited most from LSD therapy had reported mystical experiences associated with profound personality changes, suggesting that the mystical insights were responsible for the therapeutic outcomes (Kurland 1985). The psychedelic approach employed a single large dose of LSD, which was used to induce peak and mystical experiences and to bring about a profound sense of interconnectedness, unity, and meaningfulness and "a new sense of self, a new outlook, a feeling of rebirth" (Bliss 1988, 550). These experiences gave the patient a greater sense of self-control and the opportunity to make use of these insights for life changes. This was achieved through activation of repressed memories, producing catharsis and abreaction, and leading to new awarenesses and a sense of freedom (Kurland 1985). The psychedelic paradigm "recast the psychiatrist as a modern-day sha-· man" (Bravo and Grob 1989) who utilized ASC as therapeutic tools.

Systemic Effects of Psychointegrators

The conflicting perspectives of these three models of LSD effects led to a recognition of the need to assess "extrapharmacological" factors—the characteristics of "set" (personal attitudes and characteristics) and "setting" (physical location and its effects), which direct the influences of these drugs. The variation indicated that LSD produces a state of emotional lability in which experience changes as a function of expectations and environment (Yensen 1985). But although set and setting factors necessarily affect the experience, there are also physiological properties of hallucinogens which tend to promote psychotherapeutic processes when not subjected to negative set and setting influences. Langner (1967) expressed similar conclusions, noting that LSD patients had less need for therapists because they were able to directly access deeply embedded traumas and conflicts relevant to their problems. Psychointegrators stimulate memories, bringing them to consciousness, and lead to an alteration of or a dissolution of the typical sense of self, releasing one from egocentric fixations. Modifications in the relationship between the conscious and the unconscious make the patient more open to therapeutic intervention, with the depatterning influences increasing the individual's suggestibility. There are also effects on sensory processes, behavior, emotions, and cognition, which provide a basis for neurophysiological effects related to phenomenological aspects of the experiences.

Sensory Effects.   Optic and auditory processes are enhanced with low doses of LSD, which simultaneously inhibit the responsiveness of cortical systems. The result is a state of "enhanced input with diminished and more variable control" (Freedman 1984, 206). LSD effects on visual experience involve increasing absorption in internal imagery. Effects include failure to suppress prior precepts, as well as dishabituation; that is, familiar experiences and situations appear novel. An effect of hallucinogens at the sensory level is apparently the removal of customary interpretive frameworks; these effects are also reflected at the behavioral level.

Behavioral Effects.   Effects of hallucinogens on motor behavior reflect set and setting factors, but the overall effects produce a cessation of external behavior and a focus on internally generated information. In animals, whereas higher doses result in avoidance, lower dosages produce more exploratory behavior and more extensive and random routes. Hallucinogens alter behavioral habituation; they may reinstate formerly habituated arousal responses, increase arousal habituation, and disrupt behavior established under free response reinforcement (Appel and Rosecrans 1984).

Emotional Effects.   Action directly on the emotional centers of the brain (limbic system) alters emotional reactions in a variety of ways, creating heightened emotional states, feelings of personal significance, and an increase in emotional lability. Emotional effects include a wide range of emotions, mood alterations, increasing absorption in internal feelings, depersonalization, emotional lability, the coexistence of elemental feelings of fear and exhilaration, mood alterations, distorted time sense, strange body sensations, dreamlike feelings (Hollister 1984; Freedman 1984), and the emergence of unconscious conflicts and emotional issues.

Cognitive Effects.   Effects on mental functions include enhanced clarity of consciousness with diminished importance of external reality, accompanied by a shift of focus to internal experience (Freedman 1984, 209). Intact memories of both cognitive and emotional experiences permit reflection and analysis. Mandell (1985) suggested that cognitive effects are derived from improving the integration of information exchange between the two hemispheres and their specialized functions in cognition and affect, producing integration and insight. This provides a rationale for calling them "psychointegrators."

Summary

The psychointegrators heighten sensory receptivity and responsiveness to the environment, reducing or reversing habituation, dishabituating the individual from typical response patterns, and increasing arousal and responsivity to the environment. High dosages lead to a focus on the internal imagetic, emotional, and cognitive environment. The internal focus permits material from the subconscious or unconscious to enter awareness, activating repressed memories and bringing them to consciousness, where they are integrated and resolved. Psychointegrators also stimulate the primary activities of the limbic system—emotions and interpretations related to the sense of self and social attachments. Reduction of egocentric fixation and altering relationships between the conscious and the unconscious facilitate changes in self-perception and dissolution of the self. Increased interhemispheric coherence creates a greater degree of integration and insight. This facilitates therapeutic intervention through stimulation of memories to consciousness and the increased emotional lability, which enhance the individual's susceptibility to reprogramming.

NEUROTRANSMITTERS, PSYCHOINTEGRATORS, AND ORGANISMIC FUNCTIONING

Clinical effects of LSD, as well as the specific sensory, emotional, behavioral, psychological, and cognitive effects, reflect intervention in neurotransmission. The global effects of psychointegrators on consciousness are similar to the general effects of ASC (Winkelman 1991b, 1996). Laboratory studies present what mistakenly appear to be contradictory findings because of the phase- and dose-dependent characteristics in the nature, magnitude, and duration of effects (Freedman 1984) and because of the influences of set and setting factors. Dosage level, stage of the unfolding drug effect, and personal and environmental factors are all important determinants of the variations in psychointegrator-induced experiences. The diverse effects of psychointegrators also reflect different effects at different brain sites. It is the serotonergic system that mediates the primary effects of the LSD-like psychointegrators. The neurotransmitter effects of psychointegrators include the augmentation of and the repression of normal serotonergic processes, which are achieved by several means, including serving as agonists in the role of neurotransmitters, reducing habitual repressions caused by other brain mechanisms, and simultaneously stimulating processes that are normally dissociated. Psychointegrators interact with the structures ordinarily stimulated by serotonin, suppressing or modulating its effects or taking its place in neurotransmission. The systemic characteristics of neurotransmitter function of serotonin and psychointegrators provided in the following summarization are primarily derived from Aghajanian (1994), Kruk and Pycock (1991), McKim (1991), Ryall (1989), Jacobs and Gelperin (1981), and Jacobs (1984).

Serotonin and Serotonergic Projection Areas

Serotonin is a monamine neurotransmitter, a system that has nerve cells in the reticular formation and that is highly innervated in the limbic system and its "pleasure centers" and in the basal ganglia, where it plays a role in the regulation of body movement. Long, highly branched axons, slow latency and conduction, and diffuse projection to many terminal fields enable serotonin to operate more as a modulator than as a classic synaptic transmitter. Serotonin acts as a modulator across all levels of the brain, from the brain stem and limbic system to the frontal cortex. Mammalian and nonmammalian vertebrates' brains use serotonin similarly in a range of postsynaptic activities: opening and closing gated ionic channels, controlling voltage-gated channels, activating secondary messenger systems (Gerschenfeld, Paupardin-Tritsch, and Deterre 1981), and serving as a neuromodulator in the CNS (Weight and Swenberg 1981). The loci of serotonin's action include the brain stem area, raphe and reticular formations, the hippocampus and amygdala in the limbic system, and the frontal cortex, particularly the visual and auditory areas. Serotonergic psychointegrators (SPI) increase reactivity of these areas, directly and indirectly enhancing integrative processes. Effects on memory, emotions, conceptualizations, and motivation reflect action on these brain structures, affecting sensitization, habituation, memory, motivation, emotions, and experience (Freedman 1984). These and other structures affected by psychointegrators are directly responsible for a range of human capabilities central to consciousness: attention, alertness, and maintenance of waking/sleep cycles; control of organismic processes through regulation of the autonomic nervous system; integration of emotional and motivational processes; synthesis of information from the entire brain; and visual conceptualization and representation.

Serotonin (5-HT), a key neurotransmitter with a wide range of functions (Fischbach 1992; Ribeiro 1991), is the most extensive monoaminergic neurotransmitter system in the brain (Role and Kelly 1991), with profound effects on perception, cognition, and motor function (Aghajanian 1981). Serotonin plays an important role in sensory processing, in hunger and feeding, in the control of motor activity and behavior, in sleep and hallucinatory states, in the control of moods (Kruk and Pycock 1991, 122–23), and in thermoregulation and pain (Glennon 1990); 5-HT acts as a vasoconstrictor, inhibiting gastric secretions and stimulating the smooth muscles. Serotonin neurons exercise control over secretions of growth hormones, stimulating their release and participating in central regulation of blood pressure through modulating the sympathetic system. Serotonergic projections are "associated with anxiety and fear, major depression and dysthymic disorder, appetite abnormalities, sleep disturbances, schizophrenia, pain-related dysfunctions such as migraine, and psychosomatic complaints" (Ribeiro 1991, 37).

The central importance of serotonin as a neurotransmitter in many different processes reflects its primary role as a modulator involved in physiological or behavioral responses. Modulatory neurotransmitters are unconventional in the sense that they play a role in modulating the effects of other neurotransmitters or local conditions. Serotonin operates in both fast and slow transduction mechanisms and even affects nerve terminals and blood vessels, which do not have serotonergic innervation (Kruk and Pycock 1991, 116; Ribeiro 1991). Although serotonin also triggers action potentials, its overall effects are in determining the strength of the responses of the postsynaptic cells. The modulatory neurotransmitters typically have a much longer period of action and appear to play a role in response to changing levels of arousal or motivation of the organism. Serotonin controls the level of arousal and modulates the role of sensorimotor processes in behavior. The role of 5-HT in vigilance "may influence cognition, learning, perception, memory, decision making, mood, and behavior" (Glennon 1990, 39). The highest rates of firing of 5-HT neurons are during active waking periods, with their activity undergoing progressively greater reduction during quiet waking and slow wave sleep; 5-HT firing virtually ceases during REM sleep.

There are a wide range of areas of the central nervous system (CNS) that are affected by 5-HT. The primary projections are ascending, with a widespread distribution throughout the neuraxis and diffuse influences over vast neuronal populations (Parent 1981). The 5-HT neurons are concentrated along the midline area and the raphe nuclei in the brain stem, from which they project upward into the limbic system and frontal cortex. They are also found in the mammalian hypothalamus (Parent 1981), as well as in the myenteric plexus in the gut and in the peripheral tissues (Kruk and Pycock 1991). Serotonin neurons are found primarily in the raphe nuclei within the rostral pons of the midbrain, from which they project upward into the anterior hypothalamus and thalamus; the limbic system, particularly the amygdala, hippocampus, and limbic forebrain; and the corpus striatum, basal ganglia, and neocortex. The reticular activating and raphe systems are diffusely innervated projection systems that receive sensory input from axons carrying information to the cortex. The limbic system contains a large number of interconnected nuclei primarily responsible for emotion and motivation. The basal ganglia consist of two nuclei (the caudate nucleus and the putamen) located just below the cortex, which regulate voluntary movements of the body. The cortex receives inputs from many parts of the brain, integrating sensory information, initiating voluntary motor control, and coordinating bodily movements.

Different kinds of 5-HT receptors in the CNS have different effects in different parts of the brain; their characteristics are summarized here from Aghajanian (1981, 1994; cf. Schmidt and Peroutka 1989, Glennon 1990, Ribeiro 1991). The 5-HT_{1A} receptors are present in the raphe system, where they function as somatodendritic autoreceptors, mediating the responses of the serotonergic neurons with respect to their own transmitter (Aghajanian 1994, 138); and they mediate collateral inhibition of the raphe system and are affected by indoleamine hallucinogens as powerful agonists. The 5-HT_1 receptors have a high affinity for 5-HT agonists. The 5-HT cells concentrated in the rostral raphe nuclei are the primary source of serotonin projections to the forebrain. Kruk and Pycock (1991, 121–22) described two different types of 5-HT CNS axons: those of the dorsal raphe nucleus, which have very fine axons and innervate the limbic structures and striatum; and those with large-diameter axons extending from the median raphe nucleus to innervate the hippocampus and mammillary bodies. The majority of the fibers projecting from the midbrain raphe[3] ascend to the lateral hypothalamus and from there branch to a range of forebrain structures. LSD-like indoleamines have greater activity as agonists in their action at the somatodendritic 5-HT_{1A} receptors, inhibiting receptor firing (Aghajanian 1994, 140).

The principal effects of LSD-like psychointegrators result from their high affinity for 5-HT$_2$ neurons (Glennon 1990, 43). Serotonin concentrations in the limbic system are highest in the hypothalamus and basal ganglia. These 5-HT$_2$ receptors have a high affinity for 5-HT antagonists, with their sensory processing functions antagonized by LSD (Kruk and Pycock 1991). The 5-HT$_2$ receptors are found on postsynaptic neurons (Aghajanian 1994) and mediate LSD effects on the cerebral cortex, on the locus coeruleus, and on other areas of the brain. The 5-HT$_2$ neurons of the locus coeruleus (which receives numerous somatosensory and visceral inputs and which projects diffusely to most of the brain) are facilitated by LSD, which has a high affinity for 5-HT$_{2A}$ and 5-HT$_{2C}$ receptors (Miller and Gold 1993). These 5-HT$_2$ sites are implicated in the control of anxiety and the reduction of schizophrenic symptomology (Ribeiro 1991).

The 5-HT$_3$ receptors are found in the peripheral nervous system at the ANS nerve endings, where their stimulation leads to the release of acetylcholine and norepinephrine from the parasympathetic and sympathetic nerve endings, respectively; the receptors may also facilitate the release of dopamine (Kruk and Pycock 1991). The 5-HT$_3$ sites are also found in the lower brain stem and in areas of the spinal cord as well as in some areas of the limbic system (Ribeiro 1991). They have a role in the regulation of analgesia, anxiety, and schizophrenic symptoms, but they do not appear to be involved in the mediation of LSD effects (Glennon 1990). (For further discussion see Winkelman 1996.)

Psychointegrators and Consciousness

Because the overall effect of serotonin is to depress the action of target neurons in the forebrain, the overall blocking effect of LSD on serotonin neurons results in a disinhibition of their typical repression. The areas with the densest serotonin axon terminals—the limbic system's emotional processing areas and the visual areas of the cortex—have the most intense disinhibition and, therefore, the greatest effects, exemplified in the typical visual and emotional experiences. Blockage of serotonin uptake and action results in the disinhibition of the mesolimbic temporal lobe structures (Mandell 1985; Hoffmeister and Stille 1982) and permits the emergence of synchronous slow-wave discharges, which drive impulses into the frontal cortex, replacing the normal desynchronized fast-wave activity with synchronized discharge patterns.

The fact that these psychoactive substances are analogous to the

endogenous neurotransmitters suggests that the experiences they induced are the consequence of enhancement of neural functioning. For
example, releasing inhibition of the visual cortex gives rise to the visual
hyperactivity called visions or hallucinations. Action in the limbic
system and associated structures such as the reticular activating system and the hippocampus augments normal processes that MacLean
(1993) referred to as "paleomentation." The limbic system's control
of the hippocampus, a link between the reptilian brain and the frontal cortex, suggests heightened integration of hierarchically ordered
brain functions.

Psychointegrators and ASC primarily activate the paleomammalian
brain and its functions, evoking and processing important emotions
and memories. Psychointegrators also stimulate the R-complex,
maintaining alertness and awareness, interfering with routinized (habituated) behavioral routines, and providing an enhanced integration
and projection of diverse kinds of information (Winkelman 1996).
The reptilian and paleomammalian brains' information-processing
modalities involve cognitive processes that are not based on language,
but on forms of mental and social representation tied to primary
processing and nonverbal communication. These structures lack linguistic representation; but they have awarenesses, intelligence, and
consciousness; play a predominant role in managing emotional and
social life; and serve as mechanisms for shamanistic healing.

The antagonism of dopamine in the R-complex by serotonergic
psychointegrators suggests that one effect of psychointegrators is to
shut down the habitual routines related to social behavioral displays.
The psychointegrators apparently have the effect of forcing the frontal cortex to consciously process information that has been relegated
or automatized by the R-complex and paleomammalian brain. The
primary activity of LSD on serotonergic activity is thought to be
mediated by 5-HT_2 neurons of the limbic system and projections to
the frontal cortex. These effects, as well as those on the brain stem
region, particularly the locus coereleus, induce integration of diverse
stimuli and their diffuse projection throughout the brain.

Consciousness is based on the integration of the left hemisphere's
objectifying activities; the right hemisphere's integration, interpretation, and pattern construction; and the paleomammalian brain's evaluative functions and social-empathic responses, integrated with R-
complex–based behavioral routines. Human behavior requires the
coordination of information with motivations and personal significance, a linking together of emotions and the cognitive and rational

faculties. Psychointegrators induce this integration through action across the neuraxis, enhancing information integration and distribution and forcing conscious awareness of repressed materials. Attachment, emotions, and the role of social "others" in human learning and development are based in paleomammalian brain processes and elicited by psychointegrators.

Psychointegrators induce this integration by stimulating the emotionally most critical material into consciousness. Emotions are key aspects of the links between belief and physiology. Emotions are directly tied to fundamental aspects of bodily maintenance and reproduction, personal and group survival, and illness and psychopathology. Emotional functions are implicated in the instinctual drives and psychopathologies, as well as in everyday experiences.

The transcendent experiences produced by these substances suggest that they led to the evolution of uniquely human aspects of consciousness. Shamanism has been considered the first form of evolution of human consciousness to the transpersonal levels. The role of psychointegrative plants in promoting this evolution of consciousness is reflected cross-culturally in shamanism and transcendent experiences (Naranjo 1996). The typical use of the plants in infrequent ceremonials reflects adaptation to tolerance effects, as well as to the episodic nature of psychodynamic needs for their use. Psychointegrators are used to manage developmental or crises-induced needs for integration of conscious and unconscious processes. The stimulation of primary activities of the limbic system—emotions and interpretations related to emotions, self-preservation, sense of self, and social attachments—reflects the activation of evolutionarily earlier levels of cognition. Activation of these evolutionarily prior aspects of mentation nonetheless represents evolutionary developments in human consciousness through cognitive-emotional integration.

MEDITATION AS THERAPY

Shamanistic healing traditions utilize many consciousness-altering procedures for both healer and patient, which link them to meditative practices and their effects. Among these are chanting, fasting, sensory and social isolation, internal focus of attention, visualization, and austerities. There are many assessments of the therapeutic efficacy of meditation (for reviews see Taylor, Murphy, and Donovan 1997; Shapiro 1980, 1990; and Walsh 1979, 1980, 1983, 1988). Meditative practices have numerous effects in improving individual psychological and physiological well-being and appear to be particularly useful in the treatment of psychosomatic disorders (Walsh 1983). Studies have shown successful outcomes in dealing with fears, phobias, personal integration and control, stress and tension management, and a range of physical changes, including the lowering of blood pressure (Shapiro 1980). Meditation serves as a self-regulation strategy and produces a number of beneficial effects, including clinical intervention for several stress-related dependent variables (Shapiro 1980). Walsh (1980) reviewed research indicating that physical and psychosomatic benefits of meditation are found in the treatment of myocardial infarction, bronchial asthma, insomnia, cholesterol levels, and high blood pressure. Meditation improves responsiveness to medication for a range of stress-related illnesses and contributes to reductions in addictive drug use, mood elevation, and improvement in affect. Taylor, Murphy, and Donovan (1997) concluded that although meditation has been shown to be more effective than placebo effects, it is slower acting than pharmacological agents, and it is best employed in conjunction with other treatment modalities. Shapiro (1990) reviewed literature indicating that meditation induces immune system enhancement. Meditation has also been used as an ego regression technique, which prompts the manifestation of unconscious material; in assisting individuals in gaining a sense of inner directedness and increased self-responsibility; and as a means of stress management.

However, some reviews of the research literature have suggested that meditation may be no more effective in the treatment of many maladies than are other self-control strategies (e.g., progressive relaxation, hypnosis, and biofeedback) (Shapiro 1990; Pagano and Warrenburg 1983; Holmes 1987). But Alexander, Robinson, Orme-Johnson, Schneider, and Walton (1994) provided a meta-analysis of comparisons of transcendental meditation with other meditation and relaxation techniques. This analysis illustrated significantly greater effects of transcendental meditation in reducing arousal, trait anxiety, drug abuse, and hypertension and mortality in the elderly. The causes of meditation's therapeutic effects are a part of the general relaxation produced by the state of parasympathetic dominance. The beneficial effects of meditation in the treatment of psychosomatic tension states, anxiety, and phobic reactions might be generally expected of parasympathetic dominant states.

However, assessments of therapeutic efficacy of meditation are generally not dealing with the goals of meditation, nor are they based on the study of highly developed practitioners. Rather, these studies apply meditation to medical symptoms, frequently with novice meditators. Such clinical perspectives provide but scant assessment of the nature of meditative effects. Even though there is widespread evidence of the therapeutic effects of meditation, it should be recognized that the goals of meditation are not the same as those of Western psychology and psychiatry. Even when the intents of meditation and the consciousness disciplines are concerned with mental health, their states and goals may be quite different from those of the Western health sciences (e.g., dissolution of the ego, rather than ego strengthening).

Nonetheless meditation has therapeutic efficacy, as evidenced in clinical studies. Delmonte (1987b) reviewed studies that show that meditators who maintain their practice have significantly lower levels of depression than do dropouts. Studies also indicate that meditation leads to improvements in self-actualization and in reduction of anxiety, particularly for relatively healthy individuals. This may reflect the importance of motivational factors and dispositions toward self-improvement (Delmonte 1987b). Nonetheless, there is evidence of effects of meditation on arousal, stress, self-control, attention, conditioning, and insight.

Reduction of Arousal, Stress, and Anxiety

Early findings (Benson, Beary, and Carol 1974) suggested that meditation was a general hypometabolic state; but more recent (Holmes 1987) comparisons of highly trained meditators with a resting control group found that although there were reductions in arousal for both groups, there were no significant differences between them. Meditation does reduce arousal, but it may not be more effective than rest. Holmes concluded that there is no consistency in meditators' versus resting controls' levels of arousal. Holmes also assessed the evidence of whether meditators, in comparison to subjects that do not practice meditation, were more capable of controlling their arousal in threatening situations. The studies failed to support the contention that meditation has general utility in reducing stress, and in some cases, the studies indicated that relaxation, behavioral, or desensitization therapy may be more effective. One study Holmes reviewed (Goleman and Schwartz 1976) is interpreted (contrary to the authors) to indicate that meditators experience higher arousal in threatening situations and a greater sensitivity to stimulation. Delmonte (1987b) reviewed research showing that some evidence of meditation's effectiveness in reducing anxiety is a consequence of higher-than-normal anxiety among prospective meditators. There is, however, evidence that the regular practice of meditation does facilitate reduction of anxiety (Delmonte 1987b). Walsh (1983) reviewed evidence of the effectiveness of meditation in reducing anxiety and in dealing with a range of phobias. But personal reports of reduced anxiety may not be validated by behavioral or physiological indicators (Delmonte 1987b). Alexander, Robinson, et al. (1994) reviewed studies on *transcendental* meditation practices that suggested that specific forms of meditation (or regular practitioners) may reduce arousal, and they conclude that transcendental meditation produces a deep physiological rest that is distinct from ordinary resting and that provides protective and rejuvenative effects.

Meditation has been studied extensively in terms of its effects as a stress-reduction mechanism. Stress may be manifested as *fear*, an appropriate response to real danger, or as *anxiety*, an acquired or conditioned fear. The utilization of meditation as a means of combating excessive ungrounded fears has been motivated by the view of meditation as producing conditions or states incompatible with activation of the fight-or-flight response. Stroebel and Glueck (1980) suggested that the relaxed alpha states are incompatible with this stress response, making meditation useful in the treatment of chronic anxiety and stress-related and psychosomatic illness. There are, however, many different sources of alpha, as well as individual differences in response to alpha biofeedback training. This makes simple generalizations about alpha effects suspect (Orne and Wilson 1978). Pagano and Warrenburg (1983, 156) reported an extensive series of studies on transcendental meditators (TM) that "challenge the view that TM uniformly gives rise to a single, unique, wakeful hypometabolic state which persists for most, or all, of the meditation period." In order to assess whether the TM procedures produce a unique state, they compared the effects of TM with those of progressive muscle relaxation. Pagano and Warrenburg suggested that the reduction in oxygen consumption reported by Benson's (1979) early research is an artifact due to elevated baseline values and concluded that the available evidence does not support the claim that TM produces a hypometabolic state. Pagano and Warrenburg showed that TM and other relaxation techniques produce a common physiological pattern ("the relaxation response"). The somatic effects of both TM and progressive relaxation include significant decreases in heart rate, respiration, minute ventilation, and EMG, but no significant differences between them.

Although Pagano and Warrenburg do not find evidence of a unique meditation effect with TM meditators, they do report that long-term practice of TM leads to self-reported reduction of stress and to increases in well-being and internal locus of control. Controls with social-desirability measures confirm that TM is responsible for the reduction in stress. Pagano and Warrenburg concluded that TM leads to healthier self-reports, increased well-being, greater self-actualization, and lowered stress and anxiety. Rather than a unique TM or meditation effect, however, they concluded that the beneficial consequences come from "relatively nonspecific rest." This is consistent with the position of Benson, Kotch, et al. (1979) that meditation techniques allow for the body's own relaxation response to emerge. Conditions necessary for this relaxation response to occur are a quiet environment, a passive attitude, decreased muscle tones, and the use of mental devices to facilitate the shift away from the ordinary rational thought processes (Pagano and Warrenburg 1983; Benson, Kotch, et al. 1979).

Taylor et al. suggested that, nonetheless, there are findings that meditation reduces stress, as indicated in lower levels of adrenal hormones and lactates. There is a "body of evidence showing the efficacious use of yoga techniques and Hindu meditation practice in specific disorders such as hypertension, diabetes, cancer, cholesterol regulation, alcoholism, anxiety disorders, asthma, pain control, and obesity" (Taylor et al. 1997, 25). Reduction in acute and chronic anxiety has been demonstrated for both meditation and progressive relaxation conditions. Davidson and Schwartz (1984) have demonstrated that relaxation includes both somatic and cognitive components, but that the former techniques are significantly superior. They suggest that Zen practices, which combine somatic (breathing) and cognitive (mantra) techniques, are particularly effective; similar effects should be expected from shamanic practices, which combine physical activity (dancing, singing, clapping, etc.) with cognitive stimulation. Taylor et al. (1997, 116) reviewed "more than fifty contemporary studies [which show] that meditation has helped relieve addiction, neurosis, obesity, claustrophobia, headache, anxiety, and other forms of stress."

Self-Control and Systematic Desensitization

A common emphasis of the Asian psychologies is that most human behavior is mindless and unconscious. Unlearning this conditioning of thought and behavior is fundamental to realization of greater control of one's behavior and experiences. The development of this control leads to a greater awareness of the unconscious processes, with sustained attention increasing self-awareness. Meditation leads to refinement of auditory perception, to improvements in speed and accuracy in tests of perceptual-motor skills (Carrington 1987), and to increased visual sensitivity (Brown, Forte, and Dysart 1984). Meditation increases awareness of what are usually unconscious mental processes, providing insight into the nature of mental operations (Delmonte 1987a).

Meditation practices enhance awareness of unconscious processes through deautomatization, which changes perception, motor habits, and cognition from their habituated, repetitive, and routinized processes. By focusing attention, meditation enables the practitioner to develop a greater awareness of how all information, ranging from perceptual stimuli to concepts of self and the universe, is habitually processed. This increased awareness has implications for self-awareness, leading to a dissolution of the ordinary sense of self and identity and to the development of an alternate center of awareness and experience, the observing self, enhancing self-control.

Shapiro (1980, 1990) examined meditation and control-related issues, suggesting that there are different modes of self-control (positive assertive, positive yielding, negative assertive, and negative yielding), which vary along six dimensions (goal, awareness, choices, responsibility, discipline, and skill). The appropriateness of different approaches depends on the specific context and goals. Shapiro indicated that the therapeutic aspects of control strategies are related to perennial and universal issues of a personal (developmental), interpersonal (social relations), and cosmic nature (meaning) that must be addressed in all cultures. ASC traditions provide a means to maintain orientation and control across developmental life-cycle issues. ASC can serve as self-control strategies within which "others," a benevolent spirit other, provides both control and innovation without personal responsibility. Therapeutic effects derive from the close relationship that health and well-being have to a sense of control. Meditation enables greater self-awareness and control by promoting regression to areas of previous fixation, providing the opportunity to understand and to master these complexes. Studies illustrate that meditation enhances self-actualization, particularly through dealing with social conditioning and fears.

Therapeutic effects of meditation also derive from systematic desensitization, the reduction of response to threatening stimuli. Meditation creates a relaxed physical state during which unpleasant memories are slowly manifested in nonthreatening contexts. Meditation provides desensitization of distressing thoughts by permitting their occurrence in conjunction with extreme relaxation. The meditative state appears to automatically lead to the manifestation of material that is emotionally salient, an automatic consequence of reducing ordinary fixations of attention. Meditation acts through "reciprocal inhibition and counter-conditioning leading to desensitization of anxiety-evoking thoughts" (Delmonte 1987a, 46). This releases nonverbal tensions (Carrington 1987, 156), leading to relaxation, calmness, pleasurable sensations, and absorption (Pekala 1987). Insight into the processes through which the individual habitually constructs their personal version of reality enhances the possibility of changing patterns of behavior and cognition that are self-defeating (Delmonte 1987a). Meditative practices involving the stilling of the mind lead to a diminution and collapse of the left-hemisphere cognitive structures that support the individual sense of social identity, leading to a deconstruction of the self.

Those entering meditation practices often find powerful emotional experiences thrust on them, including unprocessed material, attachments, and a variety of distressing psychological phenomena and affective and cognitive sensations (Pekala 1987; Delmonte 1987a). Unpleasant phenomena include physical and emotional sensations; thoughts and images; intense feelings of anger, tension, and anxiety; and previously repressed memories and conflicts (cf. Walsh 1983). Walsh (1988) suggested that meditation can induce psychological problems, including anxiety, depersonalization, and psychosis. Delmonte (1987a) reviewed research indicating that when meditation shifts from active phases to ego receptivity, it gives rise to manifestations of the primary process mentation described by Freud and others. This primary process mentation has been viewed as the cognitive processes of the unconscious ego, conceptualized by MacLean (1990) as protomentation and emotiomentation.

SUMMARY

The therapeutic effects of ASC are widely attested to by shamanistic traditions, as well as by scientific studies. These therapeutic effects reflect a number of mechanisms, ranging from the general psychophysiological effects of ASC to specific effects of particular therapeutic modalities (e.g., psychointegrators versus meditation). The general therapeutic modalities of ASC reflect the activation of normal recuperative and integrative processes. These healing practices also reflect the symbolic power of the human mind and its interface with human biology in a variety of forms of ritual healing.

NOTES

1. The dipeptides of B-endorphin (glycyl-L-glutamine) and other pituitary neuropeptides modulate immune functioning (McCain, Bilotta, and Lamster 1987; Morley and Kay 1986).

2. These sections on "Therapeutic Effects of Hallucinogens" and "Neurotransmitters, Psychointegrators, and Organismic Functioning" are adapted from Winkelman (1996).

3. Stimulation of the 5-HT pathways in the raphe depresses neuronal firing of the dorsal hippocampus and the hypothalamic suprachiasmatic nucleus, as well as the caudate-putamen, the substantia nigra, the trigeminal nucleus, spinal-cord interneurons, spinothalamic-tract neurons, and the mesencephalic reticular formation (Aghajanian 1981, 165). The serotonergic pathways also depress amygdaloid cell firing resulting from dorsal raphe stimulation.

5

⤶

Psychophysiological Dynamics of Shamanistic Healing

CHAPTER OVERVIEW

The symbolic and ritual aspects of shamanistic healing practices provide a variety of therapeutic mechanisms for producing psychological and physiological transformations. This ability of symbolic and mental levels to cause physiological effects is recognized in cognitive science as top-down causation and in philosophy as supervenience. The basis of these mechanisms in shamanistic healing is discussed in terms of "medicine's symbolic reality" and models of symbolic healing, particularly the use of metaphor as a means of psychocognitive and psychophysiological integration. Although the classic analyses of the function of rituals have emphasized their psychological, social, or symbolic functions, the physiological effects of ritual must also be considered as a basic level of action on the body. Neurophenomenological perspectives illustrate how socialization links symbols and physiological processes, providing a mechanism for ritual healing. Shamanistic therapies manipulate physiological processes through their relationships with symbols that were established through socialization; this relationship enables them to entrain physiological processes and to produce affective responses. A neurological basis for ritual structure is illustrated by the cross-cultural similarities in the principles and characteristics of ritual and their homologies with obsessive-compulsive disorder. This suggests that one basis for shamanistic healing lies in manipulation of the processes of the R-complex (reptilian brain) and the relationship of the processes to the paleomammalian brain. A primary mechanism of symbolo-physiological action in shamanic healing is through systems of meaning. This meaning plays a central role in the management of emotional states, particularly anxiety, fear, and attachment. Rituals that curtail expression of emotions (excessive anger, depression, or grief) have important psychophysiological effects, exemplifying the psychosocial and symbolic mechanisms that cause changes in physiological processes. Ritual catharsis provides a means of relieving emotional conflicts and repressions and a socially acceptable means of expressing conflict, distress, disapproved desires, and other psychological needs. Shamanic systems for interpreting maladies have relevance for understanding modern psychodynamics, as exemplified in the *Diagnostic and Statistical Manual* (*DSM-4*) category of "spiritual emergencies" and the characteristics of contemporary spontaneous religious experiences. Spirit beliefs play fundamental roles as cognitive models of the psychosocial system, models that can be used to restructure psychodynamics, self, and social relations. The neurognostic structures utilized in shamanism are still manifested in contemporary religious experiences, illustrating the persistent relevance of shamanism for healing. The psychodynamic processes involved in possession and in the alteration of self and the emotional changes produced by meditative altered states of consciousness (ASC) illustrate the contemporary relevance of ASC-based therapies.

RITUAL HEALING: FORMS AND FUNCTIONS

Ritual has been a central feature in the analysis of shamanistic and other religious healing practices. Therapeutic efficacy can derive from the ritual transformation of identity, experience, and consciousness. Ritual affects emotional, cognitive, social, and interpersonal dynamics, producing physiological changes and providing a range of mechanisms for transformation of health. Ritual provides practitioners with a sense of conviction that they are proceeding correctly and efficaciously, reinforcing charismatic effects and patients' expectations. Confidence in the healer provides emotional assurance, which elicits the patient's own healing responses. The symbolic dimensions of shamanistic activity and their relationship to psychosocial dynamics provide mechanisms through which psychodramatic ritual enactments alter individual and collective psychodynamics. These classically recognized psychosocial processes of ritual transformation are extended in the neurophenomenological perspectives of Laughlin, McManus, and d'Aquili (1992). Entrainment of symbols and physiological processes during socialization provides bases for ritual effects of symbols on physiological processes.

Ritual has been traditionally conceived of as repetitive behavior for which no evidence exists to substantiate the technical or physical effects believed by the participants. Ritual is often an outsider's term, imputing faulty causal reasoning to the participants by the analyst who dismisses the effects participants presume their rituals to attain. Anthropological approaches have emphasized the need to distinguish presumed practical (technical) aspects of ritual from the expressive and symbolic dimensions. Rituals are then understood as acting at symbolic levels rather than at strictly technical or physical levels. But these two dimensions, the symbolic and technical, are not always separate, in practice or in effects. Symbols and rituals are found even in activities that are considered to be technical. Symbolic acts elicit associations and beliefs that transform experience, as well as physiological responses, and enhance positive expectations and commitment. Ritual techniques for altering consciousness exemplify their physiological consequences and, hence, technical effects.

Anthropological analyses of ritual have also emphasized the distinction between manifest and latent functions, the expressed intents versus the unintended, unarticulated, or unrecognized collateral effects. Because rituals generally assert means-ends relations not considered functionally possible, explanation has emphasized their latent effects on psychodynamics or social behavior. But even this perspective can fail to fully appreciate the technical aspects of social ritual's psychodrama in which important personal and social therapeutic effects are achieved *as intended by* the ritual processes. Ritual consequences for psychology, emotions, and physiological responses constitute basic technical effects of ritual. Shamanic rituals cause changes in the patient, ranging from adjustments in social relations to the alteration in the balance of the autonomic nervous system (ANS), which has direct implications for health. These physical changes are driven by the significance and psychophysiological consequences of rituals.

Prominent within anthropology has been the focus on the communicative aspects of ritual and rituals' representations of the interrelationships of values, cosmology, and social relations (e.g., see Skorupski [1976] on the symbolist traditions). Rituals are seen as symbolic statements manifesting the culture's basic values, especially humans' relationships to other humans, nature, and the cosmos. Ritual may state obligatory conditions of social life and communicate that message to participants, binding them together in a group that feels a sense of commonality (*communitas*). Rituals express the structure of society and the culturally ascribed meanings to the moral and natural order, providing an interpretive system that humans use to order experience and behavior. Ritual symbols are "multivocal," embedded in a system of meanings in which they have multiple referents. These multivocal symbols express and evoke a multiplicity of meanings, from general values to norms, roles, relationships, and beliefs. Ritual activities communicate important meanings to participants, including rules for social behavior. Didactic effects are found in rituals and associated activities, expressing traditional cultural knowledge and guidelines for social behavior.

Ritual action at symbolic and social levels can affect all levels of human functioning. Any ritual can have health implications, but those most central to healing activities are critical rituals (crises response) and rituals for social transition (rites of passage). Additionally, calendrical rituals (those held on specific days of the annual cycle, e.g., spring, deity, or harvest celebrations) may have general health effects through enhancement of social solidarity and integrative social effects. The calendrical rituals are often used as contexts for rites of social transition (passage), which recognize a stage of life development. These assist the individual and the social group with adjustments necessary to accommodate the individual's new status and the status's implications for behavior and social relations.

Rituals for social transition affect health in many ways, including the integration of the individual into new roles. Transition rituals are often directed toward the relationships between social conditions and physiological conditions (e.g., puberty). This ritual relationship demarcates certain points of the life cycle as especially significant, with social meanings and biological processes integrated in social life and personal experience—rituals at birth, naming, puberty, marriage, pregnancy, death, and so on. The ritual association of symbols and biological drives is a means of shaping and controlling human emotions and drives by providing them with explanations within cosmological frameworks. Rituals protect the individual and others during vulnerable, dangerous, and ambiguous periods of adjustment by reducing the uncertainty and stresses involved in these activities. For instance, mourning rituals may reduce behaviors (dietary intake, activity, relationships, excessive grieving, etc.) that can provoke health problems.

Rituals are means of constituting society or "significant others," reestablishing group cohesion and reducing social tension and resolving conflicts. Ritual effects on health may derive from ways in which activities affect group dynamics: reestablishing group continuity in the face of loss; dramatizing basic social values and the consequences of their violation; and modifying individual and group behavior to create social cohesion and harmony. Rituals may have social/epidemiological effects in controlling the relationship between the ill person and others. Rituals may mandate certain care for and protect the ill person, or they may protect the healthy from contact with the diseased. Rituals of purification often provide cleansing and sterilization, as well as changes in diet.

The most common recourse to ritual healing is in critical rituals or rituals of misfortune employed for illness or other malady. These healing rituals are typically psychosociophysiological therapies, manipulating all three levels through cultural and natural symbols. Critical rituals often require participation of significant others, often the entire community or the extended family. These practices often explicitly recognize causation of illness within the group's social relations. Healing rituals provide relief by reestablishing harmonious relations within the group.

Although ritual healing is often characterized as symbolic, it also involves a range of physical manipulations, including massage or rubbing of the body; application of the healer's hands on or near the body of the client with the intent of transferring healing energies; blowing or fanning on the body; sucking on the body; surgery and incisions into the body; washing and cleansing; and ingestion of a wide range of plant materials or other natural substances (Winkelman and Winkelman 1990). The physiological implications of physical manipulations are numerous. Ample evidence exists that herbal remedies are likely efficacious in treatment of physical diseases, as would be simple surgical interventions. Rubbing, massage, blowing, sucking, washing, and cleansing can be expected to induce a parasympathetic relaxation response. Sleight-of-hand can facilitate therapeutic manipulations through increasing suggestibility and psychosomatic, placebo, or psi effects (Winkelman 1982). Critical rituals also have therapeutic effects from psycho- and sociophysiological processes, as illustrated in what Kleinman (1973a,b) refers to as "medicine's symbolic reality."

MEDICINE'S SYMBOLIC REALITY

Shamanistic healing differs from traditional biomedicine in address-ing the health implications of a symbolic reality. The comparative study of healing systems reveals relationships of health to the broader cultural and social systems, even within biomedicine. Even physical diseases are experienced as symbolic and sociocultural phenomena. All healing systems are embedded within cultural systems that sym-bolically manage illness experiences through their classification and determination of specific therapeutic practices to manage illness. The meaning given by cultural symbols affects physiological responses through the attachments and evaluations they engender.

Kleinman (1973a) referred to "medicine's symbolic reality" as mediating the traditional separation of the biophysical and the psychocultural division of medicine and the sciences. This symbolic reality is involved in the evocation of psychophysiological responses through linking social events and cultural meaning to attachments, producing physiological reactions. These symbolic effects that chal-lenge the biophysical paradigm of medicine are basic to the processes of shamanistic healing.

Symbolic constructions and cultural meanings are fundamental to healing processes, beginning with the formulation of disease and its classification. Symbolic effects initiate healing functions prior to di-agnosis, a "treatment" resulting from how the patient perceives the interaction with the healing system and responds psychophysiologi-cally. Medical systems diagnose, label, classify, and treat illness, struc-turing the personal experience of illness. Classification of illness con-stitutes a part of the healing process, reducing stress, anxiety, and uncertainty and their detrimental physiological consequences. The patient's illness experience is through the cultural or symbolic reality that transforms it into events that are understandable to and man-ageable by the social group. The act of classifying an illness is a form of treatment through cognitive, personal, and social mechanisms. Symbolic mechanisms produce healing through the relationships among the cultural system, social relations, the individual's sense of self and well-being, and the cumulative effects of the mechanisms on emotions and their physiological substrate. Illness separates the sick from their normal social relations and roles, interfering with the individual's sense of well-being. Healing activities reestablish the sick person's social networks, which can reduce morbidity and mortality.

Healing occurs along a symbolic pathway of words, feelings, values, expectations, beliefs, and the like which connect cultural events and forms with affective and physiological processes. Psychosomatic and sociosomatic correlates are implicit in all medical healing relationships. Feelings and physiological responses are in some way linked to sociocultural reality via early socialization and learning. (Kleinman 1973a, 210).

This causal effect of the mental on the physical, as exemplified in psychosomatic pathologies, is also the basis for their therapeutic resolution.

This symbolic model provides a framework for explicating the effects of beliefs and cultural symbols on physiological processes. Psychophysiological responses that affect healing are linked through language and other symbolic systems during processes of socialization, enculturation, conditioning, and other forms of learning. This is based in relationships established through socialization, which create the basis for psychosomatic and sociosomatic effects by entrainment of physiological processes through their association with symbols. These symbolic processes operate not only in psychosomatic and sociosomatic conditions, but also in the shaping of all physiological responses through the interrelationships of sociocultural and psychophysiological domains. This symbolic model of healing suggests that meaning is a fundamental determinant of behavioral, perceptual, emotional, and consequently physiological responses. Shamanistic healing practices represent and manipulate social and cultural beliefs and induce psychophysiological reactions by evoking the symbolic associations established through socialization of beliefs, feelings, values, expectations, and meanings with affective/emotional processes and their physiological concomitants.

Symbolic Healing

Shamanistic healers' activities embody and express concerns of the sufferer and of society at large, with treatment processes reorganizing emotional conditions and the patient's social relations. Shamanistic healers construct a mythic world and symbolically manipulate it to elicit and to transact emotional experiences for the patient. Dow (1986) described universal aspects of symbolic healing as based in psychological processes through which symbols affect mind and consequently body. These psychological processes involve the healer particularizing for the patient a general cultural mythic view, creating an experiential reality through ritually manipulating symbols. The healer ritually enacts and elicits a commonly held mythic system and interprets the patient's condition within that system. The attachment of the patient's emotions to transactional symbols of healing allows the healer to then transform the patient emotionally through manipulating the symbols, because the social-symbol systems correspond to the self systems of the patient. A cure is produced through remodeling within the mythic world the disorder in the self and through transferring that new model to the patient to transform psychosocial and physiological dynamics.

Dow (1986) characterized the mechanisms of symbolic healing in terms of the "generalized media of social interaction" and the relationships among the hierarchies of living systems. Personality is part of a hierarchy of interrelated systems extending from the organic and somatic levels through the self and social systems. Although each level constitutes a complete system (e.g., body, self, personality), each system has control parameters based in the other systems. This provides the basis for systemic self-regulation and for causal effects across the entire organism mediated by many forms of communication. In shamanic healing, symbols provided by myth and embodied in ritual constitute the basis through which the self system and the somatic level of the patient are affected. The self system shares the unconscious thought processing of the body (somatic level) and exerts its influences through this common interface. These cognitive processes take place unconsciously, with interpretation of affective significance of symbols at the biological level in the somatic system, as well as in the self system.

Generalized symbolic media are communication devices that allow processes at a lower level in the control hierarchy to be transacted in a higher level system . . . [and are] able to affect the transaction of emotion in the self system. Thus symbolic healing allows unconscious and somatic processes to be controlled by symbolic communication occurring two levels higher in the social system. (Dow 1986, 64)

These mechanisms are reinforced through ASC, suggestion, persuasion, catharsis, social restructuring, psychodrama, and therapeutic relationships. Dow suggested that the generalized link of self and body is through emotions, with shamanistic therapies allowing the patient to catharsize, transfer, and transact emotions and other attachments. Adaptive biological aspects of symbolic healing involve linkages of emotional communication, insight, and social relations. Emotions constitute basic integrative control functions, providing higher levels of the organism with a summarization of complex processes occurring at lower levels (Dow 1986, 64). Emotions can play this fundamental linking role because although they have physiological foundations, they acquire their meaning and, consequently, patterns of elicitation from personal, social, and cultural levels. Dow suggested that symbolic healing is based on a human capacity for interpersonal communication derived from a prior capacity of humans to communicate with themselves through emotion. This intrapersonal biological control and communication mechanism was extended into later evolutionary control systems based on symbolic systems and language. Consequently, symbols can reciprocally use the emotional-meaning system to effect biological processes and produce a cure. A primary mechanism of this symbolic communication is through metaphor.

Metaphoric Processes in Healing

Kirmayer (1993) developed a theory of meaning for the mechanisms of symbolic healing, examining how language, gesture, and action perform the work of creating meaning and change. Kirmayer (1993, 162) characterized meaning as "a term for the active relationship of receiver to message of self to world worked within thought, feeling, imagination, and social transaction." Kirmayer suggested that meaning is relational and discovered by "showing what situated feelings, sensations, and actions an abstract communication or conceptualization evokes. Meaning, on this view, is equivalent to use— whether that use involves an overt action or an inferred cognitive transformation—and use is irreducibly triadic: the use *of* something *by* someone *for* some end" (162).

Kirmayer addressed the mechanisms of symbolic healing through a review of psychoanalytic and structuralist theories. Kirmayer characterized the healing efficacy of psychoanalytic approaches as derived from the revelation of warded-off truth. The patient's speech, action, and symptoms are used to reveal underlying dynamics. The symbols of psychoanalysis may heal because they provide a balance or a truce between different aspects of the self. But healing may occur not because of accurate representation or symbolic resolution, but rather because the "metaphorization of distress" provides the person with options and rhetorical supplies. In contrast, structuralism provides meaning that is derived from an examination of the coordination of sign systems and symbols. The meaning is derived from the internal logic that forms a "language" that provides meaning. Structuralist approaches, as exemplified in the analysis of myth, show meaning to be derived from the relationships in a total system of possible transformations. But although the structuralist approach illustrates how myth and symbol may function to provide a sense of social order, it does not illustrate how rituals and symbols affect the individual to reshape his or her thoughts and feelings, nor does it explain how symbols change the patient's world and experience. Kirmayer suggested that structuralists' use of physical information, psychological associations, and the social context of symbolic actions should direct society to a view of naturalism, a "biological psychology that grounds symbolic cognition in the body and in the exigencies of local power, relationships, and ecology" (1993, 167).

In Kirmayer's (1993) review of Levi-Strauss's (1963) analysis of the effectiveness of symbols in inducing childbirth, Kirmayer argued that the detailed correspondence of the mythic and metaphoric materials with the sufferer's physical condition is inadequate for an account of healing. He suggested that ritual efficacy derives from more than the analogy between the woman's body and the mythical realm; rather it involves the psychophysiological effects of metaphor. The structural relationships found in metaphor do not provide an explanation of its healing power. The finding that much of shamanic language is arcane and not understood by the participants makes the effects even more problematic. The metaphoric work is derived from expectations found in the larger social context of healing, including "bodily feelings and images evoked by nonverbal and paralinguistic aspects of ritual process" (Kirmayer 1993, 169).

Kirmayer reviewed universal aspects of symbolic healing in terms of Dow's (1986) model of the establishment of a generalized mythic world, the persuasion of the patient to particularize his or her problems within that mythic world, the healer attaching the patient's emotions to the mythic world symbols, and the manipulation of those symbols for assisting emotional transactions. Kirmayer suggested that the verbs *establish*, *persuade*, *attach*, and *manipulate* involve processes that are not explored within the structuralist approach. We must

understand the process of transduction at the level of physiological, psychological, or social mechanisms. Ultimately, what is left out of structural accounts are those nonsemiotic social (and biological) processes—establishing, persuading, attaching, manipulating, transacting—that provide both the medium and the causal structure of healing and semiosis." (Kirmayer 1993, 169)

Kirmayer (1993, 170) emphasized metaphor's power within the symbolic realm, as well as in terms of the physical body and society: "Metaphor theory does this by insisting on three levels to action and discourse: the mythic level of coherent narratives; the archetypal level of bodily-givens; and the metaphoric level of temporary constructions." Metaphor theory uses tropes linking body and society through myth and the archetype of the bodily given. By archetype, Kirmayer meant:

the bodily given—whether rooted in the nervous system or emergent in the form and exigencies of social life. Archetype stands for subjectively compelling images/experiences that seem to be presented to us before reflection or invention . . . Attempts to ground thought in basic physical actions also imply an archetypal basis to thought in the structure of the motor system and bodily constraints." (171)

Archetypes arise from the interaction of the body with social relations that constitute a universal substrate of human experience; these are the neurognostic foundations of consciousness—"knowing how."

Kirmayer characterized metaphor as involving "thinking of one thing in terms of another"; as such, metaphor constitutes the basis of creative thought. In metaphor, one transforms the topic through the juxtaposition of and interaction among sensory, affective, and cognitive elements (Kirmayer 1993, 172). Metaphors create and convey meanings or connotations derived from the juxtaposition[1] of images through reshaping of experiences provided by sensory, affective, or imagetic information.

Basic to metaphoric symbolism and healing are myth and archetype because their conflation of biological and experiential meanings collapses the false dichotomy of objective and subjective knowledge (Kirmayer 1993, 173). Kirmayer suggested that myth, metaphor, and archetype represent distinct levels of meaning, with each constructing a world view that is incommensurable with the others. The only means of reconciling these different levels is through treating them as text and deriving their meanings from an analysis of the transaction between bodily processes, metaphor, and social process. These interactions of body, imagination, and society provide the mechanisms of symbolic healing.

Kirmayer suggested that metaphors are derived from experiences of embodiment. Social relationships and the social body are embodied forces that we feel. Myth is an order of organization, the imposition of a structure on thought and behavior, which provides a social ordering of experience. The power of myth is derived from its ability to evoke and reorder experiences derived from life history, psychological development, and social behavior. The processes of myth, metaphor, and archetype represent the social, psychological, and bodily domains, respectively (Kirmayer 1993, 175).

Kirmayer (1993, 176) suggested that metaphors provide healing in three ways: "(a) by implicitly structuring conceptual domains through the qualitative logic of metaphoric implication; (b) by evoking strong sensory/affective associations that dominate or transform more abstract and rigid constructions; (c) by successfully bridging the archetypal and mythic levels of experience." The use of patients' metaphors and their sensory and emotional qualities is the essence of empathy. The healing efficacy of myths derives from their ability to unite within a narrative the disparate aspects of human experience, especially contradictions. Myths still work today when they can be interpreted in ways that tap into the patient's archetypal structures concerned with desire.

The basis of metaphoric thought is in the meaning derived from sensory and affective qualities. Metaphor becomes more complex and sophisticated with verbal expression, but Kirmayer suggested that earlier levels of meaning-making continue to contribute to abstract understanding. Kirmayer's metaphor theory provides content and specificity for meaning and knowledge through creating a twofold grounding of thought and action: one in early synesthetic and sensorimotor experience and the other in social life. In the vocabulary of Hunt (1995a), we may say that metaphor bridges presentational and representational levels of meaning with imagetic metaphors that convey meaning in both domains. The meaning of metaphors is reciprocally shared by the representational systems and the lower levels of sensory affective processing. These metaphors underlie the processes of thought and action, enabling cognition to drive physiological responses. Kirmayer (1993) suggested that central to therapy is the use of metaphors to evoke and to bridge cultural myths and bodily experience.

The effects of metaphors are derived from the immediacy of bodily felt experiences grounded in archetypal patterns shaped by cultural and social factors. This social response, a social construction, is an embodiment of metaphor. The healer uses symbols specific to the audience, with the ritual manipulation integrating different forms of meaning through linking activities from different levels of the brain. This is possible because activities of these different brain levels were symbolically entrained during socialization.

NEUROGNOSIS, BIOSOCIALIZATION, AND SYMBOLIC PENETRATION

The underlying processes of the symbolic model and mechanisms through which symbols affect health are illustrated by the neuro-phenomenological or biogenetic structuralist perspectives (Laughlin, McManus, and d'Aquili 1992). These mechanisms illustrate that socialization processes symbolically canalize physiological development and habitualize and automatize physiological responses to symbols. The development of the organism's genetic potentials requires symbolic input into the developmental canalization, habitualization of physiological responses. For humans, this input includes the cultural environment and language. Symbolic effects on physiological levels are inherent aspects of the organism and its functioning and activities because processing of environmental stimuli and their significance are fundamentally symbolic. The symbolic process is fundamental to the elicitation and elaboration of models and the development and maintenance of neural organization and experience. In its most fundamental form, perception is a symbolic process, a representation of present stimuli in terms of memories based on previous experiences. Experience, development, and socialization involve *entrainment*, the linking of neurons into networks. The brain's (and consciousness's) developmental socialization is through entrainment of neurons into networks constructing *cognized* models of the *operational* environment. The networks provide coherence and continuity to the cognized world, a symbolic model into which information is assimilated. The brain's preeminent function is to optimize adaptation through symbol systems that mediate between input (sensory) and output (behavior).

Fundamental to biological development is the repeated entrainment of networks of neurons stimulated in response to specific environmental conditions. During this developmental activity, a kind of neurological canal (a creode) forms in repetitively responding to and modeling specific stimuli. Canalization processes include the personal and cultural association patterns and their linkages across behavior, emotions, and cognition. The activation of the models may alter them by linking them together in associative chains and hierarchically organized systems, including specific and global physiological reactions (e.g., emotions). The canalizing process of neurognosis functions in ontogenesis, in social adaptation, and in the acquisition of perceptual discrimination, motor activity, conceptual differentiation, symbolic processes, and patterns of association. These adaptations are central to the development of social strategies for maintaining adaptive coordination among members of a species and for continuity of self and world view.

The relationship between cognition and action tunes the nervous system through symbolic associative processes. The biogenetic structuralist perspective recognizes events, perception, cognition, and action as interdependent aspects grounded in common neuropsychological and symbolic processes. A symbol may evoke any neural network or neurocognitive model with which it has been entrained, including autonomic and endocrine systems, brain structures, emotions, and abstract ideas. This is symbolic penetration, the effects of the neural system mediating a symbolic precept on associated physical systems. Evoking and entraining associated physiological systems allow meaning and symbols to influence physiological processes and allow physiological processes to evoke meaningful associations.

Shamanistic Healing as Ritual Symbolic Penetration

Symbolic healing processes operate on numerous associational patterns and their mediation through both the body and the ego. Laughlin et al. (1992) characterized the ego as a neural network that separates, differentiates, and integrates the environment while maintaining self-organization and adaptation to the operational environment. Outside of ego experience are structures from earlier development, automatized structures, and repressed or latent material, such as the genotypic and phenotypic progenitors of the ego. The ego tends to deny these structures that function outside of consciousness, although these complexes affect the ego and other structures of consciousness. Symbolic penetration created by ritual can evoke these structures and their intentionalities and can operate on them, mediating and transforming them outside of awareness. Symbolic healing processes can affect psychodynamic structures, destructuring the ego, evoking latent aspects of the self, transforming socioemotional aspects of the psyche, or activating and elevating deep structures into consciousness. Symbols may penetrate neurocognitive systems and reorder them to produce a cure. Rituals may reelevate, transform, and integrate latent or suppressed neural networks through symbolic penetration techniques that bypass normal inhibitory functions.

The neurophenomenological perspective provides an understanding of shamanistic healing processes as the consequence of entrainment of neural structures and networks with symbols. These processes are based in the effects of symbols on consciousness and brain processes. Rituals are mediated by specific neural networks and models and can be used to control the function of the same neural networks and associated physiological processes. Ritual healing produces cures through entraining deep levels of neurocognitive organization, evoking repressed structures and psychodynamic complexes and re-elevating them into consciousness. These repressed structures can produce conflict and collapse of the ego in development of a different relationship of self to the world. Integration of this previously unconscious material into the conscious network may result in profound changes in the individual's experience of self and world, including alteration of behavior, personality, self-understanding, and autonomic balance. Ritual communicative processes produce intraorganismic coordination of somatic systems and interorganismic (within group) coordination of the cognized environment. Shamanistic healing synchronizes consciousness through using rituals to control phases of consciousness, to synchronize the collective cognized environment of the group, and to integrate the group for concerted action (Laughlin et al. 1992, 145).

Ritual healing involves a "theater of the mind" (Laughlin et al. 1992), the use of symbols as penetrating agents that entrain with levels of neurocognitive organization and produce changes in their activity and associations. Symbolic penetration through myth, symbol, and ritual induces experiences and frames and interprets them for the participants. Myth and ritual behaviors and symbols bridge iconic and verbal levels by including elements of both domains. Metaphors are frequently used because they cross domains of meaning and cause the entrainment of different neurocognitive structures based on homology of form or relationship, or of unconscious associative processes. Myth serves as a means of molding, stabilizing, and integrating the patients' experiences, giving them meaning. Myth provides the framework for understanding the world transcending the ego and, through reciprocal assimilation, permits the integration of the ego into wider structures of mythic consciousness. This integration of previously unconscious material into the conscious network may result in profound changes in the individual. These changes are produced because the symbols have been entrained with physiological processes that are associated with: basic emotions; social attachments; needs of the self; and sense of comfort, of security and certainty, and of fears, anxieties, and other psychodynamic processes that have effects on physiological processes. Symbols may provide powerful stimulation of one's intentionality and of other physiological processes through activating neurognostic models of the phylogenetically older brain.

Rituals can also alter consciousness and physiological processes through a wide variety of mechanisms that induce retuning of the ANS balance. This retuning tends to block the dominant hemisphere's functions and produces an integrative fusion with functions of the nondominant hemisphere; this structurally synchronized state tends to resolve internal conflicts and to produce euphoric states (Laughlin et al. 1992). This synchronization depends on the elicitation of processes of lower-brain structures that are associated with basic behavior, intentionality, and emotions.

Neuroanatomical Bases of Ritual Healing

Dulaney and Fiske (1994) pointed to the cross-cultural similarity in the structure of rituals. Although studies have addressed the *meaning* of rituals, there is a lack of consideration of the component elements of rituals and their structures, "the forms of action and kinds of ideas that characterize rituals" (Dulaney and Fiske 1994, 213). They reviewed case materials and analyzed formal cross-cultural data to identify common behavioral and ideational features that rituals share with a specific neuropsychiatric syndrome—obsessive compulsive disorder. Such universal features are derived from neurognostic bases reflected in the relationship of the universal features of ritual proposed by Dulaney and Fiske to the brain systems and forms of mentation proposed by MacLean (1990).

Dulaney and Fiske (1994) suggested that rituals appear to be designed to address relationships among habitualized patterns of behavior, particularly those patterns related to the integrity of self, to the relationships with significant others, and to concerns with bodily processes, grooming, sexual impulses, and aggression. These are a basis for a homology between regular features of ritual and those of obsessive compulsive disorders (OCDs) and suggest a common physiological basis in brain functioning. Dulaney and Fiske suggested that a neurological basis for the structure of rituals is manifested in universal features of ritual and where overactive and malfunctioning in individuals is manifested in psychopathology of OCD. But in contrast to Freud's pathological attributions, Dulaney and Fiske emphasized that rituals are not collective disorders, nor are they compulsive, obsessive, or pathological because they constitute intentionally adopted cultural means of achieving culturally defined goals. But they also suggested that "the psychological proclivities that may underlie cultural rituals may be closely related to the mechanism that is malfunctioning in OCD patients" (Dulaney and Fiske 1994, 247).

Although there are fundamental differences in meaning, legitimacy, cultural values, and functions of OCDs and religious rituals, they have substantial morphological similarity, which Dulaney and Fiske (1994) illustrated through analysis of their feature-by-feature correspondences.

Rituals tend to involve precise spatial arrays and symmetrical patterns, stereotyped actions, repetitive sequences, rigidly scrupulous adherence to rules (and often the constant creation of new rules), and imperative measures to prevent harm and protect against immanent dangers. These features typify rituals, but they also define a psychiatric illness, obsessive-compulsive disorder (OCD)." (245)

The OCD features that Dulaney and Fiske considered to also be characteristic of ritual mostly coalesce around five principal categories:

1. concern with cleanliness, contamination, and bodily secretions
2. fear of harm to self or others, particularly violence
3. repetitive behaviors, including orderly arrangement of people
4. special significance of numbers (or colors)
5. unacceptable sexual impulses

Dulaney and Fiske's cross-cultural study assessing the incidence of OCD features in ritual and work found such features twice as common in ritual as in work. A number of the features have strongly significant associations with ritual:

1. concern or disgust with bodily wastes or secretions
2. fear that something terrible will happen; fear that they themselves may

cause harm to themselves or others; measures to prevent harm to self or others

3. repetitive actions

4. special significance to colors

5. attention to thresholds or entrances

The first four of five items have direct correspondence with OCD characteristics.

The similarity of the actions and thoughts in OCD and rituals suggests that the human disposition to enact rituals is the consequence of a specific human capacity or neurognostic structure. Dulaney and Fiske (1994) hypothesized that underlying cultural rituals are psychophysiological mechanisms similar to those affecting OCD patients. They cited clinical studies that indicate that OCD is a consequence of malfunction of the mammalian basal ganglia, manifested in excessive levels of serotonin (Wise and Rapoport 1989).

Similarities of the common OCD/ritual characteristics with specific forms of mentation associated with particular anatomical structures of the brain and their functions provide a basis for substantiating the hypothesis of Dulaney and Fiske. I hypothesize that the mentation processes of the R-complex and limbic system provide the common underlying features for both OCD and ritual behavior. The activation of the R-complex and limbic system is suggested by the serotonin abnormalities (excessive levels), because most serotonin of the brain is in the hypothalamus (MacLean 1990) and the hypothalamus serves as a central link between these two brain systems. The further involvement of the hypothalamus and the hippocampal septal system in the neurognostic basis of ritual is illustrated by its role in producing shamanic ASC, as detailed in chapter 3. The role of ritual as a psychosociocognitive integrative process reflects the role of serotonin as a neuromodulator and psychointegrator.

The relations of brain processes to the functions of ritual are further elucidated by MacLean's (1990) research on the physiology-behavior linkages in the brain. MacLean suggested that there are forms of human behavior mediated by the evolutionary earlier centers of the brain that are integrated into contemporary behavior in nonverbal mentation and behavior. Bateson (1972) argued that these kinisetic and paralanguage systems have been elaborated along with the development of verbal language and have become even more complex, reflecting their continued importance in human socioemotional communication. Forms of vocalization such as imitative song and chanting found in shamanic activities involve the tuning of this early communication system. MacLean suggested that these communication forms be discussed in terms of paleomentation, particularly protomentation. Protomentation involves rudimentary forms of cerebration responsible for regulating the activities of the daily master routines and subroutines in the expression of the major behavioral displays used in prosematic communication. These expressive functions are primarily managed by what MacLean (1990, 1993) referred to as the R-complex, or reptilian brain.[3] The R-complex and the striatal complex in particular are involved in the integration of the various levels and conflicting types of cortical and subthalamic mechanisms that integrate the movements and total reactions of the organism; the regulation of the animals' daily master routines and subroutines; displays of communicative social performances; and the organized expression of behavior initiated by internally derived cues. MacLean referred to these as interoperative behaviors, which operate with respect to the brain itself rather than other forms of behavior.

MacLean reviewed six forms of interoperative behavior (routinization, isopraxic, tropistic, repetitious, reenactment, and deceptive), which reflect both ritual and OCD behavior. *Routinization* of behavior involves temporal sequencing of behavior around the clock and is "dominated by a master routine, but may also have quite rigidly structured within it a number of subroutines. . . . When subroutines become rigidly structured in their patterns and time occurrence, they become known as rituals" (MacLean 1990, 142–43). *Isopraxic* refers to behavior that is acted or performed in the same way or manner. The isopraxic behaviors are "implicated in conspecific recognition and in most forms of communication involved in self-preservation and in procreation of the species" (144), permitting both species and sexual identification. *Tropistic* behavior refers to unlearned animal responses, such as innate motion patterns and fixed action patterns; fundamental elicitors of such behaviors in the animal world are colors and body direction. *Repetitious* or preservative behaviors refer to repeated performances of specific acts in which the repeated behavior contains a number of actions that are meaningfully interrelated to the actor. MacLean specifically referred to church services as an example of this periodic reenactment in human society. *Reenactment* behavior refers to "a series of actions that are repeated essentially the same way in each performance . . . ritualized subroutines . . . occurring within the daily master routine" (MacLean1990, 147); they are characterized by a rigid adherence to the same customs of behavior on a daily basis. The sixth interoperative behavior listed by MacLean is *deceptive* behavior. Although deception as such is not listed as an OCD symptom, OCD patients try to avoid bringing their OCD behavior to the attention of others because they recognize that it is abnormal. Ritual also typically has similar properties of secrecy.

The common aspects of ritual behavior and OCD involving concerns with self, violence, and sexual impulses are based in processes of the paleomammalian brain and limbic system. The limbic system serves as the major conduit for the funnelling of neural information that subserves self-preservation, feeding, fighting/defense, procreation and sexual behavior, nursing/maternal care, and audiovocal communication (MacLean 1990). Clinical findings provide crucial evidence on the role of the limbic system in the subjective experience of affect, the basic emotional needs and feelings, and the psychological information attached to sensations, perceptions, compulsions, and conceptions (MacLean 1990). Affects can occur independent of external stimuli and can persist beyond the external stimuli that may evoke them. General affects are not dependent on immediate experience but may be derived from mentation processes and memories and their associations with external objects, individuals, or situations. The limbic system is involved in the elaboration of both basic and specific affects, which provide subjective information of instrumental importance that is used to guide behavior involved in self and species preservation.

Summary

The roles of the R-complex and the limbic brain in activities related to ritual behavior and OCD are abundant. This is specifically seen in the R-complex control of master routines and subroutines and the organized expression of behavior initiated by internally derived cues. Here we find explicit similarities of routinization, isopraxic, repetitious, and reactment behaviors with the OCD and ritual characteristics. The limbic system is responsible for emotional mentation, modulating the intensity of feelings and guiding behavior required for self- and species preservation. Ritual/OCD features specific to limbic system functions include sexual feelings, compulsions, automatisms, stereotypy, species-preservation behavior, and the emotional behaviors of anger, aggression, protection, caressing, and searching. ASC predominantly evoke responses from the paleomammalian brain, suggesting that ritual induces communicative processes of the paleomammalian brain. These are not primitive forms of mentation; they provide the basis for an expansion of consciousness by integrating information from these lower systems into operational activities of the frontal brain and by establishing a synchrony with the frontal brain that permits symbolic reprogramming of the emotional dynamics and behavioral repertoires of lower-brain centers.

PSYCHOSOCIAL DIMENSIONS OF SHAMANISTIC AND RELIGIOUS HEALING

The religious aspects of shamanistic healing involve a number of different modalities. Principal among these are systems of meaning and mental processes, social relations and psychosocial processes, and emotional transactions. These are represented in the shaman's involvement with the spirit world, the community, and ASC, respectively.

Shamanistic healing represents the most primordial form of religious healing, seeking the restoration of well-being through symbolic and social interaction within a psychocognitive and emotional dimension represented as supernatural beings and a spiritual world. The worldwide presence of religious elements in healing attests to their special role in promoting well-being and psychocognitive organization and illustrates a central aspect of the therapeutic effects of mental constructs. The ubiquitous association of religion with healing practices has a functional basis in religion's ability both to organize cognition and affect and to evoke physiological responses that transform consciousness and personal experience. Religion provides fundamental assumptions, values, world views, and meanings; psychosocial representations of intra- and interpsychic dynamics and collective and intergroup dynamics; and psychosociophysiological manipulations through meanings, attachments, and their implications for well-being.

Spilka and McIntosh (1997, 67) pointed out that the persistence of religion indicates that it has a significant role in human psychology; although some psychological functions may be met by other social institutions, the "near universality begets the question of what functions religion serves uniquely or, at least, singularly well." Spiritual systems have important implications for personality theory because the universal functions and mechanisms of shamanistic healing involve fundamental aspects of the psyche, which are universally recognized within religious systems as spiritual aspects of the person that interact with external spiritual entities or powers. These external spiritual entities play a fundamental role in helping people understand problems, in meeting needs for meaning, and in enhancing self-esteem and sense of control.

Pervasive systemic influences of religion as a "mainspring of culture" make it one of the principal institutions underlying symbolic healing processes. Religion provides explanations about the nature of the world, about ultimate values and justifications, and about motivations for numerous aspects of human behavior. Religion organizes ecological, economic, familial, social, and political activities and justifies personal and social behaviors, determining many aspects of attitudes and values. Religious systems manipulate psychological and social life and cognitive structures and beliefs, triggering physiological responses, emotional reactions, and behaviors and commitments, providing powerful mechanisms for healing and change.

The therapeutic procedures of shamanistic healers share characteristics reflecting general principles involving the universal symbolic, psychological, and sociophysiological dynamics of the healing encounter. Healing involves the intercession of a socially and symbolically demarcated specialist (healer) who intends to provide relief for the sufferer through a series of ritually structured contacts. These interactions involve the identification of the nature of the malady (diagnosis) and the appropriate treatment within a culturally shared framework of meaning and explanation that connects the illness experiences of the patient to broader systems of meaning within which the malady and procedures for its resolution are understood. These interactions can reduce stress and anxiety by providing understanding and by instilling hope and expectations of improvements in health. Shamanistic healers facilitate a cure through constructing the interpersonal and social relations that are found universally in transference between therapist and patient and in which social expectations and attachments produce social and psychological change. Positive relations also produce physiological changes through elicitation of the relaxation response, or psychosomatic effects.

Shamanistic healing involves the interaction of symbolic and physiological levels through rituals that instill confidence and hope in ways that counteract anxiety and its physiological effects. The multiple mechanisms include the "biology of hope"—attitude-induced immunological system responses; persuasion and positive attitudinal induction; the restructuring of social relations and attachments; the enhancement of expectations by patient and group; the resolution of the sick role; the provision of (re)conditioning experiences or desensitization to stressful events or their representations; and psychodramatical enactments, including catharsis, which may provide a way of expressing unacceptable emotions.

Valle and Prince (1989, 151) characterized the standard healing mechanisms of self-healing religious experiences as based on producing "a sense of certainty-of-belongingness in the universe, a sense of euphoria and omnipotence which may be linked to the production under stress of the body's own morphine-like substances, the endorphins." Their study characterized religious healing experiences as dynamic functions of the psyche in reaction to problematic situations. Religious healing produces resolutions through broadening the individual's repertoire of coping abilities and his or her self-esteem. Religious healing experiences are self-healing attempts in the face of stressful life circumstances, providing a reduction of uncertainty, anxiety, and depression and a reorientation of values. Valle and Prince label the most frequent types of religious healing experiences as ecstatic, aesthetic, and hallucinatory. These are analyzed in terms of activations of the nondominant-hemisphere processes and "endogenous psychological healing mechanisms analogous to the host of well-known mechanisms for the preservation of bodily homeostasis" (164). These ecstatic (ASC) and hallucinatory (visionary) experiences are fundamental aspects of the shamanic practice interpreted as experiences of a spiritual order. These and other universal aspects of religion and religious healing reflect use of categories and constructs that represent neurognostic structures and processes and their relationship to self, others, emotions, and projections. These include fundamentals of meaning, management of emotional insecurities, constructions of relations between self and other, and the use of these systems to alter self and emotions.

Meaning, Explanation, and Assurance: Bases of Cultural Healing

Shamanistic healing incorporates a primordial psychocognitive function of religious systems in providing explanations and meaning, meeting psychological needs for a system of knowledge about the nature of life, which provides a sense of certainty and reduces anxiety (Malinowski [1925] 1954; Wallace 1966). Belief in the efficacy of religion and ritual provides assurance that can reduce anxiety and create positive expectations. Ritual systems provide a sense of control, identifying the universe of known possibilities. Religions can reduce anxiety and enhance well-being and self-confidence by focusing attention on behaviors for coping and alleviation of distress.

A central feature of religious explanation is the concept of animism, the belief in spiritual beings, and their central role in motivating humans, animals, and the forces of the natural and social world. Fundamental assumptions of religious healing rituals involve the ability to influence these agents viewed as responsible for well-being. Spirits reflect the projections and externalizations of intrapsychic dynamics and psychosocial processes. Consequently, religion can affect humans physiologically and psychologically through elicitation of emotional, behavioral, and cognitive processes based on presumptions about these agents. Religious rituals are not merely beliefs, but also systems of thought and action. These actions have consequences across all levels of humans—physical, biological, emotional, psychological, social, cognitive, and so on.

Shamanistic healing makes maladies meaningful in the context of life and cultural beliefs, an integration that may heal (make whole) the individual, relieving emotional conflicts and, consequently, symptoms of physical distress. Symbolic elements of healing may have profound effects even if the healer's interaction is brief and impersonal. These effects are part of cultural healing, a consequence of the patient's entry into the healing system, which inspires confidence, allaying the patient's concerns and contributing to mobilization of his or her own defenses (Press 1982). Healing may be induced through the unconscious manipulation by symbolic means operating through analogical processes, circumventing involvement of the ego and the rational mind.

Representations of Mental and Social Processes

Spirit beliefs play a fundamental role in religious concepts of causes of illness and processes of healing. Beliefs in "spirit aggression" theories of illness are universal (Murdock 1980; cf. Winkelman and Winkelman 1990). Spirits are the most fundamental conceptual category of religious beliefs (animism), a basic form of causation of shamanistic illness and a fundamental therapeutic mechanism of shamanistic healing. The effects of a spirit entity acting either independently or through human agency are treated through symbolic techniques involving manipulation of culturally defined spirit realities. These spirit dynamics form central themes in the psychodramatic enactments, mediating psychocognitive and physiological processes.

Durkheim (1915) showed that spirit beliefs reflect structures and patterns of relationships in society, representing abstract processes, relations, and groups. Religion is a *symbol system* that provides *meaning*, not of supernatural entities, but of social and interpersonal relations, intrapsychic dynamics, and cognitive organization and processes. Understanding spirits as representations of social groups and forces reveals ritual manipulation to involve restructuring of individual psychodynamics and collective psychosocial relations. The psychodynamic implications of spirits suggest that they be viewed as nonphysical actors in the social world, with their relationships involving social behavior (e.g., see Skorupski 1976 on the symbolist traditions). Symbolist approaches have viewed spirits as a symbolic system of social representations of norms, values, and ideal behaviors, as nonphysical actors in the social world that exemplify social ideals and reinforce them, directing people toward proper social behavior. The explicit statements of religious systems have implicit meanings and expressive functions. Spirits and supernatural beings are representations of society; of social institutions; of social attitudes and morals; of patterns of collective behavior; of social and environmental relations; of social traditions, beliefs, and processes; and of collective psychocultural dynamics. This interpretive approach (e.g., Turner's [1969] *The Ritual Process*) shows these symbolic structures to represent human needs, feelings, values, and commitments and the tensions that they produce in the relationships between the individuals and society. Swanson (1960), basing himself in Durkheim's (1915) ideas about the elementary forms of religious life, suggested that spirits and supernatural beings are personifications of society, representing social attitudes (e.g., morality), social relations, social experiences, and social purposes, particularly those of sovereign groups persisting across generations. Spirit beliefs are a language of components of intrapsychic and social dynamics and psychosocial relations. These psychodynamic implications of spirit aggression require a differentiation between possession spirits and nonpossession spirits. However, the implications share a commonality in manipulating sense of self, identity, and relations to significant others.

Structuralist approaches show that religion involves generic aspects and structures of human thought, including concepts of self and other, and structures of meaning attribution. Religious concepts organize thought, providing conceptual categories and representations to construct a basic sense of self through nonlinguistic symbolism. These conceptual categories and representations are mediated by phylogenetically older forms of representation and communication, which manage self, other, and their interdependence in producing emotional well-being.

Spilka, Shaver, and Kirkpatrick (1997) apply attribution theory to the psychology of religion, emphasizing that humans seek to make sense of experience and are always attributing meaning to occurrences. The normal human tendency to attribute enduring dispositions and traits to actors and to underestimate environmental forces constitute what Spilka et al. call a "fundamental attribution error." This fundamental cognitive tendency is embodied in the attribution of causal efficacy to spiritual actors. This attribution error is based in the metaphoric extension of the self and in its capabilities for modeling the unknown. Another important aspect of the attribution processes is their use to maintain or enhance one's own self-esteem, as well as that of one's group, through association with superior beings.

Religion's imposition of cognitive schemas for interpretation of the world is a normal aspect of human psychology. *Schemas* are structures or representations that organize information about the world, filling in the missing information with the implications provided by their conceptual framework. Schemas provide rapid mechanisms for engaging decision-making processes regarding selection of strategies and responses to challenging events. This religious function of constructing explanations has particularly salient influences on stress and the coping process. By contributing to clarification of meaning by imposing meaningful interpretations, religious systems' explanatory frameworks can reduce distress.

Both anecdotal accounts and empirical studies (e.g., see Spilka and McIntosh 1997) indicate that religion is a response often undertaken in circumstances of tragedy. Coping is a reactive and goal-directed process, addressing efforts to preserve or to reestablish important conditions. Pargament and Park (1997) reviewed research that illustrated that a central aspect of the coping response involves a "search for significance," which links religious healing to meaning-centered concerns and humans' need to understand problems of existence. Although religion has often been characterized as a coping response involving avoidance, it is better understood as a structure providing ways to evaluate and to respond to situations that fall outside of conventional understandings. Religions may provide a passive or avoidant coping strategy, but many instill a sense of control and mastery. Although coping may place responsibility in the spiritual domain, it may also insist on the individual's utilization of ritual resources, which direct behavior, attitudes, affect, and cognition toward desired goals.

The effectiveness of religious coping and its association with more favorable outcomes suggests that people find it easier to bear negative events if they can be understood within a religious framework based on benevolent principles. Religious coping is particularly important when people's coping responses have reached the limits of their personal capabilities and social resources (Spilka and McIntosh 1997, 52), which indicates that religious healing provides a unified psychosociobiological process in which personal significance (meaningfulness) plays an important role in the management of stress.

Social Relations and Well-Being: Belonging and Comfort

Ritual healing practices have numerous effects on psychosocial relations and, consequently, on individual psychodynamics and psychophysiological responses. Primary social psychological functions of religion are meeting needs for belonging and comfort in bonding the individual with society. Religious activities integrate and bond people, enhancing social cohesion through a social support system that provides material assistance, a sense of group identity, and elicitation of opioid release (see Frecska and Kulcsar 1989; chapters 2 and 3 this volume). Shamanistic healing practices incorporate all of the local group within the healing ritual. These community rituals elicit neurobiologically mediated forms of attachment and release endogenous opiates through a variety of mechanisms. Endogenous opioid release facilitates adaptive change for individuals and groups and enhances group bonding and identification through psychological and physiological mechanisms.

Religious healing practices have the power to transform a person's life through social participation and personal experience of self in relation to others. The individual is incorporated into a community of people who provide support through interpersonal relations and social networks. This incorporation satisfies social and personal needs, constituting a fundamental form of social support, which has positive effects against morbidity and mortality. Many shamanistic healing practices require that the individual take an active part in and responsibility for his or her healing through participation in other organizational activities. A healing community can transform people's lives such that they become psychologically dependent on the relationships with the community and on the emotional and social needs that they meet.

Role theory contributes to the understanding of the social psychology of religion because roles enable people to interact in regularly patterned ways, including relations with a "divine other" (Holm 1997). The processes of role-taking provide a mechanism through which personal development occurs. This role-taking through symbolic communication enables one to treat one's own identity as an object. The relations between self and role may take a variety of different degrees of internalization and identity (Sarbin 1954). A significant aspect of the development of the self is the integration of other people's roles into one's personality. This integration and identification with others provides the basis for modification of one's own behavior and identity. This identification with the social other provides the template through which one adopts relations with the "divine other."

These social role interaction experiences illustrate that spiritual entities play an important role as a social other (cf. Pandian 1995; chapters 1 and 2 this volume). Roles for individual socialization and models for the roles' developmental sequences are provided in the spirit-world symbol systems. The internalization of models for self and behavior and the capacity to express oneself through symbols provide the ability to combine memories and to transfer feelings from one situation or social object to another. These symbolic transactions link the internal cognized environment of the individual and the external social and physical environments with effects on emotional processes. These emotional attachments may produce social distress and mechanisms for therapeutic relief through expression of repressed emotions and through means to experience the self as a different person. Central psychodynamic effects of shamanistic healing evoke changes in the patient's self through the healer's projection and elicitation of models of development (Laughlin et al. 1992). Shamanic projection involves positively projecting a more-advanced state of development into another person, based on the unconscious transference of control of the individual's intentional processes to a powerful "master." An altered sense of self is provided through the ASC-induced access to another realm of experience where ritual induces cognitive, emotional, and physiological changes in the ways in which people experience themselves and the world.

Ritual Manipulation of Emotional Well-Being

Religion provides beliefs of great importance in structuring conscious and unconscious emotional dynamics. Malinowski (1925) suggested that the source of religion was in emotional life, in stress and unresolved problems, in anxieties and frustrations. These conditions are contributory to illness, providing a means through which religion can enhance health by countering these concerns. Reduction of anxiety and its physiological concomitants combined with the beneficial immunological effects of positive expectation enhance the body's capacity for resistance and recovery. Religious systems mediate the emotional impacts of disasters, illness, and death on victims and survivors, providing explanations, means of obtaining relief, assurance of survival in a spiritual afterlife, and a social support system. Ritual can alleviate habitualized high levels of pituitary/adrenal activity of the resistance stage of the stress reaction through several mechanisms: changes in emotions and ANS balance, integration of the emotional and egoic levels of the psyche, and resolution of social conflicts and disapproval.

Proudfoot and Shaver (1997) analyzed the role of religious attribution in induction of emotional experiences. Religiously defined meanings and experiences can induce and reduce autonomic arousal, providing important contributions to cognitive labeling and the interpretations individuals make of their state. Proudfoot and Shaver illustrated that religion provides powerful attributions to actors beyond individual control; however, the attribution system of shamanism establishes relationships with the spiritual world that are subject to one's control.

Kirkpatrick's (1997) applications of attachment theory to the psychology of religion illustrate attachments as a fundamental adaptive need and emotion of a biosocial behavioral system that evolved to maintain proximity between infants and caregivers. Attachments based on affectional bonds and relationships provide a secure basis for the self. Attachment relationships provide feelings of comfort and protection and a secure basis from which to explore the world. Attachment relationships are a fundamental dynamic underlying religions, providing the assurance that a powerful figure is available for protection against danger and threats. Attachment theory replaces the negative implications of Freudian concepts such as regression or dependency with an emphasis on the functions of protection and security that attachment figures provide in frightening circumstances. Attachment theory illustrates that religion contributes to emotional development, where relationships with others influence one's beliefs and adaptations, enhancing altruism and other helping behavior.

Shamanistic healing may have effects on many emotional processes, providing confession and forgiveness, eliciting repressed memories, restructuring memories of painful experiences, and resolving conflict through symbolic ritual processes. Walsh (1990) suggested that shamanic therapies create psychological and physical healing through confession, which relieves conflicts and repressions and provides for expression of unconscious concerns. Social knowledge of transgressions can exacerbate stress reactions through the social disapproval and interpersonal rejection expressed by others. Confession is often followed by social forgiveness, which can reduce social stress, reestablish harmonious interpersonal relations, and provide emotional catharsis. Catharsis—the remembering, reexperiencing, and expression of repressed emotional memories with painful attachments—is ritually structured to reduce stressful impacts on the individual.

Shamanistic healing typically provides an explanation of misfortune in ways that minimize personal guilt, a negative emotional process often resulting from intrapsychic conflict and the discrepancy between internalized ideals and actual behavior. The conflict produces an internalized emotional distress that occupies the person's attention, particularly at unconscious levels. Ritual removal of an object intruded into the body can be understood from a psychiatric perspective as releasing a "negative introject," a highly critical self-perspective derived from internalization of an attitude from a loved significant other during early childhood. The view of guilt in terms of conflicts between id impulses (considered here as processes of the paleomammalian brain) and the superego ideals (internalized standards for self-evaluation derived from significant others and enculturation) suggests that shamanistic healing mediates paleomammalian brain and neomammalian brain interactions.

The symbolic processes of rituals may also be used to evoke negative or unpleasant emotions (e.g., anger, fear) or memories, suggesting that shamanistic healers utilized the same principles of modern psychotherapy in enabling their patients to consciously confront their fears (Walsh 1990). The treatment of anxiety is linked across Western behavioral and psychopharmacological therapies in their common action of desensitization. In behavior therapies, the most common method of therapy used is exposure to feared objects, providing a learning desensitization based on a realization of one's own self-control. Although the effectiveness of pharmacotherapies is limited because cessation of medication often results in relapse, the behavioral desensitization becomes essentially irreversible once established. The treatment strategies for anxiety disorders focus on exposure to threatening, feared, or avoided objects; incorporating significant others is often a necessary part of treatment because of codependencies. Shamanic healing processes provide exposure to fearful stimuli through the shaman's dramatic enactments, with therapeutic change achieved in the confrontation of the patient's deepest fears in images that symbolize the shadow (Walsh 1990). The clients' active role in engaging the images of their fears and procedures which provide for catharsis permit reduction of the impact of the feared objects and previous traumas.

Hill (1997) addressed the relationship between cognitive and emotional processes in religious behavior and experience through a mediational or attitude-process approach that illustrates the roles of cognitive and emotional processes as the bases for attitudes. Hill suggested that the attitude concept is central to and necessary for characterizations of the spiritual and the mental aspects of religious experience. A fundamental function of an attitude is its categorization of something along some good/bad evaluative dimension. Both automatic and controlled evaluative processes are utilized in cognitive components of attitudes. Attitudes controlled by automatic processes may occur independently of higher level processing, reflecting the automaticity of affective responses. These responses reflect the anatomical basis of the emotional reactive basis described by Ledoux (1996). Ledoux's work showed how little the cognitive processes may be able to control the biologically based emotional reactions. But in contrast to this unreflective hardwiring of emotional responses and the lack of cognitive control over emotions, the outcome of ritual processes exemplifies control of emotional reactions. Attitude's evaluative processes normally have both cognitive and emotional components; however, situational, interpersonal, and other conceptual factors may determine whether cognitive or emotive processes are given priority. When individuals are operating under stress or when circumstances defy conventional explanations, it is more likely that the automatic emotional processes will take over in the evaluative processes. Rituals are used to guide these reactions to stable and adaptive states, shaping what is perceived at emotional as well as cognitive levels. Ritual can socialize and reentrain the associations that link emotional, cognitive, and behavioral levels.

The symbolic representations in spirit concepts of emotional, psychological, and social processes are basic mechanisms of shamanistic healing. The major shamanistic ASC traditions—soul journey, possession, and meditation—have different effects in structuring the relations of self, emotions, and others.

SHAMANIC ILLNESS AND SPIRITUAL EMERGENCY

The neurognostic basis of shamanistic paradigms of self and other is attested to by their persistence in contemporary religious experiences and psychological crises. Shamanic fundamentals in contemporary society are found in the prevalent religious experiences and in a new *DSM-IV* category *spiritual emergencies*. The shamanic paradigm provides a broader framework for explaining these phenomenal experiences of consciousness as natural manifestations of human consciousness and as growth and transformative opportunities rather than as pathologies. This reformulation enables one to take a more direct approach to controlling these powerful unconscious factors. Just as the shaman's initiatory crisis provides a transformation to greater health, so, too, can the shamanic perspective manage symptoms as potentials for a transformational development of the individual. Symptoms of psychosis, emotional breakdown, hallucinations, spirit encounters, and altered states can be reinterpreted as symbolic communications that provide opportunities for learning and for personal transformation of a crisis into a growth experience.

Shamanic Illness

Achterberg (1985) characterized the most central shamanic illness, soul loss, as one involving an injury to the core or essence of the person's being. This injury to one's essence is manifested as despair and has a range of physiological implications based on its effects that undermine the immune system. The decline in health status and longevity associated with profound grief is well attested to in the socioepidemiological literature. Achterberg characterized soul loss as reflecting a disharmony in terms of the meaning of life and the feeling of belonging and connection with others.

Ingerman (1991, 4) characterized *soul loss* as "losing crucial parts of ourselves that provide life and vitality." *Soul* is characterized as constituting our vital essence, the "seat of the emotions, feeling, or sentiments" (11). Soul loss is from trauma that causes some of our vital essence to separate in order to escape the impact. This separated part or aspect of ourselves carries with it the experiences that are then separated from or denied to the full person. Recovering these split off parts of one's self is central to recovery. The return of souls lost earlier in life allows the ego and the body to move forward instead of being emotionally stuck in that time and place where the loss occurred. The community awaiting the return of the lost soul is a significant aspect of the retrieval process. Based on reviews of the cross-cultural literature on soul retrieval, as well as her own work with clients, Ingerman suggested that there is great power in another person witnessing the return of the soul. The person's community or social support network plays a vital role in the recovery and healing processes.

Walsh (1990) discussed aspects of shamanistic illness with direct relevance to the new *DSM-IV* category "spiritual emergency." These include mystical experiences, which include psychotic features; spontaneous shamanic journeys; possession, which may be interpreted as domination by external structures or as the expression of archetypal patterns; and a renewal process as manifested in the death and rebirth experience. Another form of spiritual emergency is what Walsh labels "psychic opening," an experience of psychic abilities associated with shamanistic practices.

Spiritual emergencies can be managed within shamanistic world views with procedures for using these processes and neurognostic structures as constructive opportunities rather than pathologizing them. As Walsh (1990, 99) stated, "Spiritual emergencies may be newly recognized forms of perennial developmental crises. This developmental perspective allows us to view both shamanic crises and spiritual emergencies as related and difficult, but potentially valuable maturation crises." Shamanistic perspectives also suggest treatment approaches for these crises different from the traditional psychiatric use of drugs to repress the experiences. The shamanic approach suggests supportive, in-depth psychotherapy to identify the source of these spiritual emergencies and their appropriate resolution.

Central aspects of the shamanic quest involve self-empowerment. Contemporary shamanic counseling involves training the client to make his or her own shamanic journey, a visionary experience that is designed to restore personal power. The active aspect of the visionary experience helps instill a sense of mastery and control. Such self-control has important psychological and neurophysiological effects (e.g., immune system response). Harner (1988, 181) characterized shamanic counseling as "a method of personal empowerment wherein one comes to acquire respect for one's own ability to obtain spiritual wisdom without relying on external mediators."

Krippner and Welch (1992) addressed principles for the integration of shamanic healing into counseling and psychotherapy. Experiences such as spirit communication and voices, out-of-body experiences, and other religious and mystical experiences reflect neurognostic structures that can be more effectively managed within the perspectives of shamanism. Rather than marginalizing and pathologizing these experiences as psychological breakdowns and pathology, shamanism provides a framework for managing these crises as growth and development opportunities. Experiences associated with classic shamanism—the call of the spirits, their torture of the initiate, the experience of death and dismemberment—tend to be interpreted in a more constructive way from the shamanic perspective. Similarly, a range of experiences, including psychic openings, past-life experiences, and spirit intrusions, can be interpreted more constructively within the world view of shamanism. Shamanistic approaches are effective in dealing with multiple personality disorder, spiritual crises, and other anomalous traumatic experiences (Krippner and Welch 1992) because they act as a basis for growth (cf. Ingerman 1991).

Laughlin, McManus, Rubinstein, and Shearer (1986) suggested that shamanic rituals provide greater control over changes of consciousness (its different phases). Control over changes between normal phases of consciousness enhances access to transpersonal (or integrative) levels of consciousness through the replacement of ego-centered consciousness with a variety of neurognostic structures. Symbolic processes produce changes in the operating structures of consciousness, using ritual to alter consciousness and to provide new frameworks and elements for interpreting one's experiences. The penetration and evocation of neurognostic structures through symbols can enhance developmental processes by bypassing existing cognitive structures that inhibit development and growth.

Peters (1989) focused on the significance of shamanic ASC as involving access to a condition of consciousness that is qualitatively different from that associated with ordinary experience of reality. ASC central to shamanism share core features with states of other meditative traditions. Peters elaborated on the shamanic state of consciousness as being synonymous with visualizing or imaging, a kind of lucid or waking dream, a condition of "simultaneous conscious awareness of dream-ego and reality-ego" (115). The shaman's simultaneous experience of the dream realm and the ongoing flow of consciousness constitutes access to the integrative mode of consciousness. The active participation in these "waking dreams" of shamanic imagery is analogous to Jung's transcendent function, "a uniting of conscious and unconscious ways of knowing that leads to self-actualization, or 'individuation' " (Peters and Price-Williams 1981, 406). These experiences induce transformation of self. Peters (1989) suggested that an underlying similarity common to shamanic, yogic, and other meditative traditions is found in the transformational structures that entail an endogenous process of change. These transformational experiences involve acquisition of a spiritual identity used to change relationships to one's social and physical world.

An outcome of the transformational process is the experience of *communitas*—a recognition of the essential bonds that humans have with others. Turner's (1969) work illustrated the fundamental importance of the experience of communitas in providing a means of bonding members of society together in a recognition of their dependence on one another. Peters (1989) characterized communitas as an existential experience that transforms the individual in relationship to the transpersonal as well as worldly and social life. Shamans elicit feelings of communitas in transformational experiences in which the boundaries of self are dissolved into a state of unity consciousness. The unity experiences and the resultant identity with others and all life provide the basis for the development of self in an integrative style of personality and an ethos based on service to others.

Fundamental to shamanic development is the use of other points of reference for characterization of self, as embodied in the use of the animal world as a form of self-reference. Shamanistic practices provide multiple roles—participant, observer, and controller—for an active engagement with a transcendental neurognostic level of human psychodynamics. Peters and Price-Williams's (1981) experiential analysis of shamanism provided insight into the therapeutic potentials present in role-taking and development of the self. They noted specific aspects of the self that are an essential to shamanism, a self-awareness that permits communication with others during the ASC. Their perspectives on role-playing and different levels of organismic intensity and involvement in shamanic activities show that the self and the role are still differentiated, yet the shaman is involved in an intensive organismic participation through role involvement and construction of meaning.

Shamanic Roots in Contemporary Religious Experiences

The continual relevance of shamanic approaches is indicated by Stark's (1997) empirically derived taxonomy of contemporary religious experiences, all of which are central to shamanic beliefs and practices and their personal, social, and meaning-centered aspects. The principal structural aspects of contemporary religious experiences are found in shamanism's primordial beliefs and behaviors, with both reflecting psychobiological and psychosocial foundations. Stark framed religious experience as "some sense of contact with a supernatural agency" that involves: (1) sensations, perceptions, and feelings of the divine agency; and (2) the agency's awareness of, interaction and communication with, and direction and control of ourselves. These experiences have their foundation in an awareness of and in relationships between self and "divine other." This "divine other" or supernatural agency constitutes a neurognostic category, the sense of presence with volitional characteristics like ourselves; the divine other is given cultural characteristics that reflect morals, social models, and cultural psychosocial dynamics. Some of these models are central to shamanism, whereas others predominate in mediumistic possession.

Stark labeled the major types of religious experiences, ordered in terms of increasing degrees of interaction with the divine: confirming (self's awareness of divine other); responsive (divine's awareness of self); ecstatic (union of self and divine other); and revelation (messages from divine other, with varying degrees of domination of self by divine other). Variation in religious experience involves the self's experience of different degrees of relationship with and dominance by the divine other. These degrees of relationship range from awareness of the divine other to that other's awareness of self, the self's affective relationship and union with the divine other, and self's control by the divine other.

Confirming experiences involve intensification of convictions, intuitions, and feelings about the truthfulness of one's beliefs and knowledge regarding ultimate reality. Stark characterized the major subtypes of confirming experiences to involve special emotional experiences with a generalized sense of sacredness, reverence, and awe. These confirming experiences may include an awareness of the "presence of divinity," involving the sensed presence of the spirit other, in essence, animism, which lies at the basis of shamanism. Responsive experiences expand confirming awareness with the divine other's awareness of self and one's social inclusion with the divine other, with positive effects on one's well-being. Shamanism's interaction with the spirit allies and their powers is a fundamental responsive experience. Healing exemplifies the miraculous responsive experience and the divine's intervention in the physical world; this is the prototype of shamanic action. Ecstatic experiences involve an affective deepening of mutual awareness with development of an intimate relationship and union with the divine other. This ecstatic psychological upheaval is exemplified in the shaman's experience. Revelation experiences involve being a confidant and a messenger of the divine other. Revelation experiences in visual and intuitive modalities are exemplified in the soul journey of the shaman, whereas the auditory revelatory experiences exemplify the divinatory functions of possession mediums. Possession experiences may involve what Stark referred to as evil, terrorizing religious experiences, where one's thoughts and behaviors are directed by the divine other. These universal spirit-aggression beliefs are a fundamental concern of shamans' struggles with the spirit world, where the shaman attempts to recover the soul stolen from the patient or to address other afflictions caused by the spirits. These relationships to supernatural consciousness exemplified in terrorizing experiences involve the individual becoming an agent of the supernatural and subject to its control. These experiences have their roots in practices related to shamanism, specifically the shaman's initiatory crises; but the experiences have their fullest institutionalized religious development in practices associated with mediums and possession.

POSSESSION ILLNESS AND THERAPY

Although there are some cultural conceptions that view possession positively, its use normally reflects contexts in which a pathological attribution is intended. However, where possession provides a professional qualification for shamanistic healers, even illness conditions may be viewed as having positive attributes. But even in the context of shamanistic healing, possession is typically used to refer to conditions in which illness or other unexpected or unacceptable personal conditions are attributed to the activities of an aggressor spirit. Research indicates that possession is associated with a wide range of factors indicative of greater societal complexity (Bourguignon and

Evascu 1977; Winkelman 1986b), particularly political integration. However, behavioral conditions associated with temporal lobe discharges are more significant predictors of the incidence of possession than social conditions are (Winkelman 1986b, 1992). Conditions associated with possession—spontaneous illness and seizures; amnesia; tremors and convulsions; and compulsive motor behavior involving excessive, violent, and uncontrolled movements—suggest that the beliefs regarding possession may result from temporal lobe syndromes or other biologically based phenomena (cf. chapter 3 this volume). But these neurological conditions are significantly predicted by social stratification and may be caused by these social conditions. Possession is associated with societies that have considerable repression, which may provide the need for possession as a mechanism for dissociation. Because possession is significantly and independently predicted by both political integration and temporal lobe discharges (Winkelman 1986b, 1992), an explanation of the etiology and treatment processes of possession illness must consider both psychophysiological and social dynamics.

Possession Therapy

The classic treatments of possession have utilized a wide range of procedures for exorcism, including incantation, exhortation, and a variety of purgatives and punitive measures designed to drive the presumptive possessing spirit away, including beatings, starvation, and near poisonings of the patient. Ward (1989b) pointed out that although the validity of the interpretative framework may be questioned, anthropologists' reports of therapeutic benefits suggested that there is some efficacy in their treatments. In noting parallels between exorcism and psychotherapy, Ward specifically pointed out that "the therapeutic results are influenced by psychological factors and processes, such as perception, belief, expectancy, motivation, role playing, demand characteristics, and reinforcement" (135). She detailed a number of mechanisms within exorcism rituals that have the potential for therapeutic effectiveness, including the following:

1. the sick role and therapeutic processes associated with the contextualization of the experiences within a cultural system of healing beliefs that provide a meaningful representation of the condition
2. the dynamics of therapist-client relationships in which the interpersonal bond and the charismatic, authoritarian, and omnipotent characteristics

of the healer inspire the transformation of the patient's own expectations, resulting in a cure

3. spontaneous remission or physiological adjustments based in the psychodynamics of placebo reactors, who have characteristics typical of those possessed (e.g., free-floating anxiety, hypochondriacal, depressed, neurotic)

4. the cathartic discharges provided by abreactive techniques that permit a reliving and release of intense emotional experiences that underlie their psychological problems

These approaches to possession reflect conventional psychiatric perspectives. Examination of the actual processes for managing possession reflects a much wider range of therapeutic modalities. Possession plays a central role in psychodynamic transformation, providing models for the individual to reconstruct self and social identity. Possession systems can play prominent roles in the integration of cultural change, roles that are a means of incorporating and managing outside influences. Possession's sociopolitical implications and psychosocial therapeutic actions are exemplified in Stoller's (1987, 268) assessment of Songhay possession phenomena as "a form of cultural resistance . . . a psychologically stabilizing cultural response to social and cultural dissolution brought on by stressing social change." His analysis of the historical and contemporary developments of possession and spirits illustrated their central role in rejecting colonialism, Islam, and national government policies that threatened to undermine cultural identity. The possessing spirits and their behaviors were a direct affront to the externally imposed value systems, expressing cultural pride and preservation of cultural identity in the face of powerful external forces that attempted to change social mores. Sociocultural responses may also have therapeutic implications, with rituals expressing concerns about fears and externalizing and transforming these dynamics for the individual.

Kramer (1993) linked possession to the concept of *passiones*, experiences in which the self feels as if it were being acted on and affected by unwilled experience. This is expressed through mimesis—

the human faculty by which *passiones* are expressed, a pedagogical process, both embodiment of knowledge and bodying forth of knowledge. . . . Mimesis is the way in which the *habitus* is learned, through profound identification, and made self. . . . Mimesis is a two-layered notion, "a copying, or imitation, and a palpable, sensuous, connection between the very body of the perceiver and the perceived." (Boddy 1994, 425–26)

It involved internalized behavioral templates and schemas for action on the world.

The phenomena of possession illustrate the diversification of the self, incorporated as the other, as well as denial of self and responsibility in attributing responsibility for transgression to the other. Spirit possession beliefs can allow for expression of repressed aspects of the personality, enabling the sick person to behave in ways not normally permitted. Ward and Beaubrun (1980) suggested that possession provides positive advantages for victims by allowing escape from conflict and diminution of guilt by projecting responsibility onto spirits.

But Spanos (1989) rejected the notion that possession fundamentally constitutes an actor's loss of control to spiritual agencies or dissociated aspects of self. Instead, he illustrated a sociocultural basis for possession behavior in the notion of *social role enactment*. These role enactments are linked to social statuses (positions) and values involving prescribed behaviors that the possessed individual is expected to manifest. Although Spanos did not attribute possession exclusively to faking or "disinterested enactment," as opposed to subjective involvement and personal conviction, he did emphasize that the actor adopts the behavior because it constitutes a social mechanism for achievement of specific goals and relations with the social group. This enactment of possession is the means of "maintaining the behavioral control necessary to guide their actions in terms of culturally defined role prescriptions . . . [to] convincingly present themselves as the victims rather than the perpetrators of their own actions" (Spanos 1989, 97). Spanos extended this argument to "explanation" of multiple personality disorders in a similar way, characterizing psychiatrists as the major source of social influence that leads to these "enactments." But this perspective fails to explain the range of possession or typical clinical cases of multiple personality disorder.

Multiple Personality Disorder

Goodman (1988) rejected explanations of possession in terms of role-playing, faking, acting, and self-hypnosis, instead characterizing possession as a dynamic aspect of psychological functions in which personal experiences produce psychophysiological changes. Goodman suggested that the beliefs and practices associated with possession need to be understood not only in terms of cultural context and their social and psychological functions, but also in relationship to the neurophysiology of ASC and multiple personality disorder (MPD). Analyzing possession in relationship to psychophysiological processes illustrates parallels with MPD. Similarities and differences between the two shed light on both processes. The neurological variables associated with possession illustrate the importance of physiological conditions in understanding its causes and dynamics.

MPD is a severe dissociative reaction in which major aspects of psyche, emotions, and behaviors are split off from the ego. This dissociated part of the psyche acquires a large degree of autonomy and occasionally directs global control of individual intentions and behavior—mind and body. When the alternate personality dominates the organism, the egoic structures are both unconscious and subsequently amnesic. The presence of several discrete personalities or alternates in the MPD patient has obvious similarities to the possession experience. However, there are also important differences between the two: Goodman (1988) pointed to differences in the cultural perception of the phenomena and in the nature of the entities involved. The MPD experience is not interpreted in religious terms of spirits. Krippner (1987) pointed out that whereas mediums are aware of the processes through which they enter into possession states, MPD patients are generally ignorant of both the processes and the occurrences. However, there are more than just superficial similarities. Krippner studied a Brazilian physician specializing in treatment of MPD and concluded that most MPD cases have an onset between the ages of sixteen and twenty-five, the same age range (late adolescence to young adulthood) during which mediums and possession phenomena emerge cross culturally (Winkelman 1992).

Goodman (1988) reviewed laboratory research showing neurophysiological correlates of the different MPD personalities. Differences exist in evoked potentials of the EEGs of different personalities of the same individual, which contrast with the lack of EEG changes during role-playing of different personalities by the same individual. Different MPD personalities also show different diseases, allergies, and drug reactions. Goodman suggested that there are ample behavioral similarities between spirit possession and MPD—muscle tension, ASC, alternate personalities, and so on. Goodman speculated that at the neurophysiological level, possession and MPD are two different manifestations of the same human capacity. The major differences in possession and MPD lie in the lack of ritual control exercised by the latter. Cultural interpretations also play an important role in creating differences in the significance of the phenomena.

Because most MPD patients have been abused as children, Goodman suggested that the genetic endowment for dissociative ASC is utilized by these individuals in the same way that ASC are used for "brain map switching" in possession states. Goodman pointed to the general failure of Western psychiatric and biomedical treatment of MPD, suggesting that the best that has been done is to make the patient more capable of accepting the condition and coping with it. Goodman pointed out that differences between scientific ideology and the reality of experience lead to internal conflict for those suffering from MPD or possession in our society. Societies without rituals for dealing with these experiences produce inner conflict between the views of prestigious medical authorities and the afflicted person's powerful inner experiences, totally unsettling inner adjustment. Cultures with rituals of exorcism provide clients with a means of controlling these powerful experiences. Goodman reviewed the work of Ralph Allison, (cf. Allison and Schwarz 1999) who has seen aspects of the MPD that are more amenable to interpretation in the context of possession. Using exorcism rituals, he was able to cure a number of MPD patients. Krippner (1987) described how Brazilian spiritists associated with the Kardecian movements treat MPD phenomena as a form of involuntary possession or as the intrusion of a past-life personality. Goodman (1988) suggested that exorcism rituals may be an appropriate avenue to pursue therapeutically, even in cases where the MPD profile does not correspond to possession characteristics, because the rituals give the patient control. This may be achieved through exorcism, partial incorporation of the alter personalities, or merger of previous-life personalities in a psychological synthesis. Shamanistic therapies may be able to manage possession through the physiological consequences of ASC. The negative association of temporal lobe conditions with traditions of deliberately sought ASC (see chapter 3 this volume; cf. Winkelman and Winkelman 1990) suggests that shamanistic healing may affect the incidence of temporal lobe symptomology and may inhibit or prevent the incidence of possession experiences and organically based seizure phenomena (cf. Mandell 1980). Shamanistic therapeutic processes also utilize symbol systems, which provide meaning that allows for a recontextualization of the affliction and affects patients at physiological, emotional, psychological, and cognitive levels.

A contribution of shamanic approaches to modern medicine includes providing a new framework for meaning of health and illness conditions. A critical problem in modern medical encounters is interpretation because illness is fundamentally semantic. Shamanic perspectives contribute neurognostic points of reference for interpretation of symptoms and semantic realities of illness. These understandings of our inner lives, psychodynamics, and forms of self-representation in this body-based system of meaning provide a basis for a profound transformation of self and physiological responses. Meaning is important even for biologically based disease because of the role of symbols in eliciting many physiological processes.

The shaman's role involves constructing categories that provide meaning for the patient, using a mythic language that makes the situation confronting the patient intelligible. This construction of categories plays a central role in elicitation of neural structures that are responsible for mediation of experience and integration of complexes. Ritual and symbol may entrain these discrepant structures symbolically and, through ASC, elicit subconscious or unconscious processes that the shaman manipulates through symbols and metaphor. Symbol systems play a central role in integration and structural transformation of consciousness, with shamanic symbols and ritual processes facilitating healing through positive association, unification of antithetical psychic material, and the simultaneous elicitation of disconnected structural networks. These symbols typically involve the use of spirit entities to express compulsions, influences, tendencies, and behaviors. Shamanic healing involves epistemological mediation between different realms of reality, bridging social, personal, biological, psychic and spiritual, and cosmological levels of experiences in a common framework. This epistemological mediation and management is exemplified in the therapeutic dynamics of meditation.

MEDITATIVE EFFECTS ON SELF AND EMOTIONS

The dramatic emotional manifestations associated with shamanic soul recovery, possession, and exorcism are contrasted in the sedate meditative ASC. The inward focus of attention dismisses the importance of the external world and its emotional attachments in an effort to achieve emotional equanimity and nonattachment to desires. In contrast to these other traditions' dramatic enactments of self in guardian spirit entities and possessing spirits, the meditative traditions question the validity of ordinary identity and self. Instead, meditative traditions focus on development of a "true self" present beneath the socialized self.

Meditative ASC change self and emotions through development of attentional control, which enhances integration of emotion and thought, and the suspension of emotional attachments to achieve greater objectivity, detachment, and freedom from suffering. Meditators' intentional enhancement of control of attention increases awareness of mental processes and enhances control of cognitive functions and emotions. The focus of meditation on development of reflexive self-awareness creates a detached observational attitude that permits suspension of personal and social evaluative processes. Suspension or deautomatization of cognitive constructs permits emergence of somatic and organic aspects and their integration into a more complete sense of self.

A central aspect of meditation is affective development (Hunt 1995a; Wade 1996). The framework for affective development within meditative ASC is provided by the observing self, which is developed through the processes of meditation. This "witnessing consciousness" (see chapter 3 this volume) is capable of observing its own forms and developing formal affective operations that are decentered through an "other," an alternative to the ordinary self developed in meditation.

Meditative ASC play an important role in development of new ways of managing emotions. Feelings mediate social influences on the self, providing for attachments to others that define sense of self and that provide security. Alexander, Davies, et al. (1990) characterized the views of Vedic psychology on feelings as interconnecting the different levels of mind. Meditative consciousness enhances the role of feelings in providing information, linking ego, inner self, the intellect, and motivations to guide intuitive decision-making processes. Meditative ASC enable one to transcend the earlier stages of emotional development based on social constructions of self and desires and to exercise exceptional emotional control, both eliciting and suspending emotional processes. This extraordinary emotional control is manifested in experiences of rapture, bliss, and overwhelming love and compassion, which meditators are able to experience independent of any immediate stimuli for such experiences of pleasure. These developmental achievements are possible because of the control of attention and its use to develop new aspects of consciousness and self. The transpersonal self (*atman*, "true self" or witness), which is uninvolved in the world of the personal or participating self and its attachments, is consequently free from the pain and suffering of the personal self.

Meditation desensitizes one to distressing thoughts by permitting their emergence in conjunction with extreme relaxation, as exemplified in the practices of insight meditation, which focuses on arising perceptions, memories, and emotions and on the processing of their implications for self, thought, and behavior. This emergence of thoughts produces an enhanced awareness of unconscious processes, changing the ordinary sense of self and identity. Meditative practices exemplify the ASC traditions' modification of self and emotions and relationships with others. The functional basis for the effects of ASC on emotions is derived from their common bases in the limbic brain.

Carrington (1987) cited clinical evidence indicating that meditation leads to greater psychological differentiation, with a clearer understanding of one's own psychological needs and attributes, and to increases in field independence. Carrington suggested that meditation may lead to increased self-acceptance and self-esteem, enhanced self-control and confidence, increased empathy, and greater self-actualization. West (1987b) suggested that meditative experiences will necessarily lead the individual to an increase in private self-consciousness as a consequence of attention paid to the self. Inward personal attention results in self-evaluation and discovery of discrepancies between personal behaviors and standards.

Insight meditation focuses on perceptions, memories, thoughts, sensations, and emotions. This provides primary material for psychodynamic processing of patterns of thought and behavior and an opportunity for examination of the nature of personal and psychological processes. The healthful quality of meditation is widely recognized in the context of "transcendental experience." Walsh (1980) reviewed evidence that indicated that these experiences occur most frequently among those who are psychologically the most healthy. Transcendent experiences are most likely during advanced stages of psychotherapy, among those who are most self-actualized, those who are better educated and economically more successful, people who are less racist, and those who test at higher levels of psychological well-being. Not only do transcendent experiences occur among the most healthy, but they are also recognized as being responsible for long-term beneficial changes. Maslow's (1971) analysis of the hierarchy of needs placed these transcendent experiences at the apex of human development; meditation clearly supports that development.

SUMMARY

A neurophenomenological approach rescues shamanism from a premature modern demise as an atavistic delusional structure and presents it in its rightful light as a set of sophisticated traditions for managing self, emotions, and consciousness. Shamanic practices elicit neurognostic structures to facilitate the symbolic action on self, psyche, and psychobiology. Knowledge of human nature—mind and body—incorporated into shamanic beliefs and practices provides resources for modern psychodynamic adjustment and development. The different ASC traditions share effects on self and on emotions, but they differ in specific psychodynamics, reflecting different social conditions and their effects on psychological structures, self, and others.

NOTES

1. "Metaphor is a way of thinking of it in relation to a vehicle (Ortony 1979). Metaphor works by mapping the topic onto the high salience features of the vehicle, finding additional salient features and then translating back to the topic domain" (Kirmayer 1993, 172). The interaction of topic and vehicle is necessary for metaphoric relation. "Topic and vehicle are conceptual models or structures that function as operators to asymmetrically modify each other. Metaphors relate structures, not their elements" (173).

2. "Meaning is at once sensuous, emotional and conceptual [and situated] . . . in relation to body and society, archetype and myth . . . Metaphoric concepts conjoin the abstract and the concrete in experience so thought and feeling are aspects of the same image, concept, or action. Our complex thoughts and feelings are built on a foundation of simpler metaphors that involve motivational judgments that are closer to what we mean by the term emotion" (Kirmayer 1993, 184).

3. The reptilian brain (R-complex) is based in a group of ganglionic structures at the base of the forebrain, including the striatal complex consisting of a group of structures (olfactostriatum, corpus striatum, globus pallidus, and others) that belong to the basal ganglia (which has been implicated in the causation of obsessive compulsive disorder).

Bibliography

Aaronson, B., and H. Osmond, eds. 1970. *Psychedelics—The uses and implications of hallucinogenic drugs.* New York: Doubleday.

Aberle, D. 1966. *The Peyote religion among the Navaho.* Chicago: Aldine Publishing.

Abramson, H., ed. 1967. *The use of LSD in psychotherapy and alcoholism.* New York: Bobbs-Merrill.

Achterberg, J. 1985. *Imagery in healing, shamanism in modern medicine.* Boston: New Science Library Shambhala Publications.

Ackerknecht, E. 1943. Psychopathology, primitive medicine, and primitive culture. Reprinted from *Bulletin of the History of Medicine* 14: 30–67. New York: Bobbs-Merrill.

Adams, R., and M. Victor. 1977. Epilepsy and convulsive states. In *Principles of neurology.* New York: McGraw-Hill.

Adams, W. 1993. The parietal and occipital lobes and the development of consciousness: Some preliminary thoughts. *Anthropology of Consciousness* 4(3): 19–22.

Aghajanian, G. 1981. The modulatory role of serotonin at multiple receptors in the brain. In *Serotonin neurotransmission and behavior,* ed. B. Jacobs and A. Gelperin. Cambridge, Mass.: MIT Press.

———. 1982. Neurophysiologic properties of psychotomimetics. In *Psychotropic agents III,* ed. F. Hoffmeister and G. Stille. New York: Springer-Verlag.

———. 1994. Serotonin and the action of LSD in the brain. *Psychiatric Annals* 2463: 137–41.

Alexander, C., P. Robinson, D. Orme-Johnson, R. Schneider, and K. Walton.

1994. The effects of transcendental meditation compared to other methods of relaxation and meditation in reducing risks factors, morbidity, and mortality. *Homeostasis* 35 (4–5): 243–64.

Alexander, C., J. Davies, C. Dixon, M. Dillbeck, S. Drucker, R. Oetzel, J. Muehlman, and D. Orme-Johnson. 1990. Growth of higher stages of consciousness: The Vedic psychology of human development. In *Higher stages of human development: Perspectives on adult growth*, ed. C. Alexander and E. Langer. New York: Oxford University Press.

Allison, R., and T. Schwarz. 1999. *Minds in Many Pieces: Revealing the Spiritual Side of Multiple Personality.* Los Osos, Calif.: CIE Publishing.

Anand, B., G. China, and B. Singh. 1961. Some aspects of electroencephalographic studies in yogis. *Electroencephalography and Clinical Neurophysiology* 13: 452–56.

Anderson, E. 1980. *Peyote the divine cactus*. Tucson: University of Arizona Press.

Andritzky, W. 1989. Sociopsychotherapeutic functions of Ayahuasca healing in Amazonia. *Journal of Psychoactive Drugs* 21(1): 77–89.

Angus, S. [1925]1975. *The mystery religions*. New York: Dover Publications.

Antelman, S., and A. Caggiula. 1980. Stress-induced behavior: Chemotherapy without drugs. In *The psychophysiology of consciousness*, ed. J. Davidson and R. Davidson. New York: Plenum Press.

Appel, J., and J. Rosecrans. 1984. Behavioral pharmacology of hallucinogens in animal studies: Conditioning studies. In *Hallucinogens: Neurochemical, behavioral, and clinical perspectives*, ed. B. Jacobs. New York: Raven Press.

Appenzeller, O. 1987. The autonomic nervous system and fatigue. *Functional Neurology* 2(4): 473–85.

Arnheim, R. 1969. *Visual thinking*. Berkeley: University of California Press.

Asante, M. 1984. The African American mode of transcendence. *The Journal of Transpersonal Psychology* 16: 167–77.

Ashbrook, J. 1993. The human brain and human destiny: A pattern for old brain empathy with the emergence of mind. In *Brain, culture, and the human spirit: Essays from an emergent evolutionary perspective*, ed. J. Ashbrok. Lanham, Md.: University Press of America.

Atran, S. 1990. *Cognitive foundations of natural history*. New York: Cambridge University Press.

Baars, B. 1997. *In the theater of consciousness*. New York: Oxford University Press.

Barnhart, R. ed. 1988. *The Barnhart dictionary of etymology*. Bronx, N.Y.: H. W. Wilson.

Bateson, G. 1972. *Steps to an ecology of mind*. New York: Ballantine Books.

Bear, D. 1979a. Temporal lobe epilepsy—A syndrome of sensory limbic hyperconnection. *Cortex* 15: 357–84.

———. 1979b. The temporal lobes: An approach to the study of organic behavioral changes. In vol. 2 of *Handbook of behavioral neurobiology*, ed. M. S. Gazzaniga. New York: Plenum Press.

Bear, D., and P. Fedio. 1977. The quantitative analysis of interictal behavior in temporal lobe epilepsy. *Archives of Neurology* 4: 454–67.

Bear, D., K. Levin, D. Blumer, D. Chetham, and J. Ryder. 1982. Interictal behavor in hospitalized temporal lobe epileptics: Relationship to ideopathic psychiatric syndromes. *Journal of Neurology, Neurosurgery, and Psychiatry* 45: 481–88.

Bear, D., L. Schenk, and H. Benson. 1981. Increased autonomic responses to neutral and emotional stimuli in patients with temporal lobe epilepsy. *American Journal of Psychiatry* 138: 843–45.

Benedict, R. 1923. *The concept of the guardian spirit in North America*. New York: American Anthropological Association.

Benveniste, E., 1973. *Indo-European language and society*. Trans. E. Palmer. London: Faber and Faber.

Benson, H. 1979. *The mind/body effect: How behavioral medicine can show you the way to better health*. New York: Simon and Schuster.

Benson, H., J. Beary, and M. Carol. 1974. The relaxation response. *Psychiatry* 37: 37–46.

Benson, H., J. Kotch, K. Crassweller, and M. Greenwood. 1979. The relaxation response. In *Consciousness: The brain, states of awareness, and alternate realities*, ed. D. Goleman and R. Davidson. New York: Irvington Publishers.

Bird-David, N. 1999. "Animism" revisited: personhood, environment, and relational epistemology. *Current Anthropology* 40: 67–91.

Blacker, C. 1981. Japan. In *Divination and oracles*, ed. M. Loewe and C. Blacker. London: George Allen and Unwin.

Blackmore, S. 1982. *Beyond the body: An investigation of out-of-the-body experiences*. London: Society for Psychical Research.

Blagrove, Mark. 1996. Problems with the cognitive psychological modeling of dreaming. *The Journal of Mind and Behavior* 17 (2): 99–134.

Bliss, K. 1988. LSD and psychotherapy. *Contemporary Drug Problems* (Winter): 519–63.

Block, V. 1970. Facts and hypotheses concerning memory consolidation processes. *Brain Research* 24: 561–72.

Blundell, G. 1998. On neuropsychology in southern African art research. *Anthropology of Consciousness* 9(1): 3–12.

Boddy, J. 1994. Spirit possession revisited: Beyond instrumentality. *Annual Review of Anthropology* 23: 407–34.

Bodnar, R. 1990. Effects of opioid peptides on peripheral stimulation and "stress"-induced analgesia in animals. *Critical Review of Neurobiology* 6(1): 39–49.

Bourguignon, E. 1968. *Cross-cultural study of dissociational states.* Columbus: Ohio State University Press.

___. 1976a. *Possession.* San Francisco: Chandler and Sharpe.

___. 1976b. Spirit possession beliefs and social structure. In *The realm of the extra-human ideas and actions,* ed. A. Bhardati. The Hague: Mouton.

Bourguignon, E., and T. Evascu. 1977. Altered states of consciousness within a general evolutionary perspective: A holocultural analysis. *Behavior Science Research* 12(3): 197–216.

Bourguignon, E., A. Bellisari, and S. McCabe. 1983. Women, possession trance cults, and the extended nutrient deficiency hypothesis. *American Anthropologist* 85: 413–16.

Boyer, P. 1992. *The naturalness of religious ideas.* Berkeley: University of California Press.

Bravo, G., and C. Grob. 1989. Shamans, sacraments, and psychiatrists. *Journal of Psychoactive Drugs* 21(1): 123–28.

Broughton, R. 1986. Human consciousness and sleep/waking rhythms. In *Handbook of states of consciousness,* ed. B. Wolman and M. Ullman. New York: Van Nostrand Reinhold.

Brown, B. 1974. *New mind, new body.* New York: Harper and Row.

Brown, D., M. Forte, and M. Dysart. 1984. Visual sensitivity and mindfulness meditation. *Perceptual and Motor Skills* 58: 775–84.

Budzynski, T. 1986. Clinical applications of non-drug induced states. In *Handbook of states of consciousness,* ed. B. Wolman and M. Ullman. New York: Van Nostrand Reinhold.

Campbell, J. 1983. *The way of the animal powers. Vol 1, Historical atlas of world mythology.* San Francisco: Harper and Row.

Cannon, W. 1942. Voodoo death. *American Anthropologist* 44: 169–81.

Caporael, L. R. 1994. Of myth and science: Origin stories and evolutionary scenarios. *Social Science Information* 33: 9–23.

———. 1996. Coordinating bodies, minds, and groups: Evolution and human social cognition. *Journal of Social and Evolutionary Systems* 19(3): 261–75.

Carrington, P. 1987. Managing meditation in clinical practice. In *The psychology of meditation,* ed. M. West. Oxford: Clarendon Press.

Castillo, R. 1991. Divided consciousness and enlightenment in Hindu Yogis. *The Anthropology of Consciousness* 2(304): 1–6.

Chrusciel, T. 1982. General pharmacology and toxicology of alcohol. In *Psychotropic agents III*, ed. F. Hoffmeister and G. Stille. New York: Springer-Verlag.

Claxton, G. 1987a. Meditation in Buddhist psychology. In *The psychology of meditation*, ed. M. West. Oxford: Clarendon Press.

———. 1987b. Meditation: Contemporary theoretical approaches. In *The psychology of meditation*, ed. M. West. Oxford: Clarendon Press.

Cohen, D. 1979. *Sleep and dreaming: Origins, natures, and functions.* Oxford: Pergamon Press.

Cohen, S. 1968. A quarter century of research with LSD. In *The problem and prospects of LSD*, ed. J. Ungerleide. Springfield, Ill.: Charles C. Thomas.

———. 1971. Theories on the psychic effects of the psychomimetics. In *The psychodynamic implications of the physiological studies on psychomimetic drugs*, ed. L. Madow and L. Snow. Springfield, Ill.: Charles C. Thomas.

Cohen, S. and S. Syme. 1985. Issues in the study and application of social support. In *Social support and health*, ed. S. Cohen and S. L. Syme. New York: Academic Press.

Corner, M. 1985. Ontogeny of brain sleep mechanisms. In *Brain mechanisms of sleep*, ed. D. McGinty et al. New York: Raven Press.

Cosmides, L., and J. Tooby. 1992. Cognitive adaptations for social exchange. In *The adapted mind: Evolutionary psychology and the generation of culture*, ed. J. Barkow, L. Cosmides, and J. Tooby. New York: Oxford University Press.

Crapanzano, V., and V. Garrison. 1977. *Case studies in spirit possession.* New York: Wiley.

Crawford, H. 1994. Brain dynamics and hypnosis: Attentional and disattentional processes. *International Journal of Clinical and Experimental Hypnosis* 42(3): 204–32.

Csordas T. 1993. *The sacred self: A cultural phenomonology of charismatic healing.* Berkeley: University of California Press.

Cumont, F. 1956. *Oriental religions in Roman paganism.* New York: Dover Publications

———. 1960. *Astrology and religion among the Greeks and Romans.* New York: Dover Publications.

Czaplicka, M. 1914. *Aboriginal Siberia: A study in social anthropology.* Oxford: Oxford University Press.

d'Aquili, E. 1982. Senses of reality in science and religion: A neuro-epistemological perspective. *Zygon* 17(4): 361–83.

Davidson, J. 1976. The physiology of meditation and mystical states of consciousness. *Perspectives in Biology and Medicine* (Spring): 345–79.

———. 1980. The psychobiology of sexual experience. In *The psychobiology of consciousness*, ed. J. Davidson and R. Davidson. New York: Plenum Press.

Davidson, R., and G. Schwartz. 1984. Matching relaxation therapies to types of anxiety: A patterning approach. In *Meditation: Classic and contemporary perspectives*, ed. D. H. Shapiro and R. N. Walsh. New York: Aldine de Gruyter.

Davis, M., J. Kehne, R. Commissaris, and M. Geyer. 1984. Effects of hallucinogens on unconditioned behavior in animals. In *Hallucinogens: Neurochemical, behavioral, and clinical perspectives*, ed. B. Jacobs. New York: Raven Press.

Davis, V., and M. Thaut. 1989. The influence of preferred relaxing music on measures of state anxiety, relaxation, and physiological responses. *Journal of Music Therapy* 26: 168–87.

Davis, V., and M. Walsh. 1970. Alcohol, amines, alkaloids: A possible biochemical basis for alchohol addiction. *Science* 167:1005–7.

Delmonte, M. 1987a. Meditation: Contemporary theoretical approaches. In *The psychology of meditation*, ed. M. West. Oxford: Clarendon Press.

———. 1987b. Personality and meditation. In *The psychology of meditation*, ed. M. West. Oxford: Clarendon Press.

Dement, W., and M. Mitler. 1974. An introduction to sleep. In *Basic sleep mechanisms*, ed. O. Petre-Quadens and J. Schlag. New York: Academic Press.

Dobkin de Rios, M. 1984. *Hallucinogens: Cross-cultural perspectives*. Albuquerque: University of New Mexico Press.

Dobkin de Rios, M., and D. Smith. 1977. Drug use and abuse in cross-cultural perspective. *Human Organization* 36(1): 14–21.

Donald, M. 1991. *Origins of the modern mind*. Cambridge, Mass.: Harvard University Press.

Doore, G. 1987. The ancient wisdom in shamanic cultures: An interview with Michael Harner. In *Shamanism*, ed. S. Nicholson. Wheaton, Ill.: Theosophical Publishing House.

———. 1988. Shamans, yogis and bodhisattvas. In *Shaman's path*, ed. G. Doore. Boston: Shambhala Publications.

Dow, J. 1986. Universal aspects of symbolic healing: A theoretical synthesis. *American Anthropologist* 88: 56–69.

Dow, M., M. Burton, D. White, and K. Reitz. 1984. Galton's problem as network autocorrelation. *American Ethnologist* 11: 754–70.

Dulaney, S., and A. Fiske. 1994. Cultural rituals and obsessive-compulsive disorder. Is there a common psychological mechanism? *Ethos* 22: 243–83.

Durkheim, D. 1915. *The elementary forms of religious life*. London: George Allen and Unwin.

Eibl-Eibesfeldt, I. 1989. *Human ethology*. New York: Aldine de Gruyter.

Eliade, M. 1964. *Shamanism: archaic techniques of ecstasy*. New York: Pantheon Books. Originally published as *Le Chamanisme et les techniques archaïques de l'extase* (Paris: Librairie Payot, 1951).

———. 1969. *Pantanjali and yoga*. New York: Schocken Books.

———. 1974. *Gods, goddesses, and myths of creation*. New York: Harper and Row.

Ellis, R. 1986. *An ontology of consciousness*. Dordrecht, Holland: Kluwer/Martinus Nijhoff.

———. 1995. Questioning consciousness The interplay of imagery, cognition, and emotion in the human brain. In vol. 2 of *Advances in consciousness research*. Philadelphia: John Benjamins.

Emboden, W. 1989. The sacred journey in dynastic Egypt: Shamanistic trance in the context of the narcotic Water Lily and the Mandrake. In Theme issue *Shamanism and altered states of consciousness*, ed. M. Dobkin de Rios and M. Winkelman. *Journal of Psychoactive Drugs* 21(1): 61–75.

Engel, G., E. Ferris, and M. Logan. 1947. Hyperventilation: Analysis of clinical symptomology. *Annals of Internal Medicine* 27: 683–704.

Engle, G. 1980. The clinical application of the biopsychosocial model. *American Journal of Psychiatry* 137(5): 535–44.

Evans-Wentz, W. [1935] 1978. *Tibetan yoga and secret doctrines*. New York: Oxford University Press.

Fairchild, M., G. Alles, D. Jensen, and M. Mickey. 1967. The effects of mescaline, amphetamine, and four ring substituted amphetamine derivatives on spontaneous brain electrical activity in the cat. *International Journal of Neuropharmacology* 6: 151–67.

Fenwick, P. 1987. Meditation and the EEG. In *The psychology of meditation*, ed. M. West. Oxford: Clarendon Press.

Fernandez, J., ed. 1991. *Beyond metaphor: The theory of tropes in anthropology*. Stanford: Stanford University Press.

Findeisen, H. 1957. Schamanentum. *Urban-Bucher* 28: 200. As cited in Hultkrantz 1973.

Fink, M. 1978. Psychoactive drugs and the waking EEG 1966–1976. In

Psychopharmacology, ed. M. Lipton, A. Dimascio, and K. Killam. New York: Raven Press.

Fischbach, G. 1992. Mind and brain. In *Scientific American, special issue, Mind and brain* (September): 48–57.

Fischer-Schreiber, I., F. Ehrhard, and M. Diener. 1991. *The Shambhala dictionary of Buddhism and Zen*. Trans. M. Kohn. Boston: Shambhala Publication.

Flaherty, G. 1992. *Shamanism and the eighteenth century*. Princeton: Princeton University Press.

Flier, L. 1995. Demystifying mysticism: Finding a developmental relationship between different ways of knowing. *The Journal of Transpersonal Psychology* 27 (2): 131–52.

Fodor, J. 1983. *The modularity of the mind*. Cambridge, Mass.: MIT Press.

Forman, R. 1998. *The innate capacity*. New York: Oxford Press.

Forster, F., and H. Booker. 1975. The epilepsies and convulsive disorders. In *Clinical neurology*, ed. A. B. Baker and L. H. Baker. Philadelphia: Harper and Row.

Frazier, J. 1890. *The golden bough: A study in magic and religion*. New York: St. Martins Press.

Frecska, E., and Z. Kulcsar. 1989. Social bonding in the modulation of the physiology of ritual trance. *Ethos* 17(1): 70–87.

Freedman, D. 1984. LSD: The bridge from human to animal. In *Hallucinogens: Neurochemical, behavioral and clinical perspectives*, ed. B. Jacobs, New York: Raven Press.

Freedman, A., and H. Kaplan. 1967. *Comprehensive textbook of psychiatry*. Baltimore: Williams and Wilkins.

Friedrich, P. 1991. Polytrophy. In *Beyond metaphor: The theory of tropes in anthropology*, ed. J. W. Fernandez. Stanford: Stanford University Press.

Furst, P. 1976. *Hallucinogens and culture*. San Francisco: Chandler and Sharp.

Gackenbach, J., and S. LaBerge, eds. 1988. *Conscious mind, sleeping brain: New perspectives on lucid dreaming*. New York: Plenum Press.

Gambert, S., T. Hagen, T. Garthwaithe, E. Duthie, and D. McCarty. 1981. Exercise and endogenous opiates. *New England Journal of Medicine* 395: 1590.

Gardener, H. 1983. *Frames of mind: The theory of multiple intelligences*. New York: Basic Books.

Garrison, V., and V. Crapanzano. 1978. Comment on Leacock's review of case studies in spirit possession. *Review of Anthropology*. 5: 420–25.

Gellhorn, E. 1969. Further studies on the physiology and pathophysiology of tuning of the central nervous system. *Psychosomatics* 10: 94–103.

Gellhorn, E., and W. Kiely. 1972. Mystical states of consciousness: Neurophysiological and clinical aspects. *Journal of Nervous and Mental Disease* 154(6): 399–405.

Gellhorn, E., and G. Loofbourrow. 1963. *Emotions and emotional disorders. A neurophysiological study.* New York: Harper and Row.

Gennaro, R. 1995. *Consciousness and self-consciousness.* Amsterdam/Philadelphia: John Benjamins.

Gerschenfeld, H., D. Paupardin-Tritsch, and P. Deterre. 1981. Neuronal responses to serotonin. In *Serotonin neurotransmission and behavior,* ed. B. Jacobs and A. Gelperin. Cambridge, Mass.: MIT Press.

Geschwind, N. 1965. Disconnection syndromes in animals and man. *Brain* 88: 237–94, 585–644.

———. 1979. Behavioral changes in temporal lobe epilepsy. *Psychological Medicine* 9: 217–19

Geschwind, N., R. Shader, D. Bear, B. North, K. Levin, and D. Chetam. 1980. Behavioral changes with temporal lobe epilepsy: Assessment and treatment. *Journal of Clinical Psychiatry* 41: 89–95.

Gibson, J. 1979. *The ecological approach to visual perception.* Boston: Houghton Mifflin.

Glennon, R. 1990. Serotonin receptors: Clinical implications. *Neuroscience and Biobehavioral Reviews* 14: 35–47.

Goleman, D. 1977. *The varieties of meditative experience.* New York: E. P. Dutton.

———. 1978. A taxonomy of meditation specific altered states. *Journal of Altered States of Consciousness* 4(2): 203–13.

———. 1997. *Healing emotions.* Boston: Shambhala Publications.

Goleman, D., and G. Schwartz. 1976. Meditation as an intervention in stress reactivity. *Journal of Consulting Clinical Psychology* 44: 456–66.

Goodman, F. 1988. *How about demons? Possession and exorcism in the modern world.* Bloomington and Indianapolis: Indiana University Press.

Graham, R. 1990. *Physiological psychology.* Belmont, Calif.: Wadsworth.

Gray, J. 1982. *The neuropsychology of anxiety: An inquiry into the functions of the septo-hippocampal system.* Oxford: Clarendon Press; New York: Oxford University Press.

Green, C. 1968. *Out-of-the-body experiences.* New York: Ballantine Books.

Greenwell, B. 1990. *Energies of transformation: A guide to the kundalini process.* Cupertino, Calif.: Transpersonal Learning Services.

Grinspoon, L., and J. Bakalar. 1979. *Psychedelic drugs reconsidered.* New

York: Basic Books.

Grof, S. 1975. *Realms of the unconscious: Observations from LSD research*. New York: Viking Press.

———. 1980. *LSD psychotherapy*. Pomona, Calif.: Hunter House.

———. 1992. *The holotropic mind*. San Francisco: Harper Collins.

Gupta, Y. 1961. *Yoga and yogic powers*. New York: Yogi Gupta Center.

Gussler, J. 1973. Social change, ecology, and spirit possession among the South African Nguni. In *Religion, altered states of consciousness and social change*, ed. E. Bourguignon. Columbus: Ohio State University Press.

Guthrie, S. 1993. *Faces in the clouds: A new theory of religion*. Oxford: Oxford University Press.

———. 1997. The origin of an illusion. In *Anthropology of religion: A handbook*, ed. S. Glazier. Westport, Conn.: Greenwood Press.

Halifax, J. 1979. *Shamanic voices*. New York: E. P. Dutton.

Hanser, S. 1985. Music therapy and stress reduction research. *Journal of Music Therapy* 22(4): 193–206.

Harner, M. 1972. *The Jivaro: People of the sacred waterfalls*. New York: Doubleday, Natural History Press.

———. 1973a. *Hallucinogens and shamanism*. New York: Oxford University Press.

———. 1973b. The role of hallucinogenic plants in European witchcraft. In *Hallucinogens and shamanism*, ed. M. Harner. New York: Oxford University Press.

———. 1982. *The way of the shaman*. New York: Bantam Books.

———. 1988. What is a shaman? In *Shaman's path: Healing, personal growth, and empowerment*, ed. G. Doore. Boston: Shambhala Publications.

Hayden, B. 1987. Alliances and ritual ecstacy: Human responses to resource stress. *Journal for the Scientific Study of Religion* 26(1): 81–91.

Heinze, R. 1991. *Shamans of the 20th century*. New York: Irvington Publishers.

Helman, C. 1994. *Culture, health and illness*. 3d ed. Oxford: Butterworth-Heinemann.

Henricksen, S., F. Bloom, N. Ling, and R. Guillemin. 1977. Induction of limbic seizures by endorphins and opiate alkaloids: Electrophysiological and behavioral correlations. *Abstract of the Society of Neurosurgery* 3: 293.

Henry, J. 1982. Possible involvement of endorphins in altered states of consciousness. *Ethos* 10: 394–408.

Hill, P. C. 1997. Toward an attitude process model of religious experience. In *The psychology of religion*, ed. B. Spilka and D. N. McIntosh. Boulder, Col.: Westview Press.

Hobson, J. 1992. Sleep and dreaming: Induction and mediation of REM sleep by cholinergic mechanisms. *Current Opinion in Neurobiology* 2: 759–63.

Hobson, J., E. Pace-Schott, R. Stickgold, and D. Kahn. 1998. To dream or not to dream? Relevant data from new neuroimaging and electrophysiological studies. *Current Opinion in Neurobiology* 8(2): 239–44.

Hobson, J., and R. Stickgold. 1994. Dreaming: A neurocognitive approach. *Consciousness and Cognition* 3: 1–15.

Hoffmeister, F., and G. Stille, eds. 1982. *Psychotropic agents III*. New York: Springer-Verlag.

Hollister, L. 1984. Effects of hallucinogens in humans. In *Hallucinogens: neurochemical, behavioral, and clinical perspectives*, ed. B. Jacobs. New York: Raven Press.

Holm, N. 1997. An integrated role theory for the psychology of religion: Concepts and perspectives. In *The psychology of religion*, ed. B. Spilka and D. N. McIntosh. Boulder, Col.: Westview Press.

Holmes, D. 1987. The influence of meditation versus rest on physiological arousal: A second examination. In *The psychology of meditation*, ed. M. West. Oxford: Clarendon Press.

Hoyt, C. 1981. *Witchcraft*. Carbondale: Southern Illinois University Press.

Hultkrantz, A. 1966. An ecological approach to religion. *Ethos* 31: 131–50.

———. 1973. A definition of shamanism. *Temenos* 9: 25–37.

———. 1978. Ecological and phenomenological aspects of shamanism. In *Shamanism in Siberia*, ed. V. Dioszegi and M. Hoppal. Budapest: Akademiai Kiado.

Humphrey, N. 1984. *Consciousness regained*. Oxford: Oxford University Press.

———. 1992. *A history of the mind*. London: Chatto & Windus.

———. 1993. *The inner eye*. London: Vintage. (First published by Faber and Faber in 1986.)

———. 1998. Cave art, autism, and the evolution of the human mind. *Cambridge Archaeological Journal* 8(2): 165–91.

Hunt, H. 1984. A cognitive psychology of mystical and altered-state experience. *Perceptual and Motor Skills* 58: 467–513.

———. 1985. Relations between the phenomena of religious mysticism and the psychology of thought: A cognitive psychology of states of consciousness and the necessity of subjective states for cognitive theory. *Perceptual and Motor Skills* 61: 911–61.

———. 1989a. The relevance of ordinary and non-ordinary states of consciousness for the cognitive psychology of meaning. *The Journal of Mind and Behavior* 10: 347–60.

———. 1989b. *The multiplicity of dreams: Memory, imagination, and consciousness.* New Haven and London: Yale University Press

———. 1995a. *On the nature of consciousness.* New Haven: Yale University Press.

———. 1995b. Some developmental issues in transpersonal experience. *The Journal of Mind and Behavior* 16(2): 115–34.

———. 1995c. The linguistic network of signifiers and imaginal polysemy: An essay in the co-dependent origination of symbolic forms. *The Journal of Mind and Behavior* 16(4): 405–20.

Ingerman, S. 1991. *Soul retrieval.* San Francisco: Harper Collins.

Irwin, H. 1985. *Flight of mind: A psychological study of the out-of-body experience.* Metuchen, N.J.: Scarecrow Press.

Jackendoff, R. 1983. *Consciousness and the computational mind.* Cambridge, Mass.: MIT Press.

Jacobs, B., ed. 1984. *Hallucinogens: Neurochemical, behavioral, and clinical perspectives.* New York: Raven Press.

Jacobs, B., and A. Gelperin, eds. 1981. *Serotonin neurotransmission and behavior.* Cambridge, Mass.: MIT Press.

Jarrell, H. 1985. *International meditation bibliography: 1950–1982.* Metuchen, N.J.: Scarecrow Press.

Jelik, W. 1982. Altered states of consciousness in North American Indian ceremonials. *Ethos* 10(4): 326–43.

Johnson, M. 1987. *The body in the mind: The bodily basis of meaning, imagination, and reason.* Chicago: University of Chicago Press.

Johnson, M., and W. Hirst. 1992. MEM: Memory subsystems as processes. In *Theories of memory,* ed. A. Collins, S. Conway, S. Gathercole, and P. Morris. East Sussex, England: Erlbaum.

Johnson-Laird, P. 1983. *Mental models.* Cambridge, Mass.: Harvard University Press.

Jones, B. 1985. Neuroanatomical and neurochemical substrates of mechanisms underlying paradoxical sleep. In *Brain mechanisms of sleep,* ed. D. McGinty et al. New York: Raven Press.

Jorgensen, J. 1980. *Western Indians: Comparative environments, language, and culture of 172 Western American Indian societies.* San Francisco: W. H. Freeman.

Jung, C. 1971. *The Portable Jung*. Ed. J. Campbell. New York: Viking Press.

Kasamatsu, A., and T. Hirai. 1966. An electroencephalographic study on the Zen meditation. *Folio Psychiatrica & Neurologica Japonica* 20: 315–36.

Katz, R. 1982. *Boiling energy: Community healing among the Kalahari !Kung*. Cambridge, Mass.: Harvard University Press.

Kegan, R. 1982. *The evolving self*. Cambridge, Mass.: Harvard University Press.

———. 1994. *In over our heads*. Cambridge, Mass.: Harvard University Press.

Kehoe, A., and D. Gilletti. 1981. Women's preponderance in possession cults: The calcium deficiency hypothesis extended. *American Anthropologist* 83: 549–61.

Kelly, E., and R. Locke. 1981. *Altered states of consciousness and laboratory psi research: A historical survey and research prospectus*. New York: Parapsychology Foundation.

Keup, W., ed. 1970. *Origin and mechanism of hallucination*. New York: Plenum Press.

Kiefel, J., D. Paul, and R. Bodnar. 1989. Reduction of opioid and non-opioid forms of swim analgesia by 5-HT2 receptor antagonists. *Brain Research* 500: 231–40.

Kirkpatrick, L. 1997. An attachment-theory approach to psychology of religion. In *The psychology of religion*, ed. B. Spilka and D. N. McIntosh. Boulder, Col.: Westview Press.

Kirmayer, L. 1993. Healing and the invention of metaphor: The effectiveness of symbols revisited. *Culture, Medicine, and Psychiatry* 17: 161–95.

Kitchener, R. 1986. *Piaget's theory of knowledge genetic epistemology and scientific reason*. New Haven: Yale University Press.

Klein, E. 1967. *A comprehensive etymological dictionary of the English language*. Amsterdam, Netherlands: Elsevier.

Kleinman, A. 1973a. Medicine's symbolic reality. On a central problem in the philosophy of medicine. *Inquiry* 16: 206–13.

———. 1973b. Toward a comparative study of medical systems: An integrated approach to the study of the relationship of medicine and culture. *Social Science and Medicine* 1: 55–65.

———. 1980. *Patients and healers in the context of culture*. Berkeley: University of California Press.

———. 1987. *Social origins of stress and disease*. New Haven: Yale University Press.

Kleitman, N. 1970. Implications of the rest-activity cycle. In *Sleep and dreaming*, ed. E. Hartmann. Boston: Little, Brown.

———. [1960] 1972. Patterns of dreaming. In *Altered states of awareness. Readings from Scientific American*, ed. Timothy Teyler. San Francisco: W. H. Freeman.

Koella, W. 1985. Organization of sleep. In *Brain mechanisms of sleep*, ed. D. McGinty et al. New York: Raven Press.

Kramer, F. 1993. *The red fez: Art and spirit possession in Africa*. Trans. M. Green. London: Verso.

Krippner, S. 1972. Altered states of consciousness. In *The highest state of consciousness*, ed. J. White. Garden City, N.Y.: Doubleday, Anchor Books.

———. 1987. Cross-cultural approaches to multiple personality disorder: Practices in Brazilian spiritism. *Ethos* 15(3): 273–95.

Krippner, S., and P. Welch. 1992. *Spiritual dimensions of healing: From native shamanism to contemporary health care*. New York: Irvington Publishers.

Kruk, Z., and C. Pycock. 1991. *Neurotransmitters and drugs*. London: Chapman and Hall.

Kurland, A. 1985. LSD in the supportive care of the terminally ill cancer patient. *Journal of Psychoactive Drugs* 17(4): 279–90.

La Barre, W. 1970. Old and new world narcotics: a statistical question and an ethnological reply. *Economic Botany* 24: 368–73.

———. 1972. Hallucinogens and the shamanic origins of religion. In *Flesh of the gods*, ed. P. Furst. New York: Praeger.

LaBerge, S. 1985. *Lucid dreaming*. Los Angeles: J. P. Tarcher

Lakoff, G. 1987. *Women, fire, and dangerous things*. Chicago: University of Chicago Press.

Lakoff, G., and M. Johnson. 1980. *Metaphors we live by*. Chicago: University of Chicago Press.

Lambeck, M. 1989. From disease to discourse: Remarks on the conceptualization of trance and spirit possession. In *Altered states of consciousness and mental health: A cross-cultural perspective*, ed. C. A. Ward. Newbury Park, Calif.: Sage.

Langner, F. 1967. Six years experience with LSD therapy. In *The use of LSD in psychotherapy and alcoholism*, ed. H. Abramson. New York: Bobbs-Merrill.

Lansdowne, Z. 1986. *The chakras and healing*. York Beach, Me.: Samuel Weiser.

Laughlin, C. 1992a. Consciousness in biogenetic structural theory. *Anthropology of Consciousness* 3(1 and 2): 17–22.

———. 1992b. *Scientific explanation and the life-world. A biogenetic structural theory of meaning and causation.* Sausalito, Calif.. Institute of Noetic Sciences.

———. 1997. Body, brain, and behavior: The neuroanthropology of the body image. *Anthropology of Consciousness* 8(2–3): 49–68.

Laughlin, C., and J. Throop. 1999. Emotion: A view from biogenetic structuralism. In *Biocultural Approaches to the emotions*, ed. A. Hinton. Cambridge: Cambridge University Press.

Laughlin, C., J. McManus, and E. d'Aquili. 1992. *Brain, symbol, and experience toward a neurophenomenology of consciousness.* New York: Columbia University Press.

Laughlin, C., J. McManus, R. Rubinstein, and J. Shearer. 1986. The ritual transformation of experience. *Studies in Symbolic Interaction* A: 107–36.

Lawson, T., and R. McCauley. 1990. *Rethinking religion.* Cambridge: Cambridge University Press.

Ledoux, J. 1996. *The emotional brain.* New York: Simon and Schuster.

Lehrer, P., R. Woolfolk, and N. Goldman. 1986. Progressive relaxation then and now. Does change always mean progress? In *Consciousness and self-regulation: Advances in research and theory*, ed. R. Davidson, G. Schwartz, and D. Shapiro. New York: Plenum Press.

Leukel, F. 1972. *Introduction to physiological psychology.* Saint Louis: Mosley.

Levi-Strauss, C. 1962. *Totemism.* Boston: Beacon.

———. 1963. The effectiveness of symbols. In *Structural anthropology.* New York: Basic Books.

———. 1967. *The savage mind.* Chicago: University of Chicago Press.

Lewis-Williams, D., and J. Clottes. 1998. The mind in the cave—the cave in the mind: Altered consciousness in the Upper Paleolithic. *Anthropology of Consciousness* 9(1): 13–21.

Lewis-Williams, D., and T. Dowson. 1988. The signs of all times: Entoptic phenomena in Upper Paleolithic art. *Current Anthropology* 29: 201–45.

Lex, B. 1979. The neurobiology of ritual trance. In *The spectrum of ritual: A biogenetic structural analysis*, ed. E. d'Aquili, C. Laughlin, and J. McManus. New York: Columbia University Press.

Locke, R., and E. Kelly. 1985. A preliminary model for the cross-cultural analysis of altered states of consciousness. *Ethos* 13: 3–55.

Ludwig, A. 1966. Altered states of consciousness. *Archives of General Psychiatry* 15: 225–34.

Lukoff, D., R. Zanger, and F. Lu. 1990. Transpersonal psychology research review: Psychoactive substances and transpersonal states. *Journal of Transpersonal Psychology* 22: 107–47.

Lyon, M. 1993. Psychoneuroimmunology: The problem of the situatedness of illness and the conceptualization of healing. *Culture, Medicine and Psychiatry* 17: 77–97.

MacDonald, G., J. Cove, C. Laughlin, and J. McManus. 1989. Mirrors, portals, and multiple realities. *Zygon* 24(1): 39–64.

MacLean, P. 1973. *The triune concept of brain and behavior.* Toronto: University of Toronto Press.

———. 1990. *The triune brain in evolution.* New York: Plenum Press.

———. 1993. On the evolution of three mentalities. In *Brain, culture and the human spirit. Essays from an emergent evolutionary perspective,* ed. James Ashbrok. Lanham, Md.: University Press of America.

Madden, J., H. Akil, R. Patrick, and J. Barchas. 1977. Stress-induced parallel changes in central opioid levels and pain responsiveness in the rat. *Nature* 265: 358.

Maier, S. 1986. Stressor controllability and stress-induced anagelsia. In *Stress-induced anagelsia. Annals of the New York Academy of Sciences* 467, ed. D. Kelly. New York: New York Academy of Sciences.

Malinowski, B. [1925] 1954. *Magic, science, and religion.* New York: Doubleday, Anchor Books.

Mandell, A. 1980. Toward a psychobiology of transcendence: God in the brain. In *The psychobiology of consciousness,* ed. D. Davidson and R. Davidson. New York: Plenum Press.

———. 1985. Interhemispheric fusion. *Journal of Psychoactive Drugs* 17(4): 257–66.

Mani, K., P. Gopalakrishnan, J. Vyas, and M. Pillai. 1968. Hot-water epilepsy: A peculiar type of reflex-induced epilepsy. *Neurology (India)* 16(3): 107–10.

Mani, K., A. Mani, C. Ramesh, and G. Ahuja. 1972. Hot-water epilepsy—clinical and electroencephalographic features—study of 60 cases. *Neurology (India)* 20: 237–40.

Mann, S. 1984/87 *An Indo-European comparative dictionary.* Hamburg, Germany: H. Buske.

Marshall, L. 1962. !Kung Bushman medicine beliefs. *Africa* 32: 221–51.

———. 1969. The medicine dance of the !Kung Bushman. *Africa* 39: 347–81.

Maslow, A. 1971. *The farther reaches of human nature.* New York: Penguin Books.

Mauss, M. [1920–03] 1972. *A general theory of magic*. New York: W. W. Norton.

Maxfield, M. 1990. *Effects of rhythmic drumming on EEG and subjective experience*. Ph.D. diss. As cited in Wright, 1991.

McCain, H., J. Bilotta, and I. Lamster. 1987. Endorphinergic modulation of immune functioning: Potent action of the dipeptide glycyl-L-glutamine. *Life Science* 41(2): 169–76.

McClenon, J. 1994. *Wondrous events: Foundations of religious belief*. Philadelphia: University of Pennsylvania Press.

———. 1997. Shamanic healing, human evolution, and the origin of religion. *Journal for the Scientific Study of Religion* 36(3): 345–54.

McGinty, D. 1985. Physiological equilibrium and the control of sleep states. In *Brain mechanisms of sleep*, ed. D. McGinty et al. New York: Raven Press.

McIntosh, A. 1980. Beliefs about out-of-the-body experiences among Elema, Gulf Kamea, and Rigo peoples of Papua, New Guinea. *Journal of the Society for Psychical Research* 50: 460–78.

McKim, W. 1991. *Drugs and behavior: An introduction to behavioral pharmacology*. Englewood Cliffs, N.J.: Prentice-Hall.

McNeil, D. 1979. *The conceptual basis of language*. Hillsdale, N.J.: Lawrence Erlbaum Associates.

Mead, G. 1934. *Mind, self, and society*. Chicago: University of Chicago Press.

Middleton, J. and E. H. Winter, eds. 1963. *Witchraft and sorcery in East Africa*. London: Routledge and Kegan Paul.

Mikulas, W. 1981. Buddhism and behavior modification. *Psychological Record* 31 (3): 331–42.

Miller, N., and M. Gold. 1993. LSD and ecstacy: Pharmacology, phenomonology, and treatment. *Psychiatric Annals* 24(3): 131–34.

Minsky, M. 1985. *The society of mind*. New York: Simon and Schuster.

Mithen, S. 1996. *The prehistory of the mind: A search for the origins of art, religion, and science*. London: Thames and Hudson.

Molaie, M., and K. Kadzielawa. 1989. Effect of naloxone infusion on the rate of epileptiform discharge in patients with complex partial seizures. *Epilepsia* 30(2): 194–200.

Moody, R. 1975. *Life after life*. Atlanta: Mockingbird Books.

Morley, J., and N. Kay. 1986. Neuropeptides as modulators of immune system functioning. *Psychopharmacology Bulletin* 22: 1089–92.

Morris, W., ed. 1981. *The American heritage dictionary of the English language*. Boston: Houghton Mifflin.

Morris, P., and P. Hampson. 1983. *Imagery and consciousness*. New York: Academic Press.

Morrison, A., and P. Reiner. 1985. A dissection of paradoxical sleep. In *Brain mechanisms of sleep*, ed. D. McGinty et al. New York: Raven Press.

Moruzzi, G. 1974. Neural mechanisms of the sleep-waking cycle. In *Basic sleep mechanisms*, ed. O. Petre-Quadens and J. Schlag. New York: Academic Press.

Mougin, C., A. Baulay, M. Henriet, D. Haton, M. Jacquier, D. Turnhill, S. Berthelay, and R. Gaillard. 1987. Assessment of plasma opioid peptides, beta-endorphin and met-enkephalin at the end of an international nordic ski race. *European Journal of Applied Physiology* 56(3): 281–86.

Murdock, G. 1980. *Theories of illness: A world survey*. Pittsburgh: University of Pittsburgh.

Murdock, G., and C. Provost. 1973. Measurement of cultural complexity. *Ethnology* 12: 379–92.

Murdock, G., and D. White 1969. Standard cross-cultural sample. *Ethnology* 8: 329–69.

Murphy, M., and S. Donovan. 1988. A bibliography of meditation theory and research: 1931–1983. *The Journal of Transpersonal Psychology* 15 (2): 181–228.

Murray, M. 1921. *The witch-cult in Western Europe*. Oxford: Oxford University Press.

———. 1933. *The God of the witches*. London: Oxford University Press.

Naranjo, C. 1996. The interpretation of psychedelic experiences in light of the psychology of meditation. In *Yearbook of cross-cultural medicine and psychotherapy*, 1995, Sacred Plants, Consciousness, and Healing, ed. M. Winkelman and W. Andritzky. Berlin: Verland und Vertrieb.

Natsoulas, T. 1983. Concepts of consciousness. *Journal of Mind and Behavior* 4: 13–59.

———. 1991. Consciousness and commissurotomy, III: Toward the improvement of alter-native conceptions. *Journal of Mind and Behavior* 12: 1–32.

———. 1991–1992. I am not the subject of this thought. *Imagination, Cognition, and Personality* 11: 279–302.

———. 1992. The ecological approach to perception: The place of perceptual content. *American Journal of Psychology* 102: 443–76.

Neher, A. 1961. Auditory driving observed with scalp electrodes in normal subjects. *Electroencephalography and Clinical Neurophysiology* 13: 449–51.

———. 1962. A physiological explanation of unusual behavior in ceremonies involving drums. *Human Biology* 34: 151–60.

Neisser, U. 1976. *Cognition and reality*. San Francisco: W. H. Freeman.

Neppe, V. 1981. Review article: the non-epileptic symptoms of temporal lobe dysfunction. *South Africa Medical Journal* 60: 989–91.

———. 1983. Temporal lobe symptomatology in subjective paranormal experiences. *Journal of the American Society for Psychical Research* 77: 1.

Netto, C., R. Dias, and I. Izquierdo. 1986. Differential effect of posttraining naloxone, beta-endorphin, leu-enkephalin and electroconvulsive shock administration upon memory of an open-field habituation and/or a water finding task. *Psychoneuroendocrinology* 11(4): 437–46.

Newham, P. 1994. *The singing cure*. Boston: Shambhala Publications.

Newton, N. 1996. *Foundations of understanding*. Philadelphia: John Benjamins.

Noll, R. 1983. Shamanism and schizophrenia: A state-specific approach to the schizophrenia metaphor of shamanic states. *American Ethnologist* 10(3): 443–59.

———. 1985. Mental imagery cultivation as a cultural phenomenon: The role of visions in shamanism. *Current Anthropology* 26: 443–51.

Norbeck, E. 1961. *Religion in primitive society*. New York: Harper and Row.

Nutini, H., and J. Roberts. 1993. *Blood sucking witchcraft*. Tucson: University of Arizona Press.

Oakley, D. 1983. The varieties of memory: A phylogenetic approach. In *Memory in animals and humans*, ed. A. Mays. Berkshire, England: Van Nostrand Reinhold.

———. 1985. Cognition and imagery in animals. In *Brain and mind*, ed. D. Oakley. London: Methuen.

Odajnyk, V. 1993. *Gathering the light: A psychology of meditation*. Boston: Shambhala Publications.

Oesterreich, T. [1921] 1966. *Possession demoniacal and other among primitive races, in antiquity, the middle ages, and modern times*. Hyde Park, N.Y.: University Books.

Okamoto, M. 1978. Barbiturates and alcohol: Comparative overviews on neurophysiology and neurochemistry. *Psychopharmacology*, ed. M. Lipton, A. DiMascio, and K. Killam. New York: Plenum Press.

Orne, M., and S. Wilson. 1978. On the nature of alpha feedback training. In *Consciousness and self-regulation*, ed. G. Schwartz and D. Shapiro. New York: Viking Press.

Ornstein, R. 1972. *The psychology of consciousness*. New York: W. H. Freeman.

Ortony, A. 1979. Beyond literal similarity. *Psychological Review* 86(3): 161–80.

Oubré, A. 1997. *Instinct and revelation reflections on the origins of numinous perception*. Amsterdam: Gordon and Breach.

Oxford English Dictionary. 1989. 2d ed. Vol. 15. Prepared by J. A. Simpson and E. S. C. Weiner. Oxford: Clarendon Press.

Pagano, R., and S. Warrenburg. 1983. Meditation: In search of a unique effect. In Vol. 3 of *Consciousness and self-regulation advances in research and theory*, ed. R. Davidson, G. Schwartz, and D. Shapiro. New York: Plenum Press.

Pandian, J. 1997. The sacred integration of the cultural self: An anthropological approach to the study of religion. In *The anthropology of religion*, ed. S. Glazier. Westport, Conn.: Greenwood Press.

Parent, A. 1981. The anatomy of serotonin-containing neurons across the phylogeny. In *Serotonin neurotransmission and behavior*, ed. B. Jacobs and A. Gelperin. Cambridge, Mass.: MIT Press.

Pargament, K., and C. Park. 1997. In times of stress: The religion-coping connection. In *The psychology of religion*, ed. B. Spilka and D. McIntosh. Boulder, Col.: Westview Press.

Parmeggiani, P. 1985. Homeostatic regulation during sleep: Facts and hypotheses. In *Brain mechanisms of sleep*, ed. D. McGinty et al. New York: Raven Press.

Pekala, R. 1987. The phenomenology of meditation. In *The psychology of meditation*, ed. M. West. Oxford: Clarendon Press.

Penfield, W. 1975. *The mystery of the mind*. Princeton, N.J.: Princeton University Press.

Pert, C. 1986. The wisdom of the receptors: Neuropeptides, the emotions, and bodymind. *Advances, Institute for the Advancement of Health* 3(3): 8–16.

Pert, C., M. Ruff, R. Weber, and M. Herkenham. 1985. Neuropeptides and their receptors: A psychosomatic network. *Journal of Immunology* 35: 2+ (as cited in Pert 1986).

Peters, L. 1989. Shamanism: Phenomenology of a spiritual discipline. *Journal of Transpersonal Psychology* 21(2): 115–37.

Peters, L., and D. Price-Williams. 1981. Towards an experiential analysis of shamanism. *American Ethnologist* 7: 398–418.

Piaget, J. 1925. Psychologie et critique de la connaissance. *Archives de Psychologie* 19: 193–210. As cited in Kitchener.

———. 1928–1965. *Judgment and reasoning in the child*. Trans. Marjorie Warden. London: Routledge and Kegan Paul.

———. [1966] 1973. Preface. In *Dictionary of genetic epistemology*, ed. A. Battro. New York: Basic Books. As cited in Kitchener 1986.

———. 1969. *The early growth of logic in the child*. Trans. E. Luzer and D. Papert. New York: W. W. Norton.

———. 1971. *Biology and knowledge*. Chicago: University of Chicago Press.

Pivik, R. 1991. Tonic states and phasic events in relation to sleep. In *The mind in sleep*, ed. S. Ellman and J. Antrobus. New York: Wiley.

Plotkin, H., ed. 1982. *Learning, development and culture: Essays in evolutionary epistemology*. Chichester, England: Wiley.

———. 1987. Evolutionary epistemology as science. *Biology and Philosophy* 2: 295–313.

Pomeranz, B. 1982. Acupuncture and endorphins. *Ethos* 10: 385–93.

Popper, K., and J. Eccles. 1977. *The self and its brain*. New York: Springer International.

Press, I. 1982. Witch doctor's legacy: Some anthropological implications for the practice of clinical medicine. In *Clinically applied anthropology*, ed. N. J. Chrisman and T. W. Maretzki. Dordrecht, Holland: D. Reidel.

Prince, R. 1966. Can the EEG be used in the study of possession states? In *Trance and possession states*, ed. R. Prince. Montreal: McGill University Press.

———. 1982a. Shamans and endorphins. *Ethos* 10(4): 409.

———. 1982b. The endorphins: A review for psychological anthropologists. *Ethos* 10(4): 299–302.

Proudfoot, W., and P. Shaver. 1997. Attribution theory and the psychology of religion. In *The psychology of religion*, ed. B. Spilka and D. N. McIntosh. Boulder, Col.: Westview Press.

Raffman, D. 1993. *Language, music, and mind*. Cambridge, Mass.: MIT Press.

Rahkila, P., E. Hakala, K. Salminen, and T. Laatikainen. 1987. Response of plasma endorphins to running exercise in male and female endurance athletes. *Med-Sci-Sports-Exerc* 19(5): 451–55. Med-Line Search Abstracts.

Ribeiro, C. 1991. Pharmacology of serotonin neuronal systems. *Human Psychopharmacology* 6: 37–51.

Rider, M. 1985. Entrainment mechanisms are involved in pain reduction, muscle relaxation, and music-mediated imagery. *Journal of Music Therapy* 22(4): 183–92.

Rider, M., J. Floyd, and J. Kirkpatrick. 1985. The effect of music, imagery, and relaxation on adrenal corticosteroids and the re-entrainment of circadian rhythms. *Journal of Music Therapy* 22(1): 46–58.

Riegal, K. 1973. Dialectical operations: The final period of cognitive development. *Human Development* 16: 346–70.

Ring, K. 1981. *Life at death: A scientific investigation of the near-death experience.* New York: Coward, McCann and Geoghegan.

———. 1986. *Heading toward omega.* New York: Morrow.

Rogers, L. 1976. *Human EEG response to certain rhythmic pattern stimuli, with possible relations to EEG lateral assymetry measures and EEG correlates of chanting.* Ph.D. diss., Department of Physiology, UCLA.

Rogers, L. and D. Walters. 1981. Methods for finding single generators, with applications to auditory driving of the human EEG by complex stimuli. *Journal of Neuroscience Methods* 4: 257–65.

Role, L., and J. Kelly. 1991. The brain stem: Cranial nerve nuclei and the monoaminergic systems. In *Principles of neural science*, ed. E. Kandal, J. Schwartz, and T. Jessell. New York: Elsevier.

Rossi, E. 1986. Altered states of consciousness in everyday life: The ultradian rhythms. In *Handbook of states of consciousness*, ed. B. Wolman and M. Ullman. New York: Van Nostrand Reinhold.

Ryall, R. 1989. *Mechanisms of drug action on the nervous system.* Cambridge: Cambridge University Press.

Sabom, M. 1982. *Recollections of death.* New York: Harper and Row.

Sachdev, H., and S. Waxman. 1981. Frequency of hypergraphia in temporal lobe epilepsy: An index of interictal behavior syndrome. *Journal of Neurology, Neurosurgery and Psychiatry* 44: 358–60.

Sarbin, T. 1954. Role theory. In vol. 1 of *Handbook of social psychology*, ed. G. Lindzey. Reading, Mass.: Addison-Wesley.

Sargant, W. 1974. *The mind possessed.* Philadelphia: Lippincott.

Scheff, T. 1993. Toward a social psychological theory of mind and consciousness. *Social Research* 60(1): 171–95.

Schenk, L., and D. Bear. 1981. Multiple personality and related dissociative phenomena. *American Journal of Psychiatry* 138: 1311–16.

Schmidt, A., and S. Peroutka. 1989. S-hydroxytryptamine receptor "families." *Neuropsychopharmacology* 3: 2242–49.

Schoonmaker, F. 1979. Denver cardiologist discloses findings after 18 years of near-death research. *Anabiosis* 1: 1–2.

Schoun, F. 1975. *The transcendent unity of religions.* Trans. P. Townsend. New York: Harper and Row.

Schultes, R. 1972. An overview of hallucinogens in the Western hemisphere. In *Flesh of the gods*, ed. P. Furst. New York: Praeger.

Schultes, E., and A. Hofmann. 1979. *Plants of the gods.* New York: McGraw-Hill.

Schultes, E., and M. Winkelman 1996. The principal American hallucinogenic plants and their bioactive and therapeutic properties. In *Yearbook of cross-cultural medicine and psychotherapy*, ed. M. Winkelman and W. Andritzky. Berlin: Verland und Vertrieb.

Schuman, M. 1980. The psychophysiological model of meditation and altered states of consciousness: A critical review. In *The psychobiology of consciousness*, ed. J. Davidson and R. Davidson. New York: Plenum Press.

Selye, H. 1936. A syndrome produced by diverse nocuous agents. *Nature* 138: 32.

Sforzo, G. 1989. Opioids and exercise: An update. *Sports Medicine* 7(2): 109–24.

Shapiro, D. 1980. *Meditation*. New York: Aldine Publishing.

———. 1990. Meditation, self-control, and control by benevolent other: Issues of content and context. In *Psychotherapy, meditation and health*, ed. M. Kwee. London and The Hague: EastWest Publications.

Shapiro, D., and R. Walsh, eds. 1984. *Meditation: Classic and contemporary perspectives*. New York: Aldine Publishing.

Shekar, C. 1989. Possession syndrome in India. In *Altered states of consciousness and mental health. A cross-cultural perspective*, ed. C. A. Ward. Newbury Park, Calif.: Sage.

Shields, D. 1978. A cross-cultural study of out-of-the-body experiences, waking, and sleeping. *Journal of the Society for Psychical Research* 49: 697–741.

Shipley, J. 1984. *The origins of English words. A discursive dictionary of Indo-European roots*. Baltimore: Johns Hopkins.

Shore, B. 1996. *Culture in mind: Cognition, culture and the problem of meaning*. New York: Oxford University Press.

Siegel, R. 1984. The natural history of hallucinogens. In *Hallucinogens: Neurochemical, behavioral, and clinical perspectives*, ed. B. Jacobs. New York: Raven Press.

———. 1990. *Intoxication: Life in pursuit of artificial paradise*. New York: E. P. Dutton.

Siikala, A. 1978. The rite technique of Siberian shaman. In *Folklore fellows communication* 220. Helsinki: Soumalainen Tiedeskaremia Academia.

Silverman, J. 1967. Shamans and acute schizophrenia. *American Anthropologist* 69: 21–31.

Simmons, G. 1974. *The witchcraft world*. New York: Barnes and Noble.

Simons, R. C., and C. C. Hughes, eds. 1985. *The culture bound syndromes: Folk illnesses of psychiatric and anthropological interest*. Dordrecht, Holland: D. Reidel Publishing.

Skorupski, J. 1976. *Symbol and theory*. Cambridge, Mass.: Harvard University Press.

Smith, H. 1975. Introduction. In *The transcendent unity of religions*. Trans. F. Schoun. New York: Harper and Row.

———. 1976. *Forgotten truth: The primordial tradition*. New York: Harper and Row.

Spanos, N. 1989. Hypnosis, demonic possession, and multiple personality: Strategic enactments and disavowals of responsibiltiy for actions. In *Altered states of consciousness and mental health: A cross-cultural perspective*, ed. C. A. Ward. Newbury Park, Calif.: Sage.

Sperber, D. 1994. The modularity of thought and the epidemiology of representations. In *Mapping the mind: Domain specificity in cognition and culture*, ed. L. A. Hirschfeld and S. A. Gelman. Cambridge: Cambridge University Press.

Sperry, R. 1993. Psychology's mentalist paradigm and the religion/science tension. In *Brain, culture, and the human spirit. Essays from an emergent evolutionary perspective*, ed. J. Ashbrook. Lanham, Md.: University Press of America.

Spilka, B. and D. McIntosh, eds. 1997. *The psychology of religion: Theoretical approaches*. Boulder, CO: Westview Press.

Spilka, B., P. R. Shaver, and L. A. Kirkpatrick. 1997. A general attribution theory for the psychology of religion. In *The psychology of religion*, ed. B. Spilka and D. N. McIntosh. Boulder, Col.: Westview Press.

Stafford, P. 1992. *Psychedelics encyclopedia*. Berkeley, Calif.: Ronin Press.

Stahl, P. 1989. Identification of hallucinatory themes in the Late Neolithic art of Hungary. In Theme issue *Shamanism and altered states of consciousness*, ed. M. Dobkin de Rios and M. Winkelman. *Journal of Psychoactive Drugs* 21(1): 101–12.

Stark, R. 1997. A taxonomy of religious experience. In *The psychology of religion: Theoretical approaches*, ed. B. Spilika and D. N. McIntosh. Boulder, Col.: Westview Press.

Sterman, M., and C. Clemente. 1974. Forebrain mechanisms for the onset of sleep. In *Basic sleep mechanisms*, ed. O. Petre-Quadens and J. Schlag. New York: Academic Press.

Steward, J. 1955. *Theory of cultural change*. Urbana: University of Illinois Press.

Stoller, P. 1987. *Fusion of worlds: An ethnography of possession among Songhay of Nigeria*. Chicago: University of Chicago Press.

Strauss, H., M. Ostow, and L. Greenstein. 1952. *Diagnostic electroencephalography*. New York: Grune and Stratton.

Stroebel, C., and B. Glueck. 1980. Passive meditation: Subjective, clinical, and electrographic comparison with feedback. In vol. 2 of *Consciousness and self-regulation. Advances in research and theory*, ed. G. Schwartz and D. Shapiro. New York: Plenum Press.

Subrahmanyam, H. S. 1972. Hot-water epilepsy. *Neurology (India)* 20: 240–43.

Sutton, J., A. Mamelak, and J. Hobson. 1992. Modeling states of waking and sleeping. *Psychiatric Annals* 22(3): 137–43.

Swanson, G. 1960. *Birth of the gods.* Ann Arbor: University of Michigan Press.

———. 1963. The search for a guardian spirit: A process of empowerment in simpler societies. *Ethnology* 12: 359–78.

Szymusiak, R., and E. Satinoff. 1985. Thermal influences on basal forebrain hypogenic mechanisms. In *Brain mechanisms of sleep*, ed. D. McGinty et al. New York: Raven Press.

Taimni, I. 1968. *The science of yoga.* Madras, India: Theosophical Publishing House.

Tart, C. 1975. *States of consciousness.* New York: E. P. Dutton.

———. 1977. Putting the pieces together: A conceptual framework for understanding discrete states of consciousness. In *Alternate states of consciousness*, ed. N. Zinbeg. New York: Free Press.

Taylor, E., M. Murphy, and S. Donovan. 1997. *The physical and psychological effects of meditation: A review of contemporary research with a comprehensive bibliography: 1931–1996.* Sausalito, Calif.: Institute of Neotic Sciences.

Thoren, P., J. Floras, P. Hoffmann, and D. Seals. 1990. Endorphins and exercise: Physiological mechanisms and clinical implications. *Med-Sci-Sports-Exerc.* 22(4): 417–28. Med-Line Search Abstracts.

Trevarthen, C. 1993. Brain science and the human spirit. In *Brain, culture, and the human spirit. Essays from an emergent evolutionary perspective*, ed. J. Ashbrook. Lanham, Md.: University Press of America.

Turner, V. [1969] 1977. *The ritual process.* Ithaca, N.Y.: Cornell University Press.

Tylor, E. [1871] 1924. *Primitive culture.* New York: Brentano.

Valle, J. P., and R. H. Prince. 1989. Religious experiences as self-healing mechanisms. In *Altered states of consciousness and mental health: A cross cultural perspective*, ed. C. A. Ward. Newbury Park, Calif.: Sage.

van Gennep, A. [1909] 1960. *The rites of passage.* Chicago: University of Chicago Press.

Varela, F. 1997. The body's self. In *Healing emotions*, ed. D. Goleman. Boston: Shambhala Publications.

Vogel, W., D. Broverman, and E. Klaiber. 1968. EEG and mental abilities. *Electroencephalography and Clinical Neurophysiology* 24: 166–75.

Vogel, W., D. Boverman, E. Klaiber, and Y. Kobayashi. 1974. EEG driving responses as a function of monoamine oxydase. *Electroencephalography Clinical Neurophysiology* 36: 205.

Vogel, W., D. Broverman, E. Klaiber, and K. Kun. 1969. EEG response to photic stimulation as a function of cognitive style. *Electroencephalography Clinical Neurophysiology* 27: 186–90.

Wade, J. 1996. *Changes of mind: A holonomic theory of the evolution of consciousness*. Albany: State University of New York Press.

Wallace, A. F. C. 1956. Revitalization movements. *American Anthropologist* 58: 264–81.

———. 1961. Mental illness, biology, and culture. *Psychological Anthropology*, ed. F. Hsu. Homewood, Ill.: Dorsey.

———. 1966. *Religion: An anthropological view*. New York: Random House.

Wallace, R., and H. Benson. 1972. The physiology of meditation. *Scientific American* 226(2): 84–90.

Waller, M. J. C. 1996. Organization theory and the origins of consciousness. *Journal of Social and Evolutionary Systems* 19(1): 17–30.

Walsh, R. 1979. Meditation research: An introduction and review. *Journal of Transpersonal Psychology* 11: 161–74.

———. 1980. The consciousness disciplines and the behavioral sciences. *American Journal of Psychiatry* 137: 663–73.

———. 1983. Meditation practice and research. *Journal of Humanistic Psychology* 23(1): 18–50.

———. 1988. Two Asian psychologies and their implications for Western psychotherapists. *American Journal of Psychotherapy* 42(4): 543–60.

———. 1990. *The spirit of shamanism*. Los Angeles: J. P. Tarcher.

Ward, C. A., ed. 1989a. *Altered states of consciousness and mental health: A cross-cultural perspective*. Newbury Park, Calif.: Sage.

———. 1989b. The cross-cultural study of altered states of consciousness and mental health. In *Altered states of consciousness and mental health: A cross-cultural perspective*, ed. C. A. Ward. Newbury Park, Calif.: Sage.

———. 1989c. Possession and exorcism: Psychopathology and psychotherapy in a magico-religious context. In *Altered states of consciousness and mental health: A cross-cultural perspective*, ed. C. A. Ward. Newbury Park, Calif.: Sage.

Ward, C., and M. Beaubrun. 1979. Trance induction and hallucination in spiritualist Baptist mourning. *Journal of Psychological Anthropology* 2: 479–88.

———. 1980. The psychodynamics of demon possession. *Journal for the Scientific Study of Religion* 19(2): 201–07.

Wasson, R. 1980. *The wondrous mushroom: Mycolatry in Mesoamerica.* New York: McGraw-Hill.

Wasson, R., C. Cowan, F. Cowan, and W. Rhodes. 1974. *Maria Sabina and her Mazatec mushroom velada.* New York: Harcourt Brace Jovanovich.

Watkins, C., ed. 1985. *The American heritage dictionary of Indo-European roots.* Boston: Houghton Mifflin.

Wautischier, H. 1989. A philosophical inquiry to include trance in epistemology. *Journal of Psychoactive Drugs* 21(1): 35–46.

Waxman, S., and N. Geschwind. 1974. Hypergraphia in temporal lobe epileptics. *Neurology* 24: 629–36.

Wayman, A. 1969–71. Buddhism. In *Historia religionum; handbook for the history of religions*, ed. C. Bleeker and G. Widengren. Leiden, Netherlands: E. J. Brill.

Weight, F., and C. Swenberg. 1981. Serotonin and synaptic mechanisms in sympathetic neurons. In *Serotonin neurotransmission and behavior*, ed. B. Jacobs and A. Gelperin. Cambridge, Mass.: MIT Press.

Weil, A. 1972. *The natural mind; a new way of looking at drugs and the higher consciousness.* Boston: Houghton Mifflin.

Werner, H., and E. Kaplan. 1952. *The acquisition of word meanings: A developmental study.* Evanston, Ill.: Child Development Publications.

———. 1963. *Symbol formation.* New York: Wiley.

West, M. 1987a. Traditional and psychological perspectives on meditation. In *The psychology of meditation*, ed. M. West. Oxford: Clarendon Press.

———. 1987b. Meditation: magic, myth, and mystery. In *The psychology of meditation*, ed. M. West. Oxford: Clarendon Press.

White, D., M. Burton, and L. Brunder. 1977. Entailment theory and method: A cross-cultural analysis of the sexual division of labor. *Behavior Science Research* 12: 1–4.

Whitley, D. 1992. Shamanism and rock art in far western North America. *Cambridge Archaeological Journal* 2: 89–113.

———. 1994a. Shamanism, natural modeling and the rock art of far western North American hunter-gatherers. In *Shamanism and rock art in North America*, ed. S. Turpin. San Antonio: Rock Art Foundation.

———. 1994b. By the hunter, for the gatherer: Art, social relations, and subsistence change in the prehistoric Great Basin. *World Archaeology* 25(3): 356–77.

———. 1994c. Ethnography and rock art in the far west: Some archaeological implications. In *New light on old art*, ed. D. Whitley and L. Loendorf. Los Angeles: Institute of Archaeology University of California.

———. 1998. Cognitive neuroscience, shamanism, and the rock art of native California. *Anthropology of Consciousness* 9(1): 22–37.

Wierzbicka, A. 1992. *Semantics, culture, and cognition: Universal human concepts in culture-specific configurations*. New York and Oxford: Oxford University Press.

———. 1993. A conceptual basis for cultural psychology. *Ethos* 21(2): 205–31.

Wilber, K. 1977. *The spectrum of consciousness*. Wheaton, Ill.: Theosophical Publishing House.

———. 1979. *No boundary*. Los Angeles: Zen Center Publications.

———. 1980. *The Atman Project*. Wheaton, Ill. Theosophical Publishing House.

———. 1986. The spectrum of development. In *Transformations of consciousness*, ed. K. Wilber, J. Engler, and D. Brown. Boston: Shambhala Publications.

———. 1990. *Eye to eye*. Boulder, Col.: Shambhala Publications.

Wilber, K., J. Engler, and D. Brown, eds. 1986. *Transformations of consciousness*. Boston: Shambhala Publications.

Winkelman, M. 1982. Magic: A theoretical reassessment. *Current Anthropology* 23: 37–44, 59–66.

———. 1984. *A cross-cultural study of magico-religious practitioners*. Ph.D. diss. University of California, Irvine. Ann Arbor, Mich.: University Microfilms.

———. 1986a. Magico-religious practitioner types and socioeconomic analysis. *Behavior Science Research* 20(1–4): 17–46.

———. 1986b. Trance states: A theoretical model and cross-cultural analysis. *Ethos* 14: 76–105.

———. 1990a. Shaman and other "magico-religious healers": A cross-cultural study of their origins, nature, and social transformation. *Ethos* 18(3): 308–52.

———. 1990b. Physiological, social, and functional aspects of drug and non-drug altered states of consciousness. In *Yearbook of cross-cultural medicine and psychotherapy*, ed. W. Andritzky. Berlin: Verlag und Vertrieb.

———. 1991a. Physiological and therapeutic aspects of shamanistic healing. *Subtle Energies* 1: 1–18.

——. 1991b. Therapeutic effects of hallucinogens. *Anthropology of Consciousness* 2(3–4): 15–19.

——. 1992. Shamans, priests, and witches. A cross-cultural study of magico-religious practitioners. *Anthropological Research Papers #44.* Arizona State University.

——. 1993. The evolution of consciousness: Transpersonal theories in light of cultural relativism. *Anthropology of Consciousness* 4(3): 3–9.

——. 1994. Multidisciplinary perspectives on consciousness. *Anthropology of Consciousness* 5(2): 16–25.

——. 1996. Psychointegrator plants: Their roles in human culture and health. In vol. 6 of *Yearbook of cross-cultural medicine and psychotherapy 1995, Sacred Plants, Consciousness, and Healing,* ed. M. Winkelman and W. Andritzky. Berlin: Verlag und Vertrieb.

——. 1997a. Neurophenomenology and genetic epistemology as a basis for the study of consciousness. *Journal of Social and Evolutionary Systems* 19(3): 217–36.

——. 1997b. Altered states of consciousness and religious behavior. In *Anthropology of religion: A handbook of method and theory,* ed. S. Glazier. Westport, Conn.: Greenwood.

Winkelman, M., and W. Andritzky, eds. 1996. *Sacred plants, consciousness and healing: cross-cultural and interdisciplinary perspectives.* In *Yearbook of cross-cultural medicine and psychotherapy 1995.* Berlin: Verland und Vertrieb.

Winkelman, M., and M. Dobkin de Rios. 1989. Psychoactive properties of !Kung Bushman medicine plants. *Journal of Psychoactive Drugs* 21: 51–60.

Winkelman, M., and D. White. 1987. A cross-cultural study of magico-religious practitioners and trance states: Data base. In vol. 3D of *Human relations area files research series in quantitative cross-cultural data,* ed. D. Levinson and R. Wagner. New Haven, Conn.: HRAF Press.

Winkelman, M., and C. Winkelman. 1990. Shamanistic healers and their therapies. In *Yearbook of cross-cultural medicine and psychotherapy 1990,* ed. W. Andritzky. Berlin: Verlag und Vertrieb.

Winn, T., B. Crowe, and J. Moreno. 1989. Shamanism and music therapy. *Music Therapy Perspectives* 7: 61–71.

Winson, J. 1985. *Brain and psyche: The biology of the unconscious.* Garden City, N.Y.: Doubleday, Anchor Press.

——. 1990. The meaning of dreams. *Scientific American* (November): 86–96.

Wise, S. P., and J. L. Rapoport. 1989. Obsessive-compulsive disorder: Is it basal ganglia dysfunction? In *Obsessive compulsive disorder in children and adolescents*, ed. J. L. Rapoport. Washington, D.C.: American Psychiatric Press.

Wood, E. 1948. *Practical yoga, ancient and modern; being a new independent translation of Patanjali's yoga aphorisms.* New York: E. P. Dutton.

Wright, P. 1989. The "shamanic state of consciousness." In Theme issue on Shamanism and altered states of consciousness, ed. M. Dobkin de Rios and M. Winkelman. *Journal of Psychoactive Drugs* 21(1): 25–34.

———. 1991. Rhythmic drumming in contemporary shamanism and its relationship to auditory driving and risk of seizure precipitation in epileptics. *Anthropology of Consciousness* 2(3-4): 7–14.

Yensen, R. 1985. LSD and psychotherapy. *Journal of Psychoactive Drugs* 17(4): 267–77.

———. 1996. From shamans and mystics to scientists and psychotherapists: Interdisciplinary perspectives on the interaction of psychedelic drugs and human consciousness. In *Yearbook of cross-cultural medicine and psychotherapy*, ed. M. Winkelman and W. Andritzky. Berlin: Verland und Vertrieb.

Zanger, R. 1989. Psycholytic therapy in Europe. Newsletter. *The Albert Hoffman Foundation* 1(2) 1989.

Zubec, J. 1969. *Sensory deprivation: Fifteen years of research.* New York: Irvington Publishers.

Zysk, K. 1992. Reflections on an Indo-European healing tradition. Perspectives on Indo-European language, culture, and religion studies in honor of Edgar Polomé. Vol. 2. *Journal of Indo-European Studies Monograph,* #9.

Index

ABOUT THE AUTHOR

Michael Winkelman is Senior Lecturer and Director, Ethnographic Field School, Department of Anthropology, Arizona State University.

ISBN 0-89789-704-8

9 780897 897044

HARDCOVER BAR CODE